"This is a must-read volume for anybody interested in understanding both the general implications of AI in the world of defence and more specific issues, including a set of in-depth country-studies illustrating what exactly different countries are doing and trying to achieve."

Andrea Gilli, *Senior Researcher, NATO Defence College*

"This book is going to become the most important roadmap on how AI is likely to shape and influence the strategically consequential militaries of the world. No one can predict how AI is going to re-engineer wars and conflicts, but the authors offer a unique peek around the corner. And Raska and Bitzinger as co-editors remain ahead of the curve."

Dr. Chung Min Lee, *Senior Fellow, Carnegie Endowment for International Peace, University Professor, Korea Advanced Institute of Science and Technology (KAIST), and Chairman of the International Advisory Council, IISS*

"This book provides important perspectives on different national approaches to the development of artificial intelligence that offer critical insights for current debates on the military and strategic impacts of AI."

Elsa Kania, *Adjunct Senior Fellow, Technology and National Security Program, Center for a New American Security*

THE AI WAVE IN DEFENCE INNOVATION

An international and interdisciplinary perspective on the adoption and governance of artificial intelligence (AI) and machine learning (ML) in defence and military innovation by major and middle powers.

Advancements in AI and ML pose pressing questions related to evolving conceptions of military power, compliance with international humanitarian law, peace promotion, strategic stability, arms control, future operational environments, and technology races. To navigate the breadth of this AI and international security agenda, the contributors to this book include experts on AI, technology governance, and defence innovation to assess military AI strategic perspectives from major and middle AI powers alike. These include views of how the United States, China, Japan, South Korea, the European Union, and Russia see AI/ML as a technology with the potential to reshape military affairs and power structures in the broader international system. This diverse set of views aims to help elucidate key similarities and differences between AI powers in the evolving strategic context.

A valuable read for scholars of security studies, public policy, and STS studies with an interest in the impacts of AI and ML technologies.

Michael Raska is Assistant Professor and Coordinator of the Military Transformations Programme at the S. Rajaratnam School of International Studies, Nanyang Technological University, Singapore.

Richard A. Bitzinger is a Visiting Senior Fellow with the Military Transformations Programme at the S. Rajaratnam School of International Studies, Nanyang Technological University, Singapore.

THE AI WAVE IN DEFENCE INNOVATION

Assessing Military Artificial Intelligence Strategies, Capabilities, and Trajectories

Edited by
Michael Raska and Richard A. Bitzinger

LONDON AND NEW YORK

Designed cover image: © Getty Images

First published 2023
by Routledge
4 Park Square, Milton Park, Abingdon, Oxon OX14 4RN

and by Routledge
605 Third Avenue, New York, NY 10158

Routledge is an imprint of the Taylor & Francis Group, an informa business

British Library Cataloguing-in-Publication Data
A catalogue record for this book is available from the British Library

ISBN: 9781032110769 (hbk)
ISBN: 9781032110752 (pbk)
ISBN: 9781003218326 (ebk)

DOI: 10.4324/9781003218326

Typeset in Bembo
by codeMantra

CONTENTS

FIGURES

TABLES

BOXES

ACKNOWLEDGEMENTS

In March 2021, the Military Transformations Programme (MTP) at the S. Rajaratnam School of International Studies (RSIS), Nanyang Technological University, Singapore organised a virtual conference on "Building Inclusive and Trustworthy AI Governance" to draw attention to the range of emerging technology-related challenges in the international security domain. The conference took place as the multilateral AI landscape began to crystallise, notwithstanding the constraints of the global COVID-19 pandemic. With governance agendas embedded in national and regional AI strategies, international coalitions cooperating on emerging technology, and initiatives and organisations in academia and industry, there has been no shortage of stakeholders actively engaged in diplomatic and technical activities. Military partnerships, too, have begun focusing on norms and cooperation, juxtaposed by contending strategic interests and systemic competition.

The highly contending and diverse global AI governance landscape reflects different segments of the AI ethics and safety agenda – from standards and interoperability, data governance frameworks, lethal autonomous weapons systems, trustworthiness, and embedding core societal values into technology at large. The question became not how to create new AI governance in defence innovation frameworks from scratch but how to effectively navigate and coordinate between the many actors with a hand in international AI governance and cooperation. The premise of the conference has been a shared obligation to act – that is, to operationalise principles that embrace respective views on AI development in military affairs and, in doing so, help shape responsible innovation of AI in defence.

With that in mind, the MTP team embarked on a major project to bring the varying military AI perspectives together into a comprehensive edited volume, suited for a broad audience: not only as a valuable tool for scholarly communities, particularly in helping to bridge the interdisciplinary gap on different scholarly approaches to AI, but also as an essential and useful tool for policymakers in civilian and military establishments and tech-industry leaders, seeking to understand better the rapidly evolving global military AI landscape and governance. At the same time, the volume is suitable for students, especially at MA and PhD levels, in a wide range of AI-related disciplines, including political science, international relations/international security, strategic studies, science and technology studies, computer science, communications, technological ethicists, etc.

As the chapters for the volume progressed through the COVID-19 pandemic, new contentious developments began to shape international security. The intensifying Sino-US strategic competition at multiple levels and the ongoing devastating war in Ukraine have further impacted country-specific and regional military AI strategies and trajectories. For much of 2022, many authors in this volume were compelled to update their chapters and assessments.

Accordingly, the editors would like to express their sincere appreciation, first and foremost, to all the authors in this volume, across four continents, who have continuously revised their work and contributed with a truly collaborative effort. At the same time, the editors would like to thank former and current colleagues in the MTP, including Zoe Stanley-Lockman, who has co-organised the AI conference and shaped our research trajectory on AI governance in military affairs. This volume would not be possible without the assistance of Wichuta Teeratanabodee, MTP Senior Analyst, who has provided detailed scholarly feedback and critical questions for each chapter. The editors would like to express sincere gratitude to the RSIS management – particularly Ambassador Ong Keng Yong – who has supported MTP conferences and research projects over the years. Our gratitude also extends to Dr Chung Min Lee for his invaluable advisory role, support, and input to MTP over the years. We are very grateful to MTP stakeholders, particularly Tiana Desker and her team. Finally, much of our gratitude is due to the RSIS Events Unit – for organising the MTP AI conference – and the Routledge editorial team in Singapore that produced this book.

Working on this volume has enabled us to develop relevant international research networks, long-term connections, and collaborative work on military AI in Europe, East Asia, the United States, and Australia – and facilitate these connections with Singapore's academic and policy community. We see this as an essential building block for future research, particularly as the "AI wave" evolves further, bringing about novel policy, strategic, and operational challenges, particularly in the deployment of automated and autonomous systems and human-machine teaming, as well as new questions and debates ranging from future military budget priorities to issues of AI governance and ethics. Ultimately, the AI wave's ramifications mark new opportunities and risks for international cooperation by exposing limitations of established security and defence paradigms.

Michael Raska and Richard Bitzinger (editors)

ACRONYMS AND ABBREVIATIONS

4IR	Fourth Industrial Revolution
5G	Fifth-Generation (Mobile Technologies)
ACCS	Automated Combat Control System
ACS	Automated Control System
ACT	Allied Command Transformation (NATO)
ADF	Australian Defence Force
ADO	Australian Defence Organisation
AGI	Artificial General Intelligence
AGS	Allied Ground Surveillance
AHRC	Australian Human Rights Commissioner
AI	Artificial Intelligence
AI RDTE&F	Research, Development, Testing, Evaluation, and Fielding
AI-EP	AI Ethics Principles
AIDP	Artificial Intelligence Development Plan
AIS	Artificial Intelligence Systems
AM	Additive Manufacturing
AR	Augmented Reality
ARF	Advanced Research Foundation (Russia)
ARTEMIS	Architecture de Traitement et d'Exploitation Massive de l'Information Multi-Source (France)
ASD	Australian Signals Directorate
ASD	AeroSpace and Defence Industries Association of Europe
ASEAN	Association of Southeast Asian Nations
ATARS	Airborne Tactical Augmented Reality System
ATLA	Acquisition, Technology & Logistics Agency (Japan)
AUKUS	Australia, the United Kingdom, and the United States
AVM	Air Vice-Marshal

AWS	Autonomous Weapon Systems
BCI	Brain-Computer Interfaces
C2	Command and control
C4I	Command, Control, Communications, Computers, and Intelligence
C4ISTAR	Command, Control, Communications, Computers, Intelligence, Surveillance, Target Acquisition, and Reconnaissance
CAICT	China Academy of Information and Communication Technology
CBPR	Cross-Border Privacy Rules
CCDC	Combat Capabilities Development Command (US Army)
CETC	China Electronics Technology Group
CIA	Central Intelligence Agency
COVID-19	Coronavirus Disease 2019
CRS	Congressional Research Service
CSDP	EU Common Security and Defence Policy
CSIRO	Commonwealth Scientific and Industrial Research Organisation (Australia)
CSWTD	Co-operative Strike Weapons Technology Demonstrator
CT	Computed Tomography
CWIX	Coalition Warrior Interoperability Exercise
DAIC	Defence Artificial Intelligence Centre (Australia)
DAIRNET	Defence Artificial Intelligence Research Network (Australia)
DAPA	Defence Acquisition Programme Administration (South Korea)
DARPA	Defense Advanced Research Projects Agency (US)
DDMS	Digital Design, Manufacturing, and Services
DF9	Nine Digital Front-Runners
DIANA	Defence Innovation Accelerator for the North Atlantic
DIB	Defense Innovation Board (US)
DID	Data Item Descriptor
DISER	Department of Industry Innovation and Science (Australia)
DIU	Defense Innovation Unit (US)
DOD	Department of Defense (US)
DOE	Department of Energy (US)
DOS/CSET	Department of State Bureau of Cyberspace Security and Emerging Technologies (US)
DSTG	Defence Science and Technology Group (Australia)
EC	European Commission
EDA	European Defence Agency
EDF	European Defence Fund
EDIDP	European Defence Industrial Development Programme
EDTs	Emerging Disruptive Technologies

EEAS	European External Action Service
EI2	European Intervention Initiative
EP	European Parliament
ERA	Elite of the Russian Army
ESA	European Space Agency
EU	European Union
EUDIS	European Defence Innovation Scheme
EW	Electronic Warfare
FCAS	Franco-German-Spanish Future Combat Air System
FFRDC	Federally Funded Research and Development Center
GANs	Generative Adversarial Networks
GDPR	General Data Protection Regulation
GGE	UN Governmental Group of Experts
GNSS	Global Navigation Satellite Systems
GPAI	The Global Partnership on AI
GPU	Graphics Processing Unit
GRN	Genetics, Robotics, and Nanotechnology
GUNID	Scientific Research and Technological Support of Advanced Technologies
HRIA	Human Rights Impact Assessments
IC	Intelligence Community
ICBM	Intercontinental Ballistic Missile
ICRC	International Committee of the Red Cross
ICS	Information Computing System
ICT	Information Communications Technology
IEEE	Institute of Electrical and Electronics Engineers
IHL	International Humanitarian Law
IoT	Internet-of-Things
ISR	Intelligence, Surveillance and Reconnaissance
ITU	International Telecommunications Union
JAIC	Joint Artificial Intelligence Center
JASDF	Japan Air Self-Defence Force
JEF	Joint Expeditionary Force
JGSDF	Japan Ground Self-Defence Force
JSDF	Japan Self-Defence Force
JSM	Joint Strike Missile (Norway)
KAIST	Korea Advanced Institute of Science and Technology
LAWS	Lethal Autonomous Weapon Systems
LEAPP	Legal, Ethical and Assurance Program Plan
LSRAM	Long-Range Anti-Ship Missile (US)
MEAID	Method for Ethical AI in Defence (Australia)
MGCS	Main Ground Combat System
MHC	Meaningful Human Control
MIT	Massachusetts Institute of Technology

ML	Machine Learning
MND	Ministry of National Defence (South Korea)
MOD	Ministry of Defence
MRI	Magnetic Resonance Imagery
MUS	Maritime Unmanned Systems
MWS	Missile Warning System
N3	Next-Generation Nonsurgical Neurotechnology Programme
NATO	North Atlantic Treaty Organisation
NATO STO	NATO Science and Technology Organisation
NCIA	NATO Communications and Information Agency
NDAA	National Defence Authorisation Act
NDCC	National Defence Coordination Centre (Russia)
NDOC	National Defence Operations Centre (Russia)
NDPP	NATO Defence Planning Process
NGAD	Next Generation Air Dominance Programme
NIF	NATO Innovation Fund
NIST	National Institute of Standards and Technology (US)
NLP	Natural Language Processing
NORDEFCO	Nordic Defence Cooperation
NSCAI	National Security Commission on AI (US)
NSF	National Science Foundation
NSM	Naval Strike Missile (Norway)
NSW	New South Wales
OECD	Organisation for Economic Co-operation and Development
OODA	Observe, Orient, Decide, Act
PADR	Preparatory Action on Defence Research
PAI	Partnership on AI
PESCO	Permanent Structured Cooperation
PfD	Partnership for Defence
PiE	Puzzle-Solving in Ethics (Model)
PLA	The People's Liberation Army
R&D	Research and Development
R&D/T	Research and Development/Technology
R&D&I	Research, Development, and Innovation
R&T	Research and Technology
RAAF	Royal Australian Air Force
RAIC	Responsible AI Champions
RMA	Revolution in Military Affairs
SADEA	Singapore-Australia Digital Economy Agreement
SCJ	Science Council of Japan
SCORPION	Synergie du Contact Renforcée par la Polyvalence et l'Infovalorisation (France)
SDOs	Standards Development Organisations
SEAD	Suppression of Enemy Air Defence

SIGINT	Signals Intelligence
SMEs	Small and Medium Enterprises
SMF	Strategic Missile Forces (Russia)
SWAP-C	Size, Weight, Power, and Cost
TASDCRC	Trusted Autonomous Systems Defence Cooperative Research Centre (Australia)
TEVV	Testing, Evaluation, Verification and Validation
THeMIS	Tracked Hybrid Modular Infantry System
TsNII	Central-Science Research Institute (Russia)
TTPs	Tactics, Techniques, and Procedures
UACS	Unified Automated Control System
UAV	Unmanned Aerial Vehicles
UDHR	Universal Declaration of Human Rights
URSA	Urban Reconnaissance through Supervised Autonomy
USAF	United States Air Force
UUV	Unmanned Underwater Vehicles
VAULT	Visible, Accessible, Understandable, Linked, and Trustworthy
VR	Virtual Reality

INTRODUCTION

The AI Wave in Defence Innovation

Michael Raska and Richard A. Bitzinger

How are select modern armies pursuing strategies for integrating novel technologies such as artificial intelligence (AI) into their military modernisation efforts? What is the strategic impact of the development and deployment of military applications for AI? What variables influence the adoption of AI technologies in defence and military applications? These questions propel the principal aims of this comprehensive edited volume, which integrates diverse academic and policy-relevant perspectives, which in turn map out not only the varying trajectories of technical developments in military AI and autonomous weapons systems, but more importantly the ongoing debates on the strategic relevance of AI governance, ethics, and norms in defence innovation.

The starting assumption underlying this book is that the diffusion of AI systems appears to be fundamentally different from past experiences, notably the diffusion of information technologies (IT) into defence during the 1970s–2010s. This period, often called IT-driven Revolution in Military Affairs (RMA), was characterised by Western (primarily the US) superiority in the research and development of advanced military technologies, which in turn were gradually and selectively diffused, in varying paths and patterns, to allies and strategic partners, including small and middle powers in Europe and East Asia (Raska 2016). For the first time in decades, however, the United States is facing a strategic peer competitor – i.e., China – with its own advancing military capabilities, backed by novel technologies, that is challenging US military-technological primacy (Mahnken 2012). In doing so, the margins of military-technological advantages between great powers are narrowing, accelerating the strategic necessity for "disruptive" defence and military innovation. This intensifying strategic competition in advanced military technologies is embedded in the broader systemic competition over technological "leadership" in areas such as AI systems, robotics, cyber, additive manufacturing, advanced materials, synthetic biology, quantum

DOI: 10.4324/9781003218326-1

computing, directed energy, space technologies, and many others. The ability to innovate is synonymous with international influence and national power – generating economic competitiveness, political legitimacy, military power, and internal security.

However, contrary to previous decades, which, admittedly, utilised *some* dual-use technologies to develop major weapons platforms and systems, the current AI-enabled wave differs significantly in terms of the magnitude and impact of commercial-technological innovation as a key source of military innovation (Raska 2021). Large military-industrial primes are no longer the only drivers of technological innovation; rather, advanced technologies with a dual-use potential are being developed in the commercial sectors and then being "spun on" to military applications. In this context, the diffusion of emerging technologies, including additive manufacturing (3D printing), nanotechnology, space and space-like capabilities, artificial intelligence, and drones, is not confined solely to the great powers (Hammes 2016). The proliferation of AI-enabled sensors and autonomous weapons systems is also reflected in the defence trajectories of select advanced small states and middle powers such as Singapore, South Korea, Israel, Australia, and Japan, among others. These states have the potential to develop niche emerging technologies to advance their own defence capabilities and economic competitiveness, political influence, and status in the international arena (Barsade and Horowitz 2018).

Moreover, the diffusion of autonomous and AI-enabled autonomous weapons systems, coupled with novel operational constructs and force structures, challenges the direction and character of human involvement in future warfare – in which algorithms and data may shape human decision-making, and future combat that is envisioned in the use of Lethal Autonomous Weapons Systems (LAWS). As this book shows, militaries are selectively experimenting with varying technologies that use data analytics to enable warfare automation (Jensen and Pashkewitz 2019). These technologies are increasingly permeating future warfare exploration and capability development programmes. For example, some air forces are experimenting with AI algorithms as "virtual backseaters," effectively controlling the aircraft's sensors, navigation, and detection and targeting of adversary air threats, and therefore reducing the aircrew's workload (Davis 2021). Advanced militaries also increasingly use AI systems for decision support and planning of military operations. They can process a large amount of data from diverse intelligence, surveillance, and reconnaissance sensors. They are used in logistics and predictive maintenance to ensure the safety of forces and the availability of platforms and units. AI also shapes the training and simulation, cyberspace operations to detect and counter advanced cyber-attacks, and robotics and autonomous systems such as drones (Horowitz 2018).

The convergence of the three drivers – strategic competition, dual-use emerging technological innovation, and changing character of human-machine interactions in warfare – is propelling a new environment that defines and drives the AI-driven RMA wave. In other words, a military-technological tsunami is on the way that may defy previous revolutions in military affairs. While this viewpoint risks overhyping the impact of new technologies, it also shows that current ways and means of warfare – weapons, tactics, training, acquisition, and operational approaches – may become rapidly obsolete, especially in a world where strategic vulnerabilities and dependencies co-exist across a range of factors, sectors, and countries. Future warfare projections and operational concepts – such as multidomain operations – increasingly depend on the direction and character of the new AI wave in defence and military-technological innovations, including the development of advanced fighter jets paired with a team of unmanned aerial vehicles, lethal autonomous weapons systems, hypersonic missiles, directed energy or laser weapons, and technologies relevant for competing in the space, cyber, and electromagnetic spectrum (Lingel et al. 2020).

At the same time, the AI wave's diffusion trajectory inherently also poses new challenges and questions concerning strategic stability, alliance relationships, arms control, ethics and governance, and, ultimately, the conduct of combat operations (Stanley-Lockman 2021a). As this book shows, armed forces around the globe are aggressively seeking to integrate select AI systems and technologies into their arsenals to create a new competitive advantage over their adversaries. These developments beg the question of how these innovations might present challenges to current decision-making systems, trust, and military ethics. From fielded applications of artificial narrow intelligence to the looming prospect of future superintelligence, human dependency on and collaboration with machines are increasingly fraught with questions over ethics and norms. With artificial intelligence and machine learning (AI/ML) already in use in the civilian and military spheres today, present experiences are progressively shaping the norms that will define the future human-machine collaboration. Surging calls for AI safety – from practitioners and civil society alike – have bred the first generation of principles for safe, ethical usage of AI/ML, most notably the AI Asilomar Principles and IEEE Ethically Aligned Design. Building on these fundamentals, governments and militaries seek AI/ML ethics guidance. Not only is this an indispensable question of operational safety, but it is also an important signal to programmers and engineers whose criticism of "unethical" or questionable military action may short-circuit militaries' access to cutting-edge dual-use technologies.

Indeed, current and emerging international normative debates increasingly focus on the role of AI systems in the use of force, such as the diffusion of LAWS and the ability of states to conform to principles of international humanitarian law. As technological advancements move from science fiction to technical realities, states have different views on whether the introduction of LAWS would defy or reinforce international legal principles. Facing the contending legal and ethical implications of military AI applications, military establishments increasingly recognise the need to address questions related to safety, ethics, and governance, which is crucial to building trust in new capabilities, managing risk escalation, and revitalising arms control. The critical question is whether existing norms and governance mechanisms will prevent militaries from moving into a new phase of "automation warfare" in which algorithms will enable the control and actions of robotic weapons capable of selecting and engaging targets without human control. In short, there are growing tensions among different expert communities on whether militaries should focus their ethics efforts narrowly on LAWS or, more broadly, on the gamut of AI-enabled systems (Stanley-Lockman 2021b).

This book addresses these many developments, providing a comprehensive overview of AI diffusion, deployment, and use in select armies. It seeks to understand the varying conceptual and technical undercurrents of AI-defence innovation, development, deployment, and use to grasp better how AI diffusion shapes regional military modernisation paths. As such, this volume is divided into three parts. The first three chapters address the challenges facing defence innovators regarding AI governance. *Jean-Marc Rickli* and *Federico Mantellassi* begin by examining AI in warfare. According to them, AI is set to be *the* "defining technology" of the 4IR, and as AI becomes increasingly prevalent in our daily lives, its potential military applications will also grow accordingly. However, no consensus exists over AI's impact on the conduct of military operations. Enthusiasts, pragmatics, and deniers offer different interpretations regarding whether AI will revolutionise warfare. Attitudes range from believing that automation will change every aspect of how nations fight wars to believing that AI is still too immature a technology to successfully assist battlefield operations in meaningful and revolutionary ways. Rickli and Mantellassi argue that AI is already present on the battlefield, acting as an analytical enabler, disruptor, and force multiplier. These current uses of AI already entail some unique and consequential international security implications by offsetting the strategic offence-defence balance towards the offence and being subject to quick proliferation.

Next, *Tate Nurkin* explores AI and technological convergence as catalysts for national security risks. Nurkin reviews specific indicative technology interactions shaping AI across five overlapping "revolutions": in situational awareness (revolution in perception, processing, and cognition); in hyper-enabled platforms and people (revolution in human and machine performance); in new efficiencies and the impending "design age" (a revolution in manufacturing, supply chain, and logistics); in connectivity, lethality, and flexibility (a revolution in communication, navigation, targeting, and strike); and in monitoring, manipulation, and weaponisation (revolution in cyber and information operations). Nurkin argues that AI's convergences with other advanced and emerging technologies are critical to delivering new and enhanced capabilities in and across the five revolutions. Individually and collectively, the intersection of AI and advanced digital and connectivity technologies, neuro- and bioscience, augmented reality, virtual reality and other visualisation tools, additive manufacturing, synthetic biology, robotics, directed energy, and biometrics will deliver several layers of value for both security communities and militaries, as well as in many cases the industries that support these communities.

Cansu Canca next explores AI ethics and governance in defence innovation and the challenges of implementing an AI ethics framework. Canca argues that AI-enabled systems are increasingly becoming a part of military operations with applications in logistics, cyber defence, search and rescue, surveillance, and drone operations, among many others. These systems raise various ethical concerns and questions in each development and deployment stage. Currently, there is no established systematic structure to address these ethical issues effectively and promptly. As such, this chapter lays out the AI ethics landscape in a military context and presents an AI ethics framework. This framework consists of guiding tools for ethical decision-making, a process that seamlessly integrates ethics into the AI innovation and deployment cycle, and an organisational structure of employees who should carry out various ethics-related roles within the organisation.

The book's second part focuses on the strategic competition for AI. *Simona R. Soare* begins by addressing AI among European militaries and, specifically, shows how regional approaches are lagging. Soare looks at how European states adopt AI in their militaries and how military AI has accelerated at the national, EU, and NATO levels. So far, Soare argues, implementation remains fragmented, delinked from future force and capability planning, and lacks the coherence of the civilian-industrial sector. Soare lays out four variables to explain this situation. First, driven by the need to close persistent conventional capability gaps, Europeans have under-invested in future technologies like AI. Second, national defence establishments and regional security organisations like NATO have played a weak role compared to national administrations and the private sector in shaping the AI digital transformation agenda. Third, Europeans underuse regional institutional accelerators of military AI adoption, such as the EU and NATO. Finally, ambitious European military AI adoption is obstructed by self-imposed public ethical and legal restraints.

Next, *Zoe Stanley-Lockman* explores US approaches to AI governance for national security. Stanley-Lockman chronicles US security and defence policy concerning AI and how the US national security apparatus is setting up AI governance as a cornerstone of US strategy. In adopting principles for safe and ethical AI for defence, the United States has established itself as a first mover in the military AI governance space. However, implementing and operationalising these principles requires new modes of governance within the Department of Defense and across the entire US national security interagency. This chapter then explores attempts to bolster whole-of-government AI governance for national security issues. At the strategic level, a socio-technical view of US artificial intelligence governance means focusing on how the United States is trying to shape the trajectory of the technology not just to align with the values that shape democratic societies and citizenries but also to extend this to the current ideological competition by creating a contrast between democratic ways of using AI and alternative, authoritarian views. Finally, Stanley-Lockman's chapter examines the relevant US actors and their efforts govern and exploit AI in accordance with broader US goals in the international system.

Next, *Qi Haotian* addresses China's evolving processes of AI development. China is experiencing military transformation, and as a result its military is becoming increasingly reliant on artificial intelligence and associated technologies. Expecting an intelligence revolution in military affairs, China looks forward to increasing effectiveness and efficiency in intelligence, command and control, logistics, and weapons systems. Yet beneath the high promises of new technology, the strengths of such advances are limited. For the People's Liberation Army (PLA), there are still substantial obstacles to achieving revolutionary military transformation – in particular, multi-layered complexities and uncertainties that exist at the intersection of technology and strategy driving military transformation. Looking into the future, Chinese and international academic and policy communities need to voice concerns about the AI-enabled transformation's impact on the current and future conflict dynamics and take the necessary steps to enhance operational and strategic stability in an uncertain military arena.

In separate chapters, *Vadim Kozyulin* and *Samuel Bendett* analyse Russian approaches to AI. Kozyulin first examines Russia's national strategy and trajectory for AI development, mainly developments prior to the war in Ukraine. He argues that while Russia's National AI Strategy hardly touches on defence and security issues, the Russian leadership has supported AI development via a dual civil-military fusion strategy intended to strengthen the competitiveness of the Russian science and technology innovation system and to transfer AI technologies from the civilian sphere to the military. Consequently, Russia has created a system of institutions for selecting promising AI technologies in the interests of the Ministry of Defence (MoD), which in turn integrates civil and military enterprises. Civil-military integration also aims to mitigate the severe political and economic sanctions pressure from select Western countries, which have progressively intensified since 2014 (and even more so since Russia's invasion of Ukraine).

Samuel Bendett then addresses the overall development of military AI in Russia. Bendett argues that Russian AI development, testing, evaluation, and fielding by the country's military is a significant mission multiplier for the Russian MOD. The Russian military emphasises AI and robotics to make Russian military operations faster, more effective, less dependent on human costs, and more resilient to countermeasures. Russia intends to use this technology to advance its capabilities across the entire C4ISR spectrum – intelligence, surveillance, reconnaissance, command, control, communications, decision-making, electronic warfare, reconnaissance-strike and reconnaissance-fire contours, robotics/autonomy, aerial, maritime, ground, and cyber capabilities in general. Already, the Russian MOD is redefining its concept of operations and tactics, techniques, and procedures in favour of using more artificial intelligence systems and capabilities for a more effective outcome. At the same time, Bendett notes that there is a robust debate across the entire MOD establishment on the role of AI in future conflicts, and on the role of humans in the ever-increasing growth of autonomy and robotics today and in the near term. However, Russia's invasion of Ukraine is redefining some of the efforts discussed in this chapter, and the consequences of this war may have significant long-term effects on Russian AI research and development, both civilian and military alike.

Finally, the volume concludes with an exploration of AI strategies and capabilities on the part of so-called niche defence innovators. *Ryo Hinata-Yamaguchi* compares military AI strategic approaches and perspectives in Japan and the Republic of Korea (ROK or South Korea). Hinata-Yamaguchi argues that while national AI research and development (R&D) in these countries is still in their early stages compared to the United States, China, and Russia, Japan, and South Korea have taken some critical steps towards adopting and operationalising AI for national defence. These steps have involved technological advances and major policy reconfigurations, requiring a contextualised understanding of the distinct developments that have taken place in the two countries. Details as to AI military developments in Japan and the ROK are somewhat limited, not simply due to secrecy but also because of the nascent nature of the developments in place. He assesses AI developments in Japan and the ROK, adressing their perceptions towards and governance of AI from a national defence context. He also examines the varying rationales for applying AI to national defence in Japan and the ROK, followed by a discussion of national AI activities, AI governance, and applications to the defence sector. Finally, Hinata-Yamaguchi addresses the ethical debates surrounding AI-based systems and R&D and discusses the impact of COVID-19 on Seoul's and Tokyo's defence planning activities and the broader implications of these developments.

S. Kate Devitt and Damian Copeland address Australia's evolving approach to AI governance in security and defence. According to them, Australia has prioritised the development of AI, robotics, and autonomous systems in an effort to develop a sovereign capability for its military. At the same time, Australia is committed to *Article 36* of the Geneva Conventions of 1949, which requires Australia to meet its legal obligations in operating autonomous weapons systems (AWS). Australia reviews all new means and methods of warfare to ensure that weapons and weapons systems, especially AWS, are operated within acceptable systems of control. Additionally, Australia has undergone significant reviews of the risks of AI to human rights and within intelligence organisations. Its defence establishment has committed to producing ethics guidelines and frameworks in security and defence. Australia is also committed to the OECD's values-based principles for the responsible stewardship of trustworthy AI and adopting a set of national AI ethics principles. While Australia has not adopted an AI governance framework specifically for defence, Australia's Defence Science and Technology Group has published "A Method for Ethical AI in Defence" (MEAID) technical report, which includes a framework and pragmatic tools for managing ethical and legal risks for military applications of AI.

The key findings of the book show that while the AI wave may affect select countries and militaries disproportionately, its military-technological impact, amplified by political-systemic competition, is sufficiently broad to propel the next defence transformation – a rethinking of defence policy planning and management, including weapons development and R&D, defence budgetary processes, defence contractors, as well as operational and warfighting domains and concepts, alliances, and strategic partnerships. Integrating data streams and AI systems across different military platforms and organisations, to transform computers from tools into problem-solving "thinking" machines will continue to present a range of complex technological, organisational, and operational challenges (Raska et al. 2022). These include developing trustworthy algorithms that will enable these systems to better adapt to changes in their environment, learn from unanticipated tactics, and apply them on the battlefield. It would also call for designing ethical codes and safeguards for the next-generation weapons platforms and technologies. Another challenge is that technological advances, especially in defence innovation, are a continuous, dynamic process; breakthroughs are always occurring. Their impact on military effectiveness and comparative advantage could be significant and hard to predict at their nascent stages. Moreover, such technologies and resulting capabilities rarely spread evenly across geopolitical lines.

Nevertheless, critical questions remain – how much we can trust AI systems, particularly in safety-critical systems? A growing field of research focuses on how to deceive AI systems into making wrong predictions by generating false data. State and non-state actors may use this so-called adversarial machine learning to deceive opposing sides, using incorrect data to generate wrong conclusions and, in doing so, alter the decision-making processes. The overall strategic impact of adversarial machine learning on international security might be even more disruptive than the technology itself (Danks 2020). Indeed, complex AI systems and data streams also need to be linked technologically, organisationally, and operationally. For many militaries, this is an ongoing challenge: they must be able to effectively (in real time) integrate AI-enabled sensor-to-shooter loops and data streams between the various services and platforms. This includes linking diverse operational battle management systems and data; command and control, communications and networks; electronic warfare; positioning, navigation, and timing; with precision munitions. While select AI systems may mitigate some of the challenges, the same systems create new problems related to ensuring trusted AI (Cummings 2017). Accordingly, one may argue that the direction and character of the AI wave will depend on corresponding strategic, organisational, and operational agility, particularly how AI technologies interact with current and future operational constructs and force structures.

The diffusion of emerging technologies poses new challenges at the level of human involvement in warfare, the need to alter traditional force structures and recruitment patterns, and the domains in which force will be used. Modern militaries are developing their own and often diverse solutions to these issues. As in the past, their effectiveness will depend on many factors that are linked to the enduring principles of *strategy* – the ends, ways, and means to "convert" available defence resources into novel military capabilities and, in doing so, create and sustain operational competencies to tackle a wide range of contingencies. The main factors for successful implementation will not be technological innovations *per se*, but the combined effect of sustained funding, organisational expertise (i.e., sizeable and effective R&D bases, both military and commercial), and the institutional agility to implement defence innovation (Cheung 2021). The AI wave in military affairs will raise novel policy, strategic, and operational challenges, particularly in the deployment of automated and autonomous systems and human-machine teaming, that will propel new questions and policy debates ranging from future military budget priorities to issues of AI governance and ethics. Taken together, the AI wave will create both new opportunities and new risks for international cooperation by exposing the limitations of established paradigms in the ways and means of using force.

Ultimately, while emerging technologies are gradually becoming combat surrogates, the fundamental nature of warfare and strategy principles in defence innovation remains unchanged. War continues to be a contest of human wills for political ends, characterised by uncertainty and complexity, or what Prussian military theorist Carl von Clausewitz described back in the early 19th century as the "fog of war." Advanced military technologies in the militarisation of space brought by the AI-RMA also bring complexity and uncertainty to decision-making in warfare. Today's fog of war is in the uncertainties of data integrity and critical safeguards embedded in the various AI-enabled autonomous weapons systems. The underlying patterns of defence innovation – challenge, response, and adaptation – are also not changing (Ross 2010). While many defence innovations, such as AI systems, are sourced from the products in the commercial arena, nearly every military innovation continues to spark a quest for a counter-innovation in a continuous cycle of technological challenge, conceptual response, and organisational adaptation. In short, nearly every military innovation is relative to the evolving capabilities of the opposing side and, almost always, temporary in duration (as the ongoing war in Ukraine has demonstrated).

Consequently, when contemplating how AI systems may further affect security and defence trajectories, militaries must learn how to use "non-kinetic toolkits." What challenges, in turn, does this present? How will they operate in a contested environment characterised by the diffusion of sophisticated longer-range adversary capabilities and methods such as ballistic missiles, submarines, weapons of mass destruction, and offensive space, cyberspace, and information warfare assets that are all amplified by AI capabilities? This will present new challenges in a context where the battle space is crowded with both legally constituted combatants and non-combatants. In other words, the military-technological advantages of AI will not be compelling without corresponding *strategic, organisational, and operational adaptability* – from identifying new techniques, tactics, and procedures and ways and means to counter them.

The diffusion of AI systems is thus projected to have profound implications for how militaries adopt new technologies, how, on an operational level, militaries adapt to and apply new technologies, and our understanding of the future battlefield. Modern armies will have to search for their strategic-technological edge by focusing on their institutional agility to adapt to these changes. On the one hand, modern militaries will have to rethink existing conceptual templates for nearly every aspect of defence planning, organisational structures, and operational conduct. From the selection and training of soldiers, professional military education of officers, defence resource allocation, weapons selection and acquisition, and systems integration, all the way to operational and tactical conduct. On the other hand, they will have to integrate into broader national defence ecosystems by expanding their capacity for innovation through novel collaborative security and defence partnerships. And herein lies the principal challenge for implementing the AI wave: developing holistic approaches to future warfare and embracing the natural complexity of an operational environment and novel technologies requires a new mindset and new ways of thinking and operating at every echelon of military organisations. The question is whether the traditional military mindsets can incorporate disruptive innovation paths, embrace creativity and innovation, and promote the rearrangement of existing rules in varying strategic cultures.

References

Barsade, Itai, and Michael Horowitz. 2018. "Artificial Intelligence Beyond the Superpowers." *Bulletin of the Atomic Scientists*, August 16, 2018. https://thebulletin.org/2018/08/the-ai-arms-race-and-the-rest-of-the-world/.

Cheung, Tai Ming. 2021. "A Conceptual Framework of Defence Innovation." *Journal of Strategic Studies* 44, no. 6: 775–801. https://doi.org/10.1080/01402390.2021.1939689.

Cummings, Missy. 2017. "Artificial Intelligence and the Future of Warfare." *Chatham House Research Paper*, January 26, 2017. https://www.chathamhouse.org/sites/default/files/publications/research/2017-01-26-artificial-intelligence-future-warfare-cummings-final.pdf.

Danks, David. 2020. "How Adversarial Attacks Could Destabilise Military AI Systems." *IEEE Spectrum*, February 26, 2020. https://spectrum.ieee.org/adversarial-attacks-and-ai-systems.

Davis, Malcolm. 2021. "The Artificial Intelligence 'Backseater' in Future Air Combat." *ASPI Strategist*, February 5, 2021. https://www.aspistrategist.org.au/the-artificial-intelligence-backseater-in-future-air-combat/.

Hammes, T.X. 2016. "Technologies Converge and Power Diffuses: The Evolution of Small, Smart, and Cheap Weapons." *CATO Institute Policy Analysis*, no. 786, January 27, 2016.

Horowitz, Michael. 2018. "The Promise and Peril of Military Applications of Artificial Intelligence." *Bulletin of the Atomic Scientists*, April 23, 2018. https://thebulletin.org/2018/04/the-promise-and-peril-of-military-applications-of-artificial-intelligence/.

Jensen, Benjamin, and John Pashkewitz. 2019. "Mosaic Warfare: Small and Scalable Are Beautiful." *War on the Rocks*, December 23, 2019. https://warontherocks.com/2019/12/mosaic-warfare-small-and-scalable-are-beautiful/.

Lingel, Sherrill, et al. 2020. "Joint All-Domain Command and Control for Modern Warfare - An Analytic Framework for Identifying and Developing Artificial Intelligence Applications." *RAND Corporation Project Air Force Report*. https://www.rand.org/pubs/research_reports/RR4408z1.html.

Mahnken, Thomas, ed. 2012. *Competitive Strategies for the 21st Century: Theory, History, and Practice*. Stanford, CA: Stanford University Press.

Raska, Michael. 2016. *Military Innovation in Small States: Creating a Reverse Asymmetry*. New York: Routledge.

Raska, Michael. 2021. "The Sixth RMA Wave: Disruption in Military Affairs?" *Journal of Strategic Studies* 44, no. 4: 456–479. https://doi.org/10.1080/01402390.2020.1848818.

Raska, Michael, Katarzyna Zysk, and Ian Bowers, eds. 2022. *Defence Innovation and the 4th Industrial Revolution Security Challenges, Emerging Technologies, and Military Implications*. New York: Routledge.

Ross, Andrew. 2010. "On Military Innovation: Toward an Analytical Framework. *IGCC Policy Brief*, no. 1: 14–17. https://escholarship.org/uc/item/3d0795p8.

Stanley-Lockman, Zoe. 2021a. "Responsible and Ethical Military AI: Allies and Allied Perspectives." *Center for Security and Emerging Technology Issue Brief*, August 25, 2021. https://cset.georgetown.edu/publication/responsible-and-ethical-military-ai/.

Stanley-Lockman, Zoe. 2021b. "Military AI Cooperation Toolbox: Modernizing Defence Science and Technology Partnerships for the Digital Age." *Center for Security and Emerging Technology Issue Brief*, August 25, 2021. https://cset.georgetown.edu/publication/military-ai-cooperation-toolbox/.

1

ARTIFICIAL INTELLIGENCE IN WARFARE

Military Uses of AI and Their International Security Implications

Jean-Marc Rickli and Federico Mantellassi

Artificial intelligence (AI) is the defining technology of this generation. With an estimated market value of US$100 billion by 2025 and ominous remarks of world domination made by heads of state, AI is permeating into an increasing number of aspects of our daily lives. Its penetration in the military arena has already started taking place. As with many generation-defining technologies, strategic studies have seen a debate unfold over the potential strategic impact of AI to lead to the next military revolution (Raska 2021, 456). With its capacity to enable autonomous weapon systems, provide real-time battlefield data analysis, assist human-machine teaming, and support decision-making, the stage is also set for commercial AI innovations to permeate the military domain.

This chapter consists of three parts. The first part structures the debate about the impact of artificial intelligence on warfare into three schools of thought: enthusiasts, deniers, and pragmatics. These schools of thought do not differ in their recognition of the recent advances in the field of military AI, but *in their view of the potential for these advances to be utilised in a military setting, in a way which confers advantages to their adopters*. In short, the debate centres on whether and to what extent military AI influences and will influence the character of war. Enthusiasts contend that AI will increase the tempo of war and will simultaneously reduce the fog of war by providing more battlefield clarity for decision-makers, altering the character of war and potentially also its nature. AI will confer decisive advantages to adopters by growing autonomy weapon systems and decision-making. Without AI, battlefield operations will take place too quickly for human cognition alone to keep up. Pragmatics believe that AI will find its way to the battlefield, but its contributions will not change the immovable nature of war and will only impact the operational and tactical levels of war. While AI can enhance and facilitate military operations, it is still too unreliable to be used in chaotic, uncontrolled, and contested environments. Deniers

DOI: 10.4324/9781003218326-2

go further in their analysis and support the view that AI is too immature to be used by militaries that seek predictability and reliability in the fielding of new technology – something that, in their view, AI cannot yet provide. For them, the technical, organisational, and political hurdles are too high for AI to significantly impact military operations.

In the second part, the chapter takes stock of the current and prospective uses of artificial intelligence on the battlefield, showing that military AI is already a reality irrespective of views over the impact of AI on warfare, serving as an analytical enabler, disruptor, and force multiplier. As an analytical enabler, AI can provide quicker, more accurate, and reliable data analysis of much larger data sets, unburdening data-heavy aspects of military operations and assist command and control. As a disruptor, AI, through Natural Language Processing (NLP) or deepfake technology, is democratising and sophisticating the creation and spread of disinformation and propaganda, providing an affordable and impactful way for any actor to potentially reach a global influence. As a force multiplier, AI is enabling the use of increasing autonomy through sophisticated weapon systems employing battle tactics such as swarming to overwhelm enemy's forces.

Finally, the chapter concludes with a discussion about the international security implications of AI's military uses. It argues that the current and potential future military AI applications will have a substantial impact on strategic stability. By creating an international environment where speed, pre-emption, and offensive strategies have the advantage over defensive postures, AI tilts the offence-defence balance towards the former. Due to its nature as a cluster of commercial technologies, AI proliferates quickly at no cost horizontally – between states – and vertically – to non-state actors – creating an environment where multiple actors on the world stage will have access to disruptive military AI technologies.

Debating Military AI

Attitudes towards applying artificial intelligence in the military domain broadly fall into three categories: enthusiasm, pragmatism, and denial. Enthusiasts maintain that AI will revolutionise warfare, altering its character – the way war is fought – and even sometimes its nature – why wars happen. Pragmatics believe that AI will increasingly make its way onto the battlefield and military structures, albeit less revolutionising, impacting mainly the operational and tactical levels, facilitating operations, and making them more efficient. Deniers recognise advances in AI but point to various impediments – technological, organisational, socio-political, ethical, and legal – which limit the potential of AI outside very structured and controlled environments, thus rendering it suboptimal for military applications. They also argue that AI is just another technological development in warfare and that it will mainly impact the character of war, if at all.

Enthusiasts

AI enthusiasts point to Clausewitz's characterisation of war as a chameleon and his description of the character of war as constantly evolving as a basis to argue that AI will lead to the next revolution in the character of warfare (Hoffman 2018, 26). AI will change the character of warfare as it will change the way nations fight and affect military activities across the full spectrum of force and shape "all conflicts, from the lowest to highest intensity and the smallest to the largest" (Payne 2018, 8). For them, AI has clear military applications and will confer decisive advantages to successful adopters.

First, artificial intelligence will increasingly empower the deployment of autonomous systems, thereby furthering the robotisation of warfare. Fully autonomous weapons and vehicles could revolutionise warfare by autonomously conducting sophisticated battle tactics, instantly adjusting to enemy manoeuvres, and quickly exploiting opportunities on the battlefield (Davis 2019, 119). Operating at machine speed, the fielding of AI-powered systems would increase fighting speed and confer a distinct advantage to AI-adopting forces over non-AI-powered forces (Horowitz 2018, 47). Taking drone swarms as an example, Paul Scharre argues that a profound transformation in warfare is indeed underway (Scharre 2018, 387). The ability of the swarm to react to shifting events faster than humanly possible would change the way war is fought. Scharre argues that advances in artificial intelligence and machine autonomy enable these cooperative, autonomous drones, acting as one on the battlefield, to overwhelm an adversary utilising manoeuvre warfare (the iteration of warfare before swarming warfare) because of the cognitive advantages of swarming behaviour (Arquilla and Ronfeldt 2000, 7; Scharre 2018, 389).

Second, AI's usefulness in analysing vast data sets at speeds and quantities far surpasses human capacity and holds considerable military potential. As uncertainty is a driving force behind conflict, which sides continuously try to minimise, the ability to better sift through battlefield data and provide analysis is useful to militaries. The combination of increasing data flows (from the increase of machines on the battlefields that both produce and collect data), the computing power necessary to sift through the data, and the AI-powered capacity to analyse data could indeed give war fighters unprecedented visibility of the battlefield, reduce uncertainty, and would assist decision-making at all levels of fighting. This entails a reduction in the "fog" of war and its "friction", two enduring elements of warfare that, according to Clausewitz, have been central to Western and especially American military thinking since the end of the Cold War (Owens 2001).

Enthusiastic attitudes towards AI also contend that the nature of war will change due to the widespread adoption of AI in the military realm. According to Hoffman, AI will change the nature of war in several ways, as it will have an impact on all three aspects of the Clausewitz trinity model (Hoffman 2018, 30). It could weaken political direction, augment the intuition and judgement of commanders, and lessen the ability of governments to gain support and legitimacy while increasing the potential for foreign manipulations of populations. Autonomous technologies could reduce popular support for professional militaries and reduce the political consequences of engaging in conflict. Autonomy, defined as task completion without human involvement,[1] could also introduce new forms of friction (Hoffman 2018, 31). Added levels of "friction" due to the unintelligibility of AI systems are discussed in the next sub-part.

Furthermore, war's brutal, violent nature could also morph (Mallick 2019). Autonomy might further empty future battlefields, more so than it already does today. If war is to become predominantly fought by autonomous weapons, their increased accuracy and lethality make ordinary soldiers obsolete. As one contributor states: "If both sides have intelligence machines, war may become simply a case of machines being violent to other machines" (Mallick 2019). As AI enhances the capability of adversaries to spread confusion and sow dissent among populations – through disinformation campaigns, deepfakes, and cyberattacks – AI-powered hybrid tactics become a cost-effective way to wage war, and a sufficient means to internally whither nations to achieve desired political gains previously pursued through violent means. The enduring definition of war by Clausewitz (1976, 71) as "an act of force to compel our enemy to do our will" will thus be challenged as physical force will no longer be a requirement to wage war. The revolutionary prospects of AI have even led former US Defence Secretary and four-star General James Mattis, a staunch supporter of the immovable nature of warfare, to question his long-held beliefs when faced with the potential revolutionary potential of AI (Mehta 2018).

According to this school of thought, the adoption of AI in the military realm will also have critical geostrategic consequences. Horowitz has argued that innovation in AI could have "large-scale consequences for the global balance of power" (Horowitz 2018, 54). He argues that the adoption of automation could indeed favour security dilemmas. As better AI would translate into battlefield superiority, the incentive would be towards rapid development and deployment. Additionally, the difficulty in gauging a competitor's AI capabilities and progress would lead rivals to assume the worst of others (Horowitz 2018, 55). Payne builds on this point and suggests that artificial intelligence favours the offence due to its "speed, precision and acquisition and analysis of unbiased knowledge" since AI is not susceptible to the human psychological tendency for defence (Payne 2018, 26). He also maintains that AI could have implications for the risks of using force, although it is not yet clear if AI would help provoke or deter conflict (Payne 2018, 25). Rickli further argues that the combination of AI and autonomy is likely to favour offensive advantages, which will then favour strategies of pre-emption at the systemic level. The best way to defend itself against adversaries with offensive advantages is to attack first (2018, 33). This, in turn, could lead to a complete shakeout of international law as the UN Charter explicitly prohibits the use of force in international affairs through its article 2(4) (Rickli 2020a, 48).

Deniers

Proponents of this school of thought on the application of AI to the military domain maintain that both technical hurdles and organisational elements limit the usefulness and disruptive potential of artificial intelligence on the battlefield. In this view, AI will not change the nature of war and will have minor impact on its character. Its proponents also point out that AI-related technologies are relatively immature and far from being applicable to the military realm in reliable and predictable ways. The large data sets needed to train machine learning algorithms (which most AI technologies today rely on) often do not exist in the military realm. Svenmarck et al. point out that there are not enough "real world, high quality, sufficiently large datasets" that can be used to train algorithms and develop successful ML-based military AI applications (Svenmarck et al. 2018, 8).

Armies seek predictability and understandability in fielding their weapons (Holland Michel 2020, 1). The "black box" problem of AI, i.e., the incapacity of explaining the "reasoning" which led to a particular outcome, and the relative ease with which some AIs can be fooled both are seen as significant challenges for the future fielding of autonomy on the battlefield (Svenmarck et al. 2018, 9). In fact, AI has been shown to dramatically fail with relatively easy fooling techniques, such as modifying one pixel to completely misdirect image recognition software (Svenmarck et al. 2018, 7). Adversarial AI, a technique that attempts to fool models with deceptive data, questions algorithm reliability even more (Danks 2020). If inexplicability and unpredictability persist, this would severely limit and slow down the application of AI in military organisations, as both principles are essential to the commanders' decision-making in their use of force.

Organisational hurdles relating to the successful integration of autonomy in military concepts and doctrine also influence the success of AI in the military realm. Innovation alone is not sufficient to change the way armed forces operate. A recent study from Borchert, Schutz, and Verbovszky cautions against the argument that unmanned systems powered by AI will revolutionise the future of warfare. Studying recent conflicts in Libya, Ukraine, Syria, and Nagorno-Karabach, they found that the extent to which armed forces can gain an advantage over peers depends on how autonomous systems are integrated (Borchert et al. 2021, 62). Technology needs to be embedded in the broader cultural, conceptual, and organisational context, they argued (Borchert et al. 2021, 6). As one commentary has put it, "a technology alone, without new operational concept and new organisation structure, will not be able to fundamentally influence the outcome of a future military confrontation" (Gady 2015). This argument follows Colin Gray's depiction of strategy entailing 17 dimensions and his observation that incompetence in any of these dimensions can prove fatal, while dramatic improvements in any single dimension carry no guarantee of success (Gray 1999).

Finally, contrary to the belief that the integration of AI will lead to unprecedented battlefield awareness, AI might increase the "fog of war" and introduce a "fog of systems", thereby reinforcing the enduring nature of warfare (Hughes

2020). The above-mentioned inexplicability of AI decisions would then lead to increased "unawareness" of what is going on the battlefield, with events happening too fast for any meaningful human input or capacity to understand. Following Hughes' argument, friction is not reduced by the quality and quantity of information collected, but by the quality of the actions taken. Hyperawareness of the environment does not mean less friction as it is still possible to make the wrong decision (Pietrucha 2016).

Pragmatics

Clausewitzian traditionalists contend that the nature of war as violent, chaotic, destructive, and murderous cannot change (Mallick 2019). In this vein, Williamson Murray argues that advances in technology cannot do away with elements inherent to war, such as uncertainty and friction, as "no amount of computing power can anticipate [...] an enemy's capacity to adapt in unexpected ways" (Mallick 2019). Pragmatic attitudes towards AI's military applications rest on the interpretation of Clausewitz that the nature of warfare will not change, but accept that the character of war might, albeit in a relatively limited and less revolutionising way. For them, "AI is best understood as a cluster of *enabling technologies* that will be applied to most aspects of the military sphere" (Mashur 2019, 4). AI's contribution to warfare is not revolutionary but evolutionary (Cleverland et al. 2019).

Pragmatics see the most significant gains of AI in the military realm, mainly at the tactical and operational levels as facilitators of actions, and in controlled, uncontested environments. Like deniers, AI pragmatics point to the potential for adversarial fooling attacks to nuance the discussion on AI's military deployment. Due to the relative lack of resilience of some AI technologies against adversarial attacks, areas to invest in and in which military AI could have the greatest success are those that operate in these uncontested domains (Maxwell 2020). Armed forces should be weary of fielding immature and vulnerable AI systems in a contested environment, making them responsible for critical decisions (Maxwell 2020). Some such uncontested environments would be logistics, resource allocation, communications, and training. AI's data collection, analysis, and prediction capabilities could indeed help with intelligence and operational planning, and assist warfighters at the tactical level. Still, it could also help automate and make more efficient repairs and convoys (predictive logistics and autonomous convoys), communications, staff work (better allocation of time and resources), training (more personalised and realistic exercises), and reconnaissance (more efficient processing of data from different sources) (Mashur 2019, 3).

Additionally, political and social variables are important in determining how AI will permeate the military realm (Mashur 2019, 4). For example, current discussions at the UN Governmental Group of Experts (GGE) on lethal autonomous weapon systems demonstrate that the international community is profoundly divided over the future development of autonomous weapon systems.

Some countries argue for an outright ban, while others maintain that these weapons will not challenge international law and could make wars cleaner by reducing collateral damages as AI-enabled weapons would be much better at differentiating between combatants and non-combatants (Evans 2018). For pragmatists, technology is not a panacea which will propel armies forward regardless of other institutional factors which could significantly hold back the success of AI applications. AI alone will, for example, not "imbue a dysfunctional security apparatus with objectivity and the capacity for rapid decision-making" (Mashur 2019, 4). Furthermore, the adoption of AI in the military does not happen in a vacuum of other technological advancements (Mashur 2019, 4). Therefore, it should be viewed in tandem with other innovations, whose convergence with AI may take the technology in directions we cannot yet predict.

At the strategic level of warfare, Payne and Ayoub have argued that although AI will have a profound impact, strategy development will remain mainly a human endeavour. It will, however, likely see an increased level of AI assistance, yet not a total replacement by AI (Ayoub and Payne 2016, 808). Acting as a "strategic counsellor", AI could confer a distinct advantage to those adopting it (Ayoud and Payne 2016, 808). AI could, for example, anticipate and identify risks associated with strategic options, recognise patterns humans might miss, challenge accepted assumptions, and respond and adapt more rapidly to situations while not falling victim to the cognitive biases of humans. They, however, warn that the potential of AI for strategy development is limited by AI's reliance on data and its susceptibility to bias inherent to data sets, as well as by its inability to capture subjective human meanings, uncertainties, and ambiguities (Ayoub and Payne 2016, 807–808).

The three schools of thought on the military applications of artificial intelligence demonstrate that there is no agreement regarding the impact artificial intelligence and autonomy have on warfare. The following section will shed more light on the current uses of artificial intelligence in the military.

Military Applications of AI

Having taken stock of the attitudes towards the future of AI in the military domain, this section will survey the current military uses of artificial intelligence. While AI innovation is mainly being driven by the private sector and its business demands, AI has made significant inroads in the military as an analytical enabler, disruptor, and force multiplier.

AI as an Analytical Enabler

Due to its reliance on data, AI is particularly useful in data-heavy aspects of military operations where analysis of large troves of data is necessary (Sayler 2020, 10). Intelligence, surveillance, and reconnaissance (ISR) are areas where "data overload" is notoriously present (Morgan et al. 2020, 17). Consequently, ISR is one of the areas currently seeing the greatest amount of investment in military AI (Morgan et al. 2020, 20). By leveraging and integrating AI, big data, and machine learning, the aim is to automate the analysis of hours of drone footage or thousands of pages of text that analysts spend hours sifting through. Project Maven, the US DoD's much-publicised project to develop computer vision algorithms to assist drone targeting, indeed has the expressed goal to "help military and civilian analysts encumbered by the sheer volume of full-motion video data that DoD collects every day in support of counterinsurgency and counterterrorism operations" and to "turn the enormous volume of data available to DoD into actionable intelligence and insights" (Pellerin 2017).[2] Commercial advances in image recognition and computer vision have led to this field being one of the most promising for military applications. According to a Congressional Research Service report, the CIA alone has 140 projects in development that leverage AI to automate tasks such as image recognition and predictive analytics (Sayler 2020, 10). Not only can AI systems digest, categorise, and analyse more data than human analysts, but they may also find correlations in data that escape the human mind. As algorithms get better when combined with an ever-growing amount of data generated worldwide, AI systems will increasingly be capable of analysing connections between data points, flagging suspicious activity, spotting trends, fusing separate elements of data, mapping networks, and even sometimes predicting future behaviours and trends (Horowitz et al. 2018, 11). For instance, during the 2021 conflict between Israel and Hamas, the Israeli Defence Force (IDF) utilised an "advanced AI technological platform that centralised data on terrorist groups in the Gaza Strip onto one system that enabled analysis and extraction of the intelligence" (Ahronheim 2021). The IDF leveraged such AI and big data analysis capabilities to accurately map and destroy Hamas' extensive underground tunnel network (Ahronheim 2021). The IDF also utilised the "Gospel" Code: an algorithm that flags potential targets in real time and produces target suggestions for the Israeli Air Force (Ahronheim 2021).

The US and China have also invested heavily in leveraging artificial intelligence in command-and-control structures, particularly to create a "common operating picture" (Sayler 2020, 13). With an ever-increasing flow of data coming from an increasingly diversified number of sources, capabilities to centralise, analyse, and present information in a succinct way to assist decision-making are of paramount importance. With the acceleration of the speed of warfare, AI is becoming the central element to enable these platforms to assist decision-makers in a meaningful way (Dam 2020). Schubert et al. (2018) argue that when there is a premium on speed and several possible options, AI in command and control can confer a decisive advantage. In their view, sides that successfully implement AI in their command-and-control structure can make quicker decisions and gain operational advantages over their opponent (Schubert et al. 2018).

The Chinese leadership, for example, expects the tempo of operations to increase to a level where they will outpace human cognition (Kania 2018, 143–144). The People's Liberation Army (PLA) is therefore exploring the use of AI to enhance its command-and-control structure to achieve "decision superiority" in "intelligentised" warfare (Kania 2018, 141). The inaugural director of the US Joint Artificial Intelligence Center (JAIC) reached similar conclusions when he stated that

> we are going to be shocked by the speed, the chaos, the bloodiness, and the friction of a future fight in which this [AI] will be playing out, maybe in microseconds at times. How do we envision that fight happening? It has to be algorithm against algorithm.
>
> *(quoted in Johnson 2019)*

The US is therefore developing the Joint All Domain Command and Control Concept (JADC2), which aims to centralise planning for all operations by fusing data gathered from sensors in all domains (land, air, sea, space, cyber) and create a single source of information (Sayler 2020, 13). The US Air Force's (USAF) Advanced Battle Management System, a building block of JADC2 in development, leverages AI to allow Air Force and Space Force systems to "share data seamlessly" and "enable faster decision making" (Hoehn, 2021).

The United Kingdom recently fielded AI in training exercises that assisted operational command and control. British soldiers used an "AI engine" which collected and analysed data and supplied information regarding the environment and terrain, providing instant planning support and "enhancing command and control processes" (Ministry of Defence 2021). In Australia, the view is that the Armed Forces will need to be able to manoeuvre in all domains in a smarter and faster way than competitors. Warfighters will need to be trained to partner and understand AI and be able to "augment their decision-making with software-supported analysis and action" (Maddison 2020).

AI as a Disruptor

Artificial intelligence is already used today to automate and assist in the production and spread of online disinformation, eroding trust in democratic institutions and processes and sowing confusion and polarisation among populations. Disinformation is not new, but in a digital era where most of the global population is connected, disinformation is gaining traction as an effective tool of asymmetric warfare to influence and destabilise states, while remaining below the threshold of war (Kaspersen and Rickli 2016). Russia notoriously influenced the 2016 US presidential election by purchasing ads on Facebook and Google, utilising automated bot accounts on Twitter, and using troll farms to create and spread disinformation online ahead of the election and disrupt the American democratic process (Polyakova 2018; Mueller 2019). The deliberate targeting of democratic discourse is a new type of political warfare which can be "employed to disrupt free societies anywhere in the world" (Arquilla 2021, 2).

Advances in Natural Language Processing (NLP), the branch of artificial intelligence that focuses on training computers to understand, process, and replicate human language, can have very concerning applications. Open AI recently developed the ChatGPT, which can automatically generate text about any subject by learning from massive amounts of English text articles online.[3] The texts can be persuasive and nearly impossible to distinguish from text written by humans. Such capabilities have the potential to scale up a generation of misleading news articles, the impersonation of others online, the automation of the production of abusive or fake content posted on social media, or the automated production of spam and phishing content (Open AI 2019). AI enables increased dissemination of propaganda and provides "mechanisms to narrowly tailor propaganda to a target audience" (Horowitz et al. 2018, 4). With advances in machine learning and the growing amount of individual data collected on the internet, AI can profile individuals with extreme precision, predicting their preferences and behaviours (Mansted and Rosenbach 2018). This enables the kind of impact seen in the 2016 elections. It is now possible to identify those most susceptible to being influenced, targeting their fears, characteristics, vulnerabilities, and beliefs (Mansted and Rosenbach 2018). The seriousness of the threat has prompted the USAF to develop a programme with Primer (a startup company specialising in NLP) to develop a software tool to detect false narratives in public space (Tucker 2020).

Deepfake technology, which uses deep learning to alter images, videos, and audio content or even to create them from scratch in an uncanny way, further compounds AI's disruptive potential. It is, in fact, possible today to make policymakers say things they never said or create convincing portraits of non-existent people.[4] While lying and deceit are not new to military affairs, AI is compounding the problem by simultaneously democratising and sophisticating the creation of fake and misleading content (Whyte 2020, 213). This lowers the entry bar to realistic disruptive media, multiplying the numbers of actors with access to this technology and increasing their impact.

While deepfake technology is predominantly used today to create pornographic content (around 96% of deepfake videos online are pornographic), its potential for military application is clear (Ajder et al. 2019, 1). Deepfake technology fosters an environment of "plausible deniability", where the possibility of an image or video being fake erodes our trust in what we see or hear. The distinction between what is real or not is increasingly blurred (Schick 2020). In Gabon in 2018, a video of the president suspected to be a deepfake led to an attempted coup. In 2019, the pretext of a video being a deepfake shielded the Malaysian Minister of Economic Affairs from political scandal (Ajder et al. 2019, 10). In these cases, a growing awareness of deepfakes damaged political discourse and "undermined the perceived objectivity of recorded video in politically charged contexts" (Ajder et al. 2019, 10). The end of "seeing is believing" would dramatically impact political uncertainty and crisis, accelerating the spread of propaganda and disinformation online and reducing trust in democratic institutions

(Smith and Mansted 2020, 11). This phenomenon is further amplified by the fact that lies spread faster (six times) and reach a wider audience (up to a thousand times) than the truth (Vosoughi et al. 2018).

Deepfakes have also provided new tools for cyberattacks, namely through the creation and use of convincing audio imitations in phishing attacks (Stupp 2019). Geographic satellite imagery could also be faked or altered through the same technology, which could have dramatic consequences for military planning (Chesney and Citron 2019, 1783; Vincent 2021). An experiment conducted in Israel demonstrated that MRI pictures modified by CT-GAN's[5] image tampering attacks had an average success rate of 99.2% for cancer injection and 95.8% for cancer removal, which means radiologists were almost always fooled by the image manipulations (Mirsky et al. 2019). This experiment demonstrated the potential effects of malicious use of deepfakes and the concrete security implications that they could have. The disruptive potential of this technology has led the Defense Advanced Research Projects Agency (DARPA) to invest in counter-deepfake technology with two programmes dedicated to this purpose: Media Forensics (concluded in 2021) and Semantic Forensics (with a US$23.4 million budget for 2022) (Sayler and Harris 2021).

AI as a Force Multiplier

The argument for autonomy, which stipulates that military AI will be the only way for humans to keep up with the increasing speed of war, extends to weapon systems. As weapon systems will increasingly need to make some decisions autonomously to keep up with the tempo of war, and with the capacity to do so faster than enemies being key, AI as applied to weapon systems is seen by many as conferring decisive advantages to successful adopters. AI has already found its way into various weapon systems, powering autonomy to varying degrees, and is already deployed on battlefields as a force multiplier.

The International Committee of the Red Cross (ICRC) defines autonomous weapon systems (AWS) as "any weapon system with autonomy in its critical functions. That is a weapon system that can select […] and attack […] targets without human intervention" (ICRC, 2021). It is important to note that autonomous weapon systems that acquire and engage targets autonomously are not the only weapon systems utilising AI. Today, weapon systems with lesser degrees of autonomy that still rely on human operators are already using AI applications in various forms (such as for image recognition, targeting/target selections). There are broadly three categories of autonomous weapon systems with varying levels of autonomy and human supervision: *human in the loop systems, human on the loop systems, and human out of the loop systems* (Noone and Noone 2015, 28). Currently, *human in the loop* and *on the loop* systems exist and are deployed. For example, Israel's "Iron Dome" relies on predictive missiles and rockets impact location to select its firing of defensive missiles. Utilising the definition of AWS of the ICRC, one can observe that some *human out of the loop* systems have already been deployed and used operationally. While most systems that can acquire and engage targets autonomously are primarily defensive in nature,[6] loitering munitions such as the Israeli Harpy, Harop, Harpy NG, and the Orbiter 1K "Kingfisher" are, according to Boulanin and Verbruggen (2017, 115), the only operational loitering weapons that are known to be capable of acquiring and engaging targets autonomously.[7] The loitering time, geographical areas of deployment, and the category of targets they can attack are determined in advance by humans (Boulanin and Verbruggen 2017). Israel's Harpy drone, for example, can be programmed before a launch to a "loitering area" where the weapon loiters in search of targets (in this case, air defence systems) with the capacity to detect, attack, and destroy the targets autonomously (IAI, 2017). These systems can be used in a *human in the loop* configuration for high-value targets, thus maintaining a level of human oversight. In contrast, the fully autonomous configuration is utilised for Suppression of Enemy Air Defence (SEAD) missions (Boulanin and Verbruggen 2017, 54). Systems with no level of human oversight, with total freedom over the selection and engagement of targets, are not yet fielded.

Drone swarms are a prime example of the use of AI as a force multiplier on the battlefield and one of the most popular future avenues for utilising autonomous drones (Kallenborn 2021b). A drone swarm can be defined as a collection of "cooperative, autonomous robots that react to the battlefield as one at machine speed" (Scharre 2018, 385). Therefore, swarms are not just several drones together but a single, integrated weapon system that utilises artificial intelligence to coordinate its elements (Kallenborn 2021a). A swarm of drones is different from other autonomous and semi-autonomous drones insofar as its elements "self-organise", converging on behaviours to achieve a goal (Scharre 2018, 386). In what has been described as the "First AI War", Israel used a drone swarm to locate, identify and strike enemy combatants in the Gaza strip (Kallenborn 2021a). While commercial drone swarms have been around for some time – Genesis Motors flew 3,281 drones in formation above Shanghai in a record-breaking publicity stunt in 2021 – the use of a militarised drone swarm would be the first acknowledged instance of the use of a swarm in conflict. In this instance, the drone swarm co-ordinated searches and, through a command-and-control infrastructure (called Torch 750), could share data in real time with other units and weapon systems (Hambling 2021). With the capacity to self-organise, choose targets, engage, and subsequently disperse, drone swarms can be a cost-effective way to damage enemy forces (Lehto and Hutchinson 2020, 162). Hundreds or thousands of cheaply made drones could be used to overwhelm enemy air defence systems by quickly converging on targets, seamlessly re-adjusting to make up for lost individual swarm elements, and just as quickly dispersing to avoid counterattacks.

Future Prospects

In 2019, the USAF successfully conducted a flight test for the new Valkyrie drone, an unmanned aircraft designed to fly autonomously alongside a manned fighter jet. This is but one example of the increased popularity of the concept of *loyal wingman drones*, which are set to be the future of air combat. The idea of the *loyal wingman* would be to have a series of attributable autonomous drones flying alongside fighter jets to enhance the fighter jet's capabilities (reconnaissance, target engagement, and destruction) and also *sacrifice* themselves to protect the manned aircraft. Accordingly, militaries are developing these cheaper autonomous capabilities complementing fighter jets (around US$2 million a piece for the Valkyrie drone) with the USAF planning to add AI capabilities to the Valkyrie drone for it to train and learn alongside pilots, ultimately being able to respond independently to threats (Insinna 2019). The Royal Australian Air Force is equally investing in these capabilities, building similar drones with Boeing Australia. Compared to an F35 Jet, these Loyal Wingmen could prove a cost-effective way to bulk up air power capacity in contested airspaces, more cheaply protecting vital assets (Levick 2020, 33).

Loyal wingman drones are one example of the broader trend that will increasingly rely on human-machine teaming. The latter magnifies "the predictive power of algorithms with the intuitions of humans, especially in decision-framing" (Saenz et al. 2020). Armed forces are trying to capitalise on this by increasingly seeking to integrate and *enhance* the capabilities of human soldiers through seamless interaction with machinery (Gould, 2020). Here, AI is the backbone of making this interaction increasingly smooth and feasible. As put by the former director of the Joint Artificial Intelligence Center Lt Gen Jack Shanahan, AI's most valuable contribution will be in "gaining a deeper understanding of how to optimise human-machine teaming" (Konaev and Chahal 2021). Ultimately, the aim is to potentially fully integrate such drones as the "Loyal wingmen" with the human pilot. However, this is dependent on advances in other technologies, such as "Brain-Computer Interfaces" (BCI) (Vahle 2020, 16–17). One of the major trends in emerging technologies is their convergence with each other. As argued by Pauwels, "technologies are becoming complex hybrid systems that are merging and enabling each other, with drastic changes in velocity, scope and system-wide impact" (Pauwels 2019, 8). Military technological innovations do not happen in a vacuum and siloes from each other. Therefore, the prospects of AI in the military realm are deeply interwoven with advances in other emerging technologies. The convergence between AI and BCI will usher in advances which we cannot yet predict but will likely speed up and enhance the disruptive impact of these new technologies on warfare and military affairs in general (Rickli 2020b).

Though the discussion here has centred mainly on weapons operating in physical domains, the cyber domain will likely see the most deployments and active proliferation of autonomous weapon systems in the future. This domain offers fewer impediments than physical domains and provides unlimited scalability (Krieg and Rickli 2019, 106). In 2018, IBM presented a proof of concept dubbed *Deeplocker*, an AI-powered malware "highly targeted and evasive" (Stoecklin 2018). The use of AI in cyberattacks will likely be more pervasive and much harder to detect and defeat as machine learning-engineered attacks are harder to detect and less predictable (Krewell 2020; Pupillo et al. 2021).

Implications for International Security

Like many military innovations before it, AI's penetration into military affairs is not without deep implications for international security. This section argues that AI's military applications will substantially impact strategic stability by favouring offensive strategies and vertical and horizontal proliferation.

Implications for Strategic Stability

The strategic implications of artificial intelligence run deep as they have the potential to upend the fundamental calculus behind deterrence by putting the premium on offence and pre-emption (Rickli 2017). Lynn-Jones notes that "conflict and war will be more likely when offence has the advantage, while peace and cooperation are more probable when defence has the advantage" (Lynn-Jones 1995, 691). Therefore, as argued by Rickli, the impact that AWS have on the offence-defence balance is an essential element in assessing its implications for strategic stability (Rickli, 2018). The use of AI in command-and-control structures, such as automated decision-making and weapons in the form of AWS, risks tilting the balance towards the offence.[8]

First, at the tactical level, how AI-powered weapon systems are likely to be used largely favours offensive use (Rickli 2018). One such example is swarming tactics, which aim at overwhelming enemy defence systems and neutralising any advantage gained by a defensive posture. Following Lynn-Jones's argument, an environment in which defensive postures are likely to be inefficient enhances the possibility of conflict and strategic instability by incentivising pre-emptive strikes. Second, the opacity inherent to artificial intelligence algorithms similarly affects the offence-defence balance, as it leads to an incapacity to appropriately judge an adversary's capabilities and their impact (Horowitz 2018, 55). Unlike traditional military capabilities, which can be more easily observed, a state's armament in AI-related capabilities would be almost impossible for another state to measure accurately. Assessing the depth of automation of an adversary's arsenal, the quality of the code, the efficiency of the autonomous weapons, and their capabilities would prove difficult. This could create an environment where states are pushed to assume the worst of their rivals and over-estimate their capabilities (Horowitz 2018, 55).

The lack of first-hand battlefield experience of these capabilities could similarly push states to over-estimate the destructive potential of adversary's weapon systems, leading to an increased probability of arms races resulting from security dilemmas (Horowitz 2019, 779). In this case, states will not only have difficulty in discerning a state's intention but would also have trouble assessing capabilities. This adds a dimension to Jervis's traditional understanding of arms races resulting from security dilemmas, where states can measure each other's capabilities but not intentions (Horowitz 2019, 779). As posited by Price, Walker, and Wiley, understanding leadership, their intentions, and how they might react to a certain event is part of deterrence. In the case of automated decision-making and AWS, it would be impossible for a state to determine how AWS would respond to one state's action, increasing mutual unintelligibility between adversaries and strategic uncertainty (Price et al. 2018, 101).

Furthermore, in a "humans out of the loop" scenario, opportunities for de-escalation and non-use of force would be scarce. Lastly, as Horowitz argues, "the relationship between speed and crisis stability in a world of deployed LAWS [lethal autonomous weapon systems] represents one of the clearest risk factors associated with autonomous weapons" (Horowitz 2019, 781). In fact, with the expectation that hostilities will be conducted at machine speed, states might suffer from a fear of *losing quicker*, hereby creating escalation pressure and incentives to act first with a pre-emptive strike (Horowitz 2019, 782).

It is, however, worth noting that the argument of the offensive advantage provided by artificial intelligence is a disputed one. For instance, Hammes (2021) makes the opposite point by arguing that emerging technologies and AI usher in an era of defensive dominance on the battlefield because the attackers always leave multiple signatures that can be more easily identified by the defenders. While this argument holds some truth, it is limited as it assumes that strategic stability only relies on one material factor. The growing development of stealth technology also undermines the point. However, strategic stability depends on several tangible factors and relies on perceptions. Thus, we agree with Paul Scharre's doctoral thesis that "widespread deployment of fully autonomous weapons would likely undermine crisis stability, escalation control and war termination because of the risk of unintended lethal engagements" (2020, 289).

Vertical and Horizontal Proliferation: Strategic Impact of Underdogs

Artificial intelligence is inherently subject to quick proliferation due to its nature as a dual-use technology, whereby developments in the commercial sector subsequently trickle up to the military realm (Rickli and Ienca 2021). Therefore, AI is a commercial endeavour developed in the private sector to satisfy business demands (Morgan et al. 2020, 13). Private corporations are some of the most aggressive investors in the technology, including tech giants such as Microsoft investing US$1 billion in OpenAI, an AI research Lab dedicated to researching artificial general intelligence (AGI), or Google having acquired Deepmind for more than US$500 million to conduct research in the same field (Shu 2014; Vincent, 2019). In the case of AI, proliferation is not only a function of state funding and development – as is traditionally the case for nuclear armament – but also a function of private sector demands, R&D, and production. Horowitz argues that military capabilities proliferate faster when there is "an underlying commercial demand and the unit costs are low" (Horowitz 2019, 777). Therefore, the horizontal proliferation of military AI is only likely to accelerate. As stated by Morgan et al. in a RAND corporation study, "we can reasonably expect most future military applications to be adaptations of technologies developed in the commercial sector" (Morgan et al. 2020, 13).

The US benefits from a first-mover advantage in AI, with China following close behind and closing the technology gap quickly (Johnson 2021, 370). However, military AI is unlikely to remain a two-horse race due to the dual-use nature of AI and because AI research and development is taking place globally. This entails that multiple states and non-state actors will have access to at least some degree of military AI. Indeed, while China and the US are far ahead in the field, worldwide economic interdependencies and linkages mean that AI innovations are quickly diffused around the globe. Michael Raska argues that the sixth (and current) revolution in military affairs (RMAs), the AI-RMA, differs from previous RMAs in the diffusion pattern of its technologies (Raska 2021, 469). In this latest AI-driven RMA, the benefits of technological innovation will not be reaped only by major powers (Raska 2021, 473). Middle powers, such as Singapore or Israel, are developing technologies to "advance their economic competitiveness, political influence, and status in the international arena" (Raska 2021, 473). These medium powers are developing niche capabilities and will become "critical influencers in shaping future security, economics and global norms in dual-use AI" (Johnson 2021, 370). Proliferation is thus unlikely to only take place horizontally between states, but vertically too, among non-state actors and even individuals. The fact that innovation is business-driven multiplies the number of actors who have access to disruptive technologies by lowering the bar for their adoption. Furthermore, unlike traditional military capabilities such as fighter jets, algorithms, the backbone of AI, can be replicated and proliferated at little cost.

Military AI, or the ability to use AI-enabled technologies for geopolitical ends and power purposes globally, is thus no longer the sole prerogative of states as nuclear technology, for instance. As emerging technologies spread and develop, they provide non-state actors with capabilities for influence in the international arena that are similar to those that have traditionally been the prerogatives of great powers (Hammes 2016, 9). In 2018, the shadowy group called the Free Alawites Movement claimed responsibility for an attack in which 13 low-cost GPS-guided drones targeted Russia Khmeimim Air Base in Syria, allegedly destroying a US$300 million Russian Missile System[9] (Kallenborn 2020). While the attack remained relatively rudimentary (the drones were made of plywood, duct tape, and other off-the-shelf commercially available products), and irrespective of the damage it produced, the attack hints at a not-so-distant future where non-state actors have the means and intentions to employ drone swarms and other emerging technologies. Automation will only augment the efficiency and disruptive potential of such attacks.

Similarly, the Islamic State weaponised commercial drones and managed to gain temporarily tactical air supremacy over the Iraqi armed forces during the battle of Mosul in 2017 (Rickli 2020c). This led the head of the US Special Operation Command, Gen. Raymond Thomas, to acknowledge that

> this last year's [2016] most daunting problem was an adaptive enemy who, for a time, enjoyed tactical superiority in the airspace under our conventional air superiority in the form of commercially available drones and fuel-expedient weapons systems, and our only available response was small arms fire.
>
> *(Larter 2017)*

As discussed in this chapter, AI could also be instrumentalised for disinformation campaigns by non-state actors seeking to manipulate public opinion (UNCCT and UNICRI 2021, 40). These various examples demonstrate that emerging technologies and AI, once developed, can proliferate very quickly to both state and non-state actors and individuals.

In addition, the growing autonomy of technology incentivises actors to use it as a surrogate instead of manpower. Surrogate warfare is a growing feature of contemporary conflicts where state and non-state actors increasingly rely on human and/or technological surrogates to wage war (Krieg and Rickli 2019). Surrogate warfare is very appealing as it notably reduces economic and political costs by providing plausible deniability. With the development of AWS, the incentive to wage surrogate warfare through technology will likely increase steadily.

Conclusion

This chapter has sought to ground the discussion in current and potential future military uses of AI. By providing an overview of military capabilities and highlighting their international security implications, this chapter contributes to laying the groundwork and is a starting point for discussions over the more strategic and conceptual impact of AI on warfare. In doing so, the chapter has shown that no consensus exists on the ramifications that artificial intelligence will have on the conduct of military affairs. From enthusiasts to pragmatics to deniers, the field of strategic studies offers a multitude of contrasting viewpoints which suggest that discussions over the integration of AI into military affairs are timely and necessary. The views range from believing that automation will change every aspect of how nations fight wars to believing that AI is too immature technology to successfully assist battlefield operations in meaningful and revolutionary ways. Such opposing arguments indicate that the debate is still in its infancy.

Notwithstanding the varying schools of thought on AI's influence on the character and nature of warfare, one grounding reality remains: that AI has permeated into the military realm, is deployed on the battlefield, and is weaponised by some states to wield influence at a low cost below the threshold of war. On the battlefield, AI is utilised as an analytical enabler, assisting intelligence, surveillance, and reconnaissance by sifting through massive troves of texts and images, unburdening the work of analysts. As an increasing amount of data is generated on battlefields, the capacity to analyse large amounts of data faster than an adversary is critical. As the tempo of war accelerates, armed forces seek to automate command and control to gain "decision superiority" and to be able to react faster to events than an adversary (Kania 2018, 143–144). As a force multiplier, AI-related technologies already feature in weapon systems in varying forms across the globe in human-in, -on, and -out of the loop systems. With swarming set to be a promising way to utilise drones, the level of automation of weapon systems will increase. As a disruptor, AI offers smaller powers and non-state actors the ability to wield disproportionate influence on the world stage with few resources. Advances in natural language processing and deep learning are democratising and sophisticating the ability to create fictitious content, or deepfakes, through either fake text, images, or videos. Coupled with the ability to micro-target content online to maximise effects, the disruptive potential of disinformation is enhanced.

These military uses of AI have profound consequences for international security. They will likely offset the strategic offence-defence balance towards the offence and display new patterns of proliferation that are very different from those in the nuclear domain (Rickli 2019). The use of autonomous weapon systems due to their speed and offensive use in swarms will likely put the advantage on offence and pre-emption in the international system. The inherent unintelligibility of AI systems and the difficulty of gauging an opponent's AI capabilities could foster arms races and security dilemmas, creating escalation pressure (Horowitz 2019, 779). The commercial nature of AI research and development further increases the impact of AI on strategic stability, as it facilitates the proliferation of the technology, increasing the number of actors that have access to disruptive military AI. Though it is difficult to identify all the potential implications of AI on warfare, this chapter has shown that they are widespread and will profoundly shape international relations in the 21st century.

Notes

1 It is noteworthy that autonomy can be achieved without artificial intelligence through pre-planned programming of the behaviour of the machine but autonomy relying on artificial intelligence techniques, such as machine learning, offers the prospects of unintended consequences (Boulanin and Verbruggen 2017).

2 See also Brewster (2021).

3 ChatGPT builds upon the Open AI GPT-3 model. While Open AI only publicly released a small version of the GPT-2 model due to concerns over large language models being used to generate deceptive, biased, or abusive language at scale, the GPT-3 tool is accessible through Open AI's first commercial product.

4 For an example of Deepfakes, visit "thispersondoesnotexsits.com", a website which creates uncanny computer-generated portraits of non-existent people.

5 CT-GAN is a framework for automatically injecting and removing medical evidence from 3D medical scans such as those produced from computed tomography (CT) or magnetic resonance imagery (MRI). The framework consists of two algorithms

(conditional generative adversarial networks (GANs)) which perform image completion on 3D imagery (see Mirsky 2020).

6 According to Boulanin and Verbruggen, "at least 89 countries have deployed or are developing such system" (2017, 115).

7 In terms of missile systems, the few guided munitions with some target selection autonomy include the Long-Range Anti-Ship Missile (LSRAM) (US), Dual-Mode Brimstone (UK), and the Naval Strike Missile/Joint Strike Missile (NSM/JSM) (Norway) (Boulanin and Verbruggen 2017, 49).

8 See also Altmann and Sauer (2017), Johnson (2020), and Payne (2021).

9 Little is known about the Free Alawites Movement, and few attacks have been attributed to them. Russian authorities further denied that the attack resulted in any damage to the airbase or its personnel.

References

Ahronheim, Anna. 2021. "Israel's Operation against Hamas Was the World's First AI War." *The Jerusalem Post*, May 27, 2021. https://www.jpost.com/arab-israeli-conflict/gaza-news/guardian-of-the-walls-the-first-ai-war-669371.

Ajder, Henry, Francesco Cavalli, Laurence Cullen and Giorgio Patrini. 2019. "The State of Deepfakes: Landscapte, Threats and Impact." *Deeptrace*, September 2019. https://regmedia.co.uk/2019/10/08/deepfake_report.pdf.

Altmann, Jürgen, Frank Sauer. 2017. "Autonomous Weapon Systems and Strategic Stability." *Survival* 59, no. 5: 117–142. https://www.tandfonline.com/doi/abs/10.1080/00396338.2017.1375263.

Arquilla, John. 2021. *Bitskrieg : The New Challenge of Cyberwarfare*. Cambridge: Polity Press.

Arquilla, John, David Ronfeldt. 2000. "Swarming and the Future of Conflict". Santa Monica, CA: Rand Corporation National Security Research Division. https://www.rand.org/pubs/documented_briefings/DB311.html.

Ayoub, Kareem, Kenneth Payne. 2016. "Strategy in the Age of Artificial Intelligence." *Journal of Strategic Studies* 39, no. 5–6: 793–819. https://doi.org/10.1080/01402390.2015.1088838.

Borchert, Heiko, Torben Schutz, Joseph Verbovszky. 2021. "Beware of the Hype. What Military Conflicts in Ukraine, Syria, Lybia, and Nagorno-Karabakh (Don't) Tell Us about the Future of War." *Defence AI Observatory, Helmut Schmidt University*. https://doi.org/10.13140/RG.2.2.10456.62723.

Boulanin, Vincent, Maaike Verbruggen. 2017. *Mapping the Development of Autonomy in Weapon Systems*. Stockholm, SIPRI, November. https://www.sipri.org/sites/default/files/2017-11/siprireport_mapping_the_development_of_autonomy_in_weapon_systems_1117_1.pdf.

Brewster, Thomas. 2021. "Project-Maven: Startups Backed by Google, Peter Thiel, Eric Schmidt and James Murdoch Are Building AI and Facial Recognition Surveillance Tools for the Pentagon." *Forbes*, 8 September. https://www.forbes.com/sites/thomasbrewster/2021/09/08/project-maven-startups-backed-by-google-peter-thiel-eric-schmidt-and-james-murdoch-build-ai-and-facial-recognition-surveillance-for-the-defense-department/?sh=10865ba06ef2.

Chesney, Bobby, Danielle Citron. 2019. "Deepfakes: A Looming Challenge for Privacy, Democracy and National Security." *California Law Review* 107, no. 6: 1753–1820. https://doi.org/10.15770/Z38RV0D15J.

Clausewitz, Carl von. 1976. *On War*. Translated by Michael Howard and Peter Paret. Pinceton, NJ: Princeton University Press.

Cleverland, Charles T., Daniel Egel, Cristopher Oates, Eric Robinson. 2019. "AI and Irregular Warfare: An Evolution, Not a Revolution." *War on the Rocks*, October 31, 2019. https://warontherocks.com/2019/10/ai-and-irregular-warfare-an-evolution-not-a-revolution/.

Dam, Henrik Røboe. 2020. "Central to Meeting the Complexities of JADC2? Artificial Intelligence." *C4ISRNET*, May 13, 2020. https://www.c4isrnet.com/2020/05/13/central-to-meeting-the-complexities-of-jadc2-artificial-intelligence/.

Danks, David. 2020. "How Adversarial Attacks Could Destabilise Military AI Systems." *IEEE Spectrum*, February 26, 2020. https://spectrum.ieee.org/adversarial-attacks-and-ai-systems#toggle-gdpr.

Davis, Zachary. 2019. "Artificial Intelligence on the Battlefield." *PRISM* 8, no. 2: 114–131. https://www.jstor.org/stable/26803234.

Evans, Hayley. 2018. "Lethal Autonomous Weapons Systems at the First and Second UN GGE Meetings." *Lawfare*, April 9, 2018. https://www.lawfareblog.com/lethal-autonomous-weapons-systems-first-and-second-un-gge-meetings#.

Gady, Franz-Stefan. 2015. "The Fog of Peace: Why We Are Not Able to Predict Military Power." *The Diplomat*, February 4, 2015. https://thediplomat.com/2015/02/the-fog-of-peace-why-we-are-not-able-to-predict-military-power/.

Gould, Joe. 2020. "AI's Dogfight Triumph a Step toward Human-Machine Teaming." *C4ISRNET*, September 10, 2020. https://www.c4isrnet.com/congress/2020/09/10/ais-dogfight-triumph-a-step-toward-human-machine-teaming/.

Gray, Colin S. 1999. *Modern Strategy*. Oxford: Oxford University Press.

Hambling, David. 2021. "Israel's Combat-Proen Drone Swarm May Be Start of a New Kind of Warfare." *Forbes*, July 21, 2021. https://www.forbes.com/sites/davidhambling/2021/07/21/israels-combat-proven-drone-swarm-is-more-than-just-a-drone-swarm.

Hammes, T.X. 2016. "Technologies Converge and Power Diffuses." *CATO Institute*, January 27, 2016. https://www.cato.org/sites/cato.org/files/pubs/pdf/pa786-updated.pdf.

Hammes, T.X. 2021. "Defence Dominance: Advantages for Small States." *RSIS Commentaries*, 19 October. https://www.rsis.edu.sg/rsis-publication/rsis/defence-dominance-advantage-for-small-states/.

Hoehn, John R. 2021. "Advanced Battle Management System (ABMS)." *US Library of Congress. Congressional Research Service*. IF11866. https://sgp.fas.org/crs/weapons/IF11866.pdf.

Hoffman, F.G. 2018. "Will War's Nature Change in the Seventh Military Revolution." *The US Army War College Quarterly Parameters* 47, no. 4 (Winter): 19–31. https://publications.armywarcollege.edu/pubs/3554.pdf.

Holland Michel, Arthur. 2020. 'The Black Box, Unlocked: Predictability and Understand-ability in Military AI.' Geneva: United Nations Institute for Disarmament Research. https://doi.org/10.37559/SecTec/20/AI1.

Horowitz, Michael C. 2018. "Artificial Intelligence, International Competition, and the Balance of Power." *Texas National Security Review* 1, no. 3: 37–57. https://doi.org/10.15781/T2639KP49.

Horowitz, Michael C. 2019. "When Speed Kills: Lethal Autonomous Weapon Systems, Deterrence and Stability." *Journal of Strategic Studies* 42, no. 6: 764–788. https://doi.org/10.1080/01402390.2019.1621174.

Horowitz, Michael C., Gregory C. Allen, Anthony Cho, Kara Frederick, Edoardo Saravalle, Paul Scharre. 2018. "Artificial Intelligence and International Security." *Center for a New American Security*, July 10, 2018. https://www.cnas.org/publications/reports/artificial-intelligence-and-international-security.

Hughes, Zach. 2020. "Fog, Friction and Thinking Machines." *War on the Rocks*, March 11, 2020. https://warontherocks.com/2020/03/fog-friction-and-thinking-machines/.

IAI. 2017. "HARPY, Autonomous Weapon for All Weather." Accessed September 21, 2021. https://www.iai.co.il/p/harpy.

ICRC. 2021. "Autonomy, Artificial Intelligence and Robotics: Technical Aspets of Human Control." *International Committee of the Red Cross*, Geneva, August 2019. https://www.icrc.org/en/document/autonomy-artificial-intelligence-and-robotics-technical-aspects-human-control.

Insinna, Valerie. 2019. "US Air Force Looks to Fast Track Cash to Kratos Defence for More Valkyrie Drones." *Defence News*, July 17, 2019. https://www.defensenews.com/digital-show-dailies/paris-air-show/2019/06/17/us-air-force-looking-to-fast-track-cash-to-kratos-defense-for-additional-valkyrie-drones/.

Johnson, James. 2020. "Artificial Intelligence: A Threat to Strategic Stability." *Strategic Studies Quarterly*, Spring, 16–39. https://www.jstor.org/stable/pdf/26891882.pdf?refreqid=excelsior%3Ae14768b84cabb60bca7a2b612ab8a421.

Johnson, James, 2021. "The End of Military-Techno *Pax Americana?* Washington's Strategic Responses to Chinese AI-Enabled Military Technology." *The Pacific Review* 34, no. 3: 351–378. https://doi.org/10.1080/09512748.2019.1676299.

Johnson, Khari. 2019. "The US Military, Algorithmic Warfare and Big Tech." *VentureBeat*, 8 November. https://venturebeat.com/2019/11/08/the-u-s-military-algorithmic-warfare-and-big-tech/.

Kallenborn, Zachary. 2020. "A Partial Ban on Autonomous Weapons Would Make Everyone Safer." *Foreign Policy*, October 14, 2020. https://foreignpolicy.com/2020/10/14/ai-drones-swarms-killer-robots-partial-ban-on-autonomous-weapons-would-make-everyone-safer/.

Kallenborn, Zachary. 2021a. "Israel's Drone Swarm over Gaza Should Worry Everyone." *Defence One*, July 7, 2021. https://www.defenseone.com/ideas/2021/07/israels-drone-swarm-over-gaza-should-worry-everyone/183156/.

Kallenborn, Zachary. 2021b. "Meet the Future Weapon of Mass Destruction, the Drone Swarm."

Bulletin of the Atomic Scientists, April 5, 2021. https://thebulletin.org/2021/04/meet-the-future-weapon-of-mass-destruction-the-drone-swarm/.

Kania, Elsa. 2018. "Artificial Intelligence in Future Chinese Command Decision-Making." In *AI, China, Russia, and the Global Order: Technological, Political, Global, and Greative Perspectives*, edited by Nicholas D. Wright and Mariah C. Yager, 141–152. https://nsiteam.com/social/wp-content/uploads/2018/12/AI-China-Russia-Global-WP_FINAL.pdf.

Kaspersen, Anja and Jean-Marc Rickli. 2016. "The Global War of Narratives and the Role of Social Media." *World Policy*, 9 August. http://worldpolicy.org/2016/08/09/the-global-war-of-narratives-and-the-role-of-social-media/.

Konaev, Margarita, Husanjot Chahal. 2021. "Building Trust in Human-Machine Teams." *Brookings*, February 18, 2021. https://www.brookings.edu/techstream/building-trust-in-human-machine-teams.

Krewell, Kevin. 2020. "IBM, AI and the Battle for Cybersecurity." *Forbes*, 17 September. https://www.forbes.com/sites/tiriasresearch/2020/09/17/ibm-ai-and-the-battle-for-cybersecurity/.

Krieg, Andreas, Jean-Marc Rickli. 2019. *Surrogate Warfare: The Transformation of War in the Twenty-first Century*. Georgetown: Georgetown University Press.

Larter, David B. 2017. "SOCOM Commander: Armed ISIS Drones Were 2016's 'Most Daunting Problem'." *Defence News*, 16 May. https://www.defensenews.com/digital-show-dailies/sofic/2017/05/16/socom-commander-armed-isis-drones-were-2016s-most-daunting-problem/.

Lehto, Martti, William Hutchinson. 2020. "Mini-Drone Swarms: Their Issues and Potential in Conflict Situations." *Journal of Information Warfare* 20, no. 1: 159–167. https://www.jinfowar.com/journal/volume-20-issue-1/mini-drone-swarms-their-issues-potential-conflict-situations.

Levick, Ewen. 2020. "A Robot Is My Wingman." *IEEE Spectrum* 57, no. 1: 32–56. https://doi.org/10.1109/MSPEC.2020.8946306.

Lynn-Jones, Sean M. 1995. "Offence-Defence Theory and Its Critics." *Security Studies* 4, no. 4: 660–691. https://doi.org/10.1080/09636419509347600.

Maddison, Paul. 2020. "Artificial Intelligence and the Future of Command and Control." *Defence Connect*, November 30, 2020. https://www.defenceconnect.com.au/key-enablers/7286-op-ed-artificial-intelligence-and-the-future-of-command-control.

Mallick, P.K. Maj Gen. 2019. "Is Artificial Intelligence (AI) Changing the Nature of War?" *Vivekananda International Foundation*, January 18, 2019. https://www.vifindia.org/print/5778?via=Azure.

Mansted, Katherine, Eric Rosenbach. 2018. "Can Democracy Survive in the Information Age." *Belfer Center for Science and International Affairs, Harvard Kennedy*, October 2018. https://www.belfercenter.org/index.php/publication/can-democracy-survive-information-age.

Mashur, Niklas. 2019. "AI in Military Enabling Applications." *CSS Analyses in Security Policy*, no. 251: 1–4. https://css.ethz.ch/content/specialinterest/gess/cis/center-for-securities-studies/en/publications/css-analyses-in-security-policy/details.html?id=/n/o/2/5/no_251_ai_in_military_enabling_applicati.

Maxwell, Paul. 2020. "Artificial Intelligence Is the Future of Warfare (Just Not in the Way You Think)." *Modern War Institute at West Point*, April 20, 2020. https://mwi.usma.edu/artificial-intelligence-future-warfare-just-not-way-think/.

Mehta, Aaron. 2018. "AI Makes Mattis Question "Fundamental Beliefs about War." *C4ISRNET*, February 17, 2019. https://www.c4isrnet.com/intel-geoint/2018/02/17/ai-makes-mattis-question-fundamental-beliefs-about-war/.

Mirsky, Yisroel. 2020. "CT-GAN." *GitHub*. https://github.com/ymirsky/CT-GAN.

Mirsky, Yisroel, Tom Mahler, Ilan Shelef, Yuval Elovici. 2019. "CT-GAN: Malicious Tampering of 3D Medical Imagery Using Deep Learning." *arXiv*, 6 June. https://arxiv.org/pdf/1901.03597.pdf.

Morgan, Forrest E., Benjamin Boudreaux, Andrew J. Lohn, Mark Ashby, Christian Curriden, Kelly Klima, Derek Grossman. 2020. "Military Applications of Artificial Intelligence: Ethical Concerns in an Uncertain World." Santa Monica, CA: RAND Corporation, 2020. https://www.rand.org/pubs/research_reports/RR3139-1.html.

Mueller III, Robert S. 2019. *Report on the Investigation into Russian Interference in the 2016 Presidential Election*. Washington, DC: Government Printing Office.

Noone, Gregory P., Diana C. Noone. 2015. "The Debate over Autonomous Weapons Systems." *Case Western Reserve Journal of International Law* 47, no. 1: 25–35. https://scholarlycommons.law.case.edu/jil/vol47/iss1/6.

Open AI. 2019. "Better Language Models and Their Implications." Accessed July 10, 2021. https://openai.com/blog/better-language-models/.

Owens, Bill. 2001. *Lifting the Fog of War.* Baltimore MD: The John Hopkins University Press.

Pauwels, Eleonore. 2019. "The New Geopolitics of Converging Risks: The Un and Prevention in the Era of AI." *United Nations University Centre for Policy Research.* https://collections.unu.edu/eserv/UNU:7308/PauwelsAIGeopolitics.pdf.

Pellerin, Cheryl. 2017. "Project Maven Industry Day Pursues Artificial intelligence for DoD Challenges." *DoD News*, October 27, 2017. https://www.defense.gov/Explore/News/Article/Article/1356172/project-maven-industry-day-pursues-artificial-intelligence-for-dod-challenges/.

Payne, Kenneth. 2018. "Artificial Intelligence: A Revolution in Strategic Affairs." *Survival* 60, no. 5: 7–32. https://doi.org/10.1080/00396338.2018.1518374.

Payne, Kenneth. 2021. *I, Warbot:The Dawn of Artificially Intelligent Conflict.* London: Hurst and Company.

Pietrucha, Mike. 2016. "Living with Fog and Friction: The Fallacy of Information Superiority." *War on the Rocks*, January 7, 2016. https://warontherocks.com/2016/01/living-with-fog-and-friction-the-fallacy-of-information-superiority/.

Polyakova, Alina. 2018. "Weapons of the Weak: Russia and AI-driven Asymmetric Warfare." *Brookings*, November 15, 2018. https://www.brookings.edu/research/weapons-of-the-weak-russia-and-ai-driven-asymmetric-warfare/.

Price, Mathew, Stephen Walker, Will Wiley. 2018. "The Machine Beneath: Implications of Artificial Intelligence in Strategic Decision Making." *PRISM* 7, no. 4: 92–105. https://www.jstor.org/stable/26542709.

Pupillo, Lorenzo, Stefano Fantin, Alfonso Ferreira, Carolina Polito. 2021. *Artificial Intelligence and Cybersecurity: Technology, Governance and Policy Challenges. Final Report of a CEPS Task Force.* Brussels: Centre for European Policy Studies, May. https://www.ceps.eu/wp-content/uploads/2021/05/CEPS-TFR-Artificial-Intelligence-and-Cybersecurity.pdf.

Raska, Michael. 2021. "The Sixth RMA Wave: Disruption in Military Affairs?" *Journal of Strategic Studies* 44, no. 4: 456–479. https://doi.org/10.1080/01402390.2020.1848818.

Rickli, Jean-Marc. 2017. "The Impact of Autonomous Weapons Systems on International Security and Strategic Stability." In *Defence Future Technologies: What We See on the Horizon*, edited by Quentin Ladetto, 61–64. Thun: Armasuisse. https://css.ethz.ch/en/services/digital-library/articles/article.html/0654ca0d-4883-4b80-a953-9f7749e8162b.

Rickli, Jean-Marc. 2018. "The Impact of Autonomy and Artificial Intelligence on Strategic Stability." *UN Chronicle*, July 2018.

Rickli, Jean-Marc. 2019. "The Destabilising Prospects of Artificial Intelligence for Nuclear Strategy, Deterrence and Stability." In *The Impact of Artificial Intelligence on Strategic Stability and Nuclear Risk: European Perspectives*, edited by Vincent Boulanin, Vol. I, 91–98. Stockholm: Stockholm International Peace Research Institute. https://www.sipri.org/sites/default/files/2019-05/sipri1905-ai-strategic-stability-nuclear-risk.pdf.

Rickli, Jean-Marc. 2020a. "The Strategic Implications of Artificial Intelligence." In *Handbook of Artificial Intelligence and Robotic Process Automation: Policy and Government Applications*, edited by Al Naqvi and J. Munoz Mark, 41–56. London: Anthem Press.

Rickli, Jean-Marc. 2020b. "Neurotechnologies and Future Warfare." *RSIS Commentaries*, 7 December. https://www.rsis.edu.sg/rsis-publication/rsis/ai-governance-and-military-affairs-neurotechnologies-and-future-warfare/#.YXCRCy1h3EY.

Rickli, Jean-Marc. 2020c. "Surrogate Warfare and the Transformation of Warfare in the 2020s." *Observer Research Foundation*, Mumbai, 30 December. https://www.orfonline.org/expert-speak/surrogate-warfare-transformation-war-2020s.

Rickli, Jean-Marc, Marcello Ienca. 2021. "The Security and Military Implications of Neurotechnology and Artificial Intelligence." In *Clinical Neurotechnology Meets Artificial Intelligence*, edited by Orsolya Friedrich, Andreas Wolkenstein, Christoph Bublitz, Ralf J.Jox, Eric Racine,197–214. Berlin: Springer.

Saenz, Maria Jesus, Elena Revilla, Cristina Simon. 2020. "Designing AI Systems with Human Machine Teams." *MIT Sloan Management Review*, 18 March. https://sloanreview.mit.edu/article/designing-ai-systems-with-human-machine-teams/.

Sayler, Kelly M. 2020. "Artificial Intelligence and National Security." *US Library of Congress. Congressional Research Service.* R45178. https://sgp.fas.org/crs/natsec/R45178.pdf.

Sayler, Kelly M., Laurie A. Harris. 2021. "Deepfakes and National Security." *US Library of Congress. Congressional Research Service.* IF11333. https://crsreports.congress.gov/product/pdf/IF/IF11333/4.

Scharre, Paul. 2018. "How Swarming Will Change Warfare." *Bulletin of the Atomic Scientists* 74, no. 6: 385–389. https://doi.org/10.1080/00963402.2018.1533209.

Scharre, Paul. 2020. *Autonomous Weapons and Stability.* Doctoral Thesis, King's College London, March. https://kclpure.kcl.ac.uk/portal/files/129451536/2020_Scharre_Paul_1575997_ethesis.pdf.

Schick, Nina. 2020. *Deepfakes: The Coming Infocalypse.* New York: Twelve Hachette Book Group.

Schubert, Johan, Joel Brynielsson, Mattias Nilsson, Peter Svenmarck. 2018. "Artificial Intelligence for Decision Support in Command-and-Control Systems." Paper presented at the *23rd International Command and Control Research & Technology Symposium: Multi-Domain C2.* https://www.semanticscholar.org/paper/Artificial-Intelligence-for-Decision-Support-in-and-Schubert-Brynielsson/2b810c0a8f5ec30a8e4d34a8ea99af54d2d57bc1.

Shu, Catheine. 2014. "Google Acquires Artificial Intelligence Startup Deepmind for More Than $500 Millions." *Techcrunch*, 27 January. https://techcrunch.com/2014/01/26/google-deepmind/.

Smith, Hannah, Katherine Mansted. 2020. "Weaponsied Deepf Fakes: National Security and Democracy." *International Cyber Policy Centre, Australian Strategic Policy Institute*, no. 28. https://s3-ap-southeast-2.amazonaws.com/ad-aspi/2020-04/Weaponised%20deep%20fakes.pdf?VersionId=lgwT9eN66cRbWTovhN74WI2z4zO4zJ5H.

Stoecklin, Marc Ph. 2018. "DeepLocker: How AI Can Power a Stealthy New Breed of Malware." *Security Intelligence*, August 8. https://securityintelligence.com/deeplocker-how-ai-can-power-a-stealthy-new-breed-of-malware/.

Stupp, Catherine. 2019. "Fraudsters Used AI to Mimic CEO's Voice in Unusual Cybercrime Case." *The Wall Street Journal*, August 30, 2019. https://www.wsj.com/articles/fraudsters-use-ai-to-mimic-ceos-voice-in-unusual-cybercrime-case-11567157402.

Svenmarck, Peter, Linus Luotsinen, Mattia Nilsson, Johan Schubert. 2018. "Possibilities and Challenges for Artificial Intelligence in Military Applications." In Proceedings of the *NATO Big Data and Artificial Intelligence for Military Decision Making Specialists' Meeting. Neuilly-sur-Seine.* NATO Research and Technology Organisation. https://www.semanticscholar.org/paper/Possibilities-and-Challenges-for-Artificial-in-Svenmarck-Luotsinen/bf849c870b56dddf1b8e4d176a6c2a8c948afd0c.

Tucker, Patrick. 2020. "Can AI Detect Disinformation? A New Special Operations Programme May Find Out." *Defence One*, October 2, 2020. https://www.defenseone.com/technology/2020/10/can-ai-detect-disinformation-new-special-operations-program-may-find-out/168972/.

United Kingdom Ministry of Defence. 2021. "Artificial Intelligence Used on Army Operation for First Time." Accessed August 20, 2021. https://www.gov.uk/government/news/artificial-intelligence-used-on-army-operation-for-the-first-time.

United Nations Counter Terrorism Centre (UNCCT), United Nations Interregional Crime and Justice Research Institute (UNICRI). 2021. *Algorithms and Terrorism: The Malicious Use of Artificial Intelligence for Terrorist Purposes*. https://www.un.org/counterterrorism/sites/www.un.org.counterterrorism/files/malicious-use-of-ai-uncct-unicri-report-hd.pdf.

Vahle, Mark W. 2020. "Opportunities and Implications of Brain-Computer Interface Technology." *Wright Flyer Papers*, no. 75: 1–27. https://www.960cyber.afrc.af.mil/News/Article-Display/Article/2289976/opportunities-and-implications-of-brain-computer-interface-technology/.

Vincent, James. 2019. "Microsoft Invests $1 Billion in OpenAI to Pursue Holy Grail of Artificial Intelligence." *The Verge*, July 22, 2021. https://www.theverge.com/2019/7/22/20703578/microsoft-openai-investment-partnership-1-billion-azure-artificial-general-intelligence-agi.

Vincent, James. 2021. "Deepfake Satellite Imagery Poses a Not-So-Distant Threat, Warn Geographers." *The Verge*, April 27, 2021. https://www.theverge.com/2021/4/27/22403741/deepfake-geography-satellite-imagery-ai-generated-fakes-threat.

Vosoughi, Soroush, Deb Roy, Sinan Aral. 2018. The Spread of True and False News Online. *Science* 359, no. 6380, 1146–1151. https://www.science.org/doi/10.1126/science.aap9559.

Whyte, Christopher. 2020. "Deepfake News: AI-Enabled Disinformation as a Multi-Level Public Policy Challenge." *Journal of Cyber Policy* 5, no. 2: 199–217. https://doi.org/10.1080/23738871.2020.1797135.

2

AI AND TECHNOLOGICAL CONVERGENCE

Catalysts for Abounding National Security Risks in the Post-COVID-19 World

Tate Nurkin

On December 16, 2020, the United States Air Force (USAF) announced that an artificial intelligence (AI) algorithm took complete control of sensor and navigation systems on a U-2 Dragon Lady spy plane during a training exercise. The algorithm – known as ARTUμ – searched for enemy missile launchers while sharing the plane's radar with the pilot who was responsible for finding threatening aircraft (Gregg 2020). The test was the first time the US military – and possibly any military – allowed an AI agent to fully control a military system, marking an important milestone in the development of defence and security applications of AI. More broadly, the test served as another in a growing list of examples that demonstrate the growing intensity and pervasiveness of interest of defence and security communities in AI as they seek to manage an operational and tactical context that is increasingly marked by:

- *Information and Data*: Near ubiquitous and networked sensors embedded in equipment and in human operators will collect massive amounts of data that could overwhelm the capacity of humans to process – be it video, images, biometric data, signals intelligence, geospatial intelligence, or other types of information.
- *Autonomous Systems*: Autonomous uncrewed systems capable of moving and deciding at speeds exceeding those of human-operated platforms and systems will feature prominently and carry out a growing number of missions, further intensifying the need for accelerated operational and tactical decision-making that can keep up with these systems.
- *Human-Machine Teaming*: Teams of human and uncrewed systems will be connected to and operating in close conjunction with one another to carry out missions that neither could do independently.

DOI: 10.4324/9781003218326-3

- *Complexity and Expanding Threats*: The merging of traditional and difficult-to-discern unconventional and asymmetric threats – many enabled by emerging technologies or vulnerabilities in the information domain or by the natural or intentional spread of biological pathogens – will augment the complexity of future operating environments, expand mission sets for militaries and security communities, and create contingencies that sit between a state of peace and high-intensity kinetic conflict.
- *Multi-Domain Operations*: Military operations are incorporating actions, platforms, and systems functioning in and across multiple domains simultaneously, including the "new domains" of cyber, space, and the electromagnetic spectrum (Defence of Japan 2020, Special Feature 2).

But perhaps the most important feature of the future battlefield will be the remarkable *pace* at which events unfold and operations take place, which is already making AI-enabled capabilities a necessity rather than a luxury. As Brigadier General Matthew Easley, current US Army Chief Information Officer and former Director of the US Army AI Task Force, noted during the Association of US Army Exhibition in 2019, "We need AI for the speed at which we believe we will fight future wars" (Atherton 2019). In this context, AI and, especially, machine learning (ML) have become fundamental to intensifying efforts of defence and security communities throughout the world to engineer step changes – or "revolutions" – in and across five overlapping categories of intended effects (Nurkin 2020, 15):[1]

- *Towards Perfect Situational Awareness*: A revolution in perception, processing, and cognition
- *An Age of Hyper-Enabled Platforms and People*: A revolution in human and machine performance
- *New Efficiencies and the Impending "Design Age"*: A revolution in manufacturing, supply chain, and logistics
- *Connectivity, Lethality, Flexibility*: A revolution in communication, navigation, targeting, and strike
- *Monitoring, Manipulation, Weaponisation*: A revolution in cyber and information operations

However, AI and ML's impact on the future of military capabilities and conflict should not be viewed in isolation. AI converges with other advanced technologies to create disruptive and potentially transformative capabilities. Accordingly, this chapter seeks to address the issue of AI convergence with different technologies and how these convergencies further each of the five revolutions listed above. It begins with a review of specific indicative technology interactions shaping the five revolutions, including assessments of the particular values these interactions provide, and concludes with an assessment of the challenges and risks of the development and deployment of these intersections between AI and other emerging technologies.

AI Convergence and the Five Revolutions

The AI-related convergences covered in this chapter are not the only ones driving new capabilities in these five revolutions. However, they are particularly reflective of the diverse and disruptive value and effects of AI's interactions with other emerging technologies, namely those effects listed below, and the challenges of scaling the production of these benefits (Table 2.1).

- *Speeding up* data processing of large and complex data sets and enabling processing of data "at the operational edge"
- Creating *cost and time-reducing efficiencies* in critical processes such as manufacturing and training

TABLE 2.1 A List of Technologies That Are Converging with AI to Shape the Future Trajectory of Each Revolution, Including High-Level Descriptions of the Value or Effects These Convergences Can Provide

Revolution	*Key Convergences*	*Value*
Perception, processing, and cognition	5G, cloud connectivity, internet of things Virtual/augmented reality (V/AR) Microelectronics	To improve bandwidth, reduce latency, and increase security and accessibility associated with transmitting data collected and stored in the cloud To speed up the processing of data and create a more complete and real-time situational awareness To enable AI processing of raw data "at the edge"
Human and machine performance	Robotics Neuro- and biotechnologies and neural enhancements V/AR Human-machine interface technologies	To advance the development and deployment of autonomous systems To create hyper-enabled human operators with improved physical and cognitive capabilities To reduce training times and costs To facilitate human-machine teaming
Manufacturing, supply chain, and logistics	Robotics, V/AR, IoT, and cloud connectivity Additive manufacturing Synthetic biology manufacturing	To speed up frequently burdensome design, manufacturing, and certification processes To develop materials at scale with novel properties
Communication, navigation, targeting, and strike	5G and cloud enablement Directed energy Biometrics/facial recognition	To enable drone swarms To help systems detect, identify and track targets autonomously
Cyber and information operations	Biometrics Human behavioural science	To detect anomalies to secure networks at pace and scale To reduce risks and consequences of human decisions and errors related to operations in the information domain

Source: Author

- Enabling *autonomy*
- *Detecting* patterns and anomalies in complex data sets that can ensure material quality and identify threats
- *Predicting* behaviours of people and systems
- *Freeing up humans* to focus their attentions on higher-value tasks

Towards Perfect Situational Awareness: A Revolution in Perception, Processing, and Cognition

The perception, processing, and cognition revolution is foundational to the future of the ability of militaries to effectively function in the fast-moving, crowded, contested, complex, and information-saturated operating environments of the future. Humans are likely to be overwhelmed by the terabytes of information to which they will have access, absent machine assistance to filter, archive, and process this data; in short, to make it digestible and usable (Winker et al. 2019, 9–10) – and to do it all exceptionally quickly. AI/ML confers multi-layered value to overcome this challenge of collecting and processing at speed. Smart sensors possessing AI techniques such as computer vision, for example, will enhance perception.

Today, machine learning is already being used to process information for consumption by operators and even support human cognition and decision-making by evaluating data sets and recommending alternative actions. US Air Force Vice Chief of Staff General David Allvin captured this dynamic in July 2021, when he claimed that

> we are on the verge of a time in which we can collect vast amounts of data from sensors in every domain, share it with troops in every service branch, process that data to provide decision-quality information, and execute operations at a tempo that exceeds our adversary – all within the span of a typical Hollywood action sequence.
>
> *(Allvin 2021)*

AI and the Internet of Things, the Cloud, and 5G

As much as the use of AI/ML is creating opportunities in the era of big data, the collection, storage, processing, and transmission of this data is itself generating bandwidth constraints and latency of transmissions that are constraining the ability to leverage the perception, processing, and cognition advantages of AI/ML. As a result, militaries are prioritising means of combining AI with a handful of technologies, the applications of which are already bolstering the digital revolution in the commercial/industrial sector, advancing smart city development, and adding convenience to the lives of many individuals around the globe:

- *The (Battlefield) Internet of Things (IoT)*: The push to connect and collect data from all platforms, systems, people, and physical infrastructure is leading to an explosion in the production of information available to defence and security communities, including high-resolution imagery and video, biodata, and signals intelligence, among many others. Future military commanders will rely on the ability of the IoT to connect, sense, and communicate across a variety of types of sensors and devices.

- *Cloud Connectivity*: As more data and applications built upon these data become available, the ability of military platforms and systems to securely store data becomes a key priority. Remote access to centrally stored cloud data offers several advantages – ranging from enabling remote training to enhancing the autonomy of uncrewed systems to supporting near real-time and dynamic situational awareness.
- *5G*: Increased use of the cloud has led to a corresponding increase in demand for better connectivity generally and for fifth-generation (5G) mobile technologies specifically. The 5G technology uses segments of the electromagnetic spectrum that allow lower latency, faster data transfer rates, and improved bandwidth compared to fourth-generation technologies (Congressional Research Service 2021, 1). Militaries envision using 5G technologies to support the speeding up of data transmission and of AI/ML processing of information, especially data stored in the cloud. And while building or leveraging 5G infrastructure is undoubtedly one focus area of military 5G development, there are also efforts designed to enable 5G connectivity even in "areas of low bandwidth, no bandwidth and even areas with potentially contested bandwidth" (Breeden 2021) (Figure 2.1).

Nick Nilan, Director of Product Development, Public Sector for Verizon, captured the benefits of this convergence for the future of intelligence, surveillance, and reconnaissance (ISR) and the perception, processing, and cognition revolution:

> In the field, 5G and edge computing will advance surveillance and situational awareness technologies. Drones can livestream photos and videos and us AI to create digital 3D maps in near real-time, enhancing situational awareness and allowing leaders to make more informed decisions. Commanders can use platforms that gather data from IoT sensors in the field and use AI to process the data into actionable insights to inform decision-making.
>
> *(Nichols 2020)*

This statement also hints at the need for defence and security communities to push data processing "to the edge" – that is, to increase the amount of collected data that can be processed by systems that are collecting it rather than pushing data to a separate party for processing and dissemination.

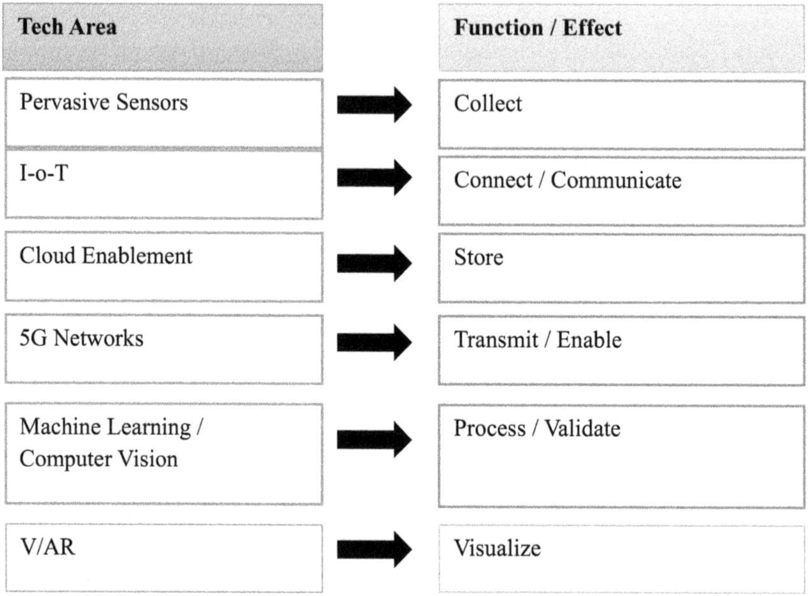

Tech Area
Function / Effect
Pervasive Sensors
Collect
I-o-T
Connect / Communicate
Cloud Enablement
Store
5G Networks
Transmit / Enable
Machine Learning / Computer Vision
Process / Validate
V/AR
Visualize

Virtual and augmented Reality (V/AR) can also contribute to the process by helping to visualise or contextualise complex data sets. These same convergences are also shaping the digital design and engineering capabilities driving the Manufacturing, Supply Chain, and Logistics Revolution discussed later in this chapter.

FIGURE 2.1 AI/ML intersects with sensors, the Internet of Things, cloud enablement, and 5G networks to increase the amount of data collected, the speed at which this information is processed, and, as a result, the pace at which humans act on this data.

TEXT BOX 2.1 TECHNICAL CHALLENGES TO LEVERAGING THE CONVERGENCE OF IOT, CLOUD CONNECTIVITY, 5G, AND AI

- **Data infrastructure**: The increase in the amount of data available places a premium on the storage, curation, and federation of that data to ensure it is useful and usable.
- **Data security**: Reliance on cloud storage, autonomy, and data collection and processing more generally raises the risks and the stakes of a successful cyber intrusion, whether it be to steal, observe, or corrupt data on which ML algorithms are developed and decisions made.
- **Spectrum management**: Increased need to transmit higher volumes of data creates spectrum management challenges in which some frequencies become while others remain unused. AI can be particularly effective in sensing spectrum activity and dynamically allocating access.

- **5G range**: In order to support 5G connectivity, three segments of the electromagnetic spectrum are used: – millimetre wave (MMW) band, mid-band, and low-band. MMW offers the highest security and data transmission rates, but its range is limited, and transmission can be disrupted by objects and landscapes.
- **Processing power and SWaP-C**: The ability to process data at the edge requires enhanced computational power. Systems such as uncrewed aerial vehicles on which this processing is taking place will need improved computing speeds without demonstrably affecting size, weight, power demands, and cost (SWaP-C) of systems

(Zhou n.d.)

A US Congressional Research Service (CRS) summary of defence and security implications of 5G technologies provides a practical example of how 5G and cloud are pushing processing to the edge, noting that

> autonomous military vehicles, like their commercial counterparts, could potentially circumvent onboard data processing limitations by storing large databases (e.g., maps) in the cloud. Safe vehicle operations would require 5G's high data rates and low latency to download off-board information and synthesise it with onboard sensor data.
>
> *(Congressional Research Service 2021, 2)*

And this is a challenge that has become more pressing for both defence and security communities and the industry that supports them. Here is an indicative example of how companies are devising solutions to complement 5G development in addressing this problem: in February 2020, *Janes* reported that sensor manufacturer SCD was developing new capabilities that place AI/ML capabilities into advanced versions of the company's short-wave IR and medium-wave IR sensors to overcome bandwidth issues (Munoz 2020b). The approach allows collected data to be processed on-board the platforms that collect it rather than being sent to off-board processing locations, accelerating the delivery of refined intelligence and recommendations to operators and decision-makers.

An Age of Hyper-Enabled Platforms and People: A Revolution in Human and Machine Performance

The human and machine performance revolution seeks to optimise the performance of people and platforms to build stronger, faster, more sustainable, and more resilient, even potentially self-healing machines and people that possess more cognitive capabilities. AI has many applications relevant to generating this increased performance, ranging from enabling autonomy to reducing soldier physical burden through AI exoskeletons to speeding-up synthetic biology production of protective materials or advanced camouflage to combining with intuitive human-machine interfaces that enable improved human-machine teaming. But the potential for human-machine hybrids – the intersection of the human and machine performance and perception, processing, and cognition revolutions – and greatly improved training stand out as notable examples of the possible benefits and risks associated with convergences of AI and other technologies that could enable humans to better compete in the crucial cognitive domain.

AI and Neuro/Biotechnologies and Neural Enhancements: Competition in the Cognitive Domain

The discussion of improving human performance enhancement and human-machine hybrids generally has tended to focus on three broad areas identified by technologist Ray Kurzweil (McShane 2016):

- *Genetics* to reprogram human biology
- *Robotics*, which includes both physical-mechanical platforms and systems and, more importantly, the AI that will allow humans to create smarter (or stronger or faster, etc.) than human agents
- *Nanotechnology*, which will allow humans to manipulate matter at the molecular and atomic scale and, as a result, design and build materials with unique and dynamic properties

The technologies supporting the genetics, robotics, and nanotechnology (GRN) construct have a history of mutually reinforcing benefits. Neuroscience has served as an inspiration for AI developers as a model for designing AI that emulates human intelligence and building neural networks that mimic brain structure. As AI advances, its data processing capability is "coming full circle" to learn more about the brain and facilitate new capabilities, such as the ability of paralysed individuals to move robotic limbs (Savage 2019). This intersection has become a focus for military and security communities seeking to better compete in the ever more critical "cognitive domain."

According to a 2019 RAND Corporation report, what matters most in a notional future operating environment is "who can bring more cognition to the battlefield and how we apply it" (Winker et al. 2019, 12). The US Army's *Cyber Soldier 2050: Human/Machine Fusion and the Implications for the Future of the DoD* report is a valuable discussion of the opportunities and challenges associated with the use of neuro- and biotechnologies to augment human cognition as well as performance in other areas. The report details how ocular enhancements, optogenetic bodysuit sensor webs, exoskeletons, and auditory enhancements can enhance the performance of human operators largely in incremental ways.

However, it also argues that combinations of AI and neuroscience will bring a revolutionary effect:

> Direct neural enhancement of the human brain for two-way data transfer would create a revolutionary advancement in future military capabilities. This technology is predicted to facilitate read/write capability between humans and machines and between humans through brain-to-brain interactions. These interactions would allow warfighters direct communication with unmanned and autonomous systems, as well as with other humans, to optimise command and control.
>
> *(US Army 2019, v)*

Exploiting the combination of neurotechnology and AI to enhance human and machine teaming aspects is also at the core of the US Defence Advanced Research Projects Agency's (DARPA) Next-Generation Nonsurgical Neurotechnology (N3) programme. In June 2019, the agency awarded six contracts to academic and applied research institutes to "develop high-performance, bi-directional brain-machine interfaces for able-bodied service members." These interfaces will be applied to the development of several military and security applications, including "control of unmanned aerial vehicles and active cyber defence systems or teaming with computer systems to successfully multitask during complex military missions," further highlighting the importance of the interaction of these technologies for both human-machine teaming and activity in the cyber domain (Sarma, n.d.).

While these hybrid capabilities are unlikely to be achieved and deployed in the immediate future, the idea of "cyber" soldiers with direct neural enhancements and thought control of uncrewed systems does create legal, ethical, perception, and social impact questions that will need to be addressed in the near term in order to influence the longer-term development of the technologies and operational concepts. In fact, among the seven main recommendations of the US Army report, two concerned developing ethical frameworks, while a third focused on the need for "efforts [to be] undertaken to reverse negative cultural narratives of enhancement technologies" (US Army 2019, vi).

AI and Augmented Reality/Virtual Reality (AR/VR): Revolutionising Virtual and Live Training

VR-enabled training has gained momentum over the last several years as the technology has developed, and the benefits, mainly the reduction of cost and time associated with training, have been more fully realised, especially in pilot training but also for other disciplines, including cyber and homeland security missions. Integrating AI into virtual training provides virtual assistance instruction and can also focus on individual training by creating a customised training curriculum for specific trainees based on their learning strengths and weaknesses. Recent breakthroughs have taken the value of the AI/AR convergence even further by applying it to live training sessions in which humans operate simultaneously in both the real and digital worlds. In November 2019, US-based companies Red 6 and EpiSci announced the successful completion of a dogfight between a human-piloted aircraft operating in the real world and an AI-generated virtual Chinese J-20 fifth-generation fighter jet (Newdick 2020). The test involved a piloted Berkut 540 experimental plane and a simulated J-20 created by EpiSci's Tactical AI technology. The J-20 was projected inside Red 6's Airborne Tactical Augmented Reality System (ATARS) headset worn by the pilot of the real world Berkut. In August 2021, the company was awarded a five-year, $70 million contract to incorporate its system on a US Air Force T-38 to enable this simultaneous real-world/virtual-world training, signalling that militaries are now investing in this AI and AR convergence in a scalable way (Insinna 2021).

Red 6 CEO Dan Robinson rightly stressed the value of the convergence, observing that it "opens spectacular possibilities for training" (Newdick 2020) – to include replicating complex environments, driving down costs of live training by removing the requirement for an expensive physical "red team" aircraft, and assisting in the experimentation of tactics, techniques, and procedures (TTPs) and operational concepts so critical to the success of effectively leveraging new technologies. The AI/AR/VR convergence in support of training also has an important "meta" value by helping to condition operators – pilots, in this case – to work with AI and operate in future contexts in which they will have to process inputs from both the physical and digital worlds. These experiences will be key to future concepts of human-machine teaming in which operators monitor and control several off-board sensors and *loyal wingman*-type uncrewed systems.

New Efficiencies and the Impending Design Age: Manufacturing, Supply Chains, and Logistics

The combination of AI and other Fourth Industrial Revolution (4IR) technologies is already changing logistics and supply chain management through predictive maintenance and cloud-based supply chain management. However, they are also beginning to reveal their potential to generate game-changing efficiencies in the design and manufacturing process by speeding up design, quality assurance, certification, and production, which reduce costs and enable *new possibilities* in terms of the nature and properties of materials used in the manufacturing process.

Digital Engineering

In September 2020, Dr Will Roper, the then head of US Air Force acquisition, announced the service had flown in the real world a prototype of a sixth-generation fighter aircraft designed digitally as part of its Next Generation Air

Dominance (NGAD) programme. According to Roper, the plane had moved from design to prototype development to manufacture to real-world test flight in less than 12 months, using AI-enabled computer models and digital engineering processes that allowed engineers to test millions of possible designs in the virtual world before building a physical aircraft to optimised design and cost standards (Gregg and Sonne 2020). According to Roper, the benefits of combining the same technologies that are so crucial to the perception, processing, and cognition revolution – smart sensors, the IoT, cloud computing, 5G, AI/ML, and VR/AR – will be far-reaching: "digital engineering is lowering overhead for production and assembly [so] you do not have to have huge facilities, huge workforces [and] expensive tooling" (Weisgerber 2020). While Dr Roper released little detailed information about the programme, the test, or even the company(s) involved, the USAF appears to be doubling down on the potential of digital engineering. In December 2020, it announced that its first Digital Engineering Pitch Day would be held in early 2021 for the industry to pitch solutions to improve software, tools, and the fidelity of models used to virtually develop new platforms and systems (Hitchens 2020).

And they are not the only ones. Defence industries worldwide are prioritising the use of digital engineering in the production of both crewed and uncrewed platforms and systems. Indeed, a January 2021 UK Ministry of Defence press release related to Project Mosquito, the UK's loyal wingman uncrewed system effort, emphasised that "by utilising the latest software development techniques and civilian aerospace engineering and manufacturing expertise, the project will deliver dramatic reductions in costs and development timelines, so their innovations can reach the front-line quicker than ever before" (UK Ministry of Defence 2021).

Scaling Disruptive Technologies: AI and Additive Manufacturing

AI is also being incorporated alongside novel manufacturing and design techniques such as additive manufacturing (AM)/3D printing and synthetic biology engineering to accelerate the scaling of the use of these technologies and their potentially transformative outputs. The AM process enables the production of typically lighter, stronger, and more complex objects than traditional manufacturing processes. Once scaled, AM can also reshape concepts of modern logistics by enabling point-of-use printing of critical supplies such as uncrewed systems, weapons, and spare parts. It also facilitates the printing of materials with dynamic – possibly even programmable – properties.

AM has been an area of growing interest for militaries around the world as the technology has developed and its benefits in prototype development and the printing of specialised parts have been demonstrated, including being used by militaries to print ventilators and personal protective equipment during the COVID-19 pandemic. Interest in 3D printing within the US DoD has become so high that, in February 2021, the DoD unveiled its first-ever comprehensive

AM strategy that seeks to establish a common vision for the use of 3D printing across the whole of DoD (Joint Defense Manufacturing Council, 2021). However, AM is still constrained by the lengthy time and high costs of design, qualification, and certification of 3D manufactured parts (Senvol 2020) – challenges AI is particularly well suited to address. Massachusetts Institute of Technology (MIT) start-up Inkbit, which works with DARPA and the US Air Force, is using both machine vision and machine learning to, in the words of CEO David Marini, endow "a 3D printer with eyes and brains." The machine vision – *the eyes* – scans the object as it is being printed, correcting errors in the printing in real time, while the machine learning – *the brain* – uses the information gathered by the eyes to predict the warping behaviour of materials and make more accurate final products ensuring the accuracy and repeatability (and even automation) of AM (Winn 2019).

The use of AI in the AM process also has implications for the types of materials that can be used in 3D printing, opening the possibility of the design and printing of new materials that can be manipulated at the molecular and atomic scale and carry novel properties. For example, the Dutch university TU Delft used AI computer models and simulations to design a super-compressible material that it was able to then print at a nano-level using additive manufacturing (TU Delft 2019).

Scaling Disruptive Technologies: AI and Synthetic Biology

Synthetic biology applies engineering principles to biological science with the intent of scaling the production of new microbes with novel properties that do not exist in nature. The applications of synthetic biology for militaries are expansive. The US Army Research Lab has identified synthetic biology as one of its ten research priorities to "help the military develop next-generation living camouflage and other never-before-seen organisms and materials" (Tucker 2019). Synthetic biology will impact several of the five revolutions, but is included in this discussion of the manufacturing, supply chain, and logistics revolution because its convergence with AI is essential to scaling the production and manufacture of synthetic biology products. The implementation and effect of ML algorithms in synthetic biology have a similar effect to that of ML's impact on AM. ML algorithms can work with synthetic biology processes to predict how changes in a cell's DNA or biochemistry will affect its behaviour and then make recommendations for the next engineering cycle along with probabilistic predictions for attaining the desired goal. This convergence between bioengineering and AI will also greatly accelerate the ponderous process of understanding cell behaviour, moving from what one researcher at the US Department of Energy's Lawrence Berkeley National Lab described as dozens of person taking years to create the anti-malarial drug, artemisinin, to creating customised new cells within a couple of weeks or months and ultimately "[revolutionising] what you can do with bioengineering" (Chao 2020).

Connectivity, Lethality, Flexibility: A Revolution in Communication, Navigation, Targeting, and Strike

The communication, navigation, targeting, and strike revolution coheres around a set of technological and operational concept innovations that are focused laser-like on enhancing capabilities to:

- *Communicate* more easily between more and more dispersed systems across multiple domains
- *Navigate* platforms and systems, even in environments in which access to global navigation satellite systems (GNSS) is denied
- *Target* platforms and systems with more precision and flexibility to reduce risk in complex, uncertain, and shifting operational environments
- *Strike, interdict, or deter* adversary capabilities and assets at short notice, at longer ranges, and in contested environments (Nurkin 2020, 20)

Several AI-enabled capabilities – such as cognitive electronic warfare and cognitive sensing for spectrum management – have a role in furthering this revolution, especially as they intersect with robotics, novel weapons systems, and 5G communication. The convergences discussed below are of particular interest because they demonstrate two important points about AI's interactions with emerging technologies. First, these interactions are now part of iterative and intense offence-defence competitions. The deployment of AI for offensive systems will likely lead to the development and deployment of AI as part of efforts to respond. Second, AI's incorporation into the future of targeting and strike, in particular, is creating ethical dilemmas and tensions that, like those associated with neuro- and biotechnologies, must be confronted before the technologies fully mature and are deployable at scale.

AI, Robotics/Uncrewed Systems, and Enhanced Connectivity: Autonomous Drone Swarms

As referenced above in the discussion of the importance of 5G for pushing data processing to the edge, including onboard autonomous systems, the intersection between AI, advanced uncrewed systems, and 5G has important implications for perception, processing, and cognition. According to the CRS primer on 5G, this convergence also enables other new capabilities for targeting and strike, including "enabling new military concepts of operations such as swarming" (Congressional Research Service 2021, 2). Natural swarming of drones involves several to several dozen or even hundreds of networked autonomous drones linked through distributed decision-making rules that allow the swarm to operate in conjunction with one another and be independent of central control. The supporting concepts and technologies are being progressed by several defence and security communities throughout the world and have expanded well beyond the usual suspects of China, the United States, and Russia. Other states are pursuing swarming programmes, too, as defence and security communities recognise that, in the words of a China Electronics Technology Group (CETC) engineer involved in a June 2017 record-setting drone swarm test, drone swarms are "a disruptive force" that will "change the rules of the game" (Tate 2017).

Israel became the first nation to deploy an intelligent drone swarm, reportedly "dozens of times," in combat during the summer 2021 conflict with Hamas in Gaza. The systems were used as an intelligence, surveillance, and reconnaissance role monitoring Hamas-held territory for missile/rocket launches and relaying that information to other strike assets (Gross 2021). But Israel's use of intelligent, autonomous, networked drone swarms almost certainly represents just the first in a series of deployments of this capability in a range of roles, including in an explicitly strike role, that point to proliferation and arms control questions. As uncrewed systems researcher Zachary Kallenborn argues, "drone swarms create risks akin to traditional weapons of mass destruction" and that as the size of swarms expands, "the degree of human control over these swarms will necessarily diminish" (Kallenborn 2021).

AI and Directed Energy: Agile Targeting at the Speed of Autonomy

Drone swarms are attractive for their agility, their ability to saturate defences, and, in the most sophisticated manifestations of the technology, the ability of the swarm to self-heal and continue the mission. Together these attributes are placing pressure on defensive capabilities. As the former head of the US DoD's Joint Artificial Intelligence Center (JAIC), Lt. General (retired) Jack Shanahan, noted during a November 2019 appearance,

> We are going to be shocked by the speed, the chaos, the bloodiness, and the friction of a future fight in which this will be playing out in microseconds at a time. If we're going to do this by humans against machines, and the other side has the machines and the algorithms and we don't, we're at an unacceptably high risk of losing that conflict.
>
> *(National Security Commission on Artificial Intelligence Conference 2019)*

Even if humans were able to match the physical and cognitive pace of autonomous systems and, especially, drone swarms, existing defensive systems built around high-cost interceptors are ill-suited to engage cheap and fast-moving threats. New weapons, such as directed energy, are required to flip current asymmetric cost curves (inexpensive offensive capabilities against exquisite and expensive defensive ones) associated with defensive systems and work with AI to ensure agile identification and tracking of targets.

Former US Department of Defence Undersecretary of Research and Engineering Michael Griffin highlighted the potential link between AI and directed energy during the Booz Allen Hamilton Directed Energy Summit in March 2019. According to Griffin,

> we require tracking and targeting mechanisms that are AI informed because you're going to be way out in front of the headlights of any human fire control person. The question of which targets to go at, and in what order, is challenging.
>
> *(Metha 2019)*

Of course, the incorporation of AI into the targeting process once again takes defence and security communities right up to important ethical lines regarding human control of the use of lethal force.

Defence communities will be able to legitimately argue that there is a difference between AI targeting missiles and uncrewed systems and using AI to target humans. Still, in complex, uncertain, and fast-moving environments distinctions between crewed and uncrewed may be more challenging to discern. As a result, the tension between the "need for speed" and the need for human control of lethal force against other humans is a persistent one that will help shape the future of the convergence between AI-enabled autonomy and robotic/uncrewed systems development and of the revolution in communication, navigation, targeting and strike capabilities.

Monitoring, Manipulation, and Weaponisation: A Revolution in Cyber and Information Operations

The intersection of AI and emerging technologies also holds relevance for the cyber and information operations revolution. However, the primary salience of the cyber and information domains for the conversation around AI interaction with other emerging technologies is the challenges and risks of implementing these convergences. To be sure, AI/ML is crucial to the future of cyber-defence (and to the design of more sophisticated cyber intrusions). By automating threat detection against the increasing pace and sophistication of cyber-attacks and using ML's ability to detect anomalies in large, complex, and diverse data sets, AI/ML will power new cyber-security solutions. It will also combine with biometrics – voice, face, pupil, fingerprint identification, for example – to create a layered system of access that eliminates the vulnerabilities stemming from weak passwords while still engaging in automated threat detection. Responses to AI-enabled disinformation and misinformation will also be shaped by the ability to incorporate computer vision and machine learning to detect synthetic activity and media, such as smart bots and deepfakes, though, as with cyber-security, the technical solutions to the challenges can only defray so much risk. Cognitive science – to include psychology, linguistics, neuroscience, philosophy, anthropology – will also play a prominent role in mitigating the risk associated with human behaviour and propensity to amplify cyber and dis- and misinformation efforts.

The Cyber Risk and Challenge

With more data being collected, stored, and transmitted, cyber intrusions become a more attractive means of attacking competitors or adversaries whether to degrade the operational capacity of a platform or system; steal money, technology, intellectual property, or sensitive personal information; or corrupt and manipulate the data on which decisions may be based, actions taken, and, significantly, algorithms are based. This risk of data and algorithm corruption is drawing more attention within security communities, especially in militaries that seek to incorporate AI and its convergences with other emerging technologies into future military capabilities and operating concepts. Jean Vettel, Chief Scientist of the US Army's Combat Capabilities Development Command (CCDC), articulated the nature of the growing concern: "once things get moved to algorithms, the idea of spoofing the data, or having infiltration into the network that actually modifies the algorithm" is acute (Munoz 2020a).

The threat of corrupted data will not just affect the efficacy of the AI-robotics convergence. Conceptually, it could lead to corrupted designs and manufacturing of AM parts or potentially to synthetic biology microbes that behave in unintended ways. The list of deleterious consequences of manipulated data and algorithms is long and perhaps largely unbound, underscoring the need not just for more robust cyber defences to protect the swelling amount of collected and stored data but also for plans to build resilience and mitigate the potentially devastating effects of future cyber intrusions.

Other Convergence Challenges and Risks

The cyber risk is just one of a handful of risks and incorporation challenges that have the potential to limit the impact of these AI-technology connections. Certainly, there are technical challenges related to developing and integrating these technologies – for example, the increasing processing of data at the edge will be energy-intensive, requiring more power for platforms and systems and potentially upsetting size, weight, and power with cost (SWAP-C) trade-offs. Disquiet about the ethical applications of emerging technologies and the potential for misuse or even unintended social consequences of many of the intersections of AI with other novel technologies stands out both as a challenge to the development of these technologies and as a risk of their deployment as well.

As the development of drone swarms or hyper-enabled humans matures, the conversation around ethics, safety, and social impact will almost certainly affect the trajectory of that development for many defence and security communities. There are already calls to consider international bans on lethal autonomous weapons systems and for states to classify intelligent AI-enabled drone swarms as weapons of mass destruction "due to the combination of mass harm and lack of controllability" (Hambling 2021). However, not all actors will be constrained by international standards for ethical use. Both state and non-state actors will continue developing and using potentially revolutionary new capabilities to gain a sustainable military advantage, placing a burden on states that seek to develop and abide by ethical norms and standards. Similarly, the risk of proliferation of these technologies and the capabilities they enable is real, especially given that many of these technologies are being developed in the commercial industry for frequently commercial purposes with fewer controls on their sale or distribution.

This proliferation dynamic has already been seen in the diffusion of commercially available drones to non-state actors, posing an increasing threat to military and security communities throughout the world. A December 2019 article in Germany's *Bundeswehr Journal* effectively described the emerging threat from commercially available drones:

> cheap drones are currently experiencing a real boom. However, their reconnaissance and payload capability, such as explosive devices can also make them a threat to military and civilian facilities. Terrorists and criminals, as well as thoughtless hobbyists, can do enormous damage with drones.
>
> *(Brugge,* Bundeswehr Journal *2019)*

A similar dynamic could take place with AI-enabled 3D printers, autonomous drones, deepfake apps, and cyber-security capabilities, all of which are (or will be) commercially available. Scaling innovation in these areas will likely make them more available, while approaches to open innovation in the biological sciences *could* create both safety and proliferation risks stemming from do-it-yourself synthetic biology labs. Even the development of AI algorithms is becoming more accessible to a wider set of actors, the 2019 RAND report stated: "the process of developing AI algorithms is becoming accessible to the novice user. In the context of warfare, this dissemination potentially places powerful military capabilities in the hands of nonstate adversaries" (Winker et al. 2019, 11).

More precise understanding and assessing the dimensions of these technical, ethical, social impact, and proliferation risks is critical to the development of AI convergences. However, there are other challenges related to ensuring the resilience and sustainability of these interactions between AI and other emerging technologies.

Disruptive if Scalable: Building Critical Infrastructure

The convergences of AI and these other technologies hold great disruptive potential, but in many cases, they are not yet scalable. Building the physical, digital, commercial, and human infrastructure to scale successful innovation at the intersection of these technologies then stands out as a vital measure for defence and security communities, seeking to achieve the salutary benefits of AI convergences. Of course, the type of infrastructure that needs to be developed will vary by technology. In some cases, 5G will require physical infrastructure, as will 3D printing as it becomes more fully integrated with digital engineering processes and the modern factory floor. Other innovative technologies will need to develop more robust data sets. The US Department of Energy's (DoE) Berkeley National Lab built its ART for synthetic biology based on what is described as "a limited set of training data" (Chao 2020), which is an impressive, if unsustainable, achievement. For the technology to achieve its potential, it will require much more data to train algorithms. Tijana Radivojevic, a data scientist and project lead on the effort, observed that "potential applications might be revolutionary given access to large amounts of data" (Chao 2020).

Of course, all data is not created equal, and access to large amounts of data may be counterproductive if that data has not been effectively curated or managed. Therefore, another component of building critical architecture to exploit these convergences is to invest in data management and data curation of these increasingly big data sets. In February 2021, the DoD's JAIC announced that it was shifting its focus from joint warfighting concepts and the development of AI-enhanced ISR initiatives towards improving the type of data management and tooling that would enable enterprise-wide AI development, especially as the requirement to collect, curate, and store images and video increases (Munoz 2021).

Infrastructure building will not just take place in the physical and digital domains. It must also emphasise the human and organisational dimensions of sustainable and scalable capability development. At a leadership level, there is an urgent need to confront a general lack of understanding about technologies of interest and to educate defence, security, and even civilian political leaders in order to build a deeper cadre of leaders and policy makers with an understanding of the underlying technologies, what the advantages of their convergence are, and how that convergence can best be achieved in order to optimise policies and priorities associated with these technologies and their intersections.

The human dimension goes deeper than educating leaders and managers. Recruiting, retaining, and training human capital will also be a challenge for defence and security organisations seeking to build scalability. One commander in the French Army emphasised the importance of aligning technological deployment with the ability of operators to understand the technologies they must use: "AI is a facilitator for soldiers but if we want to use neural networks to improve the performance of software-defined radios, there is a danger of making them more complex and less understood by the end user" (White 2021). And this alignment of human capital is not just at the end-user level. Military and security communities must recruit, train, and retain individuals at all levels of the organisation who are comfortable working with AI and other emerging technologies and improve the "flexibility" of their career development pathways and training protocols (Winker et al. 2019, 29).

A final component of building infrastructure to scale development, deployment, and integration of these intersections is generating more robust connections between defence and security community planners and procurement teams, the commercial suppliers, and academia/applied research organisations that, in many cases, are innovating in AI applications and other emerging technologies. This does not mean that the traditional defence industry does not have an important role in this process, in the development and supply of emerging technologies and capabilities, and especially as an integrator. It can also play a critical facilitation and experimentation role by partnering with the commercial industry to help develop, experiment with, and refine the operational concepts associated with these converged technologies.

But the requirement for building depth of commercial infrastructure will be more engagement between defence and security communities and non-traditional suppliers at multiple levels, including to help shape requirements and educate defence and security communities on emerging technologies, as recommended above. In addition, these efforts at enhanced engagement should include refining or reforming processes to increase incentives for fast-moving commercial companies to engage with the frequently deliberate public sector procurement process.

Conclusion

AI's convergences with other advanced and emerging technologies are critical to delivering new and enhanced capabilities in and across each of the five revolutions. Individually and collectively, the intersection of AI and advanced digital and connectivity technologies, neuro- and bioscience, AR/VR and other visualisation tools, AM, synthetic biology, robotics, directed energy, and biometrics will deliver several layers of value for both security communities and militaries, as well as in many cases the industries that support these communities.

- *Speeding up* data processing of large and complex data sets and enabling processing of data "at the operational edge"
- Creating *cost and time-reducing efficiencies* in critical processes such as manufacturing and training
- Enabling *autonomy*
- *Detecting* patterns and anomalies in complex data sets that can ensure material quality and identify threats
- *Predicting* behaviours of people and systems
- *Freeing up humans* to focus their attentions on higher-value tasks

Achieving these benefits will entail, first, fully understanding and then vigilantly and urgently addressing challenges and risks, some of which may only emerge as the technologies, operational concepts for their use, and ethical and export control frameworks mature. While technological proliferation and ethical risks will shape the future development and use of these convergences, technological resilience and scalability will also be closely tied to physical, digital, commercial, and human infrastructure investments.

Note

1 The author originally developed the "four revolutions" framework in November of 2015. Versions of the framework have been briefed and published many times since, and the framework was updated in 2019 to create a separate revolution for the cyber/information domain.

References

Allvin, David. 2021. "How We Get to Captain America-Level Battle Speeds." *Defence One*. https://www.defenceone.com/ideas/2021/07/how-we-get-captain-america-level-battle-speeds/183610/.

Atherton, Kelsey D. 2019. "Can the Army Perfect an AI Strategy for a Fast and Deadly Future." *C4ISRNet*. https://www.c4isrnet.com/artificial-intelligence/2019/10/15/can-the-army-perfect-an-ai-strategy-for-a-fast-and-deadly-future.

Breeden, John. 2021. "Why the Military Is Leading the Charge on 5G." *Defence One*. https://www.defenceone.com/ideas/2021/04/why-military-leading-charge-5g/173534/.

Brugge, Rino. 2019. "Drone Defence with Protector RWS from Kongsberg." *Bundeswehr Journal*. http://www.bundeswehr-journal.de/2019/drohnenabwehr-mit-protector-rws-von-kongsberg/.

Chao, Julie. 2020. "Machine Learning Takes on Synthetic Biology: Algorithms Can Bioengineer Cells for You." Berkeley Lab News Center. https://newscenter.lbl.gov/2020/09/25/machine-learning-takes-on-synthetic-biology-algorithms-can-bioengineer-cells-for-you/.

Congressional Research Service. 2021. "National Security Implications of Fifth Generation (5G) Mobile Technologies," updated January 26, 2021: 1, 2. https://crsreports.congress.gov/product/pdf/IF/IF11251.

Sarma, Dr. Gopal. n.d. "Next-Generation Nonsurgical Neurotechnology Program Description." DARPA.mil. https://www.darpa.mil/program/next-generation-nonsurgical-neurotechnology.

Gregg, Aaron. 2020. "In a First, Air Force Uses Artificial Intelligence Aboard Military Jet." *Washington Post*. https://www.washingtonpost.com/business/2020/12/16/air-force-artificial-intelligence/.

Gregg, Aaron, and Paul Sonne. 2020. "Air Force Seeks a Radical Shift in How Jets, Missiles, and Satellites Are Designed." *Washington Post*. https://www.washingtonpost.com/business/2020/09/15/air-force-digital-design/.

Gross, Judah Ari. 2021. "In apparent world first, IDF deployed drone swarms in Gaza fighting." *Times of Israel*. https://www.timesofisrael.com/in-apparent-world-first-idf-deployed-drone-swarms-in-gaza-fighting/

Hambling, David. 2021. "What Are Drone Swarms and Why Does Every Military Suddenly Want One." *Forbes*. https://www.forbes.com/sites/davidhambling/2021/03/01/what-are-drone-swarms-and-why-does-everyone-suddenly-want-one/?sh=43e43be32f5c.

Hitchens, Theresa. 2020. "Air Force Plans First Digital Engineering Pitch Day." *Breaking Defence*. https://breakingdefence.com/2020/12/air-force-plans-first-digital-engineering-pitch-day/.

Insinna, Valeria. 2021. "Red 6 Lands Contract to Put Augmented Reality on a T-38 Trainer Jet." *Defence News*. https://www.defencenews.com/training-sim/2021/08/16/red-6-lands-contract-to-put-augmented-reality-on-a-t-38-training-jet/.

Japan Ministry of Defence. 2020. "Defence of Japan 2020. Special Feature 2: New Domains." https://www.mod.go.jp/en/publ/w_paper/wp2021/DOJ2021_Digest_EN.pdf.

Jennings, Gareth. 2021. "UK Concludes 'Many Drones Make Light Work' with Large Scale Demonstration." Janes.com. https://www.janes.com/defence-news/news-detail/uk-concludes-many-drones-make-light-work-with-large-scale-demonstration.

Joint Defence Manufacturing Council, Office of the Deputy Director for Strategic Policy Exploitation, Office of Secretary of Defence for Research and Engineering. 2021. "DoD Additive Manufacturing Strategy." https://www.cto.mil/wp-content/uploads/2021/01/dod-additive-manufacturing-strategy.pdf.

Kallenborn, Zak. 2021. "Israel's Drone Swarm over Gaza Should Worry Everyone." *Defence One*. https://www.defenceone.com/ideas/2021/07/israels-drone-swarm-over-gaza-should-worry-everyone/183156/.

McShane, Sveta. 2016. "Ray Kurzweil Predicts Three Technologies Will Define Our Future." Singularity Hub. https://singularityhub.com/2016/04/19/ray-kurzweil-predicts-three-technologies-will-define-our-future/.

Metha, Aaron. 2019. "A DoD AI Expert Is Coming - And That Could Mean Big Things for Directed Energy." *C4ISRNet*. https://www.c4isrnet.com/pentagon/2019/03/20/a-dod-ai-expert-is-coming-and-that-could-mean-big-things-for-directed-energy/.

Munoz, Carlo. 2020a. "AUSA 2020: Service Leaders Tackle 'Deception' Attacks on AI Algorithms." Janes.com. https://www.janes.com/defence-news/news-detail/ausa-2020-service-leaders-tackle-deception-attacks-on-ai-algorithms.

Munoz, Carlo. 2020b. "SCD Develops 'Smart Imagery' Prototype Linking AI and Infrared Sensor Technology." *Jane's International Defence Review* as published on SCD's website. https://www.scd.co.il/news/scd-develops-smart-imagery-prototype-linking-ai-and-infrared-sensor-technology/.

Munoz, Carlo. 2021. "JAIC Shifts Focus to Data Management Tools, Infrastructure." Janes.com. https://www.janes.com/defence-news/news-detail/jaic-shifts-focus-to-data-management-tools-infrastructure.

National Security Commission on Artificial Intelligence Conference, Public-Private Partnerships. 2019. 27:40–28:35. https://www.c-span.org/video/?466064-2/national-security-commission-artificial-intelligence-conference-public-private-partnerships.

Newdick, Thomas. 2020. "Pilot in a Real Aircraft Just Fought an AI-Driven Virtual Enemy Jet for the First Time." *The Drive*. https://www.thedrive.com/the-war-zone/37647/pilot-in-a-real-aircraft-just-fought-an-ai-driven-virtual-enemy-jet-for-the-first-time.

Ng, Jr. 2021. "Indian Army Demonstrates UAV Swarming Technologies." *Asian Military Review*. https://asianmilitaryreview.com/2021/01/indian-army-demonstrates-uav-swarming-technologies/.

Nichols, Gregg. 2020. "Digital Fortress: 5G Is a Weapon in National Defence." ZDNet. https://www.zdnet.com/article/digital-fortress-5g-a-weapon-in-national-defence/.

Nurkin, Tate. 2020. "The Five Revolutions: Examining Defence Innovation in the Indo-Pacific." *The Atlantic Council*. https://www.atlanticcouncil.org/in-depth-research-reports/report/the-five-revolutions-examining-defence-innovation-in-the-indo-pacific-region/.

Pax. 2019. "Slippery Slope: The Arms Industry and Increasingly Autonomous Weapons." PAX. https://www.paxforpeace.nl/publications/all-publications/slippery-slope.

Savage, Neil. 2019. "How AI and Neuroscience Drive Each Other Forwards." *Nature*. https://www.nature.com/articles/d41586-019-02212-4.

Senvol Press Release. 2020. "Senvol ML to Be Used for Missile Application with US Army." Senvol.com. http://senvol.com/2020/11/18/senvol-ml-to-be-used-for-missile-application-with-u-s-army/.

Tate, Andrew. 2017. "China Launches Record-Breaking Drone Swarm." *Jane's Defence Weekly*. Firewalled.

Tucker, Patrick. 2019. "The US Army Is Making Synthetic Biology a Priority." *Defence One*. https://www.defenceone.com/technology/2019/07/us-army-making-synthetic-biology-priority/158129/.

TU Delft. 2019. "TU Delft Researchers Develop New Materials by Using AI Only." TU Delft, YouTube channel. https://www.youtube.com/watch?v=cWTWHhMAu7I.

United Kingdom Ministry of Defence. 2021. "£30 Million Injection for UK's First Uncrewed Fighter Aircraft." UK.Gov. https://www.gov.uk/government/news/30m-injection-for-uks-first-uncrewed-fighter-aircraft.

United Nations Security Council. 2021. "Letter from the Panel of Experts on Libya Established Pursuant to Resolution 1973 (2011) Addressed to the President of the Security Council." United Nations. https://undocs.org/S/2021/229.

US Army, Biotechnologies for Health and Human Performance Council Study Group. 2019. "Cyber Soldier 2050: Human / Machine Fusion and the Implications for the Future of the DoD." https://community.apan.org/wg/tradoc-g2/mad-scientist/m/articles-of-interest/300458.

Weisgerber, Marcus. 2020. "Revealed: US Air Force Has Secretly Built and Flown a New Fighter Jet." *Defence One*. https://www.defenceone.com/technology/2020/09/usaf-jet/168479/.

White, Andrew. 2021. "Connecting the Dots: AI and 5G in Tactical Communications." Janes.com. Firewalled.

Winker, John D., Timothy Marlowe, Marek N. Posard, Raphael S. Cohen, Megan L. Smith. 2019. "Reflections on the Future of Warfare and Implications for Personnel Policies of the US Department of Defence." RAND Corporation, 2019: 9–10, 12, 11, 29. https://www.rand.org/content/dam/rand/pubs/perspectives/PE300/PE324/RAND_PE324.pdf.

Winn, Zach. 2019. "A 3-D Printer Powered by Machine Vision and Artificial Intelligence." *MIT News*. https://news.mit.edu/2019/inkbit-3d-printer-0604.

Zhou, Dr. Jiangying. n.d. "μBrain Program Description (archived)." DARPA.mil. https://www.darpa.mil/program/microbrain.

3

AI ETHICS AND GOVERNANCE IN DEFENCE INNOVATION

Implementing AI Ethics Framework

Cansu Canca

Artificial intelligence (AI) systems increasingly feature in every industry and all aspects of our lives. As we often hear, AI is becoming ubiquitous, being used in all domains from finance to healthcare, from public safety to education, from transportation to entertainment. Even when we are not engaging with AI systems as consumers, we are often subjected to them, whether we realise it or not. Thus, it should not come as a surprise that AI is also becoming an integral part of military operations, armed forces, and the defence industry. In public discourse, the military use of AI often invokes images of SkyNet, Terminator, and killer robots. However, the military applications of AI are much broader, encompassing back-office operations, logistics, cyber defence, search and rescue aid, decision support in combat, and lethal autonomous weapons. AI systems can significantly impact military operations by increasing the efficiency and accuracy of many tasks. Some of these applications are ethically relatively uncontroversial, such as achieving higher success rates in personnel hiring, search and rescue missions, or medical treatment, with the use of AI. Others, however, raise serious ethical concerns: lethal autonomous weapons or decision-support tools in active combat, for example, where the use of AI may lead to ignoring the complexities of the given situation and the value of human life.

AI's most important ethical potential is its capacity to systematise good decision-making, thereby preventing ethical mistakes on a large scale. However, this is also AI's most significant risk: If an AI system has an ethical error incorporated into it, its wide-scale and efficient application may "efficiently" wrong and harm individuals and communities en masse and do so behind a veil of computational objectivity. Setting aside the more profound question of whether warfare is inherently unethical or not (Lazar 2020), tackling AI-specific issues systematically and effectively requires implementing an AI ethics framework to accompany the existing military ethics framework. As you will read in other

DOI: 10.4324/9781003218326-4

chapters of this book, most countries use AI systems, and several have already started developing such ethics frameworks.

This chapter begins with an overview of the AI ethics landscape within a military context, showing the ethical dual nature of AI tools. The chapter then defines AI ethics and situates it in relation to law and the military. Subsequently, the chapter lays out an AI ethics and governance framework called the *PiE Model* applied to the military context, detailing its core organisational components: AI ethics playbook, process, and people. And finally, the chapter concludes by presenting some further considerations, such as accountability and the role of regulations. Due to the scope of this chapter, we will not get into concerns related to an international arms race in AI.

Ethical Risks and Opportunities of AI for the Military

The military use of AI can be divided into two broad categories: non-combat and combat applications (Taddeo et al. 2021). Non-combat applications include various back-office operations, logistics, predictive maintenance, personnel management, communications, and humanitarian interventions. Like any large organisation, the military benefits from speeding up and scaling their organisational tasks most efficiently, and AI can help. As these are less domain-specific tasks, the integration of AI into such applications often does not catch public attention. However, AI systems are incredibly versatile – a resource allocation tool for logistics can technically be reprogrammed for the battlefield.

Similarly, many combat applications of AI are not military-specific technologies. An excellent example is Project Maven, where the US Department of Defence (DoD) partnered with Google to equip its drone surveillance system with better visual recognition tools. The resulting AI system can be developed for search and rescue missions, non-offensive planning purposes, or targeting. The technology has multiple uses, as is often the case with AI systems.

TEXT BOX 3.1 PROJECT MAVEN

Project Maven, formally known as the *Algorithmic Warfare Cross-Functional Team,* is a Pentagon project aiming to use computer vision technology to analyse drone footage and identify and track objects of interest. Pentagon initially collaborated with Google on this project, yet after Google employees protested in 2018 the contract, as it was initially set, was not extended.

Background

In 2009, the DoD's drones captured about 200,000 hours of footage, requiring thousands of analysts to be tasked with watching and analysing them.

By 2019, the accumulated footage reached over 4 million hours resulting in a gargantuan task of analysis that cannot be handled by humans alone. In 2017, the DoD sought to integrate AI systems, which use deep learning and neural networks, to achieve this complex task.

The Reaction

Google employees objected to Google's function in this project. In a letter to the CEO, they claimed, "Google should not be in the business of war. [...] Building this technology to assist the US Government in military surveillance—and potentially lethal outcomes—is not acceptable".

https://www.nytimes.com/2010/01/11/business/11drone.html
https://www.af.mil/News/Article-Display/Article/1781271/mq-1b-mq-9-flight-hours-hit-4-million/
https://thebulletin.org/2017/12/project-maven-brings-ai-to-the-fight-against-isis/
https://www.wired.com/story/googles-contentious-pentagon-project-is-likely-to-expand/
https://static01.nyt.com/files/2018/technology/googleletter.pdf

AI use within a military context raises various ethical concerns due to high ethical risks often inherent in these technologies. A comprehensive account of the ethical landscape of AI in the military must also account for the potential ethical benefits. AI ethics within a military context is a double-edged sword. Most tools that enable ethically preferable outcomes could also result in severe ethical problems. While this is not unique to military applications, the military domain inevitably raises the stakes by its inherent engagement with killing and dominating. To illustrate this dual aspect of military AI technologies, let us investigate a short, non-exhaustive list of ethical pairs of pros and cons.

Precision vs Aggression

A major area of AI applications for the military is about increasing precision. Project Maven is an example of that. The project aims to use computer vision algorithms to analyse hours of drone footage and tag those images that contain objects of interest. Without an AI in play, the military drowns in an exponentially growing amount of drone footage. The image recognition algorithms can technically process all this data and complete this task with higher precision than human analysts. In doing so, the system not only achieves the purpose more efficiently, but also liberates officers from the task of looking through the drone footage themselves, which allows them to focus their expertise on analysing flagged sections (see Project Maven info-box).

The military benefits of increased precision in surveillance and potentially in targeting are clear. Going beyond that, this capability may also result in ethically preferable outcomes: It may help search and rescue missions, predict and prevent deadly attacks from the opponent, and eliminate or decrease errors in defence which may have resulted in unnecessary and avoidable casualties. All of these may contribute to limiting mortality and morbidity within the conflict. However, these increased capabilities might also boost the confidence of armed forces and make them more aggressive in their offensive and defensive attacks, resulting in more armed conflict and more casualties. We can expand this example to include several similar technologies. Image-, object-, or facial recognition tools, or communication analysis tools for intel or targeting, which provide increased surveillance capacity and/or higher precision, could lead us to the same ethical conundrum: Can we ensure that accuracy and efficiency lead to ethically better outcomes with fewer lives lost or damaged than increased aggression which results in more injuries and death?

Efficiency vs Lowered Barriers to Conflict

All major organisations seek efficiency. Drones that cover wide geographies to collect intelligence, visual recognition algorithms that analyse piles of video footage, and risk analysis tools that quickly comb through big data and take multiple variables into account to aid strategic decision-making are all systems that optimise military operations. Systems that reduce the need for human resources, keep humans safe, and allow human officers to use their expertise are beneficial for the military and military personnel. If we assume that the military's purpose and reasons for its existence are ethically just – and most would argue that if nothing, then at least some form of defence is justified – then systems that optimise its operations and benefit its personnel are also ethically preferable.

The other side of the coin is the concern that increasing efficiency and safety for the military will also lower the barriers to entering a conflict. If war is both safe and low cost, what would stand in the way of starting one? One could argue that if all parties have similarly efficient and effective technologies, this might deter all parties from starting a war. But we can reasonably assume that these technologies will not be available to all, and some countries will have significant advantages over others. In that case, only those who lack the technology would be deterred from starting a war, whereas those equipped with the technology could become even more eager to escalate a conflict. Indeed, pain and suffering inflicted on the other party will not be prohibitive of starting a conflict when the goal itself is to exercise dominance over the other.

Protecting Combatants vs Neglecting Responsibility and Humanity

On the battlefield, a significant military advantage would be to shift the risk of harm from humans to machines. If a drone gathers intelligence, a route mapping machine marks and clears a minefield, a robot detonates a bomb, and an army of robots fights a war, the military personnel can remain safe and out of harm's way. Sparing military personnel's lives and keeping them safe from death and physical and mental harm that result from active combat would be a clear benefit for the military. Reducing harm to human life also constitutes an ethically positive consideration.

However, it is never that simple. These "smart" systems can be anywhere on the spectrum, from fully remotely controlled to fully automated. As soon as there is a distance between the target and the combatant, concerns regarding responsibility and humanity arise. Can an officer remotely operating a weapon feel the weight of responsibility of "pulling the trigger" as strongly when they are distant from the "other"? Can they view the "other" as possessing humanity, an inherent value, when they are no longer face-to-face with them? These are certainly not novel questions: One could argue that each technology that creates a distance between the target and the combatant, such as guns, tanks, and aircraft, has historically raised the same questions. AI systems might be one further step in this distancing. It is also worth noting how the threat presented by these remotely controlled technologies impacts the everyday lives of individuals and communities who are subject to them. Civilians and children in Pakistan, where the United States has deployed considerable numbers of drones, say that when they see a blue sky, they do not dare to go out because that is when drone strikes increase (IHR&CRC and CHRGJ 2012; Abad-Santos 2013). This is the impact on a child's life while a soldier stays safe, remotely controlling a machine.

The ethical decision-making of a human is inevitably intertwined with human psychology. How combatants feel about the situation and the other parties necessarily feature in their ethical reasoning. As the system moves further on the spectrum of machine learning and automation, how accountable and responsible *is* the combatant, and how responsible do they *feel*? And if machines fight wars, as in the case of "killer robots", can they value humanity? If an AI is sophisticated enough, one can argue that we can program these values into the system. Suppose the system is always programmed to put a high value on human life so that it requires very strict conditions ever to kill. In that case, it might even be more respectful of humanity and take it into account more consistently than a combatant who at times will "pull the trigger" because they are tired, frustrated, angry, or scared. However, complex AI systems using machine learning methods might "learn" to disregard human value. With today's AI capabilities, these questions remain hypothetical: Such value judgements are too complex and context-dependent for existing AI and, therefore, cannot be fully delegated to the AI system. Instead, these decisions must be made within a human-machine collaboration. The question then is, where, if anywhere, should we draw the line on the spectrum of automation and remote control to ensure that human officers still engage in ethical decision-making, acknowledging the weight of their decisions and their responsibility, as they operate and collaborate with AI tools?

TEXT BOX 3.2 KILLER ROBOTS/LAWS

Public discussion on the military use of AI is dominated by concerns about "killer robots". Killer robots, or lethal autonomous weapons (LAWs) as they are called, include all systems that have the capacity to kill and that engage with the target without human intervention, following the initial programming instructions. They can detect, identify, and attack their targets. LAWs are distinct from other fully or partially remotely operated military systems because they fully eliminate the need for a human officer's approval or control to complete their tasks.

The LAWs have been a topic of discussion for a good reason. They are one of the most dangerous uses of AI systems. They raise a number of ethics issues. Some of these issues are about precision, value of humanity, and responsibility: Can LAWs distinguish combatants from civilians, and can they reliably judge the context? Can they decide and act in a way that values human life? And if they operate on complex machine learning models, who is accountable for their errors? Do they create a responsibility gap in military operations?

As systems become more complex, questions arise regarding human control and accountability. Can human officers have adequate control over the functioning of these technologies in case the system makes an error? Suppose they are to be used as decision-aid tools. Will officers have sufficient comprehension of the system to judge its strengths and shortcomings rather than blindly following AI system's recommendations? If these systems are learning, who will be accountable in the event of wrongdoing? These and several other questions must be addressed for the AI tools to be developed and used ethically.

As it should be clear from this double-sided picture, AI differs from most other high-risk technologies and weapons in that it does not only pose a risk of harm to the other side of the conflict. Instead, it also has the *potential* to benefit them by reducing civilian and military casualties, protecting the components of civilisation such as historical buildings and museums, and preventing unnecessary attacks fuelled by inadequate or erroneous intel. Unfortunately, almost all these capabilities come with risks such as increased confidence to start a conflict or launch an attack, distancing parties from the humanity of each other, and losing sight of moral responsibility and accountability. Due to the dual nature of AI systems, a blanket ban of AI for military use cannot be an ethical or realistic option. Military use of AI is not a "good" or a "bad"; it is a mixed bag. For that reason, we need to create and implement frameworks for the ethical design, development, and deployment of AI systems.

What Is AI Ethics?

Before going into more detail about creating and implementing an AI ethics framework for defence innovation, let us take a step back and clarify what "ethics" means and its relation to law, AI, and the military.

Ethics vs Human Rights and Law

We talk about the ethical risks of AI systems, but what is ethics, and how does it differ from laws and regulations? Is there a space for "practising" ethics beyond legal compliance? Is ethics "just the subjective moral compass" of each individual, or is there a way of going beyond "individual taste"? Ethics is a subdiscipline of philosophy focusing on what is good/right. Applied ethics aims to systematically and analytically determine the good/right action or the just/fair policy in a given situation. For example, in the military context, is it ethically correct for an officer to blast a warehouse full of ammunition near a hospital? Is it the right policy for an intelligence agency to record all cell phone activities in the name of fighting terrorism? Answering these questions requires us to engage with concepts such as harm (to individuals and society), individual autonomy, and fairness. While these are monumental tasks, moral and political philosophy contains the relevant theories and body of work to undertake such tasks and guide ethical decision-making in real life.

Ethics has a multidimensional relation with law. Setting up "good" and "fair" regulations that would benefit society inevitably requires answering the ethical question "what is the good/fair policy" before engaging in law-making. In other words, proper law-making cannot be distinct or prior to the ethical discussion. Once the regulation is in place, the ethical reasoning must also take the legal framework into account. But this does not necessarily mean that the ethical decisions always align with legal rules since laws can also be unethical, resulting in major complexities for organisations. Even in the case of a well-crafted and ethically justified legal framework, many questions will fall into a grey area where the law does not provide definitive answers. To do the right thing, one will still have to engage in ethical reasoning and, if pressed by the legal system or the court of public opinion, present this reasoning in their defence.

Some contrast ethics with human rights, arguing that ethics fails to provide sufficient guidance, unlike the human rights framework (Hilligoss et al. 2018; Raso et al. 2018). They argue that because there are multiple competing moral and political theories, ethics cannot take us far in our decision-making. Instead, they claim, ethics is bound to remain an individual's moral compass, subject to feelings and preferences, without a binding power like the human rights framework. Some also argue that ethics fails to take the political realities and the power dynamics of the real world into account (Hao 2021). These objections are based on an erroneous understanding of the scope, concerns, and tools of applied ethics.

Applied ethics takes all aspects of the given situation into account. This includes the relevant information and data and the political, legal, and socio-economic realities of the given case. All this information provided by other disciplines feeds into the moral and political theories and ethical reasoning tools that the philosopher would then utilise. If an ethical analysis neglects these, it is not because of its limitations but rather because it is not done adequately. Therefore, suggesting that ethics fails to take politics and power into account shows a lack of understanding of the scope and work of applied ethics.

It is true that there is no one prevailing moral or political theory to rule them all. The equally well-justified and well-established theories often conflict in their recommended course of the "right" action. However, no other normative framework or discipline can solve or go beyond this conflict either. All other frameworks, including the human rights framework, are ultimately based on these theories. The general normative rules of thumb, like the articles of the Universal Declaration of Human Rights (UDHR), emphasise values that are justified through these moral and political theories, such as the value of life, liberty, well-being, privacy, self-governance, and equality. However, general rules are not sufficient when dealing with complex ethical problems. Complex ethical issues arise when, in a given case, values point in different directions, for example, in a case where protecting life and liberty requires violating privacy. In such cases, one must go beyond general rules and engage with ethical reasoning. At that stage, theories disagree about which value to prioritise among this universally endorsed set of values. Such an exercise of value trade-offs necessarily takes us to the realm of applied ethics and moral and political philosophy, even if we start from the human rights framework. And once we move beyond these universally accepted values and the general instruments such as the UDHR, there is no universal agreement about the right course of action in ethics or in the human rights framework (Canca 2019b).

AI Ethics

AI ethics has increasingly been a core area of concern across sectors, particularly since 2017, when technology-related scandals slowly started to catch the public's attention (Zetlin 2017; AI Now Institute 2018). AI ethics is concerned with the whole AI development and deployment cycle. This includes research, development, design, deployment, use, and even the updating stages of the AI life cycle, with ethical questions related to, for example, value judgements integrated into AI systems, research and project design, and responsible deployment of AI systems. Each stage presents its unique ethical questions and issues. Some of these questions are:

- Does the dataset represent the world, and if not, who is left out?
- Does the algorithm prioritise a value explicitly or implicitly? And if it does, is this justified?

- Does the dashboard provide information for a user to understand the core variables of an AI decision-aid tool?
- Did research subjects consent to have their data used? Did they consent to participate in research experiments?
- Do professionals such as military officers, managers, physicians, and administrators understand the limitations of the AI tools that they are handed?
- When provided with a risk score about an individual (such as a job candidate, an officer, or a patient) or an operation do professionals understand the scoring mechanism to avoid overreliance on imperfect tools?
- As users engage with AI tools in their professional or personal daily lives, do they agree to have their data collected and used, and do they understand its risks?

Many ethical risks with AI systems are not unique to AI or big data. What makes ethical issues AI-specific are (1) the extremely short gap between R&D and practice, (2) the wide-scale and systematic use of AI systems, (3) the increased capabilities of AI models, and (4) the façade of computational objectivity. Once an AI system is developed, it can often quickly be taken "out of the lab" to the real world and be available for widespread use, making it a part of common practice. In many instances, it became clear only after the fact that this was done while the AI system still had too many unresolved ethical issues, as in the cases of risk analysis and facial recognition tools which were biased against the Blacks (Angwin et al. 2016; Buolamwini and Gebru 2018; Obermeyer et al. 2019).[1]

Yet, the system's complexity and its computational aspect give users confidence and trick them into thinking that the AI system itself cannot have ethical issues since it is "just math and data". This façade of objectivity is extremely dangerous because it allows users, such as judges and officers, to put aside their critical approach and prevents them from questioning the system's results ("the computer said so"). Inadvertently, the AI system leads them to make ethical errors and do so systematically due to their overreliance on the AI tool. As AI becomes a part of all aspects of human life and organisational operations, it is reasonable to say that it will be impossible to have an ethical and just society or an ethical organisation if the AI systems are unjust.

AI Ethics and Military Ethics

The practice and work of AI ethics do not exist in isolation. AI is used in a context of a domain (e.g. military, healthcare, criminal justice), and the ethical questions related to the AI system are connected to the domain in which it is utilised. The military is a high-stake domain, and like other high-stake domains (such as health and criminal justice), it has a long tradition and an extensive body of work dealing with its ethical questions. An AI ethics framework in a military context should thus draw on traditional military ethics and the broader context of *just war theory* and the *laws of war.* The fundamental ethical principles for military engagement as described in laws of war – that is, necessity, proportionality, distinction, and humanity – are guiding as we deal with the ethical questions in defence innovation and the military use of AI systems. For example, the question of LAWs should not be discussed in isolation from the principle of humanity and proportionality, since the core questions related to LAWs are "Can a machine grasp the value of humanity and the context sufficiently to value each human life and kill or injure only when necessary?" and "Are the risks posed by LAWs and the damage that they might inflict proportional to their expected military benefits?"

TEXT BOX 3.3 LAWS OF WAR

Often referred to as "laws of war", international humanitarian law (IHL) is a set of international rules governing the actions during armed conflict. It regulates relations between countries, international organisations, and other entities that are subject to international law. The core element of the IHL is the Geneva Convention, which has been ratified by all 196 states, making the laws of war a universal instrument.

The four fundamental principles of the IHL are:

- "*Distinction*: There must be a clear distinction between the armed forces and civilians, and between objects that might legitimately be attacked and those that are protected from attack.
- *Military necessity*: A party to an armed conflict may use only that degree and kind of force, not otherwise prohibited by the law of armed conflict, that is required to achieve the legitimate purpose of the conflict, namely the complete or partial submission of the enemy at the earliest possible moment with the minimum expenditure of resources.
- *Humanity*: Humanity forbids the infliction of suffering, injury, or destruction not actually necessary for the accomplishment of legitimate military purposes.
- *Proportionality*: The losses resulting from a military action should not be excessive in relation to the expected military advantage".

https://www.icrc.org/en/document/what-are-rules-of-war-Geneva-Conventions
https://www.icrc.org/en/document/what-ihl
https://www.gov.uk/government/publications/international-humanitarian-law-and-the-uk-government/uk-and-international-humanitarian-law-2018

An AI Ethics and Governance Framework in a Military Context

AI systems, which previously were not evaluated for their ethical applications or their ethical design, are now the focus of ethical inquiries. Due to their high-stake operations, certain sectors are particularly subject to these inquiries, and they face demands to integrate AI ethics into their practice as they adopt novel AI systems. The military is one such sector where getting ethics right is crucial and where the lack of ethics can have catastrophic results. Luckily, as mentioned earlier, it also has the benefit of having a well-established theoretical and practical military ethics and a responsible workflow which would allow efficient integration of AI ethics into its existing ethical framework. Now the question is, how can we achieve this goal and put a robust and comprehensive AI ethics framework in place.

Core Components of the PiE Model, *an AI Ethics Framework*

Since AI-related scandals started to unfold in 2017, efforts to establish AI ethics governance practices have concentrated mainly on ethics principles and ethics boards. Over 100 sets of AI ethics principles have been published by private companies, governmental agencies, and research and professional organisations (AI Ethics Lab 2020). Many organisations have also established AI ethics boards. The idea of implementing ethics through principles and review boards is borrowed from the ethics oversight and compliance model of research ethics. However, as it should be clear from the examples in the above section, the ethical questions and issues that AI raises cannot be addressed through this traditional ethics compliance and oversight model. Neither can they be solved solely through regulation. Instead, we need a comprehensive AI ethics framework to address all aspects of AI innovation and use in organisations. One such framework is the *Puzzle-solving in Ethics (PiE) Model* (AI Ethics Lab 2019; Canca 2019a).[2]

The AI ethics framework presented in the PiE Model focuses on the organisation's AI ethics strategy and governance and details each component of this overarching strategy. The AI ethics strategy consists of (1) the *playbook component*, which includes all ethical guiding materials such as ethics principles, use cases, and tools; (2) the *process component*, which includes ethics analysis and ethics-by-design components, and structures how and when to integrate these and other ethics components into the organisational operations; and (3) the *people component*, which structures a network of different ethics roles – ranging from chief ethics officer and ethics board to ethics respondents in teams – within the organisation. These three Ps enable the organisation to systematise and seamlessly integrate AI ethics into its operations.

An extensive AI ethics framework is only slowly being adopted by the military. Some countries and political entities are at the level of adopting general roadmaps, such as the European Parliament's plenary session in January 2021 on *Guidelines on military and non-military use of Artificial Intelligence* (EP 2021).

Currently, the US Department of Defence has the more advanced AI ethics governance framework, with AI ethics principles (DoD 2020) and a *Responsible AI Guidelines in Practice* document outlining concrete steps for operationalising and implementing these principles (DIU 2021). Accordingly, in the following sections, I refer to the DoD's work as a case study to illustrate the components of an AI ethics framework.

AI Ethics Playbook

The AI ethics playbook forms the backbone of the AI ethics strategy, consisting of all guidelines and tools to aid ethical decision-making at all levels. A complete AI ethics playbook should provide a coherent and clear framework, with (i) fundamental principles to create a solid basis, (ii) accessible and user-friendly tools that help apply these principles, and (iii) use cases that demonstrate how to use these tools and bring the principles into action. An AI ethics playbook should be a living document that can be corrected, revised, and adapted according to the organisation's needs and available information.

In 2019, the US Defense Innovation Board (DIB) recommended a set of AI ethics principles: responsibility, equitability, traceability, reliability, and governability (DIB 2019a). The DoD adopted these five AI ethics principles in February 2020, making it the first defence force that took a tangible step in creating an AI ethics playbook. The DoD stated that these principles apply to combat and non-combat functions of AI use within a military context (DoD 2020).

TEXT BOX 3.4 US DEPARTMENT OF DEFENCE – AI ETHICS PRINCIPLES

1 *Responsible*: DoD personnel will exercise appropriate levels of judgement and care, while remaining responsible for the development, deployment, and use of AI capabilities.
2 *Equitable*: The Department will take deliberate steps to minimise unintended bias in AI capabilities.
3 *Traceable*: The Department's AI capabilities will be developed and deployed such that relevant personnel possess an appropriate understanding of the technology, development processes, and operational methods applicable to AI capabilities, including with transparent and auditable methodologies, data sources, and design procedure and documentation.
4 *Reliable*: The Department's AI capabilities will have explicit, well-defined uses, and the safety, security, and effectiveness of such capabilities will be subject to testing and assurance within those defined uses across their entire life cycles.

5 *Governable*: The Department will design and engineer AI capabilities to fulfil their intended functions while possessing the ability to detect and avoid unintended consequences, and the ability to disengage or deactivate deployed systems that demonstrate unintended behaviour.

https://www.defense.gov/News/Releases/Release/Article/2091996/dod-adopts-ethical-principles-for-artificial-intelligence/

AI ethics principles can be seen as the foundation of an organisation's AI ethics guidelines. Fundamentally, we can divide these principles into *core values*, which are the ultimate and inherent ethical values, and *instrumental principles*, which serve as instruments to protect, promote, and uphold these core values. As derived from moral and political theories and formulated by the *principlism* framework, (1) respecting individual autonomy, (2) minimising harm and maximising benefits, and (3) upholding justice are core values.[3] On the other hand, for example, privacy, accountability, and transparency are instrumental principles that help uphold these core values (Canca 2020).[4] Ideally, we want to uphold all three of these core values for *all stakeholders* that engage with or are subject to AI systems. However, the reality is far from ideal. These core values often conflict, forcing the decision-makers to choose between, for example, respecting citizens' autonomy and minimising harm to society. When such a conflict, either between core values or instrumental principles, arises, the AI ethics principles that the organisation has endorsed come into play. This set of principles displays a value judgement by promoting certain principles while omitting others. We can see this by mapping out the DoD's list of instrumental principles according to the core values that they most closely relate to:

1 *Responsible*: justice (DoD takes responsibility)
2 *Equitable*: justice (non-discrimination towards those who are subject to AI systems)
3 *Traceable*: autonomy (DoD personnel's rational engagement with AI systems) and justice (means to ensure accountability)
4 *Reliable*: minimisation of harm (towards all who are subject to AI systems)
5 *Governable*: minimisation of harm (towards all who are subject to AI systems)

Here we see that the DoD's principles are instrumental; each functions as a tool to uphold a core value. When classifying them according to the core value they refer to, it becomes clear that the list (intentionally) omits some of the important instrumental principles. For example, "privacy" does not feature in this list. In the DIB's supporting document accompanying the original recommendation, privacy is mentioned only a handful of times and only in the context of (i) protecting DoD employees' personal data, (ii) a general commitment to individual rights and abidance to the privacy laws of the United States, and (iii) an *equitable* design feature only to help avoid bias (DIB 2019b). Typically, however, privacy functions to help individuals exercise autonomy over their lives and their space. This function has a much broader application in relation to the development and deployment of AI systems, for example, with respect to a system's engagement with *all* subjects' personal data and its tracking and tracing capabilities. The DoD's AI ethics framework does not endorse this broader function. In fact, among the DoD's AI principles, there is no instrumental principle related to respecting individual citizens' autonomy.

Similarly, while several of the DoD's instrumental principles are about various aspects of justice, the list decidedly and explicitly omits "fairness". The DIB explains this decision by stating the following:

> We wish to acknowledge that the term "fairness" is often cited in the AI community as pertinent to [the principle of equitability]. Indeed, we use the term below. The reason we do not word this principle as such stems from the DoD mantra that fights should not be fair, as DoD aims to create the conditions to maintain an unfair advantage over any potential adversaries, thereby increasing the likelihood of deterring conflict from the outset. By intentionally seeking an unfair or asymmetric advantage, DoD can reduce the risk of armed conflict.
>
> *(DIB 2019b)*

This move takes one (debatable) aspect of fairness in war – that is, the implicit claim that to have an advantage over the other by definition creates "unfairness" – and uses it to circumvent all obligations of fairness. Broadly speaking, the core concern of the just war theory is justice and fairness. More specifically, the fundamental principles of laws of war – necessity and proportionality – are core aspects of fairness that can, and should, be part of the deployment and development of AI systems. The set of principles that the DoD has adopted is meant to guide ethical decision-making in deploying and developing AI systems. To fulfil this function, the nuances matter; what does each principle mean, what is its scope of application, how do the principles apply to different stakeholders, and, finally, which principles are omitted and why? This is a philosophically demanding task, but it directly impacts and shapes the organisation's guiding tools. Only after establishing a clear and consistent set of principles, we can move on to develop the rest of the playbook: tools and use cases.

Existing, customised, and custom-built AI ethics tools should be available as a part of the playbook. These include, for example, ethics checklists and assessments, technical tools to test accuracy and bias, and methods to improve the explainability of systems. Using case studies to illustrate how principles and tools can be applied is crucial because, without examples, principles are bound to remain abstract. Use cases should be closely related to the questions that the organisation faces in real-life applications. They should provide sufficient and accurate details to set the scenario. These cases should help the decision-maker recognise the needed and missing information, determine the relevant stakeholders, understand the ethical impact of each decision, and show, if applicable, how to use tools to help address the ethical issues. In their ethical reasoning, the decision-maker should use the organisation's AI principles to focus more in-depth on those ethical concerns and flesh out each principle's demand. As the organisation advances in its AI ethics practices, cases that they have encountered and navigated using the playbook should be added to illustrate the real-life application of guiding documents and provide an opportunity to detect and correct errors or loopholes in the playbook.

Continuing with the example of the DoD, in the follow-up document, the *Responsible AI Guidelines in Practice*, the Defense Innovation Unit (DIU) provides two real-life case studies: one on predictive health and the other on countering foreign malign influence (DIU 2021). Separating these AI projects into their planning, development, and deployment phases, the use cases also specify ethical questions that arose. However, these case studies neither guide the decision-maker to identify needed information, relevant stakeholders, and ethical impact nor do they show how one can apply the principles; for example, how should one assess and ensure the equitability of these AI systems.

AI Ethics Process

A playbook is inconsequential if there is no process to integrate it into the organisation's operations. Therefore, an essential part of an AI ethics strategy is figuring out how to add the playbook into the organisation's various operations seamlessly. The objective of the AI ethics process is to create systematic procedures for ethics decisions which include (i) structuring the workflow to add "ethics checkpoints", (ii) ethics analysis and ethics-by-design sessions, (iii) documenting ethics decisions and adding them into the playbook as use cases, and (iv) ensuring a feedback loop between new decisions and the updating of the playbook when needed. This process spans the innovation cycle including the research, development, deployment, monitoring, and updating phases as well as the procurement of AI systems.

Each of these phases in AI development and deployment raises a host of ethical questions to be answered and issues to be mitigated. Therefore, AI ethics should be an integral part of the entire AI development and deployment cycle from the very beginning. The DIU's *Responsible AI Guidelines in Practice* is an excellent example of proceeding from the playbook to the process. It aims to "explore methods for implementing these principles in several of its AI prototype projects", using "specific questions that should be addressed at each phase in the AI lifecycle" (DIU 2021). The document provides workflow templates for planning, development, and deployment phases, specifying when to ask which question to address the ethical issues in a timely manner. For example, the development phase starts with the question, "Have you created a plan to prevent the intentional or unintentional manipulation of data or model outputs and identified who is responsible for implementing this plan?" (DIU 2021).

In each phase of the AI life cycle, AI ethics analyses should lay out the ethics landscape by determining the ethics risks and ethics opportunities (that is, opportunities to solve an existing ethical issue using the AI system) concerning the development or deployment of an AI system. Once these risks and opportunities are determined, a process should be in place for ethics experts to collaborate with developers and designers to address them and find solutions. This is where *ethics-by-design* comes into play. Ethics-by-design refers to the idea of integrating ethical choices into the design – that is, the project design, the research design, the dataset and algorithm design, and, finally, the product design – thereby ensuring that the final product cannot violate these ethical choices (SIENNA 2020). As ethical decisions become a part of the design, the manoeuvring room for intentional or unintentional unethical behaviour shrinks, leaving less work to be carried out by safeguards and deterring rules. For example, an AI system may aim to achieve privacy-by-design by using federated learning and keeping all the data within the user's device. This method aims to protect against malicious actors violating user privacy without having to rely solely on safeguards such as user agreements, which malicious actors might easily disregard.

But ethics-by-design is not a cure-for-all – it may not address all ethical concerns. Therefore, a procedure for documenting ethical issues that are left unresolved is needed to put the necessary safeguards in place. This procedure should also feed back into the playbook by turning real-life cases into case studies, demonstrating the ethical decision-making process. The continuous update of the playbook should be systematised so that a strong feedback loop is created between practice and playbook. In that manner, ethics decisions function as a check on the guiding principles established in the playbook, providing opportunities for improving the playbook as needed.

AI Ethics People

In structuring the process, risk is an important aspect. How should high-, medium-, and low-risk projects be categorised? What should the process be for their respective ethics analysis and their ethics risk mitigation? Everyday low-risk questions that might arise during the development process might require developers to use ethics assessment tools or consult ethics experts. However, high-risk questions should go through in-depth ethics analysis and an expert advisory or strategy board. This brings us to the final component of the AI ethics strategy: people. Merely having an ethics board is not sufficient to implement the AI ethics strategy outlined above. Instead, a network of people who carry different roles concerning ethics should be embedded into every layer of the organisation. In the research and development phases, developers and designers face ethics questions and must make a choice as they build the AI system. Similarly, in the deployment phase, deployers are faced with ethical issues that may arise as they use the system. There should be clearly designated *ethics respondents* embedded in each division to help resolve these questions or direct them to the right forum. These ethics respondents need not be ethics experts, but rather individuals who are trained in basic ethics to assess the complexity, risk level, and urgency of the questions, find the relevant tools and guidelines that might help resolve the question at hand, and determine if the question requires an ethics expert consultation.

At the core of the AI ethics network of people in the organisation is the *ethics team* (or *ethics experts*), consisting of those who are trained in applied ethics. In a military context, this should include moral and political philosophers, experts in military ethics, and experts in ethics of technology (which includes AI ethics and data ethics). Ideally, the ethics team should also include other experts whose work directly relate to ethics, such as social scientists who investigate the ethical and social impact of military action and/or technology use and engineers who work on questions related to fairness, privacy, explainability, and similar central ethical questions. If it is not feasible to have such experts on the ethics team, the organisation should establish straightforward processes for the ethics experts to collaborate with such experts within the organisation. While the core task of determining the ethical landscape and choices fall onto ethics experts, applied ethics cannot be practised without the data and information that is provided from other related fields, and that feeds into the ethical analysis and risk mitigation.

For high-risk policy decisions, *an ethics strategy board* or *an ethics advisory board* should function as a bridge between the practitioners and ethics experts on the one hand and the leadership on the other hand. Such an ethics board should consist of high-level experts in the relevant domain (in this case, the military), technology, policy, and ethics. And finally, large organisations, such as the military, would benefit from assigning a *chief ethics officer*. This role coordinates the network of ethics people, is responsible for the ethics process, and the development and use of the ethics playbook.

It should be clear from the tasks at hand that the ethics team's work is distinct from the legal team. While there should be close collaboration between legal experts and ethics experts, the focus of legal experts and their skills and tools differ significantly from those of ethics experts. While the ethics experts do need to engage with the question "is it legal", their primary obligation is to ask, "is it ethical" – a question beyond legality. Unlike the legal team, the ethics team cannot rely on legal instruments – they must engage with the ethics instruments to navigate the regulatory landscape and the broader societal, humanitarian, and environmental landscape.

Further Considerations

As the AI ethics and governance framework described above is implemented, a crucial point is about its scope, determining which stakeholders the ethical framework applies to. Many AI systems are developed in collaboration between the military and private companies, as in the case of Project Maven. If the military's

AI ethics guidelines and requirements do not extend to these collaborations with the private sector and academia, the framework would be only partially effective. Instead, the military must find a system to ensure that its AI ethics framework is not evaded and that collaborators are also obliged to align with the ethical principles endorsed by the military.

Perhaps the most crucial question regarding AI ethics and governance in a military context is accountability: Who is accountable when the use of AI goes wrong, resulting in harm, injustice, and violation of rights? If users and even developers do not fully understand how the AI system reaches its outcome, how can they ensure that it is deployed ethically and responsibly? Questions concerning accountability arise both in relation to an individual's actions as they operate *within* the AI ethics framework and in relation to leadership's role in implementing the framework: There should be an accountability mechanism for developers and designers as they integrate ethically laden choices into the AI system and for deployers as they interact and deploy AI tools. There should also be an accountability mechanism for leadership regarding their implementation of a robust and reliable AI ethics and governance framework within the organisation. An ethics framework without an accountability mechanism would be limited to individuals' motivation to "do good" rather than functioning as a reliable and strategic organisational tool.

To that end, an AI ethics framework should be supported by AI regulation. AI regulations would function as an external enforcing mechanism to define the boundaries of legally acceptable actions and to establish a fair playing field for competition. Without national regulations and international agreements, the "wild west" competition would result in an arms race, leading to catastrophic outcomes as companies and countries with ethical principles are forced to compete with those who choose not to adopt them. Moreover, high-risk ethical issues such as "killer robots", mass surveillance tools, or artificial general intelligence, if it is ever to be achieved, should be decided collectively, with expert and citizen input. Regulations should also function to support the AI ethics framework by requiring basic components of this framework to be implemented, such as an audit mechanism for the safety, reliability, and fairness of AI systems, for establishing comprehensive and transparent guiding documents, and for proper training of officers using or developing AI systems. These regulations can also help structure the military-private sector collaborations, which have been raising many red flags. Having such a regulatory framework for AI ethics governance would also help create citizen trust. But regulations necessarily remain at a level of abstraction that cannot address every question that arises in an AI life cycle. Therefore, we always need an AI ethics framework. In a military context, where the stakes are extremely high, potentially affecting the well-being of whole societies, a well-designed, comprehensive, and robust AI ethics framework, which encompasses the whole AI life cycle and guides every decision-maker in this life cycle, is crucial. Such a framework, sustained and supported by regulation and accountability mechanisms, ensures that doing the right thing is not merely a matter of aspiration or goodwill but a matter of obligation and systematic organisational procedures for a military organisation.

Notes

1 Obermeyer et al. (2019) analysed a commercially available risk analysis algorithm that is widely used to aid prioritization in healthcare. They found that Black patients with the same risk score are sicker than White patients. When they corrected the racial bias in the algorithm, the results changed, increasing the percentage of Black patients from 17.7% to 46.5%. Buolamwini and Gebru (2018) analysed commercially available facial recognition tools. They found that while the maximum error rate for lighter-skinned males is 0.8%, for darker-skinned females the error rate is up to 34.7%.

2 The PiE Model is also in line with more recently published responsible AI frameworks such as Microsoft's (2020) and IBM's (Rossi, 2020) AI governance frameworks.

3 These three core principles were laid out in the *Belmont Report*, published by the US National Commission for the Protection of Human Subjects of Biomedical and Behavioral Research (1978), as the fundamental principles of human subject research. Later, these core principles were explained in more detail in the canonical book *Principles of Biomedical Ethics*, forming the *principlism framework* (Beauchamp and Childress 1979).

4 For a comprehensive, but not exhaustive, list of instrumental principles and their relations to core principles, see the tool, *the Box*, which is a part of the toolbox *Dynamics of AI Principles* by AI Ethics Lab (2020).

References

Abad-Santos, Alexander. 2013. "This 13-Year-Old Is Scared When the Sky Is Blue Because of Our Drones." *The Atlantic*, October 29, 2013. https://www.theatlantic.com/politics/archive/2013/10/saddest-words-congresss-briefing-drone-strikes/354548/.

AI Ethics Lab. 2019. "The Puzzle-Solving in Ethics (PiE) Model for Innovation." https://aiethicslab.com/pie-model/.

AI Ethics Lab. 2020. "Toolbox: Dynamics of AI Principles." https://aiethicslab.com/big-picture/.

AI Now Institute. 2018. "AI in 2018: A Year in Review." *Medium*, October 24, 2018. https://medium.com/@AINowInstitute/ai-in-2018-a-year-in-review-8b161ead2b4e.

Angwin, Julia, Jeff Larson, Surya Mattu, and Lauren Kirchner. 2016. "Machine Bias." *ProPublica*, May 23, 2016. www.propublica.org/article/machine-bias-risk-assessments-in-criminal-sentencing.

Beauchamp, Tom, and James Childress. 2019. *Principles of Biomedical Ethics Principles of Biomedical Ethics*, 8th edition. Oxford University Press, New York, NY.

Buolamwini, Joy, and Timnit Gebru. 2018. "Gender Shades: Intersectional Accuracy Disparities in Commercial Gender Classification." *Conference on Fairness, Accountability and Transparency, Proceedings of Machine Learning Research*, vol. 81, 1–15. http://proceedings.mlr.press/v81/buolamwini18a/buolamwini18a.pdf.

Canca, Cansu. 2019a. "A New Model for AI Ethics in R&D." *Forbes AI*, March 29, 2019. https://www.forbes.com/sites/insights-intelai/2019/03/27/rethinking-ethics-in-ai-rd/?sh=45df7b3177ba.

Canca, Cansu. 2019b. "AI & Global Governance: Human Rights and AI Ethics – Why Ethics Cannot Be Replaced by the UDHR." *United Nations University Centre for Policy Research*. https://cpr.unu.edu/publications/articles/ai-global-governance-human-rights-and-ai-ethics-why-ethics-cannot-be-replaced-by-the-udhr.html.

Canca, Cansu. 2020. "Operationalizing AI Ethics Principles." *Communications of the ACM*, December 2020, vol. 63, no. 12, 18–21. https://doi/10.1145/3430368.

European Parliament (EP). 2021. "Guidelines for Military and Non-Military Use of Artificial Intelligence." *Press Room*, January 20, 2021. https://www.europarl.europa.eu/news/en/press-room/20210114IPR95627/guidelines-for-military-and-non-military-use-of-artificial-intelligence.

Hao, Karen. 2021. "Stop Talking about AI Ethics. It's Time to Talk about Power." *MIT Technology Review*, April 23, 2021. https://www.technologyreview.com/2021/04/23/1023549/kate-crawford-atlas-of-ai-review/.

Hilligoss, Hannah, Filippo A. Raso, and Vivek Krishnamurthy. 2018. "It's Not Enough for AI to Be "Ethical"; It Must Also Be "Rights Respecting"." *Medium*, October 10, 2018. https://medium.com/berkman-klein-center/its-not-enough-for-ai-to-be-ethical-it-must-also-be-rights-respecting-b87f7e215b97.

International Human Rights and Conflict Resolution Clinic (IHR&CRC, Stanford Law School) and Global Justice Clinic (CHGJC, NYU School of Law). 2012. "Living under Drones: Death, Injury, and Trauma to Civilians from US Drone Practices in Pakistan." https://chrgj.org/wp-content/uploads/2016/09/Living-Under-Drones.pdf.

Lazar, Seth. 2020. "War." *The Stanford Encyclopedia of Philosophy*, Spring 2020 edition, edited by Edward N. Zalta. https://plato.stanford.edu/archives/spr2020/entries/war/.

Microsoft. 2020. "Putting Principles into Practice: How We Approach Responsible AI at Microsoft." https://query.prod.cms.rt.microsoft.com/cms/api/am/binary/RE4pKH5#:~:text=At%20Microsoft%2C%20we've%20recognized,inclusiveness%2C%20transparency%2C%20and%20accountability.

Obermeyer, Ziad, Brian Powers, Christine Vogeli, and Sendhil Mullainathan. 2019. "Dissecting Racial Bias in an Algorithm Used to Manage the Health of Populations." *Science*, vol. 366, no. 6464, 447–453. https://doi/10.1126/science.aax2342.

Raso, Filippo A., Hannah Hilligoss, Vivek Krishnamurthy, Christopher Bavitz, and Levin Kim. 2018. "Artificial Intelligence & Human Rights: Opportunities & Risks." *The Berkman Klein Centre for Internet & Society Research Publication Series*. https://cyber.harvard.edu/publication/2018/artificial-intelligence-human-rights.

Rossi, Francesca. 2020. "How IBM Is Working toward a Fairer AI." *Harvard Business Review*, November 5, 2020. https://hbr.org/2020/11/how-ibm-is-working-toward-a-fairer-ai.

Stakeholder-Informed Ethics for New Technologies with High Socio-Economic and Human Rights Impact (SIENNA) Project. 2020. "Ethics by Design and Ethics of Use in AI and Robotics." https://sienna-project.eu/digitalAssets/915/c_915554-l_1-k_sienna-ethics-by-design-and-ethics-of-use.pdf.

Taddeo, Mariarosaria, David McNeish, Alexander Blanchard, and Elizabeth Edgar. 2021. "Ethical Principles for Artificial Intelligence in National Defence." *Philosophy & Technology*, vol. 34, 1707–1729. https://doi.org/10.1007/s13347-021-00482-3.

US Defense Innovation Board (DIB). 2019a. "AI Principles: Recommendations on the Ethical Use of Artificial Intelligence by the Department of Defence." https://media.defense.gov/2019/Oct/31/2002204458/-1/-1/0/DIB_AI_PRINCIPLES_PRIMARY_DOCUMENT.PDF.

US Defense Innovation Board (DIB). 2019b. "AI Principles: Recommendations on the Ethical Use of Artificial Intelligence by the Department of Defence – Supporting Document." https://media.defense.gov/2019/Oct/31/2002204459/-1/-1/0/DIB_AI_PRINCIPLES_SUPPORTING_DOCUMENT.PDF.

US Defense Innovation Unit (DIU). 2021. "Responsible AI Guidelines in Practice: Operationalizing DoD's Ethical Principles for AI." https://www.diu.mil/responsible-ai-guidelines.

US Department of Defense (DoD). 2020. "DoD Adopts 5 Principles of Artificial Intelligence Ethics." *News*, February 24, 2020. https://www.defense.gov/News/News-Stories/Article/Article/2094085/dod-adopts-5-principles-of-artificial-intelligence-ethics/.

US National Commission for the Protection of Human Subjects of Biomedical and Behavioural Research. 1978. "The Belmont Report: Ethical Principles and Guidelines for the Protection of Human Subjects of Research." https://www.hhs.gov/ohrp/regulations-and-policy/belmont-report/index.html.

Zetlin, Minda. 2017. "The 3 Worst Technology Scandals of 2017, According to a New Survey." *The Inc.*, November 30, 2017. https://www.inc.com/minda-zetlin/the-3-worst-technology-scandals-of-2017-according-to-a-new-survey.html.

4

EUROPEAN MILITARY AI

Why Regional Approaches Are Lagging Behind

Simona R. Soare

Advances in artificial intelligence (AI) and its enablers (computing power, data, networking infrastructure, innovative funding, skills) are driving a global revolution in military affairs. The frontrunners, the US and China, are engaged in a race to adopt AI and other emerging and disruptive technologies. The role of the European continent in this race is often underestimated, neglected, or cast as a geopolitical and functional "third way" (Minsky 2018; Burrows and Mueller-Kaler 2019; Franke 2019). Overcoming the European AI investment lag (McKinsey 2020a; Soare 2020, 3) and coping with the geopolitical implications of European dependency on foreign digital technology are critical to European strategic autonomy and technological sovereignty. By contrast, the European public debate has focused almost entirely on AI's ethical and legal challenges. This has created a public ethical filter through which all European military AI projects are scrutinised. Against this background, there has been significantly less public information and research about European military AI projects. This creates the perception that Europeans are unwilling or unable to adopt AI in defence.

Since 2018, European AI strategy development has accelerated. While not all European states have clear military AI adoption plans, starting in 2021/22, the EU and NATO are entering a decisive but challenging implementation phase of their AI strategies. What is the strategic outlook on the adoption of AI in defence among European states? And what role do the EU and NATO play in this process? This chapter argues that Europeans find themselves at a crossroads in the adoption of military AI: either European countries overcome their reluctance and risk aversion to accelerate investment and rapid integration of AI technologies in defence over the mid-term, or they risk becoming less strategically and militarily competitive, in contradiction to political ambitions for more European autonomy, capacity, and military capability. The European approach to military

DOI: 10.4324/9781003218326-5

AI is fragmented and de-linked from threat perception and planning for future force structure, mission, and capabilities. It lacks the coherence of similar processes in the civilian-industrial sector.

Four variables explain this situation: first, there is a robust European preference for national AI adoption models where these technologies are used to incrementally optimise legacy platforms and plug enduring capability gaps. Diminishing their critical defence and technological dependencies is as important to large European states as catching up with the US and China. This leaves limited space for investments in disruptive innovation, which can ensure a continued European operational advantage against state and non-state rivals.

Second, national defence establishments and regional organisations like NATO and the EU struggle to adapt to a more discreet role in shaping technological progress, driven by commercial market forces and academia.

Third, European states underuse regional institutional accelerators of military AI adoption, such as the EU and NATO, if their initiatives do not enhance exclusive national (industrial) interests and if they impose strict financial and political commitments on the capitals.

Finally, European states exhibit self-imposed ethical and legal restraints, bordering on cultural-technological conservatism, which inhibits an ambitious European agenda on adopting military AI. Individually, these variables represent enduring features of the European military landscape. Collectively, they act as an obstacle to effective *European* collaborative AI-enabled defence innovation and provide a de facto brake on maintaining the European military technological edge.

In advancing these arguments, this chapter seeks to make a novel contribution by filling a gap in international security and emerging technologies literature about how national and regional defence actors relate to each other to accelerate or inhibit AI adoption in Europe. The novelty of this approach is that it unpacks the positive and negative dynamics between national and regional AI adoption processes, including in response to disruptive events like Brexit and the COVID-19 pandemic, which could hold insights for other similar regional organisational efforts.

The chapter's main findings are that despite its potential, European Research and Technology (R&T) cooperation in emerging disruptive technologies (EDTs) is stalling for national and industrial reasons. This breeds an uneven European playing field in military AI, which is becoming a vulnerability for European strategic autonomy and interoperability within NATO and the EU. The fragmented European landscape in military AI presents a real danger that an AI capability gap may emerge among European states and that a coherent normative and operational European governance framework for military AI may remain elusive beyond the 2020s. Unless Europeans leverage collaborative EU and NATO formats more strategically than in the past, their AI adoption efforts will be slower, capabilities will be fragmented and less interoperable, and the overall costs of European defence will increase.

The chapter proceeds in three parts. The first part takes stock of the evolution of European strategic thinking on military AI. It underlines the progress achieved in AI strategy development and highlights ongoing challenges to AI adoption in European defence. The chapter's second part outlines European states' strategic perspectives on military AI adoption into the mid-2020s. It focuses on three variables that continue to shape the process – accelerating but asymmetric and fragmented AI adoption, the underuse of institutional accelerators like NATO and the EU, and the self-imposed ethical and legal restraint in European approaches to AI adoption, particularly in connection to autonomy. The conclusion outlines the main research findings and highlights further avenues for research on adopting military AI in Europe.

Military AI Adoption in Europe

Uneven AI Playing Field

Since 2018, driven by geoeconomic and geostrategic considerations, AI has become a strategic priority for European states, the EU, and NATO (Babuta et al 2020; Gilli 2020; Sahin 2019; von der Leyen 2020; Geoană 2020). The EU has offered needed coherence, structure, and financial incentives to European efforts on commercial, civilian, and industrial AI adoption. However, the European Commission's (EC's) lead and regulatory power translated into focusing on national AI strategies in the civilian industrial sector.

The 2018 *Communication on Artificial Intelligence for Europe* and the *Coordinated Plan on Artificial Intelligence* established the priority areas for AI development and adoption in the civilian industrial and competitiveness sectors. They also broadly defined a "European approach to AI" grounded in European aspirations for human-centric AI. Subsequently, the 2020 *White Paper on Artificial Intelligence*, the updated *Coordinated Plan on Artificial Intelligence*, and the *Artificial Intelligence Act proposal* refined the EU's AI level of ambition and strategy goals, including a higher level of ambition towards creating European leadership in trustworthy AI. These programmatic documents put forward a roadmap for accelerating AI adoption, including through the creation of an ecosystem and key AI enablers (cloud, data, 5G infrastructure, cyber, semiconductors), and set AI investment benchmarks of over €1 billion annually for the next decade (European Commission 2018a; European Commission 2018b).

In June 2022, the EU adopted the *Strategic Compass*, notably the Union's defence strategy for the 2020s. The *Strategic Compass* underlines the need to invest more and better in capabilities and innovative technologies, fill strategic gaps, reduce technological and industrial dependencies, and establish a new European Defence Innovation Hub within the European Defence Agency (EDA) (European External Action Service 2022, 34–36). Given the dual-use nature of most emerging and disruptive technologies, the *Action Plan for Synergies between the Civilian, Space and Defence Industries* and the *Roadmap on Critical Technologies for Security and Defence*, the Commission has put together technology roadmaps for the development and adoption of key technologies in security and defence. Finally, the *2022 NATO Strategic Concept* outlines the importance of emerging and disruptive technologies for the Alliance's credible and efficient deterrence and defence posture.

While the EU is making progress charting the strategy and implementation tools for adopting AI in the civilian sector, European efforts to adopt AI in defence lack the same level of coherence and incentives that exist in the civilian-industrial sector. By 2022, only two European states adopted dedicated AI defence strategies, notably France and the United Kingdom (UK). Inspired by the American AI strategy, London and Paris developed AI governance (including technology accelerators, defence technology strategies, dedicated AI agencies, ethical AI governance, innovation labs, venture capital funds, and skills attraction strategies) and established national AI ecosystems. Though some areas still require work, including training, talent acquisition, new industry partnerships, exploitation of capital markets funding, and Testing, Evaluation, Verification, and Validation (TEVV), France and the UK have distinct approaches to AI-enabled defence innovation, a strategic approach to military AI and instruments to potentially accelerate its adoption. This reflects Paris and London's higher operational level of ambition, their interest in keeping up with strategic great power competition, and the ambition to enhance the competitiveness of their defence industrial sectors. Nevertheless, both London and Paris have yet to follow this progress in defence AI strategy development with concrete output-focused actions.

Not all European states have the same level of awareness, technological prowess, digitalised forces, and ambition in military AI. A growing number of European states – notably the Netherlands, Italy, Spain, Finland, Estonia, Denmark, and Turkey – develop AI adoption plans of varying scope, connected to new force generation models and capability programmes of record. In 2020, the Netherlands developed a draft military *AI Roadmap* which foresees the deployment of AI in logistics and predictive maintenance, human-machine teaming, situational awareness and decision-making support, and target acquisition. Turkey developed the National Artificial Intelligence Strategy 2021–2025 as part of the nation's "National Technology Move" towards economic and technological interdependence (Anadolu 2020; Kurç, 2023). A 2020 Italian Ministry of Defence paper called for a dedicated AI defence policy (Centro Innovazione Difesa 2020). Spain prominently featured AI in its 2021 "Estrategia de Tecnología e Innovación para la Defensa" and in the Army's new concept "Fuerza 35" (Ministerio de Defensa 2020a, 2020b). In Sweden's (2019) strategy, AI is a critical enabler of total national defence. Finland's (2017) and Romania's (2019) national AI strategies briefly reference the impact of AI on security and defence. Most European AI strategies and national AI plans include references to cyber security but not defence.

In contrast, Germany's and Norway's national AI strategies do not cover defence. Though even in such cases, there are some encouraging signs. Germany has begun to put in place at least the foundations of a defence innovation vision.

However, Berlin continues to be severely hampered by the lack of political and societal support for greater military engagement with technological innovation (Soare and Pothier 2021). In 2020, the Bundeswehr's research centre published a position paper on *Artificial Intelligence in Land Forces* focusing on three objectives: increased efficiency in routine duties, improved capabilities on operations, and addressing potential capability gaps (German Army Concepts and Capabilities Development Centre 2019). Similarly, the German Air Force prioritises using AI for electronic warfare, suppression of enemy air defences, and manned-unmanned teaming roles. However, the 2021 *Ministry of Defence Paper on the Future of the Bundeswehr* barely mentions emerging and disruptive technologies. And digitalisation continues to take priority in the German defence expenditure, according to figures released in the €100 billion Defence Fund (Hille and Werkhäuser, 2022) as the precondition for further investment in military AI. Similarly, Norway acknowledged the role of emerging technologies for defence in the high north and joined the Netherlands, France, and Sweden in the first collaborative European R&T project developing "the European capability of operating in Arctic/cold environments" (European Defence Agency 2020a).[1] However, the level of prioritisation of emerging technologies in defence remains unclear beyond isolated cases such as these.

In addition to the fragmentation of the AI strategy development landscape in Europe, European AI debates are dominated by ethical and legal concerns over the deployment of autonomous weapon systems (AWS), policy efforts towards trustworthy and democratic AI, and calls for comprehensive arms control of emerging technologies, including AI. This European cultural inclination has real strategic consequences. Though their armed forces urgently need these capabilities, since 2020, the Bundestag has blocked the acquisition of five Heron TP drones from Israel over concerns with their autonomous capabilities. The Belgian and Austrian parliaments openly called for a ban on lethal autonomy.

Adoption Challenges

European states face multiple AI adoption challenges. Weak governance (public-private partnerships and innovation ecosystems) and red tape, the lack of access to innovative and sufficient funding solutions, and the unevenly distributed key enablers (data, skills, infrastructure, and budgets) are enduring structural challenges.

First, key enablers of AI adoption are insufficiently developed across Europe. The digital economy is a strategic priority for the von der Leyen-led European Commission, which pledged to invest up to €20 billion in AI annually until 2030 despite the economic impact of COVID-19. However, EU institutions disagree about the actual level of EU investment in AI[2] (Nepelski and Sobolewski 2020, 14–17; European Parliament 2021a). Bureaucratic red tape and lengthy security clearance processes make a cooperation with national and EU authorities less appealing for tech start-ups. Even fast-tracked EU projects, including the

European Defence Fund (EDF), European Space Agency (ESA), and Horizon 2020, undertake months-long bureaucratic processes between proposal submission and acceptance, with further delays incurred for security clearances and general transfer licences. In many instances, agile procurement across Europe still means at least six-to-twelve month-long contract award processes and lengthy submission forms incompatible with start-up investment and innovation cycles.

EU instruments do not sufficiently address the asymmetric distribution of AI investment among states and regions. This situation essentially preserves the fragmentation of the European AI landscape and, at times, may even deepen existing differences. France, Germany, and the UK represent over 50% of European AI investment,[3] and 10% (27 of 266) of Europe's regions account for over 50% of R&D spending on patents, including in AI (Arjona 2020, 226). Collectively, Europe accounts for just 8% of total global private AI investment and has access to fewer and smaller innovative funding solutions, including venture capital funding.[4] European companies are less prone to adopt AI early and register fewer AI patents than US and Chinese companies. Europe is home to only three of the top 25 technology clusters in the world (McKinsey 2020b, 15–18), though the European Commission estimates that the EU landscape in AI is improving.

Second, European public and private investment in military AI is lagging significantly behind the US and China for financial, regulatory, and strategic culture reasons. Approximating European AI defence investment is a challenging undertaking. Most European states do not have dedicated AI budgets, so their R&D budgets remain largely opaque and their defence budgets vary. In 2019, the EDA surveyed EU members' AI defence initiatives. Though the results were not made public, officials assure that European defence AI investment is higher than commonly believed though not comparable to the US or China.[5] Nevertheless, the fragmentation of AI funding along national lines limits its scalability and impact in terms of economies of scale (Soare 2020, 4).

France pledged to annually invest approximately €100 million between 2018 and 2022 in defence-related AI research, and the French Agence de l'Innovation de Défense has an investment portfolio of €1 billion[6] (Ministère des Armées 2021, 1). In November 2020, the UK announced a 34.8% increase in the defence R&D budget (a £1.5 billion year-on-year increase) (Lomas 2020) and the establishment of a dedicated budget for emerging technologies. Dedicated national funding instruments have also been created, from the EU to national venture capital funds and defence innovation funds. A good example is the DefInvest venture capital fund established in 2017 by the French Ministry of Defence and operated by the French investment bank Bpifrance. The fund started with a €50 million initial investment and the ambition is to double this amount in five years. By the end of 2020, DefInvest had invested over €18 million in nine French tech start-ups, though the operational costs of running the fund remain comparatively high at reportedly €3 million (Le Figaro 2021). The UK has established several such funds, including the National Security Strategic Investment Fund (which comprises seven independent venture capital funds with over £10 million investments each) and the Transformation Fund (approximately £66 million) (Ministry of Defence of the United Kingdom 2019) with others in the pipeline.

The number of collaborative R&D projects is on the rise, primarily because of NATO and EU collaborative instruments and financial incentives, including their technological and financial overlap.[7] However, different political and strategic European preferences limit the impact of these regional instruments. Between 2014 and 2020, the NATO Science and Technology Organisation (NATO STO) implemented 855 projects on emerging and disruptive technologies, of which approximately 10% focused on AI (NATO 2020, 49). Roughly half of the long-term capability development priorities identified by the EDA in 2018 focused on emerging technologies, including AI.[8] The European Defence Fund (EDF),[9] the EDA's Innovation Challenge, and the European Network of Defence-related Regions also fund AI projects.

The EDF (2021–2027) will provide €2.65 billion for defence research, though this is half the 2019 proposed amount, of which approximately €316–632 million (4–8%) are earmarked for emerging and disruptive technologies. On average, this amounts to an EDF annual budget for emerging and disruptive technologies of €45–90 million between 2021 and 2027. In 2021, the EC allocated €58.5 million for digital transformation, €60 million for disruptive technologies (though no priority action is linked to AI), and €63.5 million for innovative technology ideas for defence applications (European Commission 2021). In 2022, the European Commission allocated approximately €40 million, or 4.28% of the annual work programme's financial envelope (thus only marginally above the minimum 4% threshold), to emerging technologies (European Commission 2022a, 32). This level of funding is lower than the estimated annual figures for the NATO Innovation Fund (roughly $70 million annually). This investment is less than the French or the British annual investment in just one emerging technology, and it is exponentially lower than American defence investment in AI, estimated at €1.5 billion ($1.62 billion) in the fiscal year 2023 (Department of Defence 2022).

Estimating the impact of EU defence instruments on collaborative defence R&D beyond the budgetary dimension remains challenging, in part because of the novelty of these instruments (EDA 2020c, 5). However, these initiatives require more coherent strategic policy guidance, synergy, and direct links to procurement processes for a more significant impact. Crossing the valley-of-death is a severe and fundamental challenge for European R&D/T in relation to emerging and disruptive technologies. Data shows fewer than 10% of EU and NATO defence research projects cross into development and procurement, and there is no publicly available tool to monitor digital (i.e., software) defence procurement by national administrations.

Increases in European defence spending since 2014 present an opportunity to invest in R&D/T. However, the European level of ambition remains linked to closing capability gaps and increasing readiness levels at the expense of investment in future capabilities and technologies. In the aftermath of the second Russian invasion of Ukraine in 2022, the European Commission focused on three priorities. These are to replenish depleted military stockpiles, replace legacy Soviet military equipment still deployed by member states with European ones, and reinforce air and missile defence (European Commission 2022b, 7). The level of investment needed to achieve these three priority gaps is tremendous, standing at an estimated €160 billion, even as European defence expenditure increases and risks squeezing the financial space for investment in innovation and new technologies (Giegerich and Soare 2022).

AI applications under development in EDF and Permanent Structured Cooperation (PESCO) directly feed into strategic platform-driven projects, such as the future air combat system or the future European drone programme. Data shows an enduring European preference towards national R&D/T and off-the-shelf procurement (EDA 2021, 9–13; EDA 2022a, 11). In 2019, collective defence R&D/T remained below the commonly agreed EDA benchmark of 2% of defence budgets and was highly concentrated. Notably, 85% of R&D/T spending in the EU originated from four members, led by the UK[10] and France. Collaborative European R&D/T continued to fall in 2019 to "the lowest level of collaborative spending ever measured by EDA" (EDA 2021, 14). European public and private R&D were estimated at €18 billion in 2019, but less than 40% of this figure was directed towards military R&D, and over a third of it was concentrated in non-EU European states, the UK, Norway, and Turkey (Aerospace and Defence Industries Association of Europe 2020, 9–10). EU-wide 2020–21 defence data shows nearly a 20% year-on-year increase in R&D and the second largest historical rise in R&T spending which tripled in comparison to 2016 figures (EDA 2022a, 10–13). This is in part justified by the EDIDP and the defence spending trends seem to point upwards, albeit they remain precarious to economic shocks and inflation.

Third, the distribution of AI skills varies significantly across European states, as does digital infrastructure. The DF9 (nine digital frontrunners) countries, notably Belgium, Denmark, Estonia, Finland, Ireland, Luxembourg, the Netherlands, Norway, and Sweden, lead in skills, data, digital infrastructure, and private sector adoption of AI technologies (McKinsey 2020b). Three-quarters of the gains from the European data-driven economy are in France, Germany, Italy, Spain, the Netherlands, and the UK, which also have higher digital adoption rates and larger data pools (European Commission 2020a, 13). France, Germany, and the UK attract 80% of AI start-up funding in Europe (Touboul 2020, 6), and the UK attracts 55% of venture capital funding for AI start-ups in Europe (OECD 2018).

Meanwhile, Central and Eastern Europe is experiencing significant constraints across all these variables. The Visegrád4 countries lack sufficiently advanced digital infrastructure and human skills to adopt AI (Szabo 2020, 8). Their military inventories are, on average, much older and less digitalised than Western European ones, which means investment in new technologies is deterred by the scale of architecture changes required to incorporate new technologies in defence systems. An inventory of Preparatory Action on Defence Research

(PADR) defence research projects shows that Visegrád4 countries participate on average in fewer projects than Western, Nordic, and Baltic countries.[11] Unlike the US and China, European regional frameworks like the EU and NATO are challenged to work across this national AI fragmentation and struggle to ensure coherence beyond the lowest AI common denominator.

European AI skills in defence present a dire situation. European defence officials acknowledge they lack AI skills in sufficient numbers to implement current AI projects.[12] Talent acquisition in the EU, NATO, and national ministries is often a very long and bureaucratic process.[13] In addition to lower remuneration than in the private sector, this significantly hinders tech talent's interest in working in the European public sector. In 2018, the EC pledged €2.3 billion for digital skills. However, there is no assessment of how many AI and data specialists European armed forces need to adopt, integrate, and operate AI-enabled military systems, how and where this specialised talent will be integrated across military institutions, and how this will change military education and talent retention policies across Europe. A 2017 RAND study of European defence skills did not even mention AI and data skills, indicating that Europeans are just beginning to consider the ramifications of AI adoption and the limitations of their abilities. In March 2020, the NATO Science and Technology Organisation warned this "growing skills mismatch may ultimately challenge the Alliance's ability to manage and absorb the disruption and exploit the opportunities presented by EDTs" (2020, 37). Recent data suggest that the EU will likely face a 40% deficit in human talent for digital technologies by 2030 (Soare and Pothier 2021, 25). Pockets of such planning are beginning to emerge in NATO and in the UK.[14] However, there is little evidence that other European governments and the EU are adjusting their digital talent retention practices in defence. Overall, the current landscape presents a real risk that this asymmetric and fragmented European AI adoption could undermine the coherence of regional approaches in NATO and the EU. It is, nevertheless, worthwhile understanding what variables shape the European landscape on military AI adoption.

Strategic Landscape of European Military AI

Accelerating, but Asymmetric and Fragmented Adoption

European states are politically and culturally disposed towards national AI initiatives over collaborative ones. The European military landscape is asymmetric and fragmented along national lines, reflecting a deep division in strategic interests, threat perception, and different levels of ambition related to military AI applications among European states. This leaves limited space for early efforts towards defence cooperation, including in AI: "Allocations made to already launched national programmes leave limited margins for manoeuvre for collaborative defence spending until the mid-twenties" (EDA 2020c, 2–3). It also makes European capitals less inclined towards regional AI governance structures if these fall below their level of ambition, don't support national industrial interests, or require financial and political commitments to less AI-advanced partners. Leading AI powers in NATO and the EU remain very reluctant to participate in collaborative AI defence projects or to transfer sensitive AI technologies to other less tech-savvy European allies.

Some obstacles to more coherent European AI cooperation are well known and much researched, including lack of trust, sensitives around data sharing, different legal, political, and policy frameworks, defence funding availability, and military digitalisation (Soare 2020; Stanley-Lockman 2020). Others are less so. First, the type and applicability of ongoing European military AI projects indicate they are more organically, rapidly, and cheaply developed at the national level, even when they are linked to multinational programmes of record. Most European AI projects are tactical or strategic, which makes them less suitable and more sensitive for multilateral cooperation (EDA 2020d). Strategic initiatives are too sensitive to share, and tactical projects are less immediately beneficial because European interoperability below the strategic and operational levels remains low and concentrated in small regional and functional pockets. A strategic-level digital architecture like the French project ARTEMIS – or *Architecture de Traitement et d'Exploitation Massive de l'Information multi-Source* – is tailored to the French military needs. ARTEMIS develops a "sovereign infostructure" (cloud-based storage for military data, big data and AI-enabled data collection, fusion, analysis and sharing, a "software factory," and predictive maintenance tools) for the French armed forces (Atos 2019). Such capabilities are less suited for multilateral cooperation than AI sub-systems integrated into open architecture platforms, like the Franco-German-Spanish Future Combat Air System (FCAS).

Second, technological co-development is rare due to its sensitive nature and maximising AI interoperability is not without financial and opportunity costs. Adding interoperability features and national optimisation packages to multinationally developed military capabilities increases their costs, complexity, and development schedules. It also implies difficult trade-offs on requirements (Soare 2021a, 21). There is no European agreement on sharing military data, and there is no agreement among leading European technological powerhouses on the operational use of AI. European states that rarely deploy together, use different military equipment, or have different threat-based defence requirements have little incentive to invest in interoperable AI early on. One avenue to consider is the role of regional formats like Joint Expeditionary Force (JEF), Nordic Defence Cooperation (NORDEFCO), European Intervention Initiative (EI2), and Visegrád4 in accelerating innovation in small coalitions of countries that coordinate defence planning and plan to operationally deploy together. Another avenue to consider is for NATO and the EU to support collaborative AI defence projects by helping to financially offset interoperability costs. NATO agreed on a Data Exploitation Policy in 2022, but its remit remains limited and far short of what is needed for allies to be interoperable in multi-domain operations.

Third, European states prioritise their freedom of action by retaining control and flexibility over capability development models and choice of partners. Countries like France are driven by excellence and export prospects, and they prefer bilateral capability development and flexible formats,[15] which inherently give Paris more political control over projects. For capitals like Paris, which want to maximise military exports and consolidate their defence industries, there is little incentive to engage early in AI cooperative development with a broad range of European partners of variable technological prowess and limited funding capacity.[16]

Smaller European states, for which capability development and security guarantees go hand in hand, are guided by their dependency on industrial and strategic partners in their choice of AI capability development. When they do not purchase capabilities off-the-shelf, Denmark, the Netherlands, and other mid-sized European states are attracted by multilateral or lead-nation models of capability development,[17] in which their (defence) industry can contribute niche technologies. In 2021, for example, the Netherland and the US agreed to facilitate access to national defence procurement for each other's defence technology companies (Selinger 2021). Nevertheless, these differences of perspective limit early and broad European cooperation in military AI projects which locks in R&D funding and could steer their procurement towards European (i.e., made-in-Europe) capabilities.

National Military Power Multiplier

The European military AI landscape is fragmented and lacks coherence because of the different national levels of military ambition. European countries see AI adoption as an enabler of enhanced *national* capabilities and a force multiplier to fill *national* capability gaps resulting from over three decades of underinvestment in defence. Furthermore, the war in Ukraine reconfirmed to Nordic, Baltic, Central, and Eastern European countries the crucial importance of hard power beyond any AI layer.[18] NATO and the EU agree on lists of capability priorities and shortfalls, driven by requirements for multilateral allied and EU Common Security and Defence Policy (CSDP) missions and operations. However, strategic national defence preferences and requirements are usually different: the Baltics and Eastern Europeans focus on territorial defence, France on counterterrorism expeditionary capabilities (though in 2022, Paris signaled it will start prioritising high-intensity inter-state conflict), and Portugal and Italy on maritime security. These differences persist even in NATO.

There is convergence in military AI use cases across Europe, particularly in intelligence, surveillance, and reconnaissance (ISR), big-data analytics, and human-machine teaming, advanced robotics, and autonomy in critical mission functions in the context of the next-generation European capabilities in the land, maritime, air, cyber, and space domains. For example, the French project SCORPION – or *Synergie du Contact Renforcée par la Polyvalence et l'Infovalorisation* – modernises land combat forces by applying novel collaborative fighting doctrine and symbiotic military units comprised of soldiers and various networked manned and unmanned combat vehicles. European sixth-generation future air combat systems – like the Franco-German-Spanish FCAS or the British-Swedish-Italian-Japanese TEMPEST – follow the same logic of developing highly interconnected data-driven battle networks comprising manned and unmanned air assets, capable of human-machine teaming and collaborative combat behaviours, including swarms.

While new programmes of record are an opportunity for Europe to accelerate AI adoption in defence, their lengthy delivery times (mid- and late 2030s) also risk delaying AI adoption among the European states. Meanwhile, Europeans pay less attention to integrating AI into legacy military platforms, which will remain the bulk of their military capabilities for the foreseeable future[19] (Soare 2020, 6). However, there are some early signs this situation may start to change. In 2021, France started upgrading its Leclerc main battle tank to use in Project SCORPION (Tanguy 2021), and the UK launched a "smart missile systems" under the Co-operative Strike Weapons Technology Demonstrator (CSWTD) focused on cooperative weapon behaviours (Jennings 2021).

Some European AI projects, such as the AI sub-systems for SCORPION, FCAS, TEMPEST, and EU initiatives in the field of digitalisation of defence, have force generation and doctrinal aspects, tentatively moving towards updated network-centric warfare and even multi-domain operations (Gady 2020). In a handful of European countries, notably in the UK, France, the Netherlands, Spain, Italy, Norway, Estonia, and Finland, there is growing consideration for counter-AI applications and the cyber security of AI-enabled battle networks. However, changes in doctrine, governance, and practices are more incremental among European states than in the US, China, and Israel. New approaches to AI-enabled capability development (agile procurement, DevSecOps, prototype warfare, algorithmic warfare, and cross-domain operations) and reflections on multi-domain operations have recently begun to circulate among a handful of European states and NATO (Watling and Roper 2019; Clare 2020). This is also an indication that Europeans see AI technologies in defence differently, as incrementally enabling the optimisation of their national military power through a decades-long defence modernisation cycle rather than as instruments of disruptive defence innovation. This is often in contrast to policy narratives calling for urgency in the uptake of military AI, as was recently the case of the UK defence AI strategy (Soare 2022).

Enabling European Strategic Autonomy?

Developing European AI technologies to enable European strategic autonomy is a priority in Brussels and other European capitals. For Europeans, the battlefield benefits of AI are as strategic as those for defence industrial competitiveness. Maintaining their geoeconomic competitiveness is as important as competing effectively against China and Russia. National prime defence contractors and European industrial consortia play a disproportionately large role in supporting and shaping ongoing European military AI projects. Part of the rationale behind military AI investment in Europe is to support or develop national champions, which acts as an obstacle to greater intra-EU technological interdependency. Relevant examples in the French context include companies like Airbus, Thales (a European leader in military cloud solutions), the Thales-Atos joint venture Athea (one of the European leaders in military big data analytics and AI solutions), and the Thales-Microsoft strategic partnership to deliver military cloud solutions to the European and NATO customers.

However, focusing on prime contractors reduces the space for meaningful governmental engagement with AI start-ups in European defence cooperation. Most European defence ministries lack adequate tech scouting capacity and rely on the traditional defence industry for insights into market newcomers. As a result, Europeans face challenges in setting up sustainable AI innovation ecosystems and engaging more broadly with non-defence private industry and academia. European defence innovation ecosystems remain underdeveloped, less geopolitically and geoeconomically competitive, and ill-equipped to support the continent's strategic autonomy.

France and the UK have dedicated SMEs defence strategies, though procurement processes and participation criteria are still lagging behind, while other European countries are just beginning to consider these aspects. For example, Spain recently prioritised correcting gaps in its national innovation ecosystem that prevent Madrid from participating in more AI defence cooperation (Ministerio de Defensa 2020a, 19). However, the policy lacks much-needed political backing for ambitious implementation. Reinforcing the European defence industry is worthwhile, though over-reliance solely on prime defence contractors for disruptive innovation may be increasingly tricky.

First, European aerospace and defence actors invest in emerging technologies significantly less than the high-tech industry and may not offer the most disruptive technological solutions (PriceWaterhouseCoopers 2020, 6). To maximise their strategic advantage, European governments need access to the broadest range of private sector and academic entities, which drive technological progress and disruptive innovation, not just to enduring and familiar industrial partners. As recently demonstrated by the COVID-19 pandemic, defence contractors need to rethink their supply chains and be more open to working with cross-border start-ups and academia to remain competitive. However, neither European defence establishments nor the primes have strong incentives to pursue technological disruption (and required procedural and financial changes) despite an innovation-focused policy narrative.

Second, large defence contractors are familiar and comfortable with waterfall-type acquisitions and procurement procedures, which are ineffective and inappropriate for disruptive technologies with shorter and iterative life cycles. While access to innovation in the private sector and academic circles is an EU and NATO priority, European acquisition and procurement models are slow to adapt to new realities. Europeans are struggling to find a balance between long-term procurement for conventional capabilities like FCAS, the Main Ground Combat System

(MGCS), and the EURODRONE and more agile procurement procedures for AI and other emerging technologies (Murray 2020). Examples of such adaptation are France's digital design, manufacturing, and services (DDMS) which uses smaller and modular procurement packages to speed product development at Airbus and Dassault, including for FCAS, the UK's future Agile Software Development Centre, or the Digital Foundry. However, these tools are novel – their effectiveness is yet to be proven. More European flexibility is needed in funding and acquisition processes to facilitate broader and early engagement with industry and academia. Addressing enduring challenges with cross-border technological-defence cooperation and investment, as well as with general transfer licences, is increasingly urgent.

Furthermore, Europeans need a new logic of software-defined defence in their capability development planning. This entails a prioritisation of software-defined architectures and data-centric battle networks running on API-enabled end-to-end elecronic workflows between sensors, deciders, and effectors. Software-defined defence approaches are platform-agnostic, can be rapidly scaled horizontally on demand, can push new software releases for added functionality frequently (i.e., in matters of days and weeks rather than years and decades as nowadays), and are better placed to rapidly capitalise on battlefield advantage stemming from rapid software technological progress (Soare et al 2023).

European defence establishments and regional institutions need agile development practices that start small, have sustainable budgets, proof problem-solving technological solutions quickly, rapidly decide on procurement, and scale them iteratively (Christie 2020). European governments must also bring industry along in changing acquisition and procurement models. For the European defence industry, low national defence investment and limited access to rare earth materials represent the most significant challenges to European defence innovation. Engagement with non-traditional partners in civilian private industry and academia is not a significant obstacle, nor are protracted procurement processes.[20] However, a review of the EU-funded Preparatory Action on Defence (PADR) and European Defence Industrial Development Programme (EDIDP) projects proves that collaboration between prime defence contractors and new, non-traditional partners is neither straightforward nor fast. Few such projects involve cross-border cooperation with small and medium enterprises (SMEs), and even fewer include new start-ups that were not already in the supply chains of European prime defence contractors.

The Great Disruptors: Brexit and COVID-19

Various external dynamics and disruptive events have contributed to regional approaches to military AI adoption. These include populism and sovereignty issues, Brexit and COVID-19, which affected the European AI landscape differently than in the US and China. Brexit is one such strategic disruptor. The departure of the UK from the EU has at least temporarily weakened European posture in military AI and diminished the latter's AI status indicators: the UK has the largest number of AI papers and patents, and British companies attracted 40% of the AI investment flowing into the EU. The UK is the second largest non-EU investor in European AI start-ups (Berger 2019, 6–8), and London has already set up venture capital funds to support AI adoption (OECD 2018, 2). The UK was the most prominent defence actor in the EU, with the largest defence budget, including the largest funding for emerging and disruptive technologies, the largest ratio of expeditionary troops and equipment, and a global military footprint. Moreover, the UK is one of the largest data pools in Europe, and UK defence companies are advanced in their AI technological development.

Brexit means one of only two European states with advanced defence strategies, budgets, governance for military AI, and influence over NATO defence innovation is now outside the EU, the EDA, and without any security or defence cooperation agreement with the Union. Meanwhile, newly established transatlantic tools with a comprehensive and structural mandate for AI cooperation, such as the EU-US Security and Defence Dedicated Dialogue and the EU-US Trade and Technology Council, do not include the UK, which is drifting closer to the US on emerging technologies, and bypass NATO. Overall, the remit for AI cooperation with the UK is significantly lower after Brexit: cooperation will continue within NATO and the alliance's Defence Innovation Accelerator (with its HQ in the UK and a regional centre in Canada) could impact closer EU-UK defence cooperation in emerging technologies. There are less optimistic prospects in other multilateral formats, such as the E2I, which do not deal specifically with AI, and the bilateral track presents a mixed picture. Franco-British defence cooperation faces significant political and practical challenges in the short term (Ellehuus and Morcos 2020), including data, digital investment, and defence market rules of cooperation. In contrast, German-British cooperation is consolidating around the UK's participation in the MGCS, albeit the scope of this British participation is uncertain given the UK government's decision to reduce land troop numbers.

COVID-19 has also been a systemic disruptor of European AI efforts. In 2020, COVID-19 travel restrictions and lockdowns did not negatively impact the traditional defence contractors, but dual-use contractors that are active in the civilian sector and are more agile in terms of disruptive technological innovation have been negatively affected.[21] If the situation continues, more significant disruptions are possible: "In the near term, acquisition programmes face disruptions by enforced changes within defence industries, which have faced their pandemic challenges" (Barrie et al. 2020). The pandemic has disrupted innovation ecosystems, too. Under pressure from lockdowns, some national innovation hubs and processes have been inactive during the pandemic,[22] affecting AI adoption prospects. Moreover, according to a 2021 Eurostat poll, COVID-19 erased 11.2% of EU-27 GDP in 2020 and is expected to exercise continued downward pressure on European economies throughout 2021 and 2022. Defence economists with Janes and IISS agree there are lingering fears about the sustainability of European defence budgets in the medium term with defence budget increases eroded by ramping inflation in 2021–22. Nominal or real terms reductions of European defence budgets will make it impossible to sustain both current programmes of record and R&D/T investments in the medium term. Finally, the pandemic has been a conversation starter for how Europeans should approach security and defence differently, focusing more on resilience and supply chains and shifting defence investment accordingly, including in AI (Barrie et al. 2020). At the same time, COVID-19 has been a positive disruptor, accelerating digitalisation of defence across Europe and incentivising the adoption of AI tools. According to the NATO Information and Communications Agency, NATO's largest military exercise, DEFENDER 2020, and other 2020 military exercises were disrupted by travel limitations. The Coalition Warrior Interoperability Exercise (CWIX) 2020 was held entirely online, accelerating the testing of new digital proofs-of-concept (NATO Information and Communications Agency 2020a).

While these considerations help us better understand the fragmented and asymmetric European landscape on military AI and the reduced role traditional defence establishments have in shaping AI adoption and governance, they also highlight the risks inherent in this continued fragmentation.

The EU and NATO – Underused Regional Accelerators of AI Adoption

The EU and NATO played an essential part in driving AI strategy development and shaping European nations' thinking about military applications of AI after 2018. However, EU defence initiatives, NATO instruments, and EU-NATO cooperation are institutional accelerators of military AI adoption that remain essentially underused by European states. As demonstrated by the rare exchanges listed in the progress reports, EU-NATO cooperation remains a particularly underused framework in emerging and disruptive technologies. The agreement between NATO Secretary General Jens Stoltenberg and the President of the European Commission, Ursula von der Leyen, to include emerging and disruptive technologies and resilience among the priority areas of EU-NATO cooperation in the third NATO-EU Joint Declaration signed in January 2023 could contribute to a change of direction in the cooperation between the two institutions. However, it is too early to assess its impact.

EU AI Initiatives in Defence

The development of the EU landscape on military AI continues to depend on the priorities of individual European Council presidencies and leading nations in the EDA framework. The European debates around strategic autonomy have done more to reveal the political divide between European states than to bridge their differences (Major and Mölling 2020). Since 2018, five EU-wide intertwined efforts have shaped the European agenda on military AI.

The first was fostered by the EU defence initiatives, notably the PADR, EDIDP, EDF, and PESCO, which fund a few AI sub-systems, generally linked to larger platform-driven capability projects. EU-backed funding for military AI is increasing, but projects are not linked to clear metrics of greater operational capacity and interoperability. To incentivise innovation, the EC sought to consolidate civil-military synergies and to establish a special advisory service to support start-up participation in the EDF, albeit eligibility criteria still mean many start-ups cannot compete in EDF bids. Less attention has been paid to reducing the bureaucratic burden and lengthy award processes. While they acknowledge that collaborative multi-year, multinational AI projects don't fit the definition of the agile model, EU officials recently offered a sobering assessment on how underused EU defence initiatives are: "The EU defence initiatives are too recent to already produce a significant and positive effect on defragmentation." The mainstream of pMS' activities in capability development is reflected in the 2018 EU Capability Development Priorities. Still, there is no evidence that they already constitute a "key reference for pMS when elaborating national plans" (EDA 2020c, 3).

The Council has also hosted military AI discussions in several working parties, including a German-led effort towards "Responsible Use in Military Artificial Intelligence" (German Foreign Office 2020, 2). However, these processes remain unconnected, reducing their strategic impact and contribution towards a coherent European approach to military AI. More recently, the EU's *Strategic Compass* prioritised actions to "jointly develop cutting-edge military capabilities and invest in technological innovation for defence and create a new Defence Innovation Hub within the European Defence Agency" (European External Action Service, 2022). However, the launch of the Innovation Hub in June 2022 revealed it hopes to deliver innovation in the long term (EDA 2022b, 2) and its initial scope is rather limited to a handful of projects.

The second process revolves around the EDA's three-step effort to develop a common taxonomy of military AI, a catalogue of AI use cases, and an AI action plan in defence (EDA 2020c).[23] The effort is noteworthy, but translating EDA AI clusters into collaborative AI projects may take a long time and may not lead to actual capabilities, even by the admission of EDA staff.[24] One promising AI cluster for EDA is the creation of an (anonymised) defence industrial "data lake" to which private industry can have access to develop defence AI applications. However, critical national barriers to sharing military operational and industrial data should not be underestimated, and so far, Europeans have not made significant progress in agreeing on a military data-sharing framework for R&D/T. As the leading EU agency seeking to support collaborative defence R&D in the field of emerging technologies, the EDA's efforts are noteworthy. However, the agency has limited legal remit in comparison to other EU bodies and its efforts sometimes fall short of bringing needed coherence to the different intra-EU stakeholders' views on military AI, including the EC, the European External Action Service (EEAS), the Council, and the member states.[25]

The third parallel effort is the EU Military Staff's May 2019 food for thought paper on the digitalisation of defence and the subsequent *Implementation Plan for the Digitalisation of the Armed Forces*. While encompassing and focused on AI as a tool for optimising current European military capabilities, their battlefield performance and interoperability, and their contribution to information superiority, the food for thought paper is cautious regarding new doctrine and operational concepts. The fragmentation of European capabilities – particularly their varying levels of digitalisation and varying cyber security capabilities – has precluded rapid European digitalisation of defence. Even predictive maintenance, arguably one of EDA's low-hanging AI clusters, is challenging because of European military infrastructure limitations at home and during deployments in the European neighbourhood.[26]

The fourth and fifth efforts respectively are the *Roadmap on Critical Technologies for Security and Defence* and the *European Defence Innovation Scheme* (EUDIS). Both initiatives have only recently been launched and do not benefit from great clarity concerning their implementation pathways. However, particularly in the case of EUDIS, worth €2 billion over seven years, there is an apparent effort on behalf of the Commission to link all defence innovation tools across different financial instruments and EU agencies for greater strategic weight.[27] The Commission plans to launch regular tenders and competitions attracting both traditional and non-traditional technology and industry partners to develop defence solutions using advanced technologies. Their methodology is sound and in line with best practices in the US, for example. However, the process underpinning these efforts still seems comparatively long, cumbersome, and bureaucratic.

Consequently, the EU landscape on military AI remains fragmented among the different relevant EU bodies, and acquisition processes remain too long, complicated, and bureaucratic to incentivise innovation and early adoption of military applications of AI technologies. European defence planners view AI as an opportunity to incrementally optimise their capabilities, an added layer to existing platforms and capabilities. Meanwhile, China and Russia are seen more as geoeconomic challenges than military AI competitors. It remains to be seen whether Russia's war of aggression against Ukraine will fundamentally shift the Europeans' threat perspections.

NATO 2030 and AI

In 2021, the alliance adopted the first *NATO Implementation Strategy on Artificial Intelligence*, a follow-up to the 2019 NATO *Emerging and Disruptive Technologies Roadmap*. The strategy's core objective is to accelerate and mainstream the adoption of AI technologies in defence in support of the alliance's three core tasks – collective defence, crisis management, and cooperative security. The strategy also aims to provide a "common policy basis" for accelerating the integration of AI technologies in military applications, protect and monitor AI technologies from potential adversaries, and safeguard against potential malicious uses of AI by state and non-state actors (NATO 2021a). The document identifies six principles of responsible use of AI technologies in defence – namely, lawfulness, responsibility and accountability, explainability and traceability, reliability, governability, and bias mitigation – and seeks to map out the means and ways to operationalise them and standardise them for the purpose of enhanced interoperability. The allies simultaneously agreed on a *Data Exploitation Framework Policy*, including "actions to treat data as a strategic asset, develop analytical tools, and store and manage data in the appropriate infrastructure" (Stanley-Lockman and

Christie Hunter 2021). However, the publication of the *NATO AI Strategy* also revealed an important lack of internal coherence among the allies and different parts of the NATO innovation ecosystem along the policy and military lines regarding the adoption of AI in defence.

In June 2021, NATO leaders established a Defence Innovation Accelerator for the North Atlantic (DIANA), with headquarters in the UK and Canada, which will support transatlantic civil-military cooperation in the development and adoption of seven critical emerging and disruptive technologies, including AI (NATO 2021c). In October 2021, 17 allies, excluding the US, France, and Turkey, signed the Letter of Intent to establish the NATO Innovation Fund (NIF), an off-budget $1 billion fund intended to work as a venture capital fund made up of national contributions and bring allies closer to start-ups and academia to facilitate spin-in and innovation (NATO 2021d). Though NATO officials hoped the US would join DIANA and the NIF by the time of the NATO Madrid Summit in June 2022,[28] their participation remains uncertain. DIANA is preparing to launch its first set of ten challenges in April 2023, reportedly with a budgetary envelope of over $20 million and it is putting in place an acquisition liaison process to enhance adoption. Meanwhile, the NIF has seen its first €8 million budgetary pledges from Italy's new government in late 2022.

In 2020, the Group of External Experts appointed by Secretary-General Jens Stoltenberg to advise him on the NATO 2030 process emphasised the urgency of AI adoption. In particular, the group's report highlighted the need to embed democratic values into emerging and disruptive technologies, primarily through NATO's role in standardisation and industry forum, as well as to translate the objectives of the upcoming AI Implementation strategy into priority capabilities in the NATO defence planning process (NDPP) (Mitchell and Maizière 2020, 29–31). These recommendations were echoed and further developed by the NATO Defence Innovation Board group of external experts in early 2021.

These recent initiatives signal the alliance is moving from reflection towards implementation and AI adoption. Interoperability of AI-enabled capabilities has emerged as a major concern for the alliance, and NATO staff are preoccupied with the significant differences among the allies regarding AI adoption. Some solutions, such as "data lakes" and "software factories," were informally advanced within the alliance. However, it is uncertain whether they are sufficient to prevent a real risk of an intra-alliance digital divide and AI capability gap in the 2020s (Soare 2020, 6; Soare 2021a, 7–8). Limiting factors such as the general US disinterest in technology transfers, scepticism of the Alliance's function to foster innovation, the fragmentation of AI adoption along national lines, the EU's agenda on technological sovereignty, and the regulation of AI applications could further contribute to suboptimal interoperability.

It is also worth mentioning that the alliance is already supporting AI projects with military applications, demonstrating its potential as a military AI accelerator. AI-enabled capability packages are deployed as part of NATO satellite-imagery and intelligence analysis, the Allied Ground Surveillance (AGS) system, the Tracked Hybrid Modular Infantry System (THeMIS), the 2018-established Maritime Unmanned Systems (MUS) initiative, and the NATO Communications and Information agency (NCIA) cloud-based "software factory." NATO Allied Command Transformation (ACT) and its Innovation Branch are also developing several AI projects, including AI algorithms for intelligence gathering and dissemination (project TEXAS), management of air-to-air refuelling (project JIGSAW), back-office communication and workflow tasks (project AI FELIX), and multi-domain operations (project MUAAR). However, only mail management AI is deployed on NATO systems, and slow procurement processes a severe shortage of AI skills and uncompetitive project budgets hamper progress.

Furthermore, joint military exercises have been a good opportunity to showcase new proofs of concept involving AI-enabled capabilities and incentivise allies to adopt military AI applications. TRIDENT Juncture (2018) tested over 20 different AI-enabled capabilities, including the capability to autonomously detect, diagnose, and deliver care to wounded soldiers; autonomous military robots; human-machine teaming; and information warfare (Tucker 2018). The Coalition Warrior Interoperability Exercise (CWIX) 2020 tested over 160 new capabilities, including upgraded digital networks for more secure and interoperable data-sharing and a health surveillance capability called "syndromic surveillance" (NATO Communications and Information Agency 2020b). In July 2021, the UK operationally used an AI application for ISR during Exercise "Spring Storm" in Estonia (Cranny-Evans 2021). However, integrating proof of concept into alliance exercises and training may also require reconsidering how to jointly fund expensive industry demonstrations of technology solutions as part of NATO exercises. Finally, large allies like the UK are increasingly testing new technologies during military exercises or as part of innovation pilots. However, so far there is little evidence of how these technologies transition to actual procurement.

Moreover, more clarity and transparency are needed on how these AI-allied goals will translate into concrete AI projects; Research, Development, and Innovation (R&D&I) spending; NDPP capability priorities (Soare 2021a, 8); and organisational adaptation. The NATO AI strategy is a step in the right direction. However, the strategy is more of a political statement and signalling tool than a technological adoption guide which is evident from the fact that it does not connect NATO means, ways, and ends in AI technological adoption; it does not align the roles of the different NATO and national innovation bodies; and it runs parallel to the subsequent processes of the 2019 NATO Military Strategy (Soare 2021).

Negotiations over the NDPP cycle (2023–2027) are an excellent opportunity to embed AI among the list of capability priorities, reflect on counter AI capabilities and new operational concepts, and optimise defence planning practices. Furthermore, investing in technology demonstrators, testing and verification-as-a-service and proof of concept for specific AI military applications that are featured in multinational exercises and joint training could further enhance allied appetite for early AI adoption.

Military AI Adoption in Europe – Moral Exceptionalism or Cautious Self-Restraint?

Perhaps the defining variable of the European military AI landscape has been – and will continue to be – the focus on ethical, legal, and values-driven AI, responsibly used and with positive outcomes for society at large. Human-centric AI that respects and fosters European values is at the centre of EU, NATO, and national AI strategies. In relation to military applications of AI technologies, four issues have galvanised the public and political debate in Europe and underlined the contradiction between AI's military strategic benefits and the political, legal, and ethical requirements for due process (European Commission 2020b, 7).

The first issue is the public acceptability of AI technologies relative to human and political-democratic responsibility, accountability, and compliance with international law (IL) and international humanitarian law (IHL). The development and use of autonomous weapon systems (AWS) raise significant ethical and legal issues for *all* European states. Most of them express the view that while IL and IHL strictly apply to all weapon systems, including AWS, IHL provisions may not be sufficient or sufficiently clear in the case of AWS. Ethical and safety concerns about the operation of AI applications, particularly fully autonomous armed drones, are prominent in European public and political discourse. Numerous European political figures and institutions call for a ban on autonomous weapon systems, including the Austrian government, the Belgian parliament, the Swedish government, and the European Parliament.[29] Others support stricter regulation of lethal autonomy (Soare and Pothier 2021, 15).

There are different European approaches to the ban on AWS. Technological conservatism, political left entities, and disarmament advocacies have nearly monopolised public European debate on AI. They combine forces in condemning AWS and call for a comprehensive ban on "killer robots" on the basis that autonomous capabilities do not meet the ethical principles of human agency and human dignity (Marischaka 2020). This approach conflates AI with autonomy and the realm of technological possibility with that of actual certified operational uses for given categories of autonomous weapons. Its proponents demand a comprehensive blanket ban against such capabilities, including their public or private research and development.[30] However, no concrete proposals have been put forward on the enforceability and verifiability of the proposed ban – fundamental aspects of any arms control initiative.

The second issue is "meaningful human control" (MHC) over the operation of AI capabilities. European states and the EU participating in the Group of Governmental Experts on Emerging Technologies in the Area of Lethal Autonomous Weapon Systems agree that states should exercise MHC over lethal autonomous capabilities, one of the 11 principles agreed by the group in its 2019 session (United Nations 2019). However, there are significant legal nuance and interpretation differences among the European states regarding the nature, type, and timing of MHC. European states believe that MHC should be exercised at all life-cycle stages of AI capabilities and that human-machine teaming is central to ensuring sufficient and appropriate human control over autonomous capabilities. Nevertheless, they differ on the types of control measures (Boulanin et al. 2020) and the degree of legal, normative, and operational regulation and oversight needed for weapon systems based on emerging and disruptive technologies (United Nations 2020).

Nearly half of European states have not yet outlined a national position on military AI, AWS, or MHC. France and the UK take an institutional (MoD) approach in developing ethical guidelines for AI in defence, whereas others, like Germany, Belgium, and the Nordic countries, adopt a national and general-purpose approach to AI ethical principles. Traditional institutions such as national parliaments perform public scrutiny duties, often at odds with national executive bodies. This fragmentation of national and intra-European institutional views complicates any attempt to negotiate a common European or NATO position. Different bodies of the Council and the EEAS have been involved in drafting the EU positions presented at the UN Governmental Group of Experts (GGE) LAWS. However, no EU common position on the matter is in sight. NATO has shown more interest in mundane use cases for AI, including intelligence analysis, ISR, cyber defence, and back-office tasks, and paid less attention to AWS, currently seen as over-the-horizon capabilities (Hill and Marsan 2018; Smallegange et al. 2018).

Several European states (France, the UK, Germany, and the Netherlands) confirmed they are not developing or planning to develop fully autonomous weapon systems in the foreseeable future.[31] Indeed, former NATO officials acknowledge national positions are still very far apart:

> while [individual NATO allies' AI] strategies use some of the same vocabulary in calling for more clarity on the legal and ethical frameworks of military AI, there is a real risk of a lack of meeting of the minds about the substantive content of these frameworks.
>
> *(Hill 2020, 151)*

In short, the EU and NATO will struggle to increase R&D&I levels and accelerate AI adoption without a clear and coherent European vision of using military AI.

Other important stakeholders and shapers of the European debate on military AI have been private industry, civil society, and academia. Defence establishments and even regional security actors like NATO and the EDA have been less prominent in shaping AI strategies, governance, and adoption processes compared to the private sector. In the UK, France, NATO, and the EU, defence innovation is perceived as a function of the broader industrial policies. Defence ministries, NATO, and the EDA are not the key drivers and shapers of normative, technological, procurement, or governance aspects of AI adoption but rather clients of commercial and technological progress and contributors to a whole-of-government AI strategy. This is a major shift to which European military organisations are just beginning to adapt. Cooperative fora like the NATO- and EDA-Industry

Forums and their respective conferences of national armaments directors play an essential role in revealing deep-seated challenges in broader engagement with private industry.[32] Still, they are increasingly regarded as too slow and inadequate for engaging the far more dynamic private sector focused on disruptive, cutting-edge innovation. Private companies and defence industry associations are also developing their ethical AI compasses, a further aspect for national governments to consider. For example, in 2019, the AeroSpace and Defence Industries Association of Europe (ASD), the Brussels-based defence industry association, developed a dedicated working group on ethical aspects of AI.[33]

The third issue is trust in the operation, resilience, and reliability of AI-enabled capabilities, which is central to the European approach to AI in military applications. On the one hand, this goes to the core of the concept of "human-machine teaming" and the application of AI ethical and legal guidelines for defence. On the other hand, it has implications for assessing the level of technological maturity for R&D, TEVV, technological standards, procurement, regulation of weapons review processes, and rules of engagement procedures. Trust has been central to the EC effort to develop and adopt ethical and legal guidelines for trustworthy AI. In 2019, the EC High-Level Group of External Experts adopted a set of seven key ethical guidelines for trustworthy AI, endorsed by the EC's Communication on *Building Trust in Human-Centric Artificial Intelligence* (2019), and developed them into an *Assessment List on Trustworthy AI* that same year (European Commission 2021). The test-run of the Assessment List was conducted in 2019–2020, and in mid-2020 it became an official EC work instrument. However, in 2020 only one EU state – Italy – publicly expressed an interest in adopting the Assessment List as a risk assessment and ethical screening tool. In the military field, trust in AI technologies is an even more complex undertaking – it refers to the trustworthiness, robustness, and reliability of the technology,[34] the commander's trust to deploy the technology, and the trust in the responsible use of the technology on the battlefield. No tool equivalent to the civilian Assessment List currently exists in the military. This is where the operationalisation of the *NATO AI strategy's* six principles of responsible use for military AI could significantly influence governmental development and choice between AI applications based on a clear understanding of risk, impact, and opportunity.

Europeans also differ on how to achieve trust in military AI. In the 2021 EC proposal of the *Artificial Intelligence Act*, the focus is on targeted regulation of specific use cases rather than a blanket regulation of AI to protect the safety and human rights of European citizens, avoid legal discrimination generated using AI systems, harmonise compliance, and provide a European governance structure for AI. By contrast, the EP has called for strict regulation in civilian and military domains of high-risk, high-impact AI. According to the EP, "a common European legal framework with harmonised definitions and common ethical principles, including the use of AI for military purposes," "an EU-wide strategy against LAWS and a ban on so-called 'killer robots,'" and "highly intrusive social scoring applications" by public authorities are needed (European Parliament 2021, 8–10).

Conclusion

This chapter sought to make a novel contribution to international security and emerging technologies literature by outlining how the interplay of national and regional dynamics may accelerate or inhibit European AI adoption in defence. It has demonstrated that while NATO and EU awareness of military AI is more advanced, cooperative regional approaches are slower to emerge. Four variables explain this situation: a European preference towards national R&D/T and capability development; a slowly changing defence innovation culture in which defence establishments play a more discrete role in shaping the AI agenda by comparison to civilian actors; the underuse of regional institutions like the EU and NATO to accelerate military AI adoption in Europe; and a strong cultural technologic conservatism and a self-imposed European ethical and legal restraint on military AI.

This chapter's key findings demonstrate that the European military AI landscape's fragmentation and lack of coherence are a significant strategic vulnerability that inhibits rapid AI adoption across the continent. Europe's approach to AI in defence remains cautious and incremental, limited by objective and material factors (investment, skills, networks, and data) as well as by a sense of moral and legal self-restraint. Continuing down this path will leave European states struggling to keep up with the threat landscape, with technological developments, with close allies and with geopolitical competitors.

Notes

1 Though this is a worthy avenue for research, space considerations limit this chapter from covering the role of regional defence cooperation formats such as NORDEFCO, the Joint Expeditionary Force, the European Intervention Initiative, or the Visegrád4 in supporting the integration of emerging and disruptive technologies in security and defence.
2 The EC estimates EU AI investment to be between €7 and €8.4 billion – roughly 35%–40% of the EU's target, whereas the EP places it between €2.4 and €3.2 billion, which is significantly lower that the core target.
3 Available data (2016–2020) in this paper includes the UK among the members of the EU. However, since January 1, 2020, the UK is no longer an EU member state.
4 Through the average number and overall value of the private investment in AI in the EU has increased over the past years, most investments remain relatively small value and EU and European venture capital funds remain under the average capitalisation of similar instruments in the US and China (OECD 2018, 2–3).
5 Interview with EDA official, December 2019.
6 Albeit it is unclear how much of this budget is spent on AI technologies and how much it is dedicated to ongoing procurement programmes of record.
7 NATO Center for Maritime Research and Experimentation (CMRE) is implementing a Data Knowledge and Operational Effectiveness (DKOE) AI project co-funded by participating countries, NATO ACT, and EU Horizon 2020 Project RANGER. European Commission, Horizon 2020 project page "RANGER: RAdars for loNG distance maritime surveillancE and SaR operations," https://cordis.europa.eu/project/id/700478 [accessed January 7, 2021].
8 Interview with EDA official, December 2019.
9 Including precursor programmes, the Preparatory Action on Defence Research (PADR), Permanent Structured Cooperation (PESCO), the European Defence Industrial Development Programme (EDIDP).

10 The latest available defence data at the time of writing was for 2019, when the UK was part of the European Union.

11 Between 2019 and 2021 the Visegrád4 countries have discussed several options to collaborate closer in bids for EDF projects as well as in accelerating their adoption of emerging and disruptive technologies for defence.

12 Author interviews with EDA and EUMS officials, December 2019.

13 On average, it takes between six months and two years to occupy a position in either the EU or NATO, whereas the mobility of tech talent is measured in weeks at most.

14 In April 2021 the UK has published a Digital Strategy for Defence which will guide the implementation of a digital transformation of the UK armed forces towards multi-domain operations, contribute to building the digital data-driven backbone of the UK's armed forces, and develop digital skills across the military enterprise.

15 Examples of bilateral capability development projects relevant in this context include the Franco-British cooperation or the Franco-German cooperation for the Main Ground Combat System (MGCS), whereas examples of flexible formats preferred by France are the regional defence association OCCAR.

16 However, often technological defence cooperation is coalesced with arms exports revealing the need for clear classification and definitions of the two phenomena. For example, in 2021 Paris hosted a conference on Defence Cooperation in the framework of the European Intervention Initiative (EI2). The event focused on the operational benefits of air combat mass through a combination of manned and unmanned air platforms, notably the FCAS and the Next Generation Weapon System (NGWS) which draw on AI, military cloud, and edge computing.

17 Preferences are specifically for cooperation with the US and the UK rather than continental European partners.

18 Author interviews with Norwegian, Finish, Estonian, and Polish governmental experts, 2022.

19 This is a serious concern. Apart from UAVs which have delivery deadlines in the mid-2020s, most high-profile next-generation capability projects, like the FCAS, the NGWS, and the MGCS which include AI sub-systems, have estimated delivery times in the late 1930s and early 1940s. And even then, these capabilities will not immediately replace legacy equipment.

20 Interview with AeroSpace and Defence Industries Association of Europe (ASD) representative, April 2021.

21 EDA Annual Conference, December 2020.

22 ECFR workshop, November 2020.

23 The EDA has studied the impact of AI (and other emerging and disruptive technologies) on defence before 2018, as part of the Key Strategic Activities (KAS). This effort is more comprehensive and entails a mapping of funding opportunities, industrial capacity, technological progress, required skills, and ongoing research and capability priorities of the EU member states.

24 Interview with EDA official, December 2019.

25 There are multiple stakeholders involved in the EU emerging and disruptive technologies agenda, including the EC, the EEAS, SECDEFPOL and EUMS, the Council, and others, which often compete for the power to shape EU initiatives. For example, during the EDF and EDIDP negotiations, the EC refused to give the EDA powers over all or parts of the implementation (as it had done for the PADR) or to even make it a permanent member in EDF comitology. Instead, the EDA can provide invited input on specific projects upon request and the EC established a new Direction General for Defence, Industry and Space (DG DEFIS) to manage implementation.

26 Interview with EDA official, December 2019.

27 Author interview with DG DEFIS representatives, 2022.

28 Author interview with NATO official 2021.

29 In these cases, different national and European authorities called for a ban on autonomous weapon systems that do not abide by the principle of "meaningful human

control," have situational awareness, and can fully autonomously plan and implement missions and select and engage (human) targets.

30 A version of the 2018 European Parliament resolution on "Autonomous Weapon Systems" seen by the author featured a blanket ban on the research, development, production, and use of LAWS as well as common position of the EU member states establishing a ban on the development and use of these military capabilities.

31 See national statements in the format of GGE on LAWS, especially 2019/20 sessions.

32 Interview with EDA official, December 2019.

33 Interview with ASD representative, November 2019.

34 This refers to how the AI algorithms work in optimal operational conditions. However, increasingly European states are also considering the implications of cyber security risks to their military AI applications which carry implications for the trustworthiness of the respective application.

References

Aerospace and Defence Industries Association of Europe. 2020. "The Aerospace and Defence Industries Association of Europe: 2020 Facts & Figures". https://www.asd-europe.org/sites/default/files/atoms/files/ASD_FactsFigures_2020.pdf.

Anadolu Agency. 2020. "Turkey Soon to Launch National AI Strategy, Technology Minister Says". December 2. https://www.dailysabah.com/business/tech/turkey-soon-to-launchnational-al-strategy-technology-minister-says.

Arjona, Román. 2020. "Science, Research and Innovation Performance of the EU 2020: A Fair, Green and Digital Europe". *European Commission*. May. https://ec.europa.eu/info/sites/default/files/srip/2020/ec_rtd_srip-2020-report.pdf.

Atos. 2019. "The French Defense Procurement Agency Selects the Consortium Led by Atos for Project Artemis, Phase II". March 23. https://atos.net/en/2019/press-release_2019_05_23/the-french-defense-procurement-agency-selects-the-consortium-led-by-atos-for-project-artemis-phase-ii#_ftn1.

Babuta, Alexander, Oswald, Marion and Janjeva, Ardi. 2020. "Artificial Intelligence and UK National Security: Policy Considerations". *RUSI Occasional Paper*. April. https://rusi.org/sites/default/files/ai_national_security_final_web_version.pdf.

Barrie, Douglas et al. 2020. "Defence Spending and Plans: Will the Pandemic Take Its Toll?". *IISS Military Balance Blog*. April 1. https://www.iiss.org/blogs/military-balance/2020/04/defence-spending-coronavirus.

Berger, Roland. 2019. "The Road to AI - Investment Dynamics in the European Ecosystem. AI Global Index 2019". *France Digitale*. January 1. https://www.rolandberger.com/en/Insights/Publications/The-road-to-AI.html.

Boulanin, Vincent. 2020. "Limits on Autonomy: Identifying Practical Elements of Human Control". *SIPRI* and *International Committee of the Red Cross*. October. https://www.sipri.org/sites/default/files/2020-06/2006_limits_of_autonomy.pdf.

Burrows, Matthew and Mueller-Kaler, Julian. 2019. "Europe's Third Way". *Atlantic Council*. March 14. https://www.atlanticcouncil.org/content-series/smart-partnerships/europes-third-way/.

Centro Innovazione Difesa. 2020. "Aree di Sviluppo dell'Intelligenza Artificiale ambito difesa". *Italian Ministry of Defence*. http://www.difesa.it/SMD_/Staff/Reparti/III/CID/Conferenza_Innovazione_Difesa/Documents/read_ahead/Linee_di_indirizzo_IA.PDF.

Christie, Edward Hunter. 2020. "Artificial Intelligence at NATO: Dynamic Adoption, Responsible Use". *NATO Review*. November 24. https://www.nato.int/docu/review/articles/2020/11/24/artificial-intelligence-at-nato-dynamic-adoption-responsible-use/index.html.

Clare, Phil. 2020. "The Answer Is Multi-Domain Operations - Now What's the Question?". *Wavell Room*. February 13. https://wavellroom.com/2020/02/13/the-answer-is-multi-domain-operations-now-whats-the-question/.

Ellehuus, Rachel and Morcos, Pierre. 2020. "Sticking Together Or Drifting Apart: The Future of Franco-British Defense Cooperation". *CSIS Commentary*. October 28. https://www.csis.org/analysis/sticking-together-or-drifting-apart-future-franco-british-defense-cooperation.

European Commission. 2018a. "Communication from the Commission to the European Parliament, the European Council, the Council, the European Economic and Social Committee and the Committee of the Regions on Artificial Intelligence for Europe. COM(2018) 237 Final". *European Commission*. April 25. https://ec.europa.eu/digital-single-market/en/news/communication-artificial-intelligence-europe.

European Commission. 2018b. "Communication from the Commission to the European Parliament, the European Council, the Council, the European Economic and Social Committee and the Committee of the Regions - Coordinated Plan on Artificial Intelligence. COM(2018) 795 Final". *European Commission*. December 7. https://ec.europa.eu/digital-single-market/en/news/coordinated-plan-artificial-intelligence.

European Commission. 2020a. "Digital Economy and Society Index (DESI)". *European Commission*. October 28. https://digital-strategy.ec.europa.eu/en/policies/desi.

European Commission. 2020b. "Public Consultation on the AI White Paper: Final Report". *European Commission*. November. https://www.standict.eu/sites/default/files/2021-02/PublicConsultationAIWhitePaper_Finalreportpdf.pdf.

European Commission. 2021. "European Defence Fund (EDF) Call for Proposals for 2021". *European Commission*. June 30. https://ec.europa.eu/defence-industry-space/edf-calls-2021-factsheet_en.

European Commission. 2022a. "Commission Implementing Decision of 25.5.2022 on the financing of the European Defence Fund established by Regulation (EU) No 2021/697 of the European Parliament and the Council and the adoption of the work programme for 2022 – Part II". *European Commission*. May 25. https://defence-industry-space.ec.europa.eu/system/files/2022-05/C_2022_3403_1_EN_ACT%20and%20Annex%201.pdf.

European Commission. 2022b. "Joint Communication to the European Parliament, the European Council, the Council, the European Economic and Social Committee and the Committee of the Regions on the Defence Investment Gaps Analysis and Way Forward." *European Commission*. May 18. https://commission.europa.eu/system/files/2022-05/join_2022_24_2_en_act_part1_v3_1.pdf.

European Defence Agency. 2020a. "New R&T Project to Improve Resilience of Cold Weather Operations". *European Defence Agency* Press Release. April 23. https://eda.europa.eu/news-and-events/news/2020/04/23/new-r-t-project-to-improve-resilience-of-cold-weather-operations.

European Defence Agency. 2020b. "Pilot Project and Preparatory Action on Defence Research". *European Defence Agency*. November 3. https://www.eda.europa.eu/what-we-do/activities/activities-search/pilot-project-and-preparatory-action-for-defence-research.

European Defence Agency. 2020c. "CARD Report 2020: Executive Summary". *European Defence Agency*. November 12. https://www.eda.europa.eu/docs/default-source/reports/card-2020-executive-summary-report.pdf.

European Defence Agency. 2020d. "Artificial Intelligence: Joint Quest for Future Defence Applications". *European Defence Agency*. August 25. https://www.eda.europa.eu/info-hub/press-centre/latest-news/2020/08/25/artificial-intelligence-joint-quest-for-future-defence-applications.

European Defence Agency. 2021. "Defence Data 2018-2019: Key Findings and Analysis". *European Defence Agency*. January 28. https://eda.europa.eu/docs/default-source/brochures/2019-eda-defence-data-report.pdf.

European Defence Agency. 2022a. "Defence Data 2020-2021: Key Findings and Analysis". *European Defence Agency*. December 8. https://eda.europa.eu/docs/default-source/brochures/eda---defence-data-2021---web---final.pdf.

European Defence Agency. 2022b. "Hub for EU Defence Innovation (HEDI)." *Factsheet*. May 16. https://eda.europa.eu/docs/default-source/brochures/hedi-factsheet-(final).pdf

European External Action Service. 2022. "A Strategic Compass for Security and Defence." March 24. https://www.eeas.europa.eu/sites/default/files/documents/strategic_compass_en3_web.pdf.

European Parliament. 2021a. "AI Rules: What the European Parliament Wants". *European Parliament* Press Release. January 21. https://www.europarl.europa.eu/news/en/headlines/society/20201015STO89417/ai-rules-what-the-european-parliament-wants.

European Parliament. 2021b. "Report on Artificial Intelligence: Questions of Interpretation and Application of International Law in So Far as the EU Is Affected in the Areas of Civil and Military Uses and of State Authority Outside the Scope of Criminal Justice (2020/2013(INI)). A9-0001/2021". *European Parliament*. January 4. https://www.europarl.europa.eu/doceo/document/A-9-2021-0001_EN.pdf.

Franke, Ulrike. 2019. "Not Smart Enough: The Poverty of European Military Thinking on Artificial Intelligence". E*CFR Policy Brief*. December. https://ecfr.eu/publication/not_smart_enough_poverty_european_military_thinking_artificial_intelligence/.

Gady, Franz Stefan. 2020. "Network-Centric Warfare: Can Europe Be Ready?". *Wavell Room*. December 21. https://wavellroom.com/2020/12/21/network-centric-warfare-europe-defence/.

German Army Concepts and Capabilities Development Centre. 2019. "Artificial Intelligence in Land Forces Position paper". *Bundeswehr*. https://www.bundeswehr.de/resource/blob/156026/79046a24322feb96b2d8cce168315249/download-positionspapier-englische-version-data.pdf.

German Foreign Office. 2020. "Minister's Declaration at the Occasion of the Conference "2020. Capturing Technology. Rethinking Arms Control". *German Foreign Office*. November 6. https://rethinkingarmscontrol.de/wp-content/uploads/2020/11/Ministerial-Declaration-RAC2020.pdf.

Giegerich, Bastian and Soare, Simona. 2022. "'Replenish, replace and reinforce' – Europe's gap filler defence." *IISS Military Balance Blog*. 1 June. https://www.iiss.org/blogs/military-balance/2022/06/replenish-replace-and-reinforce-europes-gap-filler-defence.

Gilli, Andrea. 2020. "NATO-Mation": Strategies for Leading in the Age of Artificial Intelligence". *NATO Defence College* Research Paper no. 15. December. https://www.ndc.nato.int/news/news.php?icode=1514.

Hill, Steven. 2020. "AI's Impact on Multilateral Military Cooperation: Experience from NATO". *American Journal of International Law* special edition "How will artificial intelligence affect international law?". Vol. 114. https://www.cambridge.org/core/journals/american-journal-of-international-law/article/

ais-impact-on-multilateral-military-cooperation-experience-from-nato/3AEF22AA22550A10B75DD74A806D4D18.

Hill, Steven and Marsan, Nadia. 2018. "Artificial Intelligence and Accountability: A Multinational Legal Perspective". *NATO STO paper STO-MP-IST-160 PP-4-1*. June. https://www.sto.nato.int/publications/STO%20Meeting%20Proceedings/Forms/All%20MPs.aspx?RootFolder=%2Fpublications%2FSTO%20Meeting%20Proceedings%2FSTO%2DMP%2DIST%2D160&FolderCTID=0x0120D5200078F9E87043356C409A0D30823AFA16F602008CF184CAB7588E468F5E9FA364E05BA5&View=%7B72ED425F-C31F-451C-A545-41122BBA61A7%7D.

Hille, Peter and Werkhäuser, Nina. 2022. "The German military's new shopping list." *DW*. March 6. https://www.dw.com/en/how-will-the-german-military-spend-100-billion/a-62020972.

Joint Research Centre of the European Commission. 2020. "AI Watch National Strategies on Artificial Intelligence a European Perspective in 2019". *European Commission*. https://publications.jrc.ec.europa.eu/repository/bitstream/JRC119974/national_strategies_on_artificial_intelligence_final_1.pdf.

Kurç, Çağlar. 2023. "Enabling Technology of Future Warfare: Defense AI in Turkey." *Defence AI Observatory*. DAIO Study 23/08. January. https://defenseai.eu/wp-content/uploads/2023/01/DAIO_Study2308.pdf.

Le Figaro and AFP. 2021. "Definvest, le fonds d'investissement des Armées, réalise sa première cession." May 18. https://www.lefigaro.fr/flash-eco/definvest-le-fonds-d-investissement-des-armees-realise-sa-premiere-cession-20210518.

Lomas, Natasha. 2020. "UK to Invest in AI and Cyber as Part of Major Defence Spending Hike". *TechCrunch*. November 19.

Major, Claudia and Moelling, Christian. 2020. "Less Talk, More Action". *Internationale Politik Quarterly*. Issue 1. https://ip-quarterly.com/en/less-talk-more-action.

Marischaka, Christoph. 2020. "Artificial Intelligence in European Defence: Autonomous Armament?". *GUE/NGL*. January 18. https://documentcloud.adobe.com/link/track?uri=urn%3Aaaid%3Ascds%3AUS%3A1884c966-f618-4110-a5f3-678899e4c8ee.

McKinsey & Company. 2020a. "Notes from the AI Frontier: Tackling Europe's Gap in Digital and AI". *McKinsey & Company*. February. https://www.mckinsey.com/~/media/mckinsey/featured%20insights/artificial%20intelligence/tackling%20europes%20gap%20in%20digital%20and%20ai/mgi-tackling-europes-gap-in-digital-and-ai-feb-2019-vf.pdf.

McKinsey & Company. 2020b. "How Nine Digital Frontrunners Can Lead on AI in Europe". *McKinsey & Company*. https://www.mckinsey.com/business-functions/mckinsey-digital/our-insights/how-nine-digital-front-runners-can-lead-on-ai-in-europe.

McGee, Patrick and Chazan, Guy. 2020. "The Apple Effect: Germany Fears Being Left Behind by Big Tech". *Financial Times*. January 29. https://www.ft.com/content/6f69433a-40f0-11ea-a047-eae9bd51ceba.

Ministère des Armées of France. 2021. "Actualisation Stratégique 2021". *Ministère des Armées*. January 22. https://www.defense.gouv.fr/dgris/presentation/evenements/actualisation-strategique-2021.

Ministerio de Defensa of Spain. 2020a. "Estrategia de Tecnología e Innovación para la Defensa". *Ministerio de Defensa*. December. https://www.tecnologiaeinnovacion.defensa.gob.es/es-es/Estrategia/Paginas/Defensa.aspx.

Ministerio de Defensa of Spain. 2020b. "Resumen Ejecutivo 'Fuerza 35'". *Ministerio de Defensa*. https://ejercito.defensa.gob.es/en/estructura/briex_2035/resumen_ejecutivo_fuerza_35.html?__locale=en.

Ministry of Defence of the United Kingdom. 2019. "Army Robotics Receive £66-Million Boost". *Ministry of Defence* Press Release. March 5. https://www.gov.uk/government/news/army-robotics-receive-66m-boost.

Minsky, Carly. 2018. "One Former Google Exec Says There's No Hope for Europe's Artificial Intelligence Sector". *Sifted*. December 14. https://sifted.eu/articles/interview-google-kaifu-lee-ai-artificial-intelligence/.

Misuraca, Gianluca and van Noordt, Colin. 2020. "Overview of the Use and Impact of AI in Public Services in the EU". https://joinup.ec.europa.eu/collection/elise-european-location-interoperability-solutions-e-government/document/report-ai-watch-artificial-intelligence-public-services-overview-use-and-impact-ai-public-services.

Mitchell, Wess A. and de Maizière, Thomas. 2020. "NATO 2030: United for a New Era. Analysis and Recommendations of the Reflection Group Appointed by the NATO Secretary General". *NATO*. November 25. https://www.nato.int/nato_static_fl2014/assets/pdf/2020/12/pdf/201201-Reflection-Group-Final-Report-Uni.pdf.

Murray, Rob. 2020. "Building a Resilient Innovation Pipeline for the Alliance". *NATO Review*. September 1. https://www.nato.int/docu/review/articles/2020/09/01/building-a-resilient-innovation-pipeline-for-the-alliance/index.html.

NATO. 2020. "NATO Annual Report 2020". *NATO*. https://www.nato.int/nato_static_fl2014/assets/pdf/2020/3/pdf_publications/sgar19-en.pdf.

NATO. 2021a. "Summary of the NATO Artificial Intelligence Strategy". *NATO*. October 22. https://www.nato.int/cps/en/natohq/official_texts_187617.htm.

NATO. 2021b. "Defence Expenditure of NATO Countries (2014-2021)". *NATO*. June 11. https://www.nato.int/cps/en/natohq/news_184844.htm.

NATO. 2021c. "Brussels Summit Communiqué". *NATO*. June 14. https://www.nato.int/cps/en/natohq/news_185000.htm.

NATO Communications and Information Agency. 2020a. "NATO Exercise Proceeds Remotely during COVID-19 and Tests Health Tracking". *NCIA* Press Release. June 9. https://www.ncia.nato.int/about-us/newsroom/nato-exercise-proceeds-remotely-during-covid19-and-tests-health-tracking.html.

NATO Communications and Information Agency. 2020b. "NATO Interoperability Exercise Concludes". *NCIA* Press Release. June 25. https://www.ncia.nato.int/about-us/newsroom/nato-interoperability-exercise-concludes.html.

NATO Science and Technology Organisation. 2020. "Science & Technology Trends 2020-2040: Exploring the S&T Edge". *NATO*. https://www.nato.int/nato_static_fl2014/assets/pdf/2020/4/pdf/190422-ST_Tech_Trends_Report_2020-2040.pdf.

Nepelski, Daniel and Sobolewski, Maciej. 2020. "Estimating Investments in General Purpose Technologies. The Case of AI Investments in Europe". *Joint Research Center of the European Commission*. https://publications.jrc.ec.europa.eu/repository/handle/JRC118953.

OECD. "Private Equity Investment in Artificial Intelligence." December. https://www.oecd.org/sti/ieconomy/private-equity-investment-in-artificial-intelligence.pdf.

PriceWaterhouseCoopers. 2020. "Defence Trends 2020: Investing in a Digital Future: 23rd Annual Global CEO Survey". *PriceWaterhouseCoopers*. https://www.pwc.com/gx/en/ceo-agenda/ceosurvey/2020/trends/defence.html.

Quintin, Audrey. 2020. "Progress on the Scorpion Program: France's Plan to Upgrade Its Motorised Capacity". *Finabel*. February 26. https://finabel.org/progress-on-the-scorpion-program-frances-plan-to-upgrade-its-motorised-capacity/.

Sahin, Kaan. 2019. "AI and Warfare: Pending Issues for Europe". *International Security Forum Bonn*. https://www.aicgs.org/site/wp-content/uploads/2020/04/Sahin-ISFB-Report-2019.pdf.

Selinger, Marc. 2021. "Dutch Firms Gain Boost in Seeking US Defence Work". *Jane's*. June 23. https://customer.janes.com/Janes/Display/BSP_885-JDIN.

Silfversten, Erik et al. 2017. "Key Skills and Competences for Defence: Governmental Domain". https://eda.europa.eu/docs/default-source/news/rand_europe_ksc_for_defence_governmental_domain_executive_summary.pdf.

SIPRI. 2020. "Global Arms Industry: Sales by the Top 25 Companies Up 8.5 Per cent; Big Players Active in Global South". *SIPRI*. December 7. https://www.sipri.org/media/press-release/2020/global-arms-industry-sales-top-25-companies-85-cent-big-players-active-global-south.

Smallegange, Antoine et al. 2018. "Big Data and Artificial Intelligence for Decision Making: Dutch Position Paper". *NATO STO Paper STO-MP-IST-160 PP-1-1*. June. https://www.sto.nato.int/publications/STO%20Meeting%20Proceedings/Forms/Meeting%20Proceedings%20Document%20Set/docsethomepage.aspx?ID=43455&FolderCTID=0x0120D5200078F9E87043356C409A0D30823AFA16F602008CF184CAB7588E468F5E9FA364E05BA5&List=7e2cc123-6186-4c30-8082-1ba072228ca7&RootFolder=/publications/STO%20Meeting%20Proceedings/STO-MP-IST-160.

Soare, Simona R. 2020. "Digital Divide? Transatlantic Defence Cooperation on AI". *EUISS Brief* no. 3. March 5. https://www.iss.europa.eu/content/digital-divide-transatlantic-defence-cooperation-ai.

Soare, Simona R. 2021a. "What If... the Military AI of NATO and EU States Is Not Interoperable?" in Gaub, Florence. 2021. "What If ...Not? The Cost of Inaction". *EUISS* Chaillot Paper no. 163. January 22. https://www.iss.europa.eu/sites/default/files/EUISSFiles/CP_163.pdf.

Soare, Simona R. 2021b. "Algorithmic Power, NATO and Artificial Intelligence". *IISS* analysis. November 18.

Soare, Simona R. and Pothier, Fabrice. 2021. "Leading Edge: Key Drivers of Defence Innovation and the Future of Operational Advantage". *IISS*. November 2021. https://www.iiss.org/blogs/research-paper/2021/11/key-drivers-of-defence—innovation-and-the-future--of-operational-advantage.

Soare, Simona R. 2022. "Thinking clever - the UK's Defence AI Strategy." *IISS Military Balance Blog*. July 8. https://www.iiss.org/blogs/military-balance/2022/07/thinking-clever-the-uks-defence-ai-strategy.

Soare, Simona R., Singh, Pavneet, and Nouwens, Meia. 2023. "Sofwtare-Defined Defence: Algorithms at War." IISS. Forthcoming February.

Sprenger, Sebastian. 2021. "German Defense Minister Vows to Keep Fighting for Armed Drones". *DefenseNews*. April 16. https://www.defensenews.com/global/europe/2021/04/16/german-defense-secretary-vows-to-keep-fighting-for-armed-drones/.

Stanford University. 2019. "AI Index Report 2019". *Stanford University*. https://hai.stanford.edu/sites/default/files/ai_index_2019_report.pdf.

Stanley-Lockman, Zoe. 2020. "Futureproofing Transatlantic Relations: The Case for Stronger Technology Cooperation. In Soare, Simona R. ed. 2020. "Turning the Tide: How to Rescue Transatlantic Relations". *EUISS*. October 22. https://www.iss.europa.eu/content/turning-tide-how-rescue-transatlantic-relations.

Stanley-Lockman, Zoe and Christie Hunter, Edward. 2021. "An Artificial Intelligence Strategy for NATO". *NATO Review*. October 25. https://www.nato.int/docu/

review/articles/2021/10/25/an-artificial-intelligence-strategy-for-nato/index.html.

Szabo, Septimiu. 2020. "Transition to Industry 4.0 in the Visegrad Countries". *Joint Research Centre Economic* Brief 052. https://ec.europa.eu/info/sites/info/files/economy-finance/eb052_en.pdf.

Touboul, Emmanuel. 2020. "How Germany, UK, France and Israel compete to become financial leaders in AI." *Roland Berger.* January 7. https://www.rolandberger.com/en/Insights/Publications/The-road-to-AI.html

Tucker, Patrick. 2018. "How NATO's Transformation ChiefIs Pushing the Alliance to Keep Up in AI". *Defence One.* May 18. https://www.defenseone.com/technology/2018/05/how-natos-transformation-chief-pushing-alliance-keep-ai/148301/.

Tucker, Patrick. 2020. "France, Israel, S. Korea, Japan, Others Join Pentagon's AI Partnership". *Defense One.* September 16. https://www.defenseone.com/technology/2020/09/france-israel-s-korea-japan-others-join-pentagons-ai-partnership/168533/.

United Nations Group of Governmental Experts on Emerging Technologies in the Area of Lethal Autonomous Weapons System. 2019. "Report of the 2019 Session of the Group of Governmental Experts on Emerging Technologies in the Area of Lethal Autonomous Weapons Systems". *UN GGE LAWS.* September 25. https://undocs.org/pdf?symbol=en/CCW/GGE.1/2019/CRP.1/REV.2.

United Nations Group of Governmental Experts on Emerging Technologies in the Area of Lethal Autonomous Weapons System. 2020. "Commonalities in National Commentaries on Guiding Principles". *UN GGE LAWS.* March. https://documents.unoda.org/wp-content/uploads/2020/09/Commonalities-paper-on-operationalization-of-11-Guiding-Principles.pdf.

United States Department of State. 2020. "Declaration of the United States of America and the United Kingdom of Great Britain and Northern Ireland on Cooperation in Artificial Intelligence Research and Development: A Shared Vision for Driving Technological Breakthroughs in Artificial Intelligence". *United States Department of State.* September 25. archived website https://2017-2021.state.gov/declaration-of-the-united-states-of-america-and-the-united-kingdom-of-great-britain-and-northern-ireland-on-cooperation-in-artificial-intelligence-research-and-development-a-shared-vision-for-driving/index.html.

United States Department of Defence. 2022. "Defense Budget Overview. United States Department of Defence Fiscal Year 2023 Budget Request." Office of the Under Secretary of Defence. April. https://comptroller.defense.gov/Portals/45/Documents/defbudget/FY2023/FY2023_Budget_Request_Overview_Book.pdf.

von der Leyen, Uursula. 2020. "State of the Union". *European Commission.* September 16. https://ec.europa.eu/commission/presscorner/detail/en/SPEECH_20_1655.

Watling, Jack and Roper, Daniel. 2019. "European Allies in US Multi-Domain Operations". *RUSI* Occasional Paper. September 23. https://rusi.org/publication/occasional-papers/european-allies-us-multi-domain-operations.

5

US GOVERNANCE OF ARTIFICIAL INTELLIGENCE FOR NATIONAL SECURITY

Competitive Advantage from the Moral High Ground?

Zoe Stanley-Lockman

As machine learning (ML) advancements raced ahead in the 2010s, governments worldwide awoke to the need to match the strategic potential of the technology with their roadmaps, investment and talent pipelines, and governance plans. The emphasis on governance is uniquely vital because artificial intelligence (AI) is a general-purpose technology, and its impact spans all sectors of the economy and society (Bresnahan and Trajtenberg 1995; Brynjolfsson and McAfee 2014). By extension, adoption is likely to consolidate further the connections between "artificial intelligence, digital security, physical security, and political security" (Brundage et al. 2018, 64). In the current era of strategic competition, these connections further extend to economic security and systemic rivalries insofar as the design and usage of the technology reflect human values and the cultural nexus between humans and machines.

With this as the departure point, governments have approached AI strategy as a holistic, whole-of-government endeavour. The European Union has established itself as a normative first mover in AI policy, first through its trustworthy AI principles and subsequently in its broader digital agenda. Chinese technology policy stresses the military and civilian implications of the technology as intertwined. International organisations have prioritised opportunities for international cooperation to enhance AI safety that promotes human rights, peace, and beneficence for humanity. While many countries have improved military investments in AI/ML, the majority of strategy and governance initiatives focus on cross-sectoral, civilian issues.

This international context is important because it illuminates a fundamental difference in the US approach to AI governance: instead of starting with a whole-of-government, civilian-oriented approach that can then be tailored to the military realm, it is the Department of Defense (DoD) that has thus far led US leadership in the AI agenda. Under President Trump, the White House used

DOI: 10.4324/9781003218326-6

executive orders to launch an American AI Initiative[1] and adopted the AI principles issued by the Organisation for Economic Co-operation and Development (OECD). Institutionally in the US government, the DoD has done more on AI governance than other agencies. Accordingly, one of the marked differences between the United States and other countries prioritising AI governance as a new technology policy area is that US efforts are "spinning out" of the military rather than civilian governance efforts spinning in.

DoD leadership in the US government is evident in efforts to govern the safe, ethical, and legal aspects of artificial intelligence and machine learning (AI/ML). With DoD in the lead, the question for the US government now is how to diffuse lessons from the unique bureaucracy and institutional culture of DoD to the broader, national security interagency. This means that the US bureaucracy is catching up to ensure its policy efforts and investments meet the pervasive demands of this general-purpose technology. To this end, the National Security Commission on AI (NSCAI) has become an influential voice in the US AI policy since its establishment in 2018, given its mandate to "comprehensively address the security and defence needs of the United States" (Congress 2020, Section 1051). The focus on comprehensiveness means not only further empowering the DoD to maintain its strong position in AI policy, but also extending authority to the White House; Departments of State, Energy, and Commerce; the 17 agencies comprising the intelligence community (IC); and the National Science Foundation, among others. Further, AI policy could not be considered comprehensive without accounting for relationships with the private sector, academia, and international actors.

In this context, this chapter chronicles the US security and defence policy on AI/ML to answer: how is the US national security apparatus organising itself to focus on AI governance? After defining the stakes of US government AI governance in the current strategic context, an answer is provided in three sections. The first section focuses on the DoD, explaining how it cemented its leadership role in AI/ML governance relative to other segments of the US government. This leads to the second section, which assesses how the NSCAI is attempting to promote a more comprehensive AI policy across all national security organs of the government. Then, in the third section, the analysis turns towards external relationships with the private sector, academia, and international actors to assess their influence on US AI governance for national security.

US AI Governance in an Era of Strategic Competition

Machine learning is a "computational process," but progress in AI can be more holistically measured in societal impact (Hwang 2018). The focus on AI governance in this chapter is used to equally acknowledge both the technical and societal aspects of AI/ML. In other words, it adopts the view that AI is inherently "socio-technical" and cannot be reduced to either half of the equation, just as AI systems themselves cannot be reduced merely to inputs and outputs. This allows the analysis to centre on social structures that feature in the diverse elements of strategic competition. In doing so, the connections between AI governance and strategic competition offer an analytical lens to help understand the technology race that the United States perceives and seeks to dominate through a range of policy measures and investments.

The concept of technology cannot be disassembled from human intention and thus from social structures through which humans interact. Brian Arthur defines technology as "a means to [always] fulfil a human purpose" (Arthur 2009, 28), which Alex Roland echoes in his conception of technology as a "purposeful human manipulation of the material world" and "a process of altering the material world to serve some human purpose" (Roland 2016, 5). These connections to human purpose make technology extend logically to "social institutions that cohere around artefacts" (Herrera 2006, 36). Seeing technology as socio-technical helps analyse the "complex of associated social institutions" relevant to international politics (Herrera 2006, 36).

With specific regard to AI/ML, Virginia Dignum, Catelijne Muller, and Andreas Theodorou provide a useful definition that encompasses its relevance to social institutions. They refer to AI as interactive, adaptable technologies that produce statistical results and also comprise the socio-technical systems around the hardware, software, and data (Dignum et al. 2020). This means comprising the societal impact of an AI system's development and/or deployment in the definition while also understanding that the technology does not link cause and effect (Dignum et al. 2020). In other words, values are incorporated into AI systems, but the technology itself cannot be seen as a moral agent with any awareness or understanding of the impact of the decisions it enables. Humans, not AI systems, are moral agents and are obligated to adhere to their moral code of conduct when interacting with moral entities like AI technology.

Maintaining this human centricity is critical because it puts the onus on human beings and organisations to emphasise the *interactions* between technology and social structures.[2] As is relevant to this chapter, the social structures in question include those at the intersection of AI governance and strategic competition. Unpacking the terms "governance" and "strategic competition" helps further clarify this concept.

The term "governance" acts as a common denominator for the range of issues described below. In its most basic form, governance entails the management or control of a social system – not limited to just states – through tools such as laws, norms, language, power, and the distribution of authority across that system.[3] As Mark Bevir writes, "governance refers to processes of rules wherever they occur" (Bevir 2012, 3), which can include norms and informal networks through which social practices are coordinated. For technology, relevant entities – in the public and private sectors, civil society, academia, etc. – as well as more nebulously defined networks – like subcultures in scientific communities[4] – steer development and innovation. This chapter focuses on the US government as one set of key actors in a broader governance ecosystem.

This chapter also centres on the unique challenges that emerging technologies imply. For emerging technologies, governance means contending with the endemic mismatch between scientific discovery on the one hand, and the slow, traditional pace of governance on the other.[5] Technological reform is structurally stymied: while it is easy to shape regulation very early in the history of technology, it is not necessarily possible to know how the technology will unfold in its early days. By the time a technology's impact becomes clear, it will be too entrenched and too late to influence its overall trajectory. In other words, parameters for monitoring and control often only become apparent once they are inevitable.[6] The governance of any emerging technology, including AI/ML, thus requires coordination in the international system to shape norms, develop benchmarks and standards, and cooperate on essential socio-technical features like trustworthiness as early as possible before its entrenchment is irreversible. As Annika Björkdahl notes, norms "are often discussed before a consensus is reached" and that "the manner in which states talk about norms is often just as important" as their patterns of behaviour in constituting norms in the international system (Björkdahl 2002, 13).

To this end, governments play a time-sensitive role in setting the stage for AI governance, and this is especially true of national security. Relatedly, whether the design of governance is centralised or decentralised has important implications for the ability of states, organisations, and networks to manage the trajectory of technology (Cihon et al. 2020). In other words, governance depends on organisational structures and institutional methods at the local, national, and international levels.

Governing technology in the international system also requires a deeper understanding of the strategic context in which technologies are introduced. For the United States, the return to an era of strategic competition is the primary feature of the international system that guides the government's approach to technology. Instead of focusing narrowly on bilateral rivalries, it is helpful to think of strategic competition here as the conditions that culminate in a broader context that challenges the presumed advantages of a particular state or bloc (Mazarr et al. 2018, 37). This broader context is multi-vectored, comprising technological, normative, ideological, political, economic, military, geographic, informational, and cultural elements.[7] In fact, the current strategic environment may be better described as a set of multiple, simultaneous competitions that takes place under different sets of rules (Raska 2019). Norms, ethics, standards, and governance thus form a linchpin in the battleground between contesting powers.

As a general-purpose technology, AI/ML cuts across each of these vectors of strategic competition. Its pervasiveness is not only measured by changes in informational advantage, economic competitiveness, or military superiority but also in the interactions between ideologies. At the strategic level, a socio-technical view of US AI governance means focusing on how the United States is trying to shape the trajectory of the technology, not just to align with the values that shape democratic societies and citizenries but also to extend this to the current ideological competition by creating a contrast between a democratic way of AI and alternative, authoritarian views. For military operations, responsible AI innovation depends largely on safety. How this strategic goal trickles down into operational and tactical levels remains to be seen, but it sets a clearer stage for the US view of AI governance for national security, starting first with DoD efforts and then expanding outwards to other relevant actors.

US Department of Defense: Safe and Ethical AI in US Military Strategy and Operations

DoD holding up AI ethics principles is a way to equally (1) ensure that the military complies with national and international legal obligations in a new age of technological and societal transformation; (2) further the state's role in fostering scientific discovery and technological prowess by aligning robustness with democratic values; and (3) actively shape norms as the character of warfare shifts, in line with the systemic-superiority view of democracy prevailing over authoritarianism. To analyse the ability of the United States to achieve these goals, it is first necessary to overview the role of DoD in AI safety and ethics. Then, the section turns towards DoD governance efforts to implement and operationalise safe and ethical AI.

Principles for Safe and Ethical AI

In October 2019, following a 15-month study, the Defense Innovation Board adopted five principles for safe and ethical AI. The advisory board to the DoD took the consultative process seriously, engaging a wide range of stakeholders in public listening sessions, closed-door roundtable discussions, and two tabletop exercises, including one on autonomy in weapons systems. The resulting principles are purposefully broad enough for their value- and safety-centric focus to resist the test of AI advancements over time. They concluded that AI should be responsible, equitable, traceable, reliable, and governable, and issued two documents with extended definitions of these terms (Defense Innovation Board 2019a). In February 2020, the DoD adopted these five principles (hereafter "the DoD principles") (US Department of Defense 2020), meaning that department-wide implementation could begin. In doing so, the United States became the first military to adopt AI ethics principles, joining a group of more than 80 other organisations around the globe that had issued such guidelines (Jobin et al. 2019).

Rather than expanding the definitions of the DoD principles – a task which the Defense Innovation Board's supporting document on AI Principles amply achieves – it may be of interest to compare the DoD approach to other AI ethics guidelines. The DoD principles differ from prevailing civilian AI ethics terminology on two main counts: the DoD does not use the terms "alignment" and "fairness." Alignment is a subset of beneficence, a core value meaning that AI development and use should benefit humanity by aligning with human values.[8] This does not preclude the alignment of AI with democratic values or ensure AI and autonomous systems "are hopefully aligned with written laws and written codes of professional ethics" (IEEE Global Initiative on Ethics of Autonomous and Intelligence Systems 2018). But insofar as beneficence requires emancipating benefits to others, it is contrary to the organising principle of militaries to control and consolidate their competitive advantages. The Defense Innovation Board was more explicit about its decision not to employ the term fairness, which is included in 80% of AI ethics guidelines (IEEE Global Initiative on Ethics of Autonomous and Intelligence Systems 2018). The Board acknowledged the "DoD mantra that fights should not be fair, as DoD aims to create the conditions to maintain an unfair advantage over any potential adversaries, thereby increasing the likelihood of deterring conflict from the outset" (Defense Innovation Board 2019b, 31–32). Apart from these differences, which aim to allow DoD to concentrate power, the DoD principles echo uncontroversial threads seen in civilian AI ethics documents: upholding values, complying with legal obligations, and advancing robustness and reliability.

While all five DoD principles are relevant to this study, it is worth calling specific attention to "governable AI" (Defense Innovation Board 2019b, 4) to make clear that its focus on governability has less to do with organisational elements of technology management or governance, so much as it is a technical question of engineering and systems performance (Defense Innovation Board 2019b, 40–41). The governability to which DoD refers here is largely a safety question that concentrates on anticipating and preventing failure modes when deploying AI in unfamiliar operational environments rather than pertaining to moral dilemmas.

When announcing the adoption of these principles, then-Director of the Joint Artificial Intelligence Centre (JAIC) Lieutenant General Jack Shanahan indirectly responded to President Putin's belief that the nation that rules AI will be the leader of the world (Russia Today 2017). General Shanahan said that "While we firmly believe that the nation that *masters* AI first will *prevail* on the battlefield for many years, we also believe that the nation that successfully *implements* AI principles will *lead* in AI for many years" [emphasis added] (Deasy and Shanahan 2020). In other words, arriving at the finish line first does not ensure dominance, as the Russian president has provocatively suggested. Instead, in focusing on AI ethics for defence, the United States is placing its bet that principled leadership will confer an advantage. In its interim report, NSCAI similarly stated that "ethics and strategic necessity are compatible," citing an "ethical imperative to accelerate the fielding of safe, reliable, and secure AI systems that can be demonstrated to protect the American people, minimise operational dangers to US service members, and make warfare more discriminating, which could reduce civilian casualties" (National Security Commission on Artificial Intelligence 2019, 16–17).

Public signals also reinforce this message. For example, former Secretaries William Cohen, Leon Panetta, Chuck Hagel, and Ash Carter explicitly name a purpose that is also served in DoD's five AI ethics principles. They write: "If we do not lead its [AI's] development and ensure it reflects our values, authoritarian regimes will ensure it reflects theirs" (Cohen et al. 2020). Their message includes "deliberately and carefully" embedding democratic values into the technology. This is not merely to avoid leaving a vacuum for competitors or adversaries to fill but to drive the US government to play a more proactive, normative role. Further, Avril Haines, Michèle Flournoy, and Danielle Chefitz connect ethical development and the use of AI to measures of effectiveness. Echoing General Shanahan's statement on the necessity of ethics for AI leadership, they write:

> Fielding AI systems before our competitors may not matter if DOD systems are brittle and break in an operational environment, are easily manipulated, or operators consequently lose faith in them. [...] Adversary advancements will likely increase pressure to field AI-enabled systems faster, even if testing and assurance are lacking. [...] However, it shouldn't be a race against our competitors to field AI systems at any cost. It's a race to field robust, lawful, and secure AI systems that can be trusted to perform as intended.
>
> *(Flournoy et al. 2020, 4)*

Insofar as there is an "American way of AI" (National Security Commission on Artificial Intelligence 2019, 17), the DoD is tying safety initiatives to the US commitment to uphold legal obligations, most notably international humanitarian law (IHL), by increasing trust in more reliable, more robust AI/ML. As discussed below, the extent to which these ethical commitments also prioritise less functional, more virtuous visions of moral character is more challenging to expound from current implementation efforts.

For uses of AI/ML at the tactical edge, it may be that the *ability* to act legally and ethically is tied to AI safety, testing, and trust efforts – and that the *willingness* to do so is less about AI so much as it is a question of strategic culture and commitment to the rule of law. Indeed, ethical questions pose even definitional concerns for accuracy. Accuracy for ML is defined as the fraction of correct predictions a model gets right (Google 2020). While seemingly simpler than the definition of accuracy for PGMs, the fraction can be misleading if measuring the wrong thing. Algorithms may in fact have *higher* average levels of accuracy when discriminating against groups (human or otherwise) or may only be accurate at *lower* levels of explainability (Whittlestone et al. 2019).

These trade-offs mean that accuracy levels are not fixed. They cannot be linearly measured and may inadvertently conceal critical features of C4ISR systems relied on to determine precision. For decision-support systems, the inherently flawed features of accuracy for ML may thus be problematic not just for precision in targeting but also when measuring the performance for other tasks ranging from mission planning to ISR, to logistics, to human resources, and enterprise management. Broadening the discussion beyond the tip of the spear means treating compliance with IHL on par with other concerns related to accountability, security, privacy, and civil liberties. Indeed, NSCAI recommends that developers across the government (not just DoD) "document value considerations based on how trade-offs with accuracy are handled" (National Security Commission on Artificial Intelligence 2019, 244).

Related to questions of autonomy and human control, the DoD may also informally review Directive 3000.09, which established the legally binding parameters for "Autonomy in Weapon Systems" in 2012.[9] A future AI directive may incorporate aspects from this autonomy guidance to focus more on operationalising testing and ethical principles, rather than changing course on US policy towards lethal autonomous weapons systems (LAWS), which are largely beyond the scope of this article (Shanahan 2020).

The United States has other motivations to ensure ethical and legal AI that are not necessarily shared with Russia and China, namely signalling to partners and allies that upholding the rule of law is crucial for political cohesion and operational safety. Discriminating between combatants and civilians is not only an IHL principle in place to reduce civilian and *hors du combat* casualties, but the US military has the added layer of motivation of promoting interoperability. Compliance with IHL is thus an important signal to US allies and partners – not only because Washington takes its commitment to the rule of law and cohesion based on values seriously but also because it is necessary to minimise risks related to unpredictable behaviour in coalition settings. This burden may not necessarily weigh as heavily on China and Russia, which are less likely to operate in coalitions.

Implementation and Operationalisation

An examination of other documents, including legislation and advisory reports, hints at the DoD approach to operationalising the DoD principles. For the DoD, implementation entails "developing procurement guidance, technological safeguards, organisational controls, risk mitigation strategies and training measures" (Deasy and Shanahan 2020). While some of these elements fall outside of DoD's remit, as the next section explores, elements such as procurement guidance or training measures are specific to the defence realm.

Early implementation of ethics guidelines can also be seen in select initiatives. For instance, the JAIC launched the "Responsible AI Champions" (RAIC) and "Drive AI" pilot programmes in 2020. RAIC aimed to develop a cross-functional approach to train personnel on what AI ethics implicate for individuals' respective roles and also seek to guide JAIC policy as it scales to affect the broader DoD workforce (Harper 2020). With 85 initial participants, Drive AI took place from October 2020 to November 2020 with the more targeted aim of training acquisition and requirements professionals (Beall 2020), who will be involved in the front-end design and development of AI systems, where ethical design questions first arise.

The Urban Reconnaissance through Supervised Autonomy (URSA) program "aims to use unmanned agents to autonomously detect hostile forces and establish positive identification of combatants in the complex, uncertain, and unsafe urban battlefield" in order to "detect and discern (and defeat) the enemy long before physical contact is ever made" (Kennedy 2018, 72). While humans still make the final decision, the Institute of Defence Analyses has worked with DARPA to ensure that the higher level of autonomy in the URSA incorporates "law and ethics to analyse the system's technological dependencies and components from its inception" as a possible, multidisciplinary "path forward for ethical military AI development" (Daniels and Williams 2020). As a federally funded research and development centre (FFRDC), the Institute of Defence Analyses allows the government to benefit from a broader swatch of research expertise that it may not be able to recruit and retain internally (Gallo 2017). Consistent with the NSCAI recommendation to leverage FFRDCs and DoD university-affiliated research centres to shore up US leadership in AI/ML, these partnerships may increase importance for AI ethics and safety.

Universities with experience in human subject research may have experience from which the military can benefit, such as sharing challenges with other academics to advance the state of the art collaboratively (Jacobs 2020). For this kind of sharing, ethical commitments can entail more transparency than the military is set up – culturally and legally – to handle. In response, the Air Force has set up a new data-sharing arrangement to work more effectively with the Massachusetts Institute of Technology (MIT) to create the Visible, Accessible, Understandable, Linked, and Trustworthy (VAULT) data platform. VAULT "provide[s] a centralised, secure and accessible place for hosting both public and controlled Air Force data sets" (Jimenez 2020). While serving the practical, operational goal of setting up training models for GPS alternatives for the Air Force, VAULT also relates to safety and ethics by opening up datasets for independent analysis and data competitions ("datathons"). As the acronym implies, this new mode of data sharing allows for new levels of collaboration on classified and unclassified networks for non-DoD experts to scrutinise datasets for elements such as bias, privacy, and explainability.

Beyond the Pentagon's five walls, the JAIC also focuses on "shaping norms through democratic values" as one of its three pillars of international engagement (Barnett 2020). The other pillars of international military AI policy – "ensuring data interoperability and working to create pipelines to enable the secure transfer of technology" (Barnett 2020) – also partially depend on ethics, safety, principles, and regulations. In September 2020, the inaugural meeting of the Partnership for Defence (PfD) convened delegations from Australia, Canada, Denmark, Estonia, Finland, France, Israel, Japan, Norway, the Republic of Korea, Sweden, and the United Kingdom and the United States to "shape what responsible AI looks like" (Joint Artificial Intelligence Centre 2020). In follow-up meetings, Germany, the Netherlands, and Singapore joined the PfD.

Broader National Security Interagency

The rest of the broader national security interagency may ride the coattails of DoD's first-mover experience in order to come up to speed on issues related to AI governance and strategic competition. This section covers these efforts by describing relevant NSCAI recommendations and analysing the forthcoming AI governance bureaucracy. It explains what a new AI governance bureaucracy for national security may look like beyond the five walls of the Pentagon. The State Department may be the highest-priority, most-underfunded department to advance a digital democracy agenda. The intelligence community has followed the DoD lead with the issuance of its own ethical AI principles (hereafter, the IC principles). Still, it has fewer statutory and policy tools at hand to assess the implementation of its AI ethics guide.

In addition to diplomacy and intelligence, other stakeholders – including the National Institute of Standards and Technology (NIST) and Bureau of Industry and Security in the Department of Commerce, and National Science Foundation – play crucial roles in US AI governance. More specifically, they relate to establishing trustworthiness in AI, coordinating the development of standards, and implementing ethical reviews.

State Department

Of the proposals above, the State Department is most relevant because the issues at hand are cross-cutting and global in nature – and also because it is currently underequipped to meet the challenge. Incorporating emerging technologies into diplomacy is important, insofar as it means developing shared approaches to democratic AI that safeguard against authoritarian views. Most concretely, this would be accomplished through coordination on standards, talent exchanges, and technology coalitions. While it remains too early to address how the Biden administration is taking this on, it is notable that they have announced the Bureau of Cyberspace and Digital Policy, building on an initial 2019 recommendation to establish the Department of State Bureau of Cyberspace Security and Emerging Technologies (DOS/CSET) intended to position US diplomacy to "secure cyberspace and its technologies, reduce the likelihood of cyber conflict, and prevail in strategic cyber competition" (Lyngaas 2019). Turf wars over its placement in Foggy Bottom have delayed its implementation (Mazanec and Marinos 2020), which has also impacted the broader emerging-technology agenda.

This differs from the Trump administration's view on an organisational level because it entails re-investing in the State Department,[10] and on a policy level, insofar as it means integrating "promote" and "protect" strategies. In October 2020, the White House issued a new "National Strategy for Critical and Emerging Technologies" that sees the promotion of the national security innovation base and the protection of technology advantage as separate pillars (Office of the President of the United States 2020). Their integration, per NSCAI's recommendation, includes safeguarding technology by creating alternative global markets and spurring innovation aligned with democratic values (National Security Commission on Artificial Intelligence 2020, 50).

The international dimension may turn more proactive, with carrots to incentivise innovation among like-minded countries rather than just relying on sticks to disincentivise partners and allies from decoupling with China (Stanley-Lockman 2020). More specifically, AI diplomacy could mean the United States creates "a coalition of like-minded countries and companies built on trust principles and shared values that use 'trusted' vendors and networks to protect citizens' privacy, secure sensitive data, and prevent IP theft" (National Security Commission on Artificial Intelligence 2020, 222–224). The NSCAI also recommends that State build expertise in AI/ML beyond DOS/CSET by creating a senior-level council to raise AI/ML as a strategic issue for leadership and by dedicating a cadre of technology officers to staff embassies and consulates. This is important insofar as AI governance entails shaping norms. With the narrow exception of LAWS, the fact that the DoD has led international efforts on AI/ML has meant that issues on technology and the international system are seen through a primarily military lens.

Furthermore, State has lagged behind its counterparts, which have begun to hone expertise in AI diplomacy and cooperation.[11] It is worth noting that this is largely consistent with the US militarisation of foreign policy, but is seen in the expert community as insufficient given the broad reach of this general-purpose technology. One of the former founders of the State Department Centre for Analytics has advocated that diplomacy is the right venue for a digital democracy agenda, calling AI the third "grey rhino," alongside pandemics and the climate crisis, with which the national security community will have to urgently contend (Dukeman 2020).

Intelligence Community

While not substantively different from the DoD principles, the intelligence community has issued a semantically separate set of its principles: (1) respect the law and act with integrity; (2) provide transparency and accountability; (3) be objective and equitable; (4) be human-centred in development and use; (5) be secure and resilient; (6) be informed by science and technology (Office of the Director of National Intelligence 2020b). Over time, the establishment of common technical standards would build on these IC principles in tandem with best practices and industry standards. In addition to more technical standards, this could also include "technologies and operational policies that align with privacy preservation, fairness, inclusion, and human rights, documentation of value considerations and trade-offs" (National Security Commission on Artificial Intelligence 2020, 81).

In the meantime, the IC principles also correspond to a framework that intends to drive implementation, including questions to guide personnel "on how to procure, design, build, use, protect, consume, and manage AI and related data" (Office of the Director of National Intelligence 2020a). The framework emphasises risk management and documentation heavily in its six categories: balancing goals with a risk assessment in the design of a system; partnering with legal and policy teams, including civil liberties and privacy professionals; defining the role of a human in decision-making for judgement and accountability purposes; mitigating undesired bias; testing for accuracy, bias, security, and other risks; accounting for the evolution of the system over its life; documenting purpose, parameters, limitations, and design outcomes; and determining the explainability and interpretability in line with the 2015 Principles of Intelligence Transparency (Office of the Director of National Intelligence 2015).

Given the secret nature of the work, it is difficult to assess the broader framework in which this ethics guidance enters. The NSCAI recommends that the intelligence community issue a classified technology annex to the National Intelligence Strategy to solve operational intelligence problems (National Security Commission on Artificial Intelligence 2020, 79), although this may wait until 2022. Further questions about resources and training are also left unanswered, although it is notable that Avril Haines is conversant in issues around trust and testing. NSCAI has also recommended granting the Director of Science and Technology the statutory authority to become the Chief Technology Officer for the intelligence community. This would empower a centralised voice for the 17 intelligence agencies to establish policies and supervise the whole development lifecycle for AI/ML (National Security Commission on Artificial Intelligence 2020, 78). While the DoD has an equivalent of this role, there is a ceiling for how the intelligence community is able to issue policies and fund their implementation without it.

National Institute of Standards and Technology (NIST) and National Science Foundation (NSF)

Undergirding AI ethics implementation is the concept of trustworthiness. Developing trust in AI/ML is difficult because the technology, particularly deep learning systems, is not necessarily explainable. As Carol Smith writes, "human-machine teams are strongest when human users can trust AI systems to behave as expected, safely, securely, and understandably" (Smith 2019). As the intelligence community approach to AI ethics suggests, these qualities are well suited for a risk management framework, so that humans teaming with machines can understand the associated risks if a machine is going to behave in an unpredictable or unsafe way, and then make decisions about the safety, security, legality, and morality of deploying AI-enabled systems accordingly.

The US government sees trustworthiness initiatives as important to incentivise responsible AI innovation for use in the economy and across society. However, it is also deemed critical for military effectiveness, given the emphasis on human-machine teaming in US strategy and policy planning documents.

Indeed, to emphasise the importance of trust between operator and machine in military operations, the Army has adapted the concept of human centricity to "soldier-centred design" (Thornton 2020). In and of itself, trust is not one of the five DoD principles. It is nevertheless present in US legislation that aims to help implement the principles.

In the Fiscal Year 2021 National Defence Authorization Act (FY 2021 NDAA), Congress offers a four-pronged definition of "harm" against which AI/ML would have to protect to be deemed "trustworthy." These harms are adversarial attacks, privacy and security, uncontrollable AGI, and bias against protected classes.[12] In a separate section on the Department of Energy, the NDAA defines trustworthiness differently, with three key components: "(A) algorithmic explainability; (B) analytical methods for identifying and mitigating bias in artificial intelligence systems; and (C) safety and robustness, including assurance, verification, validation, security, and control" (Congress 2021, Section 5501). Taking these overlapping definitions of trustworthiness together, NIST has been charged with developing a voluntary risk management framework with the National Science Foundation, Department of Energy, and private-sector collaborators over the next two years (Congress 2021, Section 5301).

The NSCAI has recommended practices for human-AI interaction that closely align with value and safety considerations. On the process level, this includes defining the functions and responsibilities of human operators, issuing policies to define the task of humans across the AI lifecycle (including for machine-human handoff), documentation for traceability and understanding, and training. Other recommendations are more technical, such as the development and use of algorithms that support interpretability, as well as the design of systems (including the user interface) to "provide cues to human operator(s) about the confidence a system has in its results or behaviours" (National Security Commission on Artificial Intelligence 2020, 244).

Related to questions of trustworthiness, documentation is a relevant mechanism to trace the design, development, and deployment of a model or dataset to perform audits throughout a system's lifecycle. This includes using a model or dataset for a different application other than its original one. Owen Daniels and Brian Williams provide a layman's definition of how documentation can be used as an explainability metric for AI models used by the government:

> We are not referring to explainability in a forensic sense of understanding the underpinnings of deep-learning systems. Rather, at the outset of system development, developers should also be able to describe how their system will function in the field, including the objectives it aims to achieve and the tasks it will undertake, the technologies it will rely on to do so, and the technical, legal, and ethical risks inherent to using those technologies.
>
> As updates to system designs occur and recur, legal and ethical implications should continuously be re-examined and evaluated. In complex systems of systems, developers' focus on cracking individual technical

> components can overshadow considerations of system end-use goals and operational context, thereby leaving these difficult explanatory questions unanswered.
>
> *(Daniels and Williams 2020)*

This relates to the DoD principle of traceable AI and the IC principle of transparency and accountability. Model documentation includes information to "characterise how the model was built, what its characteristics are, how it was tested, what's its performance" (Horvitz 2020) for any use. For data, best practices include annotating training metadata to mark the origins, the intent behind creation, authorised uses, and descriptive characteristics (such as which populations are underrepresented/excluded). On the socio-technical level, other best practices in the FY2021 NDAA also include "standards for privacy and security of datasets with human characteristics" (Congress 2021, Section 5301). Like model documentation, this annotation can be designed to be portable. As Timnit Gebru and Emily Bender note in their research on the data intensiveness of current ML systems, "a methodology that relies on datasets too large to document is therefore inherently risky. […] While documentation allows for potential accountability, […] undocumented training data perpetuates harm without recourse" (Hao 2020). In tandem, documentation and annotations can be used to promote the auditability of AI systems. More broadly, the government approach to wean machine learning systems off massive training datasets and shape norms of AI research to consider societal impact may then be constituents of an "American" or "democratic" way of AI.

To this end, NIST and NSF play crucial roles in documentation practices to be implemented along the lifecycle of an AI system. As a standards organisation, NIST aims to cultivate trust in AI by "develop[ing] tools, technical guidance, and best practice guides, that accurately measure and understand the capabilities and limitations of AI technologies and the underlying data that catalyse them" (National Institute of Standards and Technology 2020). As is the first step to defining future benchmarks or standards, NIST has already established a taxonomy for the safety and security of ML.[13] Current work on defining measurement for ML adopts a socio-technical view of the technology, including privacy and security and benchmarks for accuracy, transparency, verifiability, and safety assurance.[14] The forthcoming voluntary risk management framework from NIST includes lifecycle-long documentation to account for value considerations for accuracy-related trade-offs and for "systems that rely on representations of objective or utility functions," as well as "disallowed outcomes," *i.e.*, what not to use the model and training data for (National Security Commission on Artificial Intelligence 2020, 244).

While the Biden administration may take a different approach to AI-related regulation than President Trump has (Vought 2020), the voluntary nature of this type of work – risk management frameworks, vendor-agnostic benchmarks, and shared best practices – is likely to persist. As norms develop, the elucidation of standards may become more feasible, taking these early measures into account. For the United States, governmental incentives to shape norms and best practices are equally important to defining an American way of AI. They increase the robustness of systems used for national security and economic competitiveness. Although it is difficult to extricate safety from advancements in the technology race, one related national security prerogative may be eventual cooperation with strategic competitors for "safe competition" (Imbrie and Kania 2019; Horvitz 2020).

For its part, in the next 18 months, NSF will require ethics statements as part of grant proposals to account for "potential societal benefits," "foreseeable or quantifiable risks to society," and "how technical or social solutions can mitigate such risks" (Congress 2021, Section 5401). This approach appears to be gaining traction in the AI research field more broadly. For instance, the leading AI/ML conference, the Conference on Neural Information Processing Systems, began ethics reviews this year (Lin et al. 2020). Separately, NSF has also expressed intent to conduct a study on the "governance of research in emerging technologies" with the National Academies of Sciences, Engineering, and Medicine (Congress 2021, Section 5401). In this context, governance may refer to the responsible actors, accountability processes and goals, and external oversight support (National Security Commission on Artificial Intelligence 2020, 244).

Non-Governmental Influences on US AI Governance for National Security

The range of governmental actors above seeks closer collaboration with international, private, and academic actors. It is also true that these actors influence US AI policy. The governance agenda for national security will reasonably be impacted by interactions with these non-governmental players, particularly through pressure to cooperate in international formats and with the domestic AI ecosystem.

International Cooperation and Competition

Both competitors and partners pressure the US government to drive international AI governance. As mentioned above, the democratic AI agenda entails pushing back against authoritarian uses of technology. In this vein, the NSCAI has identified several international efforts that the United States should engage in for "AI to Benefit Humanity": the Freedom Online Coalition, G-20, International Telecommunications Union (ITU), African Union, Organization for Security and Co-operation in Europe, and United Nations Secretary General's High-level Panel on Digital Cooperation (National Security Commission on Artificial Intelligence 2020, 222–224). Apart from the ITU, given the importance of standards, these do not appear to be the primary formats for US engagement to advance its own AI interests.

Further, while the Trump administration took a passive approach to AI by following Franco-Canadian leadership in the OECD and Global Partnership on AI, the US national security community sees US leadership in democratic AI governance as a strategic necessity. With so many international initiatives already in place, the question will be what gap the United States seeks to fill, and in which formats it can project credibility vis-à-vis AI policy first movers, such as the European Commission, given the domestic state of technology regulation and control over industry.

Relations with the Domestic AI Ecosystem

By the time the Defense Innovation Board adopted its principles for safe and ethical AI, more than 20 other US organisations had already issued their own guidelines (Jobin et al. 2019). In companies, research institutes, and industry associations alike, such ethics frameworks were already in vogue in no small part due to pressure from investigative journalism and civil society. This pressure on the industry also extended to companies working with the military, most notoriously causing Google to announce in 2018 that it would not renew its "Project Maven" contract with DoD. Project Maven was a wake-up call that showed how misinformation on US military capability development could impact the relations with the commercial tech sector that is deemed crucial to maintaining technological superiority. Observers were quick to label the contract as a gateway to lethal autonomous weapons, despite lower levels of autonomy in the decision-making tool that analysed which Wide Area Motion Imagery data should be elevated to human reviewers. It was Google, not DoD, that stipulated in its contract that the Department could not mention the company's involvement – and in fact, the Maven controversy was a main driving force that led Google to issue its own AI ethical principles (Afifi-Sabet 2018).

Other episodes demonstrate that such incidents are not isolated, such as the "No Tech for ICE" movement following exposure of Amazon's work with the Department of Homeland Security during the Trump administration's controversial policies on immigration enforcement (Denham 2019). As these and other episodes show, civil society is organised to impact corporate behaviour and shape US AI policy at the local, state, and federal levels. The extensive civil society focusing on civilian digital policy issues and banning lethal autonomous weapons systems are both well covered in other literature (Zhang and Dafoe 2019). Fewer voices comment on national security and military issues beyond the tip of the spear. A recent survey concluded that "most AI professionals are positive [38%] or neutral [39%] about working on DOD-funded AI projects," with a willingness to work with DoD increasing for humanitarian projects (Aiken et al. 2020, 2).

In addition to humanitarian assistance and disaster relief, lucrative infrastructure contracts also help solidify civil-military technology relationships. In November 2019, Google's Chief Legal Officer Kent Walker called Project Maven a one-time result and, sitting next to JAIC Director Lieutenant General Jack

Shanahan, Walker said, "we're eager to do more" (Freedberg 2019). Half a year later, Google Cloud signed an initial "seven-figure" contract with the Defence Innovation Unit (Fried 2020). Active-duty, reservists and retired personnel are increasingly taking up posts in Big Tech companies, potentially constituting a new digital revolving door.

University partnerships are also beginning to include ethics, safety, and governance issues as part of their collaboration with the military. Carnegie Mellon University – renowned for its School of Computer Science – hosted the US Army Chief AI Ethics Officer in 2019 while setting up the hub of the Army AI Task Force (Nagel 2018). MIT collaborates with the Air Force, including through the MIT-Air Force AI Accelerator. The accelerator seeks to make AI real for the workforce through pilot projects, education, and "dialogue in AI, ethics and safety" (Smith 2020), with the aforementioned VAULT data transfer mechanism as an example of this commitment.

Beyond the military alone, the health of the US AI ecosystem may depend partially on the industry's relations with academia, given that academic researchers often act as interlocutors for multidisciplinary policy areas. Mohamed Abdalla and Moustafa Abdalla have revealed that 58% of AI ethics faculty look to Big Tech to finance their academic research, noting its importance because "governmental bodies rely on academics' expert advice to shape policy regarding Artificial Intelligence" (Abdalla and Abdalla 2020).

Relatedly, the non-profit coalition Partnership on AI (PAI), which was co-founded by Amazon, Facebook, Google, DeepMind, Microsoft,[15] and IBM in September 2016 (with Apple joining as a founding member in January 2017), also focuses on AI and robotics policy. PAI is an important force in AI governance conversations due to participation with the United Nations and Human Rights Watch, and has both gained and lost international partners in 2020 (PAI Staff 2020). Efforts to include civil society and Chinese voices have floundered. In 2020, both Baidu, the only Chinese member, and Access Now, an international digital and human rights organisation, left PAI. With Sino-US tensions on the rise and Access Now citing "an increasingly smaller role for civil society" (Johnson 2020) as its reason for departure, PAI's influence in AI governance circles may come to be constrained as a dialogue between Big Tech and the US government rather than a more inclusive forum.

Conclusion

AI ethics and AI safety are overlapping spheres, with safety mechanisms as the means by which ethical principles can be transposed. The United States is betting that AI cannot be ethical if it is not safe, but this does not mean that safe, reliable AI ensures that the development and deployment of AI will be ethical. As seen in departmental guidance, NDAA appropriations, and incoming leaders conversant in AI ethics and safety, the United States has many tools to incentivise responsible AI innovation. At the same time, the focus on safety and reliability does little to assuage credibility concerns. A review of US commitment to law and ethics may be equally telling about US values, as are AI-centric efforts themselves. On the normative front, cyber powers conferred to the Central Intelligence Agency, which open the door to offensive cyber operations – potentially including cutting off electric grids and financial institutions (Dorfman et al. 2020) – are fundamentally at odds with the 11 cyber norms and principles the United States has led and endorsed at the United Nations.[16] Organisationally, the DoD is the only government agency to have not yet passed an audit, which is relevant given the importance of auditability to ensure accountability for safe and ethical AI. After delaying the start of the audit process for years, it has failed the past three audits from 2018 to 2020 (Mehta 2020).

This is not to dispute the good-faith efforts to ensure that US usage of AI/ML in the international system coheres with law and ethics, but rather to say that systemic issues – on the legal, normative, and organisational fronts – with ostensibly little to do with this new technology may undermine claims of "democratic" AI. The same may be said of industry's behaviour, where "surveillance capitalism" (Zuboff 2019) goes largely unchecked due to the conflict between Big Tech business models and privacy. To maintain moral superiority against strategic competitors, attempts to create contrast between a democratic, "American way of AI" and digital authoritarianism may also come up against these shortcomings.

Nevertheless, this exposure to accusations of hypocrisy may increase the influence of two strategic differentiators that the United States benefits from *vis-à-vis* its competitors: civil society and alliances. Through open forums of discussion, the United States sees both as "asymmetric advantages" that can shape the normative level of governance for AI in the international system. Thus far, on both counts, the two-way dialogue has proved beneficial to shaping the US approach to safe and ethical AI. If not for the Project Maven controversy, the JAIC may not have heralded ethics as a core function. Without civil society organisations engaging in the Defense Innovation Board listening sessions, the US government may have been less attuned to the concerns of key academic and industry stakeholders that are critical to ensuring US AI competitiveness. As a new administration increases technology dialogues with other democratic nations, the US government may feel pressured to take more principled action to secure its leadership role.

Whether the moral high ground can confer an advantage is an elusive question in the competition for influence in governance initiatives. Strategically, safe and ethical AI is crystallising as a frontier in ideological competition – one that the United States is likely to increase efforts to "win" as it dedicates more resources to segments of the national security apparatus beyond DoD. Operationally, AI ethics ushers in a new era of robustness and reliability functions that will be critical to economic competitiveness and military advantage. For now, whether the United States will occupy the moral high ground may depend on how these strategic and operational goals intersect.

Notes

1 In launching the American AI Initiative, President Trump issued five Executive Orders related to AI on 11 February 2019: See https://www.whitehouse.gov/ai/.
2 This view largely evolved from decades of work from robo-ethicists and machine intelligence ethicists, and has gained even more credence among a wide range of AI stakeholders concerned with governance in the past three years.
3 Mark Bevir provides the following definition: "Governance refers, therefore, to all processes of governing, whether undertaken by a government, market, or network, whether over a family, tribe, formal or informal organization, or territory, and whether through laws, norms, power, or language. Governance differs from government in that it focuses less on the state and its institutions and more on social practices and activities." See Bevir (2012).
4 One example of an informal network that exerts influence is the "effective altruism" community.
5 Remarks from Wendell Wallach (20 May 2020).
6 Remarks from Wendell Wallach (20 May 2020).
7 The report above (*op. cit.* 20) divides strategic competition into economic, military, geopolitical, and informational aspects, identifying 13 different means of competing – military power and investments in technology two among them.
8 This definition is extrapolated from Jobin, Ienca, and Vayena (2019, 395).
9 The 2012 policy – which was based on study of the usage of Patriot and Aegis systems – was affirmed in 2017 and remains in place. If this informal review transitions to a formal review, changes would likely not take effect until the mid-2020s. This may be triggered if Patriot and Aegis are deemed outdated representatives of the level of autonomy of military capability development, not necessarily because of a change in the US position on LAWS.
10 The Department has suffered budget cuts, morale and retention issues, and low ratings for candidates for the foreign service officer test.
11 One example is Germany, whose Ministry of Foreign Affairs has ownership over these issues.
12 The language from Section 5108 of *H.R. 6395 – National Defense Authorization Act for Fiscal Year 2021* reads:

> (A) high-risk systems that lack sufficient robustness to prevent adversarial attacks; (B) high-risk systems that harm the privacy or security of users or the general public; (C) artificial general intelligence systems that may become self-aware or uncontrollable; and (D) artificial intelligence systems that may perpetuate societal biases against protected classes of persons, including on the basis of sex, race, age, disability, color, creed, national origin, or religion, or otherwise automate discriminatory decision-making.

13 The taxonomy, which focuses largely on adversarial attacks, is "intended to inform future standards and best practices for assessing and managing the security of ML components" (Tabassi et al. 2019).
14 For NIST, measurement focuses on privacy and security, hardware, data management, safety and robustness (including assurance, verification, validation, security, control, and the ability to withstand adversarial AI), auditing and benchmarks for accuracy, transparency, verifiability, and safety assurance.
15 Eric Horvitz, a PAI co-founder from Microsoft, is also one of the 15 NSCAI commissioners.
16 One limiting norm that the United States sought to include is: "A State should not conduct or knowingly support ICT activity contrary to its obligations under international law that intentionally damages critical infrastructure or otherwise impairs the use and operation of critical infrastructure to provide services to the public" (United Nations General Assembly 2015).

References

Abdalla, Mohamed, and Moustafa Abdalla. 2020. "The Grey Hoodie Project: Big Tobacco, Big Tech, and the threat on academic integrity." *arXiv*. https://arxiv.org/pdf/2009.13676.pdf.

Afifi-Sabet, Keumars. 2018. "Google publishes ethical code for AI following Project Maven fallout." *IT Pro*. https://www.itpro.co.uk/machine-learning/30891/google-publishes-ethical-code-for-ai-following-project-maven-fallout.

Aiken, Catherine, Rebecca Kagan, and Michael Page. 2020. "'Cool projects' or 'expanding the efficiency of the murderous American war machine?' AI professionals' views on working with the Department of Defense." *Centre for Security and Emerging Technology*. https://cset.georgetown.edu/research/cool-projects-or-expanding-the-efficiency-of-the-murderous-american-war-machine/.

Arthur, Brian M. 2009. *The Nature of Technology: What It Is and How It Evolves*. London: Penguin Books.

Barnett, Jackson. 2020. "Why the Pentagon can't go it alone on AI." *FedScoop*. https://www.fedscoop.com/experts-urge-us-nato-not-to-go-it-alone-on-developing-artificial-intelligence/.

Beall, Mark. 2020. "Building an AI-ready defence partnership and workforce" with Brian Katz and Lindsey Sheppard. *Centre for Strategic and International Studies*. Audio. https://www.csis.org/events/online-event-building-ai-ready-defense-partnership-and-workforce.

Bevir, Mark. 2012. *Governance: A Very Short Introduction*. Oxford: Oxford University Press.

Björkdahl, Annika. 2002. "Norms in international relations: some conceptual and methodological reflections." *Cambridge Review of International Affairs* 15, 1: 9–23. https://doi.org/10.1080/09557570220126216.

Bresnahan, Timothy F., and M. Trajtenberg. 1995. "General purpose technologies: engines of growth." *Journal of Econometrics* 65, 1: 83–108. https://doi.org/10.1016/0304-4076(94)01598-T.

Brundage, Miles, Shahar Avin, Jack Clark, Helen Toner, Peter Eckersley, Ben Garfinkel, Allan Dafoe et al. 2018. "Malicious uses of AI." Future of Humanity Institute. https://maliciousaireport.com.

Brynjolfsson, Erik, and Andrew McAfee. 2014. *The Second Machine Age: Work, Progress, and Prosperity in a Time of Brilliant Technologies*. New York: W.W. Norton & Company.

Cihon, Peter, Mattijs M. Maas, and Luke Kemp. 2020. "Should artificial intelligence governance be centralised? Design lessons from history." *arXiv*. Accessed January 9, 2022. https://arxiv.org/abs/2001.03573.

Cohen, William, Leon E. Panetta, Chuck Hagel, and Ash Carter. 2020. "America must shape the world's AI norms - or dictators will." *Defence One*. https://www.defenseone.com/ideas/2020/02/america-must-shape-worlds-ai-norms-or-dictators-will/163392/.

Congress. 2020. "S.1790 - National Defence Authorization Act for fiscal year 2020." https://www.congress.gov/bill/116th-congress/senate-bill/1790/text.

———. 2021. "H.R.6395 - William M. (Mac) Thornberry National Defence Authorization Act for fiscal year 2021." https://www.congress.gov/bill/116th-congress/house-bill/6395/text.

Daniels, Owen, and Brian Williams. 2020. "Day zero ethics for military AI." *War on the Rocks*. https://warontherocks.com/2020/01/day-zero-ethics-for-military-ai/.

Deasy, Dana, and Jack Shanahan. 2020. "Department of Defense Press briefing on the adoption of ethical principles for artificial intelligence." *US Department of Defense*.

https://www.defense.gov/Newsroom/Transcripts/Transcript/Article/2094162/department-of-defense-press-briefing-on-the-adoption-of-ethical-principles-for/.

Defense Innovation Board. 2019a. "AI principles: recommendations on the ethical use of artificial intelligence by the Department of Defence." https://media.defense.gov/2019/Oct/31/2002204458/-1/-1/0/DIB_AI_PRINCIPLES_PRIMARY_DOCUMENT.PDF.

———. 2019b. "AI principles: recommendations on the ethical use of artificial intelligence by the Department of Defense - supporting document." https://media.defense.gov/2019/Oct/31/2002204459/-1/-1/0/DIB_AI_PRINCIPLES_SUPPORTING_DOCUMENT.PDF.

Denham, Hannah. 2019. "'No tech for ICE': protesters demand Amazon cut ties with federal immigration enforcement." *Washington Post*. https://www.washingtonpost.com/business/2019/07/12/no-tech-ice-protesters-demand-amazon-cut-ties-with-federal-immigration-enforcement/.

Dignum, Virginia, Catelijne Muller, and Andreas Theodorou. 2020. "First analysis of the EU whitepaper on AI." *ALLAI*. Accessed January 9, 2020. https://allai.nl/first-analysis-of-the-eu-whitepaper-on-ai/.

Dorfman, Zach, Kim Zetter, Jenna McLaughlin, and Sean D. Naylor. 2020. "Exclusive: secret Trump order gives CIA more powers to launch cyberattacks." *Yahoo News*. https://news.yahoo.com/secret-trump-order-gives-cia-more-powers-to-launch-cyberattacks-090015219.html.

Dukeman, Ryan. 2020. "Winning the AI revolution for American diplomacy." *War on the Rocks*. https://warontherocks.com/2020/11/winning-the-ai-revolution-for-american-diplomacy/.

Flournoy, Michèle A., Avril Haines, and Gabrielle Chefitz. 2020. Building trust through testing: adapting DOD's test & evaluation, validation and verification (TEVV) enterprise for machine learning systems, including deep learning systems." *WestExec Advisors*. https://cset.georgetown.edu/wp-content/uploads/Building-Trust-Through-Testing.pdf.

Freedberg Jr, Sydney J. 2019. "Google to Pentagon: 'we're eager to do more'." *Breaking Defense*. https://breakingdefense.com/2019/11/google-pentagon-pledge-to-work-together-were-eager-to-do-more/.

Fried, Ina. 2020. "Scoop: Google lands cloud deal with Defence Department." *Axios*. https://www.axios.com/google-cloud-deal-defense-department-da619f1b-4d84-4d57-8e5d-4ddc1c0bf46b.html.

Gallo, Marcy E. 2017. "Federally Funded Research and Development Centers (FFRDCs): background and issues for Congress." *Congressional Research Service*: 1–2. https://fas.org/sgp/crs/misc/R44629.pdf.

Google. 2020. "Machine learning glossary." https://developers.google.com/machine-learning/glossary.

Hao, Keren. 2020. "We read the paper that forced Timnit Gebru out of Google. Here's what it says." *MIT Technology Review*. https://www.technologyreview.com/2020/12/04/1013294/google-ai-ethics-research-paper-forced-out-timnit-gebru/.

Harper, Jon. 2020. "Pentagon grappling with AI's ethical challenges, National Defence Magazine." *National Defence Magazine*. https://www.nationaldefensemagazine.org/articles/2020/11/10/pentagon-grappling-with-ais-ethical-challenges.

Herrera, Geoffrey L. 2006. *Technology and International Transformations. The Railroad, the Atom Bomb, and the Politics of Technological Change*. New York: State University of New York Press.

Hwang, Tim. 2018. "Computational power and the social impact of artificial intelligence." *SSRN*. http://doi.org/10.2139/ssrn.3147971.

Horvitz, Eric. 2020. "Eric Horvitz on AI and allies." *Eye on AI* hosted by Craig Smith. https://www.eye-on.ai/s/Eric-H-Q3-final.docx.

IEEE Global Initiative on Ethics of Autonomous and Intelligent Systems. 2018. "Ethically aligned design: a vision for prioritising human well-being with autonomous and intelligent systems." *New York: Institute of Electrical and Electronics Engineers*: 113–30.

Imbrie, Andrew, and Elsa Kania. 2019. "AI safety, security, and stability among great powers options, challenges, and lessons learned for pragmatic engagement." *Centre for Security and Emerging Technology*. https://cset.georgetown.edu/wp-content/uploads/AI-Safety-Security-and-Stability-Among-the-Great-Powers.pdf.

Jacobs, David. 2020. "Collaboration for new AI solutions: digital report 2020." *USAF-MIT AI Accelerator*.

Jimenez, Rita. 2020. "Historic agreement opens defence data to academia." *US Air Force*. https://www.af.mil/News/Article-Display/Article/2386640/historic-agreement-opens-defense-data-to-academia/.

Jobin, Anna, Marcello Ienca, and Effy Vayena. 2019. "The global landscape of AI ethics guidelines." *Nature Machine Intelligence* 1: 389–399. https://www.nature.com/articles/s42256-019-0088-2.

Johnson, Khari. 2020. "Access now resigns from partnership on AI due to lack of change among tech companies." *Venture Beat*. https://venturebeat.com/2020/10/14/access-now-resigns-from-partnership-on-ai-due-to-lack-of-change-among-tech-companies/.

Joint Artificial Intelligence Centre. 2020. "JAIC facilitates first-ever International AI dialogue for defence." https://www.ai.mil/news_09_16_20-jaic_facilitates_first-ever_international_ai_dialogue_for_defense.html.

Kennedy, Fred. 2018. "Enterprise disruption." *Defence Advanced Research Projects Agency 60 Years: 1958–2018*.

Lin, Hsuan-Tien, Maria Florina Balcan, Raia Hadsell, and Marc'Aurelio Ranzato. 2020. "What we learned from NeurIPS 2020 reviewing process." *Medium*. https://neuripsconf.medium.com/what-we-learned-from-neurips-2020-reviewing-process-e24549eea38f.

Lyngaas, Sean. 2019. "State Department proposes new $20.8 million cybersecurity bureau." *CyberScoop*. https://www.cyberscoop.com/state-department-proposes-new-20-8-million-cybersecurity-bureau/.

Mazanec, Brian M., and Nick Marinos. 2020. "CYBER DIPLOMACY: state has not involved relevant federal agencies in the development of its plan to establish the cyberspace security and emerging technologies bureau." *Government Accountability Office*. Letter to Congress. https://www.gao.gov/assets/710/709563.pdf.

Mazarr, Michael J., Jonathan Blake, Abigail Casey, Tim McDonald, Stephanie Pezard, and Michael Spirtas. 2018. "Understanding the emerging era of international competition: theoretical and historical perspectives." *RAND Corporation*. https://www.rand.org/content/dam/rand/pubs/research_reports/RR2700/RR2726/RAND_RR2726.pdf.

Mehta, Aaron. 2020. "The Pentagon failed its audit again, but sees progress." *Defence News*. https://www.defensenews.com/pentagon/2020/11/16/the-pentagon-failed-its-audit-again-but-sees-progress/.

Nagel, Matthew. 2018. "Army AI task force selects carnegie mellon as new hub." *Carnegie Mellon University*. https://www.cmu.edu/news/stories/archives/2018/december/army-ai-task-force.html.

National Institute of Standards and Technology. 2020. "AI research - foundational." Accessed December 6, 2020. https://www.nist.gov/topics/artificial-intelligence/ai-research-foundational.

National Security Commission on Artificial Intelligence. 2019. "Interim report." https://www.nscai.gov/wp-content/uploads/2021/01/NSCAI-Interim-Report-for-Congress_201911.pdf.

———. 2020. "NSCAI interim report and third quarter recommendations memo." https://www.nscai.gov/wp-content/uploads/2021/01/NSCAI-Interim-Report-and-Third-Quarter-Recommendations.pdf.

Office of the Director of National Intelligence. 2015. "Principles of intelligence transparency for the intelligence community." https://www.dni.gov/files/documents/ppd-28/FINAL%20Transparency_poster%20v1.pdf.

———. 2020a. "Artificial intelligence ethics framework for the intelligence community." https://www.intelligence.gov/images/AI/AI_Ethics_Framework_for_the_Intelligence_Community_1.0.pdf.

———. 2020b. "Principles of artificial intelligence ethics for the intelligence community." https://www.intelligence.gov/principles-of-artificial-intelligence-ethics-for-the-intelligence-community.

Office of the President of the United States. 2020. "National security for critical and emerging technologies." https://www.whitehouse.gov/wp-content/uploads/2020/10/National-Strategy-for-CET.pdf.

PAI Staff. 2020. "Building responsible AI with new international partners." *Partnership on AI.* https://www.partnershiponai.org/building-responsible-ai-with-new-international-partners/.

Raska, Michael. 2019. "Strategic competition for emerging military technologies: comparative paths and patterns." *PRISM Journal of Complex Operations* 8, 3: 64–81. https://ndupress.ndu.edu/Portals/68/Documents/prism/prism_8-3/prism_8-3.pdf.

Roland, Alex. 2016. *War and Technology: A Very Short Introduction*. Oxford: Oxford University Press.

Russia Today. 2017. "Whoever leads in AI will rule the world': Putin to Russian children on Knowledge Day." https://www.rt.com/news/401731-ai-rule-world-putin/.

Shanahan, Jack. 2020. "Department of Defense Press briefing on the adoption of ethical principles for artificial intelligence." *US Department of Defense*. https://www.defense.gov/Newsroom/Transcripts/Transcript/Article/2094162/department-of-defense-press-briefing-on-the-adoption-of-ethical-principles-for/.

Smith, Carol J. 2019. "Designing trustworthy AI: a human-machine teaming framework to guide development." *arXiv*. https://arxiv.org/pdf/1910.03515.pdf.

Smith, William. 2020. "Michael Kanaan on the USAF/MIT AI accelerator." *Business Chief.* https://www.businesschief.com/interviews/michael-kanaan-usafmit-ai-accelerator.

Stanley-Lockman, Zoe. 2020. 170–188 "Futureproofing transatlantic relations: the case for stronger technology cooperation." In *Turning the Tide: How to Rescue Transatlantic Relations*, edited by Simona Soare. Paris: European Union Institute for Security Studies.

Tabassi, Elham, Kevin J. Burns, Michael Hadjimichael, Andres D. Molina-Markham, and Julian T. Sexton. 2019. "A taxonomy and terminology of adversarial machine learning." *National Institute of Standards and Technology*. https://nvlpubs.nist.gov/nistpubs/ir/2019/NIST.IR.8269-draft.pdf.

Thornton, David. 2020. "Building trust in AI is key to autonomous drones, flying cars." *Federal News Network*. https://federalnewsnetwork.com/defense-main/2020/08/building-trust-in-ai-is-key-to-autonomous-drones-flying-cars/.

United Nations General Assembly. 2015. "Group of governmental experts on developments in the field of information and telecommunications in the context of international security." https://www.un.org/ga/search/view_doc.asp?symbol=A/70/174.

US Department of Defense. 2020. "DOD adopts ethical principles for artificial intelligence." https://www.defense.gov/Newsroom/Releases/Release/Article/2091996/dod-adopts-ethical-principles-for-artificial-intelligence/.

Vought, Russell T. 2020. "Guidance for regulation of artificial intelligence applications." *Office of Management and Budget.* https://www.whitehouse.gov/wp-content/uploads/2020/11/M-21-06.pdf.

Whittlestone, Jess, Rune Nyrup, Anna Alexandrova, Kanta Dihal, and Stephen Cave. 2019. "Ethical and societal implications of algorithms, data, and artificial intelligence: a roadmap for research." *Nuffield Foundation.* https://www.nuffieldfoundation.org/sites/default/files/files/Ethical-and-Societal-Implications-of-Data-and-AI-report-Nuffield-Foundat.pdf.

Zhang, Baobao, and Allan Dafoe. 2019. "Artificial intellignce: American attitudes and trends." *Centre for the Governance of AI at the Future Humanity Institute.* https://governanceai.github.io/US-Public-Opinion-Report-Jan-2019/us_public_opinion_report_jan_2019.pdf.

Zuboff, Shoshana. 2019. *The Age of Surveillance Capitalism: The Fight for a Human Future at the New Frontier of Power.* New York: Public Affairs.

6

CHINA'S EVOLVING AI DEVELOPMENT

Emergent Process Transcending Instrumentalism and Morality

Qi Haotian

Technology is not an apolitical or amoral force. Contemporary technological advances are not just about algorithms as abstract artefacts but are endowed with a specific structuring function and develop as emerging phenomena. Technological transitions or transformations do not only involve instrumental changes in the scientific and technical sense. They also consist of changes in socio-political elements such as practices, regulation, industrial networks, infrastructure, and socially, politically, and culturally constructed meanings. No technological transition takes place linearly or smoothly. In the technological and socio-technical evolution phase we are witnessing, no other technology has generated as much expectation and anxiety as artificial intelligence (AI). Most practitioners and observers involved in the development of AI believe that it is the most unique, powerful, and quintessential general-purpose and enabling technology in our (and future) age. It provides crucial inputs to essential processes in almost every area of human society. AI also generates complementary innovations in related technological domains.

The complex systems in the existing socio-technical configuration are deeply intertwined, creating structural and institutional costs of change. Advances often occur in non-linear, uncertain, and indeterminist ways, as the process of AI's development has shown. Evolutional changes are hard to actualise in an environment characterised by technological challenges and organised complexity, with different actors interacting in a highly complicated manner (Weaver 1948).

Two lines of argument help further explain the processes of technological evolution. The first perspective understands evolution as a process with technological regimes that create inertia for established technologies (Nelson and Winter 1982). The second identifies socio-technological transitions as processes with "new combinations" of elements that further lead to trajectories of change (Schumpeter 1934). Either way, evolution is characterised by uncertainties, costs, and failures than successes. When it comes to AI's development, especially in

DOI: 10.4324/9781003218326-7

highly unpredictable, uncertain, complex, and contentious scenarios of military conflicts, many "expected" achievements and images of *intelligentised* military transformation are far from both the reality and the future.

There are varying optimistic and prudent/pessimistic opinions on the advances of AI in both technical senses and its political-social impact. Technological optimists believe that the ongoing breakthroughs in AI development will eventually lead to the birth of artificial general intelligence (AGI). The prudent view holds that this process would take decades along the current technological path, if not never. Meanwhile, social optimists tend to look at the bright side of technological advances in different application scenarios, such as greater creativity, higher efficiency, more fairness in resource allocation, value distribution, greater individual achievement, and better coordination. However, the social pessimists remind us of the negative and even existential impact on humanity as the machine keeps rising.

Whether positive or negative, the impact of AI is felt in almost every aspect of individual and social activities, in both civilian and military realms. With the progress in big data, computing power, and machine learning (ML), the current AI can optimise predictive reasoning by learning how to identify and classify patterns. With unprecedented computing efficiency, deep learning offers unmatched investigative opportunities, for good or bad.

Like any AI-enabled technology and military capabilities, if AI's development is not well managed, it could cause security relations to go awry. There are concerns that the development of AI in military affairs can harm the stability between major military powers like the United States and China (Bidwell and MacDonald 2018). In all fields of AI utilisation, the following concerns address the current and future roles of AI: accountability, safety and security, reliability, explicability, adaptability, human control, and responsibility. AI – along with its associated technologies and risks – can potentially contribute to strategic and operational instability.

AI Development in China

China's political and economic elites count on AI to empower a new round of national growth. In recent years, economic growth has been slowing down in China. The country is looking towards a future that re-empowers national economic growth and solves the difficulties created as a by-product of the reforms of the last three decades, such as urban-rural duality, inequality, and pollution. It is widely believed that economic foundation and advanced production power, enabled by leading new technologies, will eventually determine future social and political superstructures. China sees the advances in AI as ways to enhance its national competitiveness and security in both civilian and military domains.

Digital services in general and AI in particular feature a natural global monopoly structure due to their low marginal costs. Accordingly, many in China see AI development and technological advances as unavoidable competition across national or industrial borders. Thus, the image of competition involving AI has two facets: one on the development of AI per se, the other enabling spill-over effects of AI in related technological and economic realms.

China's AI development includes an extraordinary commitment, including the S&T sector, industry, and the party-state. In 2017, the State Council issued the New Generation Artificial Intelligence Development Plan (AIDP). With the goals depicted in the Made in China 2025 plan (China State Council, 2015), AI communities aim to achieve indigenous AI capabilities to match or even surpass the West. As AIDP states,

> …Artificial intelligence has become a new focal point of international competition, and it is a technology with a strategic weight that will lead in the future. Major developed countries in the world are taking the development of AI as the main strategy to enhance national competitiveness and protect national security.
>
> *(China State Council 2017)*

The government's call to action, endorsed and backed by the top leadership, is to bring China into the top ranks in theoretical research on AI and occupy the high ground in critical and AI core technologies. To do so, the acceleration of AI development in China is primarily led by the technological industry and companies. The tech giants and pioneering firms hire large numbers of talented AI experts, build research facilities, and compete with their Western counterparts such as Amazon, Google, or Microsoft on every possible front.

While China is still behind the leading countries in AI, especially the United States, it has advantages, such as fewer and lower obstacles to data accessibility for research and training. In commercial markets, the health care sector, and the public safety realm, this advantage has already given rise to social, political, and economic returns. At the same time, however, it also created AI governance concerns. There is a debate on managing competition and potential conflicts in both civilian and military spheres. Despite these concerns, though, most leading players in China's AI development, civilian and military, pay more attention to AI's instrumental and functional aspects and how to pursue advances in AI more proactively. The country has been devoting a lot of resources to advancing AI's development.

Currently, China has the most AI-related paper publications and highly cited AI papers globally. Higher education institutions are the dominant contributor to papers published in the field of AI. Among the top 100 institutions with the highest number of papers worldwide, 87 are universities. The trajectory of China's highly cited papers has taken an upward swing, with China overtaking the United States and topping the global list. In terms of disciplinary distribution, computer science, engineering, and automatic control systems are the top three disciplines for AI articles. Over 40% of China's highly cited papers have been published through international collaboration.

China also has the largest number of AI patents globally, slightly ahead of the United States and Japan. The combined number of patent disclosures of these three countries amounts to 74% of the global total. Patent applications worldwide are mainly centred on sub-disciplines such as speech recognition, image recognition, robotics, and machine learning. Among the top AI patent-holding institutions in China, research institutes and universities are evenly matched with the business community regarding their patent output. Most patented technologies are in the fields such as data processing systems and digital information transmission, compared to relatively less-focused areas such as image processing and analysis.

China has the second highest number of AI talents globally, albeit with a low proportion of outstanding ones. Universities and research institutes are the primary seedbeds for AI talents. Tsinghua University and the Chinese Academy of Sciences have become the institutions with the most significant AI talent investment worldwide. However, only 977 Chinese researchers are characterised as outstanding talents based on their h-index scores (a metric that measures the research performance of a scientist), less than one-fifth of that in the United States and ranking sixth in the world. Corporate talent investment is still relatively low in China; most companies with intensive talent investment are American. Huawei is the only Chinese company among the global top 20 in this regard. Internationally, machine learning, data mining, and pattern recognition are among the fields that bring together the most AI talents, while in China, their research areas are more fragmented.

The challenges facing China in AI development are mainly in three areas: AI algorithms, framework software, and chips.

AI Algorithms

The most popular AI algorithms include decision trees, random forests, logistic regression, support vector machines, and the Naive Bayes algorithm. Major universities in China have been conducting in-depth research on these technologies but are seeing a sluggish transformation of their research outcomes. The difficulty lies in integrating the algorithms and practical engineering applications to implement technology research into production. In this regard, the business community has got a higher grade. Tech R&D teams led by Huawei, Alibaba, Tencent, and other companies have transformed algorithm technologies into practical applications by integrating the algorithms with their apps.

At the bottom layer, the research of underlying math libraries has always been an unpopular subject due to the difficulty of technology transformation and restricted research areas. Only a few teams in China are focusing their research on this discipline. With a different focus, the corporate sector has been carrying out research from the perspective of underlying hardware development through the optimisation of math libraries to optimise hardware efficiency. On the one hand, the research community focuses on optimising scripted algorithms to improve processing quality. On the other hand, businesses focus more on applying mature algorithms to practical engineering projects to realise AI industrialisation based on their development needs. This is one of the areas where significant gaps exist between China and leading countries such as the United States.

Framework Software

China's AI framework software sector is gradually taking shape, starting to embrace open source, and cultivating its ecosystem. China needs to advance the mutual adaption between its own AI framework software, AI chips, and hardware and push for performance optimisation and application promotion to build an integrated platform of software and hardware for industrial applications and promote this converged technology in different industries. There are still formidable challenges in this regard.

AI framework software has lowered the technical threshold through a collection of built-in algorithms, libraries, and tools. Such computing frameworks save the need for developers to start coding from creating complex neural networks; instead, they can turn to existing models as needed and quickly enable the application. Framework software offers a series of machine learning and deep learning components, in which general AI algorithms have been scripted and integrated. A new algorithm can be used, if required, by identifying needs and calling the function interface of the deep learning framework to create a user-defined algorithm. As these open-source frameworks are widely used across the globe, tech giants have gradually taken control over the AI application ecosystem: almost all AI chips, systems, and platforms need to be adaptable to these mainstream frameworks.

China's AI industry has primarily adopted framework software developed overseas. Its domestically developed AI frameworks are still a relatively non-mainstream option; most of them are being used internally in the few companies engaged in early AI algorithm research. However, technological advances have led to increasingly extensive applications of AI frameworks and a growing number of open-source releases. A few of the more well-known frameworks in China include:

- *Baidu's PaddlePaddle: AI computing framework in China.* It is an open-source deep learning platform that integrates a core deep learning framework, a basic model library, an end-to-end development kit, tool components, and a service platform. Assumed from the market acceptance, it is still in its infancy with a smaller user group and needs more R&D investment and market cultivation.
- *Megvii's Brain++*: Megvii's self-developed AI algorithm platform. As a unified underlying architecture, Brain++ supports algorithm training and model improvement processes. For algorithm development, Megvii has developed MegEngine, its own open-source deep learning framework (one of the core components of Brain++). With Brain++, Megvii can create a

self-improving and more automated production line for algorithms and design a rich and growing portfolio of algorithms for the fragmented needs of different vertical industries.

- *SenseTime's Parrots*: A training framework with an engine for dynamic compilation and scheduling at its core. SenseTime's Parrots applies real-time dynamic compilation technologies, where all codes are compiled on-the-fly during runtime and put on computing chips or engines for a massive parallel execution. It has both the scalability of traditional static deep networks and the flexibility of contemporary dynamic programming models.
- *Huawei's MindSpore*: An officially open-sourced computing framework that could be used for mobile, edge, and cloud scenarios. MindSpore has improved runtime efficiency and computing performance through its technological innovation and the synergy with Huawei's Ascend-Max AI chipsets.

Chips

Generally, AI chips can be defined as "chips with accelerators specifically designed for AI algorithms." There are four types of AI chips based on their technical architecture: GPUs, FPGAs, ASICs, and brain-inspired chips. Academics have proposed somewhat developed AI algorithmic models as early as the 1980s. Still, for a long time, the intrinsic value of these models was never really realised, mainly due to the difficulty of providing the computing power needed for deep neural network training and reasoning processes with the hardware available back then. Today, AI chips have considerably accelerated the processing of data, especially big data, which is a significant advantage compared with traditional CPUs. Different types of chips have their strengths and weaknesses in terms of versatility, application compatibility, programming complexity, performance, and energy efficiency. They are applicable to different scenarios such as training and reasoning. The features, strengths, and weaknesses of different types of AI chips are shown in Table 6.1.

TABLE 6.1 Features, Strengths, and Weaknesses of Different Types of AI Chips

Type	*Programming Complexity*	*Versatility*	*Energy Efficiency Ratio*	*Main Application Scenarios*
GPUs	High	Fairly strong	Medium	Reasoning + training
FPGAs	High	Medium	Medium	Reasoning
ASICs	Medium	Weak	High	Reasoning + training
Brain-inspired chips	High	Strong	Low	Reasoning

Source: Author.

TABLE 6.2 Major Chinese and Overseas AI Chip Manufacturers

Type	*Foreign Manufacturers*	*Chinese Manufacturers*
GPUs	NVIDIA, AMD, Intel	Hygon
FPGAs	Xilinx, Intel	Pangomicro
ASICs	Google, Qualcomm Zeroth, Intel	Cambricon, Huawei, Alibaba, Vimivro, Bitmain, Horizon Robotics, Baidu
Brain-inspired chips	IBM	None

Source: Author.

Today, the core technologies and markets of AI chips are monopolised by American manufacturers. There is still a wide disparity between Chinese chip makers and the global giants regarding technical maturity and market share (Table 6.2).

- *GPUs*: There is a predominance of GPUs in the current AI market. In China, Hygon is advancing the development of GPU-like (DPU) chips according to its expected timelines and has already achieved milestones in that process.
- *FPGAs*: FPGAs have the second largest market share among the four types of AI chips. They are completely monopolised by two US companies, Xilinx, and Intel, with a global market share of 90%. Chinese manufacturers engaged in the R&D of FPGAs are Pangomicro (with its Titan series) and Shanghai Fudan Microelectronics. Their FPGA products are one generation behind their American counterparts, and the performance of their products only equals the mid- to high-level performance of the same series of products of the previous generation made by foreign brands, which is no match for their overseas competitors yet.
- *ASICs*: In China, ASIC chip architecture is the primary carrier for innovation. There is a relatively narrow gap between ASIC chips manufactured at home and abroad, especially in terms of their performance and energy efficiency. Chinese chip makers such as Cambricon have already ramped their chips into mass production. However, there are still inherent gaps between Chinese manufacturers and the global behemoths, including the lack of their integrated software ecosystems.

AI in the People's Liberation Army

China has been engaging in an AI-enabled military modernisation process that shares many features of Western countries' structural, doctrinal, and technological transformations. China is behind the other major AI powers in basic research on algorithms, software frameworks, and the manufacturing of high-end chips. But China has some advantages, such as fewer data collection and usage obstacles, which enable more accessible algorithm training. China uses a "military-civil fusion" approach – which, as the name suggests, integrates civilian and military resources – to develop capabilities, such as autonomous command and control (C2) systems, predictive operational planning, and a better fusion of intelligence, surveillance, and reconnaissance (ISR).

The People's Liberation Army (PLA) envisions the military operationalising AI and related technologies, including cloud computing, big data analytics, and unmanned systems. This combination of AI applications, in the context of military transformation, is leading towards a shift in the character of conflict, understood in the Chinese study of military science as an evolution of war, from "informatised warfare" (*xinxihua zhanzhen*) towards "intelligentised warfare" (*zhinenghua zhanzheng*) (Ministry of Defence of the People's Republic of China 2019).

During a 2020 press briefing, Senior Colonel Ren Guoqiang acknowledged that, although PLA forces are working towards informatisation, the PLA is still a long way from establishing robust informatised warfare capabilities (Ministry of Defence 2020). For now, the Chinese military has been primarily focusing on AI's functional and instrumental enabling effects. These include, for example, information management and processing, intelligence assessment and prediction, autonomous offence and defence systems, cyber-electronic-magnetic warfare, logistics and support, training, simulations, etc. The PLA is in the process of moving from the "realisation of mechanisation" to informatisation and has deemed AI and associated technologies vital to the improvement of speed, accuracy, and efficiency in all missions, from logistics and intelligence to battle planning and strategic decision-making.

In general, the Chinese military is still in the early stages of the ongoing transformation in military affairs, exploring where the future of warfare may lead and what the AI-enabled modernisation will mean for international and regional stability. Some preliminary consensuses, however, have been formed. These include general guidelines of technological governance covering the legal, ethical, and operational aspects of new types of conflicts. But few of them are being formalised and institutionalised. A mismatch, not only witnessed in China but in other countries as well, in perceptions of the strategic and operational impact of AI-enabled capabilities can be detrimental to the entire international AI community.

Civilian AI Applications: Ethical Concerns and Governance Attempts

We are witnessing a swelling global public anxiety about the possible loss of control and risks generated by algorithms. In the algorithmic world of machines, what is happening seems to be escaping our modes of understanding and trust. Societies are increasingly influenced by human-made technologies and the rule of law, and many worry that this influence will one day evolve into the dominant control of the machine. Therefore, one of the principal concerns at the heart of AI governance becomes how to avoid technological control by either machines or the people behind it. As most of us do not understand the nature of the design and functions of technologies like AI, strategic ramifications of technological utilisation cannot be precisely anticipated.

At the same time, challenges such as biases and adversarial attacks are significant for the current state of AI or ML. If not managed properly, the fragility and lack of resilience in the complex system of and surrounding AI can exacerbate inequality, social cleavage, conflict tendency, and many more risks. In this context, we see a lot of work on norm creation regarding AI's ethical and safe governance. One important example is the European GDPR (General Data Protection Regulation), which regulates how data can be accessed, used, and controlled. There are many other examples of these kinds of regulations, including the G20 AI Principles, OECD AI Principles, Proposed Additional Protocol to the Convention on Certain Conventional Weapons, Singapore's AI Governance Model, Canada's Directive on Automated Decision-Making, and various stakeholders' initiatives around the globe, such as GNI, IEEE, Google, Tencent, and Baidu.

But regulation and management can also be problematic. In general, it is often hard to forecast what the next generation of technology will look like, and it is even harder to predict what the implications will be for different industries and political-societal structures. In dealing with a complex system like the development of AI technology and its impact, it is natural to expect attempts to reduce the risk of failure by introducing more safety measures, training, and redundancy. The contribution of the human component can improve the reliability of such a complex system. Nevertheless, in any complex system, the development of AI will always exhibit unpredictability and nonlinearity. Adding remedies or fixes to the existing complexity may ironically introduce further unforeseen interactions and increase the likelihood of failures (Perrow 1999). That said, the mainstream argument still holds that regulating intervention in the development of AI is necessary.

In the eyes of some Western observers, a popular image depicts non-liberal democratic states as having a strong tendency to be solely or at least primarily interested in maximising the benefits of AI or related technology in information gathering, processing, monitoring, and controlling. The Chinese government indeed enjoys advantages in the lower costs of collecting and utilising data. There are, however, increasingly widespread public voices supported by political and legal processes to better regulate and manage the utilisation of AI. Domestic stakeholders from various social, political, and economic backgrounds have been working together to find a suitable governing structure for technological advancement in China. A series of initiatives have been converging bottom-up and top-down processes, with strong endorsement from the government. It is shifting away from a traditional image of hierarchical procedure to an emerging polycentric and, in some areas, market-oriented process.

Take some recent cases of AI governance initiatives in China, for example.

- *"Six Principles of AI," Tencent Institute (April 2017)*
  The Tencent Principles, developed by the tech giant's Tencent Institute in cooperation with a research organisation led by the Chinese Academy

of Sciences, consist of six overarching and relatively theoretical principles: freedom, justice, well-being, morality (or ethics), security, and responsibility. The Tencent principles are designed to guide both Tencent's corporate governance and promulgate standards for the safe development of AI.

- *"Beijing AI Principles," Beijing Academy of Artificial Intelligence (May 2019)*
  The Beijing AI Principles were developed by the Beijing Academy of Artificial Intelligence, a consortium of China's top universities in Beijing, national-level think tanks and institutes, and Beijing-based tech companies. These principles are designed with AI research and development teams, the government, and users themselves in mind. Accordingly, the principles are organised into three separate categories: research and development, use, and governance. Aside from the slightly more abstract "harmony and cooperation," the Beijing AI Principles, among these documents, offer perhaps the clearest statement of values for future governance priorities: optimising (human) employment, adaptation and moderation of guidelines and regulations, followed by a commitment to refinement and implementation, and a focus on long-term planning (towards a stated social benefit).

- *"Governance Principles for the New Generation of AI," National Governance Committee for New Generation Artificial Intelligence (June 2019)*
  The New Generation Principles were issued by the National Governance Committee for the New Generation of Artificial Intelligence, a committee led by China's Ministry of Science and Technology, intended for all relevant stakeholders. The principles are relatively abstract in their framing and include safety and controllability, fairness and justice, privacy inclusiveness, and responsibility.

- *"Artificial Intelligence Industry Code of Conduct (Consultation Version)," Artificial Intelligence Industry Alliance (June 2019)*
  AIIA, a vast nationwide industry alliance, released their code of conduct for public consultation and feedback in 2019. The AIIA Code of Conduct splits its nine principles into four "general rules," which share many overlapping themes with the New Generation Principles, though with slight variations in word choice.

Military AI Applications: Between Instrumentalism and Moral Concerns

Unlike the established polycentricity and diversity in civilian governance, the Chinese military primarily focuses on AI's functional and instrumental enabling effects. Military and security practitioners and scholars share three general perspectives regarding the values of AI in creating a significant new military transformation and revolution. The first is the basic functional application in enhancing data processing and information. AI offers the possibility to speed up the information gathering and interpretation processes, freeing human agency for higher-level missions. This aspect is not different from the utilisation of AI in most other major militaries. For example, Project Maven in the US military seeks to use algorithms to interpret imagery more rapidly from drone surveillance feeds. From image recognition to processing of publicly available or classified information databases, processing applications of AI could help militaries more accurately and quickly interpret information.

The second perspective is human-machine interaction, such as creating unmanned wingmen in different scenarios and missions. Especially with algorithms that help respond in cases where human coordinators cannot directly guide the machines, for example, swarms, the Chinese military sees this as an opportunity to create a new balance between itself and technologically superior opponents. The third aspect involves a higher level and idealised military transformation. Most Chinese military thinkers and planners share the idea of a revolutionary transformation brought by the development and diffusion of AI and associated technologies. This view holds that the speed and complexity of conflicts are increasing not only quantitatively but in a qualitative sense, in terms of either a shortened OODA (observe, orient, decide, act) loop, the increasing velocity of military platforms and munitions, or the expanded network that is connecting all the nodes. From decision-making to the functioning of kill chains, individual platforms are increasingly embedded in a complex network or even a network of networks.

The amount and complexity of data are growing exponentially as the tempo of modern conflicts increases across multi-dimensional layers. Battlefield information sensors have spread over the land, sea, air, outer space, and electromagnetic domains. In this context, the Chinese military attempts to pursue new C2 architectures that would enable linkages between the different domains. These systems require open architectures that allow rapid development and integration of new applications and seamless interoperability between forces. The need for rapid information sharing and the ability to leverage various resources are critical for these systems to be feasible and practical. When AI-enabled systems span a large area, they will be able to assist commanders in assessing the availability and suitability of resources, units, and assets. AI systems can also alert commanders to adjust mission targets and optimise asset deployment and use.

Another major area of AI application (and associated technologies) in China is military unmanned aerial vehicles (UAVs). AI, coupled with other new technologies, such as cloud computing, has promoted the development of UAVs. The primary concerns and goals of the military UAV development contain three aspects: the first involves enhancing the interoperability of unmanned systems and their integration in systemic confrontations. The second is to strengthen autonomous combat capabilities, especially the efficiency, effectiveness, and adaptability of unmanned systems in uncertain battlefield environments in the future. The third aspect involves solidifying cyber defence, information protection, and electromagnetic defence.

C2 and UAV are just two broad categories of efforts – with each comprising many specific projects – of the modernisation and transformation, which (will) make the PLA increasingly reliant on algorithms to coordinate intelligence, command, logistics, and weapon systems. Computer vision and speech recognition are becoming increasingly important in information processing and intelligence management at tactical, operational, and strategic levels. Chinese military leaders believe that a more capable command, control, communication, computers, intelligence, surveillance, and reconnaissance (C4ISR) system may, in the future, not only facilitate but also oversee planning and decision-making (Wang 2015; Work 2015; Gong et al. 2016; Chai 2019); Jin 2017; Li 2017; Lin 2017; Liu 2018a).

In addition to the efficiency-focused functional orientations of AI utilisations, there are concerns regarding the potential risks of military AI. The PLA's concerns are not unique, but the sources of concerns and moral stance have different political-philosophical inputs. While the underlying ethical concerns can also be captured in terms such as accountability, safety, security, reliability, explicability, human control, and responsibility, deep beneath these terms and conceptualisations is an inner "tug of war" between the technological determinism based on Dialectical Materialism and Chinese Communist Party-Military's decades-long tradition of emphasis on human agency and creativity. Both continue serving as the philosophical foundation of education and indoctrination of Chinese military thinkers and practitioners. At the core, a balance must be achieved regarding a trade-off between costs, efficiency, and human control. Two broad vistas can be found. One focuses on the ontological relationship between and roles of man and machine. The other focuses primarily on technological advancement per se and its instrumental meanings.

The instrumentalists cheer the improvement of technological foundations without any reservations and do not attach much weight to the issue of ethics and governance from a moral angle. They primarily focus on using new AI advancement to effectively strengthen soldiers and commanders, streamline the command chain, and enhance systemic efficiency. When they emphasise the "human-in-the-loop" requirement, it is less for moral consideration but more about effectiveness. When they envision a possible future fully autonomous conflict, there is less fear and concern, but more embracement and expectation (Shen et al. 2014; Wang 2015; Guo et al. 2016; Zhu 2017; Chen 2018; Li 2018; Qiu 2018).

To a certain extent, this technology worshipping results from the Chinese military (and political) elites' deep-seated feeling of insecurity because of decades-long inferior positioning when faced, challenged, and threatened by technologically superior opponents. AI is believed to offer an opportunity for "overtaking on bend" (*wan dao chao che*) on competitors or potential adversaries when the latter continue paying attention and costs on mature and old systems (Li et al. 2016; Pang 2016; Wang et al. 2016; Zhao 2018; Zou 2019).

The technologically determinist voices embrace strong expectations of what AI can change to make warfare different. Along this line, some argue that emerging technologies can give their military an upper hand in potential future confrontations (Guo 2016; Shen et al. 2014; Guo et al. 2016; Zhu 2017; Chen 2018; Li 2018, 2019; Qiu 2018). Thus, to a certain extent, when they are dealing with risk management, the question is often turned into one of military effectiveness. That is, to make technology more advanced to repair imperfect systems. However, this efficiency and effect-oriented approach does not address the challenges arising from the very potential of AI and associated technologies.

When the instrumental school of thought talks about the limitations and risks of AI, it is less concerned about moral questions but more focused on the military effectiveness question. To a large extent, the viewpoints here are based on the Clausewitzian tradition of "the fog of war," friction, and uncertainties. For instance, there are concerns about programming AI systems for contingency and reliability. The current AI systems are trained for specific tasks. In the domain of military competition and confrontation, however, the environment can change rapidly and in a non-linear fashion. If the context for a given AI system changes, it may not be able to adapt. The already complex operational environments in varying military scenarios amplify the use of AI systems. However, this level of complexity may undermine the ability of these systems to interpret data reliably and correctly. Accidents and mistakes happen.

The arguments focusing on human agency, however, take a human-centred perspective. Their concerns originate from the questions of what emerging technology means for the humanity and how to ensure that humans will prevail over the ascendant machines and regulate who and how will pull the triggers in future military domains.[1] In this context, to manage relevant risks, there must be a balance between these two perspectives. The instrumental viewpoint is far from the primary focus, but it is not unquestionably dominant in China's military. One crucial factor cannot be overlooked – the military-civil integration (*jun min rong he*). China's civil-military fusion strategy has amplified deep and widespread concerns in the West. However, different types of civil-military integration can be also found in many Western countries. Taken together, in the military realm, China is ambitiously developing AI and, at the same time, increasingly gaining broader knowledge and a culture of caution regarding its utilisation and influence. From an overwhelming focus on instrumental values, the military is learning to balance ontological and functional dimensions between ethics/morality challenges and AI-enabled military efficiency/effectiveness. AI can be both a sword and a shield. Beyond the rhetoric of military effectiveness, the PLA is learning to move more cautiously concerning the role and impact of AI.

Debunking Myths

There is no doubt that AI has significant advantages over humans in searching, computing, storing, and optimising tasks. However, when more targets and complex missions are present, it is very challenging for AI to form correct or effective general situational awareness, as expected in the aforementioned transformational efforts (Jia and Wang 2020). Unlike human cognition, AI is a solely computer-centred and statistics-based tool. It remains a daunting job to introduce the human cognitive model into AI to function as reasoning instead of computing, decision-making instead of matching, and memorising instead of storing. As already mentioned, AI's most significant potential impact on the future character of warfare is its creation of a new model of general situational awareness. Situational awareness is composed of two parts. One is the mechanical part, that is, the formalisation of symbols. The other is the organic part, which involves the intentional actions of understanding, explaining, and thinking. The mechanical part can be optimised computationally, but the organic component is only possible when cognitive processing occurs.

In essence, in the current age of AI, computers are simply tools to realise informal intentionality, a process that reflects physical rules and psychological traces through mathematics and physics. There is no place for "common sense" in AI, but common sense is the very essence of cognition. With its organic framework of cognition, human intelligence is seen especially in highly competitive and complex environments such as militarised conflicts. This cognition goes far beyond what a machine can do today. It is not only physical but also psychological, physiological, ethical, and characterised by time and space topology. With no such comprehensive cognition, AI is nothing but statistical inputs and probabilistic outputs.

With this foundational constructive feature, mainstream AI relies on a strong assumption of rational choice. This implies that the individuals or groups in decision-making have high levels of behavioural homogeneity. However, this assumption, in the context of war and conflicts, neglects vital differences between different warring parties and "anomalies" in interpretations of fluid environments and unstable processes. Researchers and thinkers have been trying to deconstruct and rebuild mainstream intelligence science by bringing in the heterogeneity of individual behaviours to solve this problem. Here, the bottleneck of human-machine integration is not the simple interaction between human and machine but the fusion of cognition and computation.

The limitations of AI come from a weak theoretical foundation and vulnerable algorithm robustness due to the lack of effective approaches to cognitive brain simulation. The causes lie in the following issues: we have not so far achieved fundamental breakthroughs in the cognitive mechanisms of the human mind; mainstream AI is still limited to the classical logic and statistical thinking by using knowledge acquired from large amounts of data; support from massive training data and high-performance computing platforms is indispensable; big data is never "big" enough, as a real intelligent machine in the current model would need an infinite amount of data, while the human brain does not require unlimited data or tremendous energy to operate; AI's performance relies on parameter optimisation, and its models are devoid of explicability; small trepidations in the data and parameters of a neural network can cause significant deviations, something that has yet to be satisfyingly addressed.

Some of these issues are related to current AI paths. Without an entirely new approach, bottlenecks cannot be solved. But some other problems are considered more technically controllable and manageable and thus have raised specific concerns, such as the questions of adaptability, perturbations, and ethics. When related technical, operational, and policy challenges are met appropriately, it is believed that AI in this current form – for instance, characterised by deep learning – can still vastly improve military effectiveness and efficiency on the battlefield. But due to the limitations, in the sense of both science-philosophy and technology, AI is generally not suitable for general-purpose applications. In addition, it is computationally intensive in training, requiring more experienced people to adjust parameters (that is, to set the frame and the super-parameters) to increase efficiency.

Having discussed all these limitations, a balanced view should be taken when we assess the strengths and weaknesses of AI from a Chinese perspective. Debunking the myths of both promises and risks associated with AI is the basis for a comprehensive understanding of the prospect and consequences of Chinese and other countries' long march in AI development, especially in the military context.

Adaptability

A common view holds that systems for intelligent warfare are based on established rules, experience, and knowledge that cannot independently innovate for an unpredictable future, and that once an opponent's style of warfare deviates from past patterns, the system would not know "from whom to learn what." As a result, one would be unable to make the corresponding decisions or judgements in time, thus significantly increasing the risk of failure. This pervasive view can point out the general limitations of AI, but it is not entirely accurate. Machine learning can be divided into supervised, unsupervised, and semi-supervised learning. Supervised learning is used when training samples are available, and unsupervised learning is used when training samples are not available. So even if unsupervised learning is not possible, supervised learning can still be adopted.

Supervised learning is a common technique for training neural networks and decision trees. It learns a function (model parameters) from a given set of training data, and when new data arrives, the results can be predicted based on this function. Supervised learning is the most common classification problem, in which the existing training samples (i.e. known data and their corresponding outputs) are trained to obtain an optimal model (the model belongs to a certain set of functions and optimal means under specific evaluation criteria). Then this model is used to map all the inputs to the corresponding outputs and make simple judgements on the results to achieve the purpose of classification, thus also having the ability to classify unknown data. The goal of supervised learning is often for the computer to learn the classification system (model) that we have created.

In unsupervised learning, the input data is not labelled, and there is no definitive result. The class of the sample data is unknown. The sample set needs to be classified according to the similarity of the samples (clustering) to minimise the intra-class difference and maximise the inter-class difference. In layman's terms, in practical applications, the sample labels are not known in advance, i.e. there is no training sample corresponding to the class, and thus the classifier design can only be learned from the original sample set without sample labels.

In the supervised learning approach, the result of data identification is expressed in the labelling of the data categories. However, unsupervised learning methods only have the dataset itself to be analysed without any prior labelling. Suppose the dataset is found to exhibit some aggregation. In that case, it can be classified according to the natural aggregation but not be labelled with some pre-categorised label to match the number. The unsupervised learning approach looks for regularities in the dataset that do not necessarily serve the purpose of dividing the dataset, i.e. "classification." On this point, the unsupervised learning approach is more versatile than supervised learning. In short, the idea that there are natural limits to AI cannot be faulted, and the ideal situation is not always guaranteed. But the potential of AI's enabling roles has not been "exhausted" in the current technological possibilities.

Adversarial Attack and Disruption

We often see AI systems being disrupted and attacked, resulting in errors. Such examples are also widely used to demonstrate the limited nature of AI technology and associated risks. For example, by modifying image pixels, someone has successfully tricked Google's image recognition system into mistakenly identifying a puppy as two skiers; wearing specially designed glasses can cause most face recognition systems to misjudge; adding specific words to a sentence or intentionally misspelling words can completely interfere with natural language understanding systems used for text analysis. Once a person with malicious intent against our side analyses the algorithm's logic on which our intelligent system relies, they can cause the system to miscalculate through deception or disguise. AI systems are not sufficiently robust and are relatively vulnerable to attack and disruption.

At the same time, however, the potential for development in the current AI framework is far from exhausted. For example, in 2020, the face recognition system for motor vehicle exams in Guangzhou had successfully identified a twin substitution situation. In another example in 2018, Google proposed the Bert algorithm – an unsupervised self-training model pre-trained before the text input model to calculate the weight of each word in a sentence and the relationship with the context. If a particular word in a sentence breaks the structure, Bert's attention mechanism will mitigate the problem by allowing the decoder to look back at the hidden state of the source sequence. The weighted average is then fed to the decoder as an additional input, giving the new words a lower weight and ultimately having little impact on text comprehension.

Ethical Misjudgement

If an AI system fails to meet human moral standards, will automation spell disaster? This is a very legitimate concern. No deep learning algorithm is 100% accurate, and AI algorithms are bound to make mistakes, resulting in unnecessary mistakes and casualties in conflictual scenarios. A purely technical solution does not exist yet, which is why it is crucial to make governance a social and political process. AI is, at the same time, both strong and weak, enabling and limiting, promising and self-failing. In the military context, there is a clear borderline within which AI can and will dramatically shift the way major powers fight future wars. If neglected, select myths can lead to wrong and empty expectations for AI's impact. Without the breakthrough of many emerging technologies such as efficient chips and advanced quantum computers, the future development of AI will be fundamentally limited. Through the lens of this balanced perspective, we should see the impact that AI and associated technologies might have already created in interstate interactions, especially in the highly complex military arena. The challenges to stability and risks of loss of control exist in terms of AI's strengths and weaknesses. However, this does not mean the potential for AI utilisation and governance will necessarily be exhausted.

Embedded, Evolutionary, and Emergent Development of AI in China

The development of AI technologies and policies in China is the product of a complex system similar to most other countries. This system involves various actors with different identities, knowledge, preferences, and biases. At the stages of development, integration, utilisation, and regulation of technology, actors from all aspects should get involved to strike a balance between capability-effectiveness and reliability-moral risks. Without collaboration between the various stakeholders, the development of AI and future innovation stalls. With increasing interactions, however, complexity grows. Higher complexity means greater uncertainty but also a greater possibility of better regulation and governance.

Technically speaking, the potential opportunities and risks caused by AI development can and should be solved by focusing on fundamental values shared by people from different backgrounds. Making machines learn and understand human values is ultimately the only way to fulfil the promises of technological advances while at the same time decreasing the probability of system failure. In either military or civilian sphere, AI can become reliable tools, partners, or even peers only when the machines are made to understand human values rather than being programmed to behave as if they follow the ethical principles. Finding a common denominator regarding the future development of AI is not just a mission for different stakeholders within a national border but a shared enterprise among nations. As AIDP, China Academy of Information and Communication Technology (CAICT), and various other Chinese institutes or initiatives suggested, the competition mindset should be avoided, be it arms race or technological marathon analogy. Global cooperation on rules, regulations, standards, and laws should be deepened and transcend different political values and economic interests.

Such a global network would be even more complex and prone to fail. For this very reason, the AI development in China and other countries should be understood and treated as an evolutionary and emergent process. The impact of and response to the development of AI both take place in a non-linear way. AI is technology, not tools on its own. The influence and opportunities of AI depend on how it is developed, applied, and governed in complex scenarios. The impact and policy responses are embedded in both technological and socio-political-strategic logic. How AI shapes the future of either a particular country or the international community is not solely determined by its functional meanings. The impact and policy responses are embedded in the holist and complex processes of technological development and its utilisation. In these processes, the strategies and policies of AI development and the actions in governing AI acquire functional and social meanings in an emergent pattern. The same processes are happening in China and other countries and regions.

Note

1 See Zhao (2017), Zhao et al. (2017), Dong (2018), Liu (2018b), Mu (2018), Zhao (2018), Gu (2019), Gu et al. (2019), Zhao et al. (2019), Chen et al. (2020), Yuan (2017), and Long et al. (2020).

References

Bidwell, Christopher and Bruce MacDonald. 2018. "Emerging Disruptive Technologies and Their Potential Threat to Strategic Stability and National Security," Federation of American Scientists Special Report. September 2018.

Chai, Shan. 2019. "The Essence of Winning Intelligent War." *PLA Daily*. June 4, 2019.

Chen, Hanghui. 2018. "Artificial Intelligence: How to Subvert the Future War." *China National Defence News*, pp. 1–2. January 2, 2018.

Chen, Qi et al. 2020. "Why Worry about AI Impacting International Security." *People's Forum*, March, 2020: 124–127.

China State Council. 2015. "Made in China 2025." July 7, 2015.

China State Council. 2017. "New Generation Artificial Intelligence Development Plan." Order no. 35. July 8, 2017.

Dong, Qingling. 2018. "The Ethics of New War: Norms and Constraints." *International Observer*, vol. 4: 51–66.

Gong, Chunke et al. 2016. "Artificial Intelligence Makes Unmanned Combat Platforms Like Tigers with Wings." *PLA Daily*, pp. 1. November 3, 2016.

Gu, Jingchao. 2019. "Four Issues to Avoid on Intelligent Combat Research." *PLA Daily*. February 21, 2019.

Gu, Jingchao et al. 2019. "On Intelligent Command 'Independent Decision-Making'." *PLA Daily*. March 26, 2019.

Guo, Fenghai. 2016. "On 'Intelligent Revolution' and 'Military Intelligence Revolution'." *Journal of Xi' an University of Political Science*, vol. 29, no. 6: 106–110. December 2016.

Guo, Yanjiang et al. 2016. "How Artificial Intelligence Will Change Future Wars." *China Aerospace News*, pp. 1–3. April 12, 2016.

Jia, Zifang and Wang, Dong. 2020. "The Impact of Artificial Intelligence to the Pattern of Warfare and Its Strategic Implications." *International Politics Studies*, vol. 6: 36–59.

Jin, Xin. 2017. "Current Situation and Development of Intelligentization of Command and Control." *Command Information System and Technology*, no. 4: 10–18.

Li, Daguang et al. 2016. "How Intelligent Unmanned Weapons Can Change the Future Combat Style." *Study Times*. February 18, 2016.

Li, Minghai. 2018. "What Is Driving the Evolution of War to Intelligence?" *PLA Daily*, pp. 1–2. November 6, 2018.

Li, Minghai. 2019. "Where Does the Winning Mechanism of Intelligent War Change." *PLA Daily*. January 15, 2019.

Li, Renbo. 2017. "Intelligent Equipment Will Change the Rules of War." *PLA Daily*. December 15, 2017.

Lin, Yanfeng. 2017. "Will Artificial Intelligence Replace Battlefield Commanders?" *PLA Daily*, p. 1. June 23, 2017.

Liu, Shucai. 2018a. "Armed Drones and the Evolution of War: From the Perspective of Socio-Technical Systems." *International Security Studies*, vol. 36 no. 2: 72–90.

Liu, Yangyue. 2018b. "Autonomous Weapons Arms Control from the Perspective of Global Security Governance." *International Security Studies*, vol 36 no. 2: 49–158.

Long, Kun et al. 2020. "Arms Control of Lethal Autonomous Weapon Systems-Dilemma, Solution and Engagement Strategy." *Guo Ji Zhan Wang*, vol 14 no. 2: 78–102, 152.

Ministry of Defence. 2020. Press Release. November 26, 2020. http://www.mod.gov.cn/1dzx/2020-11/26/content_4874645.htm.

Ministry of Defence of the People's Republic of China. 2019. China's National Defence in the New Era. http://www.gov.cn/zhengce/2019-07/24/content_5414325.htm.

Mu, Huaiyu. 2018. "Who Promotes RMA, Is It Technology Or Theory?" *China Youth Daily*, pp. 11. February 1, 2018.

Nelson, Richard R. and Winter, Sidney G. 1982. *An Evolutionary Theory of Economic Change*. Cambridge, MA: Harvard University Press.

Pang, Hongliang. 2016. "The Dawn of Intelligent Military Revolution." *PLA Daily*. January 28, 2016.

Perrow, Charles. 1999. *Normal Accidents: Living with High-Risk Technologies*. Princeton, NJ: Princeton University Press.

Qiu, Hao. 2018. "The Winning Mechanism of Traditional Wars Will Be Overturned." *PLA Daily*, pp. 1–2. November 8, 2018.

Schumpeter, J. A. 1934 (2008). *The Theory of Economic Development: An Inquiry into Profits, Capital, Credit, Interest and the Business Cycle*. Translated from the German by Redvers Opie. New Brunswick, NJ and London: Transaction Publisher.

Shen, Xueshi et al. 2014. "Disruptive Technology Becomes the Commanding Height of the Military Game of Great Powers." *National Defence Science, Technology and Industry*, vol. 2: 35–37.

Wang, Fujun et al. 2016. "Unmanned Combat System: Subverting the Rules of Future War." *PLA Daily*. November 3, 2016.

Wang, Qingbo. 2015. "Unmanned Combat Platforms Change Traditional Combat Rules." *China Social Science Daily*. March 20, 2015.

Weaver, Warren. 1948. "Science and Complexity." *American Scientist*, vol. 36: 536–544.

Work, Robert. 2015. The Third US Offset Strategy and Its Implications for Partners and Allies. Speech Delivered at the Willard Hotel, Washington, DC. January 28, 2015. https://www.defence.gov/Newsroom/Speeches/Speech/Article/606641/the-third-us-offset-strategy-and-its-implications-for-partners-and-allies/.

Yuan, Yi. 2017. "Will Artificial Intelligence Command Future Wars?" *China National Defence News*, pp. 1–2. January 12, 2017.

Zhao, Ming. 2017. "Getting on the Fast Train of Intelligent Military Development." *PLA Daily*, pp. 1–3. November 14, 2017.

Zhao, Xiangang. 2018. "Intelligentization Is Not Simply Unmanned." *PLA Daily*. November 20, 2018.

Zhao, Xiangang et al. 2017. "Unmanned Combat: Who Has the Ultimate 'Right to Fire'." *PLA Daily*. August 11, 2017.

Zhao, Xiangang et al. 2019. "Unmanned Combat Must Still Be Manned." *PLA Daily*. April 4, 2019.

Zhu, Qichao. 2017. "Artificial Intelligence Knocks the Door of Intelligent War." *China National Defence News*, pp. 1–4. January 23, 2017.

Zou, Li. 2019. "Where Should Intelligent Combat Be." *PLA Daily*. January 24, 2019.

7

ASSESSING RUSSIA'S NATIONAL STRATEGY FOR AI DEVELOPMENT

Vadim Kozyulin

"Artificial intelligence is the future, not only for Russia, but for all humankind. It comes with colossal opportunities but also threats that are difficult to predict. Whoever becomes the leader in this sphere will become the ruler of the world," President Vladimir Putin said during the all-Russian open lesson on September 1, 2017 (Russia Today 2017). Since then, hundreds of domestic and foreign commentators have repeated this phrase as confirmation that the Russian leader is striving for world domination. No one has been misled by the words that Putin uttered next. "If we become leaders in this area, we will share this know-how with the entire world, the same way we share our nuclear technologies today." Putin's words became a kind of epigraph to a broad discussion of the phenomenon of a global AI dominance and a possible appearance of the "world ruler." The Russian President may have liked this created image of himself. Speaking to the Federal Assembly in March 2018, he declared Russia's leadership in designing "weapons based on new physical principles" and presented the advanced systems "Burevestnik," "Poseidon," "Avangard," "Kinzhal," and "Peresvet" (RIA Novosti 2018).

Since then, the topic of artificial intelligence has become almost mandatory at conferences and meetings of managers at various levels, and it has firmly entered the Russian media agenda. Most likely, the President's interest and even love for the subject of artificial intelligence was inspired by the President and Chairman of the Board of Sberbank, German Gref, whom Vladimir Putin met back in 1991 while working in the administration of St Petersburg. In 1999, Gref headed the Centre for Strategic Research, created by Putin's initiative under the government of the Russian Federation. In 2000, the Centre developed the "Strategy-2010." Besides the fact that both of them received a law degree from Leningrad State University, it is obvious that the President respects German Gref for his strategic vision.

DOI: 10.4324/9781003218326-8

Mikhail Mishustin, the country's chief tax officer from 2010 to 2019, has become a prominent figure on Russia's "digital honour board." In 1989, he received his education in computer-aided design systems and then completed his postgraduate studies. When Mishustin headed the national tax service, he completed the digitisation of this department. Tax collection increased by 36.5%, with the economy growing by only 3.2%, according to the official Russian statistics (which many experts consider highly inflated). Today Mikhail Mishustin is the prime minister of Russia. In his view of the future, he noted:

> Now, there is a lot of talk about what will replace and complement the digit. Let's list: biometrics, big data, biotechnologies, 3D printing, mobile applications, cryptocurrency, electronic payments, blockchain, high-density image, Internet of Things, smart dust, mixed reality, augmented reality, artificial intelligence, digital twins.
>
> *(Бутрин 2019)*

Prime Minister Mishustin is in favour of reducing the state apparatus; he believes "the state should become a digital platform" (TASS 2020a). Digital services do cut government spending and make life easier for ordinary citizens, and most importantly, they make the life of citizens more transparent and more controllable.

National Strategy for the Development of Artificial Intelligence

"We say at Sberbank today: if you do not use AI in every process, no matter what part of your business, then you are losing time, you are in history, you are lagging behind competitors. And this applies to every company; it concerns every process," to quote German Gref (TASS 2019a). In May 2019, the Russian government authorised the Sberbank to write the national roadmap for the development of artificial intelligence (Балашова 2019). In October 2019, the *National Strategy for the Development of Artificial Intelligence for the Period up to 2030* was approved (CSET 2019). In addition to the largest state-owned bank, market leaders such as Gazprom Neft and tech giants Yandex and Mail.ru Group participated in the document preparation. This state policy in the field of digitisation based on digital super corporations was consolidated with the formation of the AI-Russia Alliance, which, in addition to the named corporations, included MTS PJSC and the Russian Direct Investment Fund (Ястребова 2019). Ministries and departments did not play a significant role in the strategy's formation, which was reflected in the letter and spirit of the document. For example, the words "defence" or "military" are absent in the text. The document states (CSET 2019, 17):

> Taking into account the current situation on the global artificial intelligence market and medium-range forecasts for its development, the implementation of the Strategy at hand is a necessary condition for the Russian

> Federation's entry into the group of world leaders in the field of the development and introduction of artificial intelligence technologies, and consequently, for the country's technological independence and competitiveness.

It plans to achieve this goal by supporting scientific research, developing software, increasing the availability and quality of data and hardware, supporting the export of Russian products, training and attracting foreign specialists, as well as attracting private investment. There are two benchmarks in the strategy's implementation:

- By 2024, Russia should demonstrate a significant increase in the number of scientific articles in leading world scientific publications and registered results of intellectual activity, as well as applied technological solutions, increase the level of participation of Russian specialists in the international exchange of knowledge, their contribution to the creation of open libraries of artificial intelligence, create infrastructure support for domestic organisations, including high-performance data centres, and significantly increase the number of AI specialists.
- By 2030, Russia and Russian companies should join the group of leaders in the global market.

The document does not contain any financial obligations:

> Financial support for the implementation of this Strategy shall be provided from Russian Federation budgetary system budget funds, state extrabudgetary foundation funds, and extrabudgetary sources, including the funds of development institutions, state-owned corporations, state-owned companies, and joint-stock companies with state participation, as well as private investments.

On October 26, 2021, Russia's leading technology companies adopted the *Code of Ethics in the Field of Artificial Intelligence*. The Code of Ethics proclaimed a human-centred and humanistic approach to the development of AI technology, based on the principles of non-discrimination, data security, and information security; identification of AI in communication with humans; respect for the autonomy of the human will; and responsibility for the consequences of the use of AI. The document underlined that the recommendations of this Code were designed for AI systems used exclusively for civil (not military) purposes. In addition to a set of ethical principles and rules, the Code recommended developing and using an AI systems risk assessment methodology. It encouraged a risk assessment to be conducted through the involvement of a neutral third party or authorised official body when doing so would not harm the performance and information security of the AI systems and would ensure the protection of the intellectual property and trade secrets of the developer. In order to implement the Code, a commission for the implementation of the Code in the field of AI ethics was established. The Code founders welcomed Russian and foreign AI actors to join the Code on a voluntary basis.[1]

The Digital Sovereignty of Russia

Despite a section on defence and national security absent, the abovementioned strategy regards technological sovereignty as one of the principles for the development and use of AI technologies, namely, "the assurance of the necessary level of Russian Federation self-sufficiency in the field of artificial intelligence, including that achieved through the predominant use of domestic artificial intelligence technologies and technological solutions developed on the basis of artificial intelligence" (CSET 2019).

> "Ensuring the improvement of the well-being and quality of life of its population, ensuring national security and the rule of law, and achieving the sustainable competitiveness of the Russian economy, including leading positions the world over in the field of artificial intelligence" is viewed as one of the goals of AI development in addition to ensuring the growth of the welfare and quality of life of its population.
>
> *(Government of the Russian Federation 2019, 12).*[2]

As part of the creation of a comprehensive system for regulating public relations, the strategy allows for "delegating the possibility of individual decision-making to information systems that function on the basis of artificial intelligence," but "with the exception of decisions that might infringe upon the rights and legitimate interests of individuals" (Government of the Russian Federation 2019).[3]

Artificial intelligence has become a key term in another important strategic document, the National Programme "Digital Economy of the Russian Federation," which is designed to accelerate the introduction of digital technologies in the Russian economy and its social sphere (Russian Ministry of Digital Development, Communications and Mass Media, n.d.). The Programmes include projects on regulating the digital environment, training, infrastructure, information security, developing digital technologies, and digital government. For example, this document instructs the Deputy Minister of Digital Development, Communications and Mass Media of the Russian Federation to create "a technology with the use of AI for processing information security incidents to increase the automation level of decision-making processes and reduce the response time to incidents by December 31, 2021" (Analytical Centre for the Government of the Russian Federation 2019, 22). The "Digital Economy" National Programme includes more than ten targets. For the period from 2019 to 2024, it calls for:

- the number of digital economy specialists should increase from 30,000 to 270,000;
- the number of basic data processing centres in federal districts should increase from three to eight; and
- the average downtime of state information systems due to computer attacks should decrease from 48 hours to 1 hour (TASS 2019b).

Russia's doctrinal documents on AI development rarely touch upon the national security issue. "The Concept for the Development of Regulation of Relations in the Field of Artificial Intelligence and Robotics Technologies until 2024," dated August 19, 2020, considers it unacceptable "to use AI and robotics technologies that pose a clear threat to the country's defence and state security" (p. 5). According to the Concept (p. 7), at least until 2024, the Russian legislation should allow the "delegation" of certain decisions to artificial intelligence systems only provided that they "do not pose a threat to fundamental human rights and freedoms, the country's defence and state security." The document prescribes to assess the risks of "the implementation of threats to the country's defence and state security" in the field of AI technologies and robotics, as well as to ensure "technological sovereignty, which provides the necessary level of independence of the Russian Federation in the field of artificial intelligence and robotics, taking into account the state policy in the field of information technologies development and import substitution" (GARANT 2020). It can be noted that the Concept is initially oriented towards the country's interior and intended to fix a certain balance of interests of the regulator, business, science and society. It almost does not touch upon the political component of the issue.

Still, it declares the need to create an ethical environment for developing AI technologies based on "human-centrism." The Concept notes the need to create a regulatory environment "based on the balance of interests of a person, society, state, companies – developers of artificial intelligence systems and robotics, as well as consumers of their goods, works, services. However, ideas about this balance differ significantly" (Government of the Russian Federation 2020, 3). The authors consider the Concept as a tool "to achieve the convergence of the interests of man, society, state and business in the area under consideration in the coming years."

The following basic principles serve to preserve human control in the AI age:

- Adoption of restrictive norms if the use of artificial intelligence and robotics technologies carries an objectively high risk of causing harm to participants in public relations, human rights, and the interests of society and the state.
- Expansion of the use of settlement and self-regulation tools, the formation of codes of ethical rules for the development, implementation, and application of artificial intelligence and robotics technologies.
- Technological sovereignty provides for the necessary level of independence of the Russian Federation in the field of artificial intelligence and robotics, taking into account the state policy in the field of information technology development and import substitution.
- The Concept states that AI technologies should be based on basic ethical standards and provide for the priority of protecting fundamental human rights and freedoms, human control, projected compliance with the law, and prevention of unlawful manipulation of human behaviour.
- The Concept supports the development of self-regulation of market participants, including the adoption of codes of ethical rules.

- The Concept recognises it expedient

> to stimulate the development and consolidation by developers and manufacturers of appropriate systems of ethical standards in the field of information processing (including personal data), conscientious information about the main functional features of artificial intelligence systems and robotics, as well as the introduction of voluntary certification systems for compliance with such standards.

- In personal data protection, the Concept considers it necessary to adopt legislation to create special data access regimes, subject to the human right to privacy.
- In terms of technocratic solutions using AI algorithms, the Concept declares that the Russian Federation can allow "only pointwise" delegation "of certain decisions to artificial intelligence systems, where it is objectively expedient and does not pose a threat to fundamental human rights and freedoms." At the same time, for the implementation of individual elements of "delegation," it is proposed to use the tool of experimental legal regimes ("regulatory sandboxes").

At the same time, the adoption of "The Concept for the Development of Regulation of Relations in the Field of Artificial Intelligence and Robotics Technologies until 2024" does not mean that Russia has firmly chosen its path of digital development. The leadership of Russia has to determine its approaches to many problems that, in the context of modern political conflicts, reach the level of national security, in particular, the limits of information openness in Russia, the issue of foreign information influence on the territory of Russia, and the limits of permissible interference of law enforcement and other government services using technical control and surveillance systems in the private life of Russian citizens.

First, on the limits of information openness, Russia has become a source of big data for foreign IT corporations and a field for overseas e-commerce applications and Internet payments today. This phenomenon increasingly worries the Russian authorities. Russian regulatory bodies require foreign corporations to store all data collected in Russia on Russian territory. However, not all foreign operators comply with this requirement even after receiving a court order.

The second issue concerns foreign information influence on the territory of Russia. The Western technological dominance in the Russian Internet space is perceived as a direct destabilising factor in an atmosphere of increasing confrontation with the United States and NATO countries that might require special regulation. The *National Security Strategy of the Russian Federation* states in this regard:

> Traditional Russian spiritual, moral and cultural and historical values are being actively attacked by the United States and its allies, as well as by transnational corporations, foreign non-profit non-governmental,

> religious, extremist and terrorist organisations. They have an informational and psychological impact on an individual, group and public consciousness through the dissemination of social and moral attitudes that are contrary to the traditions, convictions and beliefs of the peoples of the Russian Federation.
>
> *(The National Security Strategy of the Russian Federation 2021)*

The Russian authorities consider it necessary to conclude an international agreement on regulating the activities of Internet companies and increasing the role of states in the global governance of the Internet. Director of the Department for International Information Security of the Russian Ministry of Foreign Affairs, Andrey Krutskikh, said in his interview with *Mezhdunarodnaya Zhizn Journal*:

> Regulation of the Internet exclusively by the private sector, where the role of states that are the guarantor of the rights and freedoms of their citizens and play a major role in the economy, security and stability of critical information infrastructure has been levelled, has long been ineffective.

Krutskikh believes that this kind of problem can be solved by developing new standards and protocols for the Internet, for which the International Telecommunication Union should be given appropriate powers (Russian Ministry of Foreign Affairs 2021). Finally, the issue of the limits of permissible interference of law enforcement and other government services using technical control and surveillance systems in the private life of Russian citizens has not been fully resolved either. The discussion in Russian society on this issue is just beginning. On the eve of the elections to the State Duma, the pro-government "United Russia" party published a *Digital Manifesto*, in which it proposed to prohibit the state from transferring key functions and decision-making power from a person to AI or digital platforms in areas of activity affecting the constitutional rights of citizens: medicine, law, education, private property, the right to work, etc. The manifesto proposes to protect a person from cyber fraud and crime, digital discrimination, and violation of privacy in the digital environment, a state's priority. Deputies of the "United Russia" propose to ban "extra-legal means of digital assessment and discrimination of citizens, in addition to laws and courts, such as social ratings, digital trajectories that violate the equality of citizens before the law" (Корнев and Галимова 2021).

AI in the Russian Military

Russia inherited the problem of imbalance between military and civilian industries from the Soviet Union (USSR). More than a third of all national material, financial, scientific, and technical resources went to the development of the military-industrial complex in the USSR. The Russian leadership attempted to transform the defence-industrial complex towards producing civilian products. The most notable campaign began with the Federal Law "On the Conversion of the Defence Industry in the Russian Federation," dated April 13, 1998, No. 60-FZ, signed by then-President Boris Yeltsin (Government of the Russian Federation 1998). It ended ingloriously and remained a model of bureaucratic voluntarism in the national memory.

The modern military-industrial complex of Russia shrunk several times compared to the Soviet time. President Vladimir Putin inherited the same problem, "The strategic task is to increase the share of nonmilitary products to 30% of the total volume of defence industry production by 2025, and 50% by 2030" (TASS 2018). He sees a solution to this problem by integrating military and civilian sciences. In 2012, President Vladimir Putin spoke out in favour of using Russia's scientific potential to enhance the country's defence capability. In his keynote article, he wrote,

> Without a doubt, the normal development of military research is impossible without partnership with civil science, without using the potential of our leading universities and the State Scientific Centre. Scientists must have sufficient information about the state and development prospects of the Army and weapons systems to be able to orient their future research, bearing in mind, among other things, their possible defence use.
>
> *(The International Affairs 2012)*

> I believe that we also need to more actively involve the potential of civil universities to programmes for the modernisation of the defence industry. Large 'defence' orders can become another source of development for our leading universities and research centres. It is sometimes argued that the revival of the military-industrial complex is a yoke for the economy, an unbearable burden that ruined the USSR at one time. I am convinced that this is a deep delusion.
>
> *(Rossiyskaya Gazeta 2012)*

Engaging citizen scientists with military contracts, he also hopes that military technologies could find application in the civilian sphere.

> It is necessary to comprehensively analyse and evaluate the test results of advanced weapons systems. I would like to note that successful research and development in these high-tech areas is of great importance for the development of the civil sector, for increasing the competitiveness of science, for creating advanced industries and infrastructure, and the digital economy, said Putin.
>
> *(TASS 2019c)*

The Russian military authorities implement this plan in practice today. Major General Andrei Goncharov, head of the Main Directorate for Research Activities of the Russian Ministry of Defence, said, "We need to transfer AI technologies from the civil to the military sphere. Today, Russia implements national programmes for developing high-tech sectors of the economy. The results of these projects can and should be usable for the defence needs" (ЯRobot 2020a). According to Ruslan Tsalikov, First Deputy Defence Minister of the Russian Federation, there is already feedback when military science leads in "breakthrough areas," and then military technologies serve as a locomotive for civil ones. "We already implement in practice what has not even been even scientifically researched and formalised to the end," he said at the conference on "Artificial Intelligence: Problems and Solutions" in 2018 (Тигров 2018).

It is challenging to provide an in-depth assessment of the level of AI technologies in Russian military developments due to their classified nature. Federal Law No. 5485-1, "On State Secrets," dated July 21, 1993 (Government of the Russian Federation 1993), has been repeatedly supplemented with new articles. According to this law, state secrets include the following subjects today:

- Information on the content or results of the implementation of targeted programmes, research and development work on the creation or modernisation of weapons and military equipment
- Information about the tactical and technical requirements, tactical and technical characteristics, and the ways of the combat use of weapons and military equipment
- Information revealing tendencies of development and the content of the development of weapons and military equipment
- Information revealing the design and manufacturing technology of weapons and military equipment
- Information revealing the physical and chemical properties and isotopic composition of materials used in the creation of weapons and military equipment
- Information revealing the combat, physical, chemical, or nuclear properties of weapons and military equipment
- Information disclosing the procedure for the use or exploitation of weapons and military equipment
- Information revealing the state of metrological support of weapons and military equipment, technical or metrological characteristics of military standards, means of metrological support, and defining a qualitatively new level of weapons and military equipment
- Information revealing the main directions and programmes for the development of standardisation or the content of standards in the field of weapons and military equipment
- Information about the achievements of science and technology, about technologies that can be used in the creation of fundamentally new products, and technological processes in various sectors of the economy
- Information on the achievements of science and technology, defining a qualitatively new level of capabilities of weapons, military equipment, increasing their combat effectiveness

- Information disclosing the content or focus of targeted programmes, research and development, design work carried out for the benefit of defence, state security
- Information disclosing the tendencies of development of means and technologies of dual use. Information on the use of dual-purpose means, technologies for military purposes
- Information disclosing predictive estimates of scientific and technological progress in the Russian Federation and its socio-economic consequences in areas that determine the defence capability and state security
- Information disclosing the cost of funds for research and development work on the creation of weapons and military equipment
- Information disclosing the expenditure of funds for orders, development, production or repair of weapons, military equipment and security facilities

Some conclusions, however, can be drawn from open data and public statements by Russian officials. Speaking at a specialised conference, Sergey Garbuk, Deputy Director General of the Advanced Research Foundation, named the main areas where AI is used to process data for defence purposes (Garbuk 2018):[4]

- Analysis of intelligence obtained from various sources
- Identification of security threats based on the analysis of large volumes of heterogeneous data
- Support for decision-making on the management of forces and assets
- Formation of terrain maps based on the results of aerospace surveys and other information
- Unmanned traffic control
- Targeting in conditions of uncertainty of the angle and variability of the shape of the target, in difficult visibility conditions, and in other interfering factors
- Automation of decision-making on the use of lethal weapons
- Detection, localisation, and classification of infrastructure objects, weapons, military and special equipment
- Intelligent biometrics (human recognition by face image, gait, gestures)
- Speech recognition in a complicated noise environment

A significant part of procurements and supplies for defence research is carried out through the electronic platform "Automated System of Bidding for the State Defence Order," which is not accessible to the public.[5] Some applications can be found on open trading electronic services, like the public website "Unified Information System in the Field of Procurement."[6] For example, the "Sozvezdie" Concern, a manufacturer of military command and control systems, placed an order for "revision of the software for decision-making support by officials of the combat control centre" (United Procurement Information System 2019a). In 2017, the "Granit Electron" Concern, a Russia-based manufacturer of radio-electronic warfare systems and information management systems for Naval Forces, ordered the development of a structural and functional model for analysing the target environment and selection by unmanned aerial vehicles equipped with an active phased array antenna (United Procurement Information System 2017). The "Avtomatika" Concern, a Russia-based holding company focusing on the development and production of information security technologies, has been interested in the supply of "means of influence on unmanned aerial vehicles" (United Procurement Information System 2018), and the State Research Institute of Aviation Systems requested research on foreign UAVs (United Procurement Information System 2019b). In 2020, the Ministry of Defence of the Russian Federation announced a closed tender for "research on the creation of an experimental model of a complex for the development, training and implementation of deep neural networks for a new generation of military systems with artificial intelligence" with a budget of 390 million rubles (US$5 million) (Interfax 2020). The "Rostec" state corporation includes more than 700 defence enterprises that are united into 11 holding companies (1Prime.ru 2012). Many of them actively develop and use AI applications.

Deputy Prime Minister Yuri Borisov has been in charge of Russia's military artificial intelligence development. He received his military education at the higher command college of the air defence electronics and later graduated from the Faculty of Computational Mathematics and Cybernetics of Moscow State University. Being the Deputy Minister of Defence, he was responsible for the military-technical policy of the Armed Forces and the creation, development, and modernisation of weapons and military equipment. Currently, as a member of the Russian government, he oversees the development of the military-industrial complex.

GUNID

The Main Directorate of Scientific Research and Technological Support of Advanced Technologies (GUNID) is the centre point for the Russian MoD in AI innovations (Russian Defence Ministry, n.d.-a). Its function is to simplify the military deployment of advanced developments that enterprises then carry out independently. Andrei Goncharov, head of the GUNID, acknowledges that the development of group-role control for drones and an increase in their autonomy became the priority areas in the military use of AI and neural networks in 2020 (TVZvezda.ru 2020). GUNID monitors modern technologies and developments of Russian enterprises and institutions, conducts scientific and technical expertise on selected projects, and submits them for consideration by a special commission. If approved, the most promising projects and technologies can be submitted to the Scientific and Technical Council of the Ministry of Defence of the Russian Federation, which may propose to include them in the State Defence Order (Елистратов 2020). GUNID reports directly to the Deputy Minister of Defence, the Army General Pavel Popov. Another Deputy Defence Minister,

Alexei Krivoruchko, keeps in hand the Central Research Institute №46 and the Centre for Special Projects[7] of the Russian MoD and the Scientific and Technical Committee for Arms Development.[8]

The Central Research Institute №46 of the Russian MoD designs the State Armament Programmes and participates in shaping the State Defence Order and Russian military standards in partnership with many research organisations of the Ministry of Defence and the industry (Russian Defence Ministry, n.d.-b). The Russian Ministry of Defence has research organisations and practice grounds for designing and testing new equipment and weapons.[9] For example, the third Central Scientific Research Institute of the Russian MoD researches the automation of command and control, reconnaissance, and support of missile and artillery weapons. The third Institute, in turn, includes several research centres and departments.[10]

The ERA Military Innovative Technopolis

In 2019, an extraordinary military facility called the Elite of the Russian Army (ERA) Military Innovative Technopolis appeared on the Black Sea coast.[11] The most talented recruits throughout the country are selected for service here. On the one hand, this centre is a place for scientific research and implementation of breakthrough military technologies and, on the other hand, an institution for educating junior military scientists in 14 priority areas:

- Artificial intelligence technologies
- Small spacecraft
- Robotics
- Information security
- Automated control systems and IT systems
- Energy supply technologies. Life support apparatus and machines
- Technical vision. Pattern recognition
- Informatics and computer technology
- Biotechnical systems and technologies
- Nanotechnology and nanomaterials
- Hydrometeorological (meteorological) and geophysical support
- Hydroacoustic object detection systems
- Geographic information platforms for military purposes
- Weapons based on new physical principles

ERA compiles an inter-agency database on advanced civil technologies and AI applications with the aim to test the most promising of them in the military technopolis (Кашемиров 2020). Thirty-seven leading defence enterprises, including the Kurchatov Institute, Kalashnikov, Sukhoi, Vega, and Uralvagonzavod, opened their offices in the laboratory cluster of the technopolis (Галанина et al. 2018). ERA residents receive property and tax benefits similar to the inhabitants of special economic zones (TASS 2019d).

Advanced Research Foundation (ARF)

The Advanced Research Foundation (ARF) was established in 2012 and is considered an analogue of the American Defense Advanced Research Projects Agency (DARPA). The ARF works in three research areas – information, physical-technical, and chemical-biological (Телеканал Санкт-Петербург 2018) – and also deals with the AI standardisation in four classes: image decryption, speech processing, control of autonomous robotic systems, and information support for the life cycle of weapons and equipment (Морозова 2018). In particular, ARF researches autonomous systems and studies control methods of group use and interaction of drones from multiple domains – land, sea, and air (ЯRobot 2020b). The foundation also designs an AI technology for recognising objects, such as cars and aircraft, in space images of the Earth. The fund expects that the technologies of image recognition, autonomous navigation, human speech processing, and predicting complex systems' behaviour will become the most in-demand (Advanced Research Foundation 2020). One of the foundation's AI programmes allows for identifying a network attack with an accuracy of 90%, indicating the attack class, the number of network packets, and the exploited software vulnerability (TAdvisor.ru 2019).

The foundation is working on the advanced designing engines for high-velocity vehicles, holding a tender for a convertible aircraft concept and algorithms for small-sized copters capable of autonomous high-speed flights in complicated conditions. To avoid duplication of projects among teams that often "reinvent the wheel," ARF created the National Centre for the Development of Technologies and Basic Elements of Robotics, which coordinates work in this area. The centre integrates projects and provides developers with the opportunity to use the best scientific and technical solutions (ЯRobot 2020b).

MoD AI Department

"The Ministry of Defence has decided to create a Department for Artificial Intelligence," announced Mikhail Osyko, the Member of the Military-Industrial Commission under the Government of the Russian Federation, at the *Intelligence of Machines and Mechanisms Forum*. The Department with its own budget should be completed by December 1, 2021, and it will shape the national defence order for AI-based military hardware. Russia's requirements for AI for military purposes should be standardised. "I think that we will face a new concept of 'military artificial intelligence' in the very near future, as it was with robots," according to Osyko (Interfax 2021).

"Intellectualise Everything Automated"

Like many leading military powers, Russia produces varying autonomous military systems for use in the sky, at sea, and on the ground. Autonomous robots are the most visible exhibits at the annual Patriot Expo. However, robots are hardly the defining direction of the development of Russian military thought today. Following the global trend of building a network-centric warfare system, Russia has been creating its multi-domain C3ISR network for over a decade. On December 1, 2014, the National Defence Operations Centre of the Russian Federation (NDOC) took up combat duty, and it immediately became a showcase for the new look of the Russian army. The NDOC keeps the Armed Forces ready for combat use, provides the MoD high command with information on the situation in the country and the world, and serves the operation of the country's leadership during events in the situation room. "Hardware and software systems combine information flows of heterogeneous automated systems into a single information and control complex along the entire vertical, from strategic to tactical levels of control," according to the head of the NDOC, Colonel-General Mikhail Mizintsev (Заквасин and Комаров 2020). The National Centre unites three control centres (Zvezda Weekly 2020):

- Strategic Nuclear Forces Command and Control Centre
- Combat Control Centre
- Day-to-Day Operations Control Centre

The NDOC became the pinnacle of the world's first unified automated control system (UACS), Akatsiya-M, for all Russian armed forces' military units. Akatsiya-M is a kind of military analogue of the Internet, and Russian military commands began receiving it in 2005. UACS allows troops to stay in the same information space both in places of permanent deployment and during combat missions. This system is constantly improving; new units of the Army and Navy, as well as centres of the Ministry of Emergency Situations, enterprises of the military-industrial complex, and transport logistics services, get access to it (Zvezda Weekly 2020). This system permanently integrates space and air intelligence assets and supplements tactical reconnaissance means equipped with the Strelets C3ISR sets during combat operations (Курильченко 2019). During his visit to the NDOC in December 2014, Vladimir Putin noted: "Everything is done exclusively on Russian technologies, with very powerful computer software, which has no equal in the world today." The President stressed that the Centre will work for all Collective Security Treaty Organization (CSTO) countries: "I am sure this will increase the controllability of the national defence systems, our troops, and improve coordination" (TVZvezda.ru 2014).

In January 2020, it was announced that the National Defence Control Centre was awaiting modernisation. The updated system will add AI elements that will assist top military leaders in making decisions. Pavel Laptaev, General Director of the RTI company, which is leading this project, explained: "The military is not planning to delegate decision-making to artificial intelligence. We are developing the system in a slightly different direction. It will assist in making decisions." Artificial intelligence will help commanders take into account the available forces and assets, assess the situation in subordinate military units, and suggest possible solutions (NEWS.ru 2020).

The second area of modernisation of the centre is forecasting emergency situations. The system will forecast floods and fires based on historical data. AI will accelerate the mobilisation of forces and assets of the Emergencies Ministry, the National Guard, and the Ministry of Defence in specific locations. RTI also solves the NDOC's cybersecurity issues; in particular, it transfers equipment to domestic software, processors, and systems, which significantly increases the security and cyber stability of the centre (REGNUM News 2020).

The Strategic Missile Forces (SMF) traditionally rely on an Automated Control System (ACS), which consists of two independent but interfaced elements: an Automated Combat Control System (ACCS) and an Information Computing System (ICS). ACCS provides for the transmission of orders, signals, and reports in any security situation. ICS ensures the planning of the combat use of the SMF and managing daily activities. The ACS has been continuously modernised since its inception. In August 2014, the United Instrument-Making Corporation presented the fifth-generation ACS for the SMF (RussianElectronics.ru 2014). In December 2017, speaking at the Military Academy of the SMF named after Peter the Great, Vladimir Putin suggested that AI could help Russia restore the disturbed balance of power. The President noted that America spent ten times more on defence than Russia. It was possible to maintain parity utilising artificial intelligence (Комаров 2018).

The US missile defence system deployment near Russian borders requires new solutions for the Russian ICBMs. One of such projects, called "Vozzvanie," allows the SMF headquarters to quickly re-target missiles and divert them from an anti-missile attack, changing the order of targets engagement and the number of required charges. The "Vozzvanie" processes these decisions and transmits them to missile sites within a few minutes (Txnomania.ru 2013). Elements of the US missile defence system deployed near the Russian borders are the main concern for the Russian leadership, as noted by President Putin:

> A guarantee against disrupting the global balance of power can be either the creation of our own, very costly and still ineffective missile defence system, or the ability to penetrate any missile defence system and protect the Russian retaliatory capacity, which is much more effective. Russia's military-technical response to the global US Missile Defence and its segment in Europe will be effective and asymmetric. And it will fully comply with the steps of the United States in the field of missile defence.
>
> *(Rossiyskaya Gazeta 2012)*

Neural networks will become an essential component in the Russian response. The SMF exploits AI in support of decision-making systems, onboard control systems for various assets, and the automation of professional activities (Russian Defence Ministry, n.d.-c). It is no coincidence that the Military Academy of the SMF was the first of the MoD universities to start training AI specialists in 2020

(Петров 2020). The Academy, in particular, created a neural network model for assessing the capacity and remaining life expectancy of missiles, launchers, service, and security systems (Валагин 2018).

Russia introduces artificial intelligence into the means of defence. The Missile Warning System (MWS) is undergoing an upgrade, where each radar will be converted to digital technology. MWS will receive a data processing centre using machine learning and big data analysis. Machine learning will significantly speed up the determination of the signature, types of detected objects, and flight directions. AI-based radars track more targets with greater accuracy and speed. MWS assets will be united in a single information system, "which will transmit the necessary information for making decisions," according to Pavel Laptaev, the RTI Director General (TASS 2020b).

The Russian Aerospace Forces also deploy the ACS with AI elements for Air Defence Systems. This command and control (C2) system connects anti-aircraft missile assets of different classes with modern radar systems. The ACS automatically analyses the air situation and issues scenarios for weapons employment. The ACS will empower Air Defence Systems to automatically repel a massive missile attack through the deployment of several types of anti-aircraft systems, as well as set up several air defence lines (Круглов et al. 2018).

According to some sources, even the top secret Russian military project, the Perimeter Automatic Control System for a massive retaliatory nuclear strike (known in Western Europe and the United States as *Dead Hand*), also adopted AI elements. The new AI-empowered brain of the Perimeter system has replaced the autonomous control and command system, which aimed to independently decide to effect a retaliatory nuclear strike in case the Russian population showed no signs of life (Хроленко 2017).

Creating a New Class of Intelligent Robots

The annual Russian Military Expo in the Patriot Park convincingly demonstrates the progress of the Russian defence industry: armoured vehicles of the last century gradually acquire the features of intellectual weapons of the 21st century, and new autonomous systems are born that will serve the Russian armed forces at sea, in the sky, and on the ground. The Russian Defence Ministry holds the International Military-Technical Forum ARMY-202x at the Patriot Park in August every year.[12] With their latest defence technologies, new combat drones have become a vital component of this military show. In addition to showcasing the latest ground, air, and sea projects, the Russian Military Expo in Patriot Park brings together autonomous systems developers to meet and discuss the strategic trends of Russian military robotics and military AI. A target recognition system, for example, has been one of the topics essential for most combat systems. It may look like a universal module that can be mounted on drones, aerial vehicles, helicopters, and ships, as well as on ground vehicles. Design based on the modular principle is becoming increasingly ubiquitous.

Technopolis ERA develops a universal software and hardware complex for the research and testing of AI technologies. Among other tasks, this complex can be used to identify targets on the battlefield. Currently, its databank includes 100,000 images of objects in the optical range and 5,000 targets in the radar band. Designers aim to reach the maximum automation of Russian reconnaissance and combat systems. The ERA-based Machine Learning Centre teaches the neural network on virtual images and weapon models, and forms a database for implanting it into advanced military platforms (Заквасин and Комаров 2020).

The Rostec Corporation presented a neural network to control groups of combat drones at the Army-2020.

> The intelligent system is software for automated weapons control. After satellite, drone or radar reconnaissance detects a target, they send the data to the mobile control centre. The system processes the information and generates a command to the means of destruction, i.e., advanced missile, rocket or artillery robotic systems,

Rostec reported. "The new automated control system for drones can be used to equip the Armed Forces and other law enforcement agencies within the same framework of shaping a single information space." The neural network processes information from satellites or reconnaissance drones online and independently selects the mode of target acquisition. Testing has shown that the system's efficiency increased three times without human intervention. The neural network not only decides to resort to arms against a target but also chooses the type of weapon. The system has missile, rocket, or artillery systems in its arsenal now (Радыгин 2020). The ERA technopolis works on one of the most promising tasks in military robotics today, i.e., designing control of a swarm of diverse autonomous vehicles in the air, at sea, and on land (TVZvezda.ru 2020).

In conclusion, since 2014, Russia has experienced severe political and sanctions pressure from select Western countries. The concentration of military and civilian resources served as Russia's response to defend its national interests. The primary Russian documents on the national regulation of artificial intelligence – *the National AI Strategy and the Concept for the Development of Regulation of Relations in the Field of Artificial Intelligence and Robotics Technologies until 2024* – bypass the weapons and national defence issues. However, Russian authorities seek to amplify the potential of the defence industry to propel the national economy and, at the same time, utilise the capabilities of civil engineers for the needs of the Ministry of Defence.

Notes

1 See http://a-ai.ru/code-of-ethics/.

2 Статья V. Цели и задачи развития искусственного интеллекта, п.23 (Chapter V. Goals and main objectives of artificial intelligence development, Article 23, p. 12). http://publication.pravo.gov.ru/Document/View/0001201910110003?index=2&rangeSize=1.

3 Статья V. Цели и задачи развития искусственного интеллекта, п.49 (с) (Chapter V. Goals and main objectives of artificial intelligence development, Article 49(c), p. 22). http://publication.pravo.gov.ru/Document/View/0001201910110003?index=2&rangeSize=1.
4 (Author's notes from the conference). Sergey V. Garbuk, Deputy Director General and Head of Information Research at the Advanced Research Foundation, at the conference "Strategy for the Development of Technologies in the Field of Artificial Intelligence to Ensure the National Security of the Russian Federation," *Russian Military Expo Army 2018*, August 24, 2018.
5 See http://www.astgoz.ru/page/index.
6 See https://zakupki.gov.ru.
7 For more information on Centre for Special Projects of the Russian Defence Ministry, see https://ens.mil.ru/science/SRI/information.htm?id=11739@morfOrgScience.
8 For more information on the Scientific and Technical Committee for Arms Development, see https://structure.mil.ru/structure/ministry_of_defence/details.htm?id=12405@egOrganization.
9 For more information on R&D Organization, see https://ens.mil.ru/science/SRI.htm.
10 For more information on the 3rd Institute, see https://ens.mil.ru/science/SRI/information.htm?id=10994@morfOrgScience.
11 See ERA Technopolis's website at https://www.era-tehnopolis.ru.
12 See https://www.rusarmyexpo.ru/visiting/forum-maps/obiekty.

References

1Prime.ru. 2012. "Ростехнологии" сократят число холдингов до 13 с 17 (Rostechnologies will reduce the number of holdings to 13 from 17)." https://1prime.ru/Machines/20121218/757970597.html.

Advanced Research Foundation. 2020. "ФПИ создаст технологию дешифровки снимков из космоса с помощью искусственного интеллекта (ARF will create a technology for decrypting images made from space by using AI)." https://fpi.gov.ru/press/media/fpi-sozdast-tekhnologiyu-deshifrovki-snimkov-iz-kosmosa-s-pomoshchyu-iskusstvennogo-intellekta/.

Analytical Centre for the Government of the Russian Federation. 2019. "Паспорт национальной программы "Цифровая экономика Российской Федерации" (Passport of the national program "digital economy of the Russian Federation")." https://digital.gov.ru/uploaded/files/natsionalnaya-programmesma-tsifrovaya-ekonomika-rossijskoj-federatsii_NcN2nOO.pdf.

CSET. 2019. "Translation: decree of the President of the Russian Federation on the development of artificial intelligence in the Russian Federation (Указ Президента Российской Федерации "О развитии искусственного интеллекта в Российской Федерации")." https://cset.georgetown.edu/research/decree-of-the-president-of-the-russian-federation-on-the-development-of-artificial-intelligence-in-the-russian-federation/-:~:text=The following document is Russia's national strategy for, to build Russia into a leading AI power.

GARANT. 2020. "Распоряжение Правительства РФ от 19 августа 2020 г. № 2129-р Об утверждении Концепции развития регулирования отношений в сфере технологий искусственного интеллекта и робототехники на период до 2024 г. (Decree of the Government of the Russian Federation No. 2129-R of August 19, 2020 on approval of the concept of development of regulation of relations in the field of artificial intelligence and robotics technologies for the period up to 2024)." http://www.garant.ru/products/ipo/prime/doc/74460628/.

Government of the Russian Federation. 1993. "Закон РФ "О Государственной Тайне" От 21.07.1993 N 5485-1 (Последняя Редакция) (Law of the Russian Federation "on state secrets" of 21.07.1993 N 5485-1 (last edition)." http://www.consultant.ru/document/cons_doc_LAW_2481.

———. 1998. "Федеральный Закон От 13.04.1998 г. № 60-ФЗ (Federal Law of 13.04.1998 No. 60-FZ) (Federal Law of 13.04.1998 No. 60-FZ) (Federal Law No. 60-FZ of 13.04.1998 "about the conversion of the defence industry in the Russian Federation)." http://www.kremlin.ru/acts/bank/12216/page/1.

———.2019. "Указ Президента Российской Федерации "О Развитии Искусственного Интеллекта в Российской Федерации" (Decree of the President of the Russian Federation on the development of artificial intelligence in the Russian Federation)." http://static.kremlin.ru/media/events/files/ru/AH4x6HgKWANwVtMOfPDhcbRpvd1HCCsv.pdf.

———. 2020. "Government Decree No. 2129-r on the "concept for the development of regulation of relations in the field of artificial intelligence and robotics technologies until 2024". http://static.government.ru/media/acts/files/1202008260005.pdf.

Interfax. 2020. "Минобороны собралось создать искусственный интеллект на основе нейронных сетей за 390 млн руб (The Ministry of Defence is going to create artificial intelligence based on neural networks for 390 million rubles)." https://www.interfax.ru/russia/701920.

———. 2021. "Минобороны РФ создаст заказчика в сфере искусственного интеллекта (The Russian Ministry of Defence will create a customer in the field of AI)." https://www.interfax.ru/russia/769661.

NEWS.ru. 2020. "Искусственный интеллект поможет военному руководству России (Artificial intelligence will help the military commanders of Russia)." https://news.ru/technology/iskusstvennyj-intellekt-pomozhet-voennomu-rukovodstvu-rossii/?utm_source=yxnews&utm_medium=desktop.

REGNUM News. 2020. "Национальный центр управления обороной РФ применяет искусственный интеллект (The National Defence Control Center of the Russian Federation applies artificial intelligence)." https://regnum-ru.turbopages.org/regnum.ru/s/news/2836730.html.

RIA Novosti. 2018. "Путин рассказал о лидерстве в создании оружия на новых физических принципах (Putin spoke about leadership in creating weapons based on new physical principles)." https://ria.ru/20180301/1515531535.html.

Rossiyskaya Gazeta. 2012. "Владимир Путин: "Быть сильными: гарантии национальной безопасности для России" (Vladimir Putin: "to be strong: guarantees of national security for Russia)." https://rg.ru/2012/02/20/putin-armiya.html.

Russia Today. 2017. "'Whoever leads in AI will rule the world': Putin to Russian children on Knowledge Day." https://www.rt.com/news/401731-ai-rule-world-putin/.

Russian Defence Ministry. n.d.-a. "Главное управление инновационного развития Министерства обороны Российской Федерации (The Main Department of Research and Technological Support of Advanced Technologies (innovative research) Ministry of Defence of the Russian Federation)." https://structure.mil.ru/structure/ministry_of_defence/details.htm?id=11376@egOrganization.

———. n.d.-b. "46 Центральный Научно-Исследовательский Институт Министерства Обороны Российской Федерации (Central Research Institute NO 46 of the Ministry of Defence of the Russian Federation)." https://ens.mil.ru/science/SRI/information.htm?id=11391@morfOrgScience.

———. n.d.-c. "Искусственный интеллект в военном деле (Artificial intelligence in military affairs)." https://encyclopedia.mil.ru/encyclopedia/dictionary/details_rvsn.htm?id=13200@morfDictionary.

Russian Ministry of Digital Development, Communications and Mass Media. n.d. "«Цифровая экономика РФ» ("Digital economy of the Russian Federation")." https://digital.gov.ru/ru/activity/directions/858/.

Russian Ministry of Foreign Affairs. 2021. "Интервью директора Департамента международной информационной безопасности МИД России А.В.Крутских «Глобальная киберповестка: дипломатическая победа» журналу «Международная жизнь» (Interview of the Director of the Department of International Information Security of the Ministry of Foreign Affairs of Russia A.V. Krutskikh "global cyberagenda: diplomatic victory" to International Affairs magazine)." https://www.mid.ru/main_de/-/asset_publisher/G51iJnfMMNKX/content/id/4778945.

RussianElectronics.ru. 2014. "АСУ пятого поколения для РВСН использует только отчественные электронные компоненты (The fifth-generation automated control system for the Russia's Strategic Missile Forces uses only domestic electronic components)." https://russianelectronics.ru/asu-pyatogo-pokoleniya-dlya-rvsn-ispolzuet-tolko-otchestvennye-elektronnye-komponenty/.

TAdvisor.ru. 2019. "«Инфосистемы Джет» построили для Фонда перспективных исследованийнейросеть,выявляющуюсетевыеатаки(JetInfosystemshasbuiltaneuralnetworkfortheAdvancedResearchFoundationthatdetectsnetworkattacks)."https://www.tadviser.ru/index.php/Проект:Фонд_перспективных_исследований_(ФПИ)_(Разработка_решения_по_превентивному_выявлению_сетевых_атак).

TASS. 2018. "Путин рассказал о планах нарастить долю гражданской продукции в ОПК до 50% к 2030 году (Putin spoke about plans to increase the share of civilian products in the defence industry to 50% by 2030)." https://tass.ru/armiya-i-opk/4899582.

———. 2019a. "Греф объяснил, за что в Сбербанке любят искусственный интеллект (Gref explained why Sberbank loves artificial intelligence)." https://tass.ru/ekonomika/7092550.

———. 2019b. "Основные Задачи и Показатели Нацпроекта "Цифровая Экономика" (The main objectives and indicators of the national project "digital economy")." https://tass.ru/info/6101510.

———. 2019c. "Путин обсуждает с военными возможности использования искусственного интеллекта (Putin discusses with the military the possibility of using artificial intelligence)." https://tass.ru/armiya-i-opk/7277167.

———. 2019d. "Резиденты технополиса "Эра" получат налоговые льготы (Residents of technopolis "era" will receive tax benefits)." https://tass.ru/armiya-i-opk/6459925.

———. 2020a. "Мишустин заявил, что власти серьезно работают над цифровизацией (Mishustin said the authorities are seriously working on digitalization)." https://tass.ru/ekonomika/9765889.

———. 2020b. "Проект модернизации станций СПРН России будет готов до конца года (The project of modernisation of the Russian Ballistic Missile Early Warning System stations will be ready by the end of the year)." https://tass.ru/armiya-i-opk/7575667.

The International Affairs. 2012. "Владимир Путин: «Быть сильными: гарантии национальной безопасности для России» (Vladimir Putin: "to be strong: guarantees of national security for Russia")." https://interaffairs.ru/news/show/8286.

The National Security Strategy of the Russian Federation. 2021. "Указ Президента Российской Федерации От 02.07.2021 № 400 "О Стратегии Национальной Безопасности Российской Федерации" (Decree of the President of the Russian Federation of 02.07.2021 No. 400 "on the national security strategy of the Russian Federation")." http://publication.pravo.gov.ru/Document/View/0001202107030001.

TVZvezda.ru. 2014. "Национальный Центр Управления Обороной РФ Будет Работать Для Всех Стран ОДКБ (The National Defence Control Center of the Russian Federation will work for all CSTO countries)." https://tvzvezda.ru/news/vstrane_i_mire/content/201412232053-sdcf.htm?utm_source=tvzvezda&utm_medium=longpage&utm_campaign=longpage&utm_term=v1.

———. 2020. "Форум «Армия-2020»: интервью с Начальником ГУНИД МО РФ Андреем Гончаровым (Forum "Army-2020": an interview with the Head of the Main Department of the Ministry of Defence of the Russian Federation Andrei Goncharov)." https://tvzvezda-ru.turbopages.org/tvzvezda.ru/s/news/live_stream/content/20208271726-6DwBu.html.

Txnomania.ru. 2013. "Россия создает цифровую систему управления МБР (Russia is creating a digital ICBM control system)." https://texnomaniya.ru/voennaya-texnika/rossija-sozdaet-cifrovuju-sistemu-upravlenija-mbr.html.

United Procurement Information System. 2017. "ЗАКУПКА №31705409671 (Purchase No. 31705409671)." https://zakupki.gov.ru/223/purchase/public/purchase/info/common-info.html?regNumber=31705409671.

———.2018."ЗАКУПКА№31806660500(PurchaseNo.31806660500)."https://zakupki.gov.ru/223/purchase/public/purchase/info/lot-list.html?regNumber=31806660500.

———. 2019a. "ПРОСМОТР ИЗВЕЩЕНИЯ О ЗАКУПКЕ №31908468210 (Review of the purchase notification No. 31908468210)." https://zakupki.gov.ru/223/purchase/public/purchase/info/lot-info.html?lotId=11595524&purchaseId=8733066&purchaseMethodType=IS.

———. 2019b. "ПРОСМОТР ИЗВЕЩЕНИЯ О ЗАКУПКЕ №31907446370 (V review of the purchase notification No. 31907446370)." https://zakupki.gov.ru/223/purchase/public/purchase/info/lot-list.html?regNumber=31907446370.

Zvezda Weekly. 2020. "Все инфопути к победе ведут в Национальный центр управления обороной (All info paths to victory lead to the National Defence Control Center)." https://zvezdaweekly-ru.turbopages.org/zvezdaweekly.ru/s/news/t/20208172016-kGYTT.html.

Балашова, Анна (Balashova, Anna). 2019. "«Цифровой Экономике» Подберут Новых Кураторов Среди Госкомпаний ("Digital economy" will get new curators among state-owned companies)." РБК. https://www.rbc.ru/technology_and_media/30/05/2019/5cf0198b9a794757ac2fd762.

Бутрин, Дмитрий (Butrin, Dmitry). 2019. "«С России Берут Пример, к Нам Приезжают Учиться» Михаил Мишустин Об Инновационных Технологиях ФНС ("They take an example from Russia, they come to study with us," Mikhail Mishustin about innovative technologies of the federal tax service)." Коммерсантъ. https://www.kommersant.ru/doc/4165008.

Валагин, Антон (Valagin, Anton). 2018. "Искусственный Интеллект Для РВСН Испытали На Кондиционере (Artificial intelligence for the Russia's Strategic Missile Forces tested on an air conditioner)." Rossiyskaya Gazeta. https://rg.ru/2018/01/15/reg-cfo/iskusstvennyj-intellekt-dlia-rvsn-ispytali-na-kondicionere.html.

Галанина, Ангелина (Galanina, Angelina), Дмитрий, Людмирский (Lyudmirsky, Dmitry), and Роман, Крецул (Roman, Kretsul). 2018. "Оружие Разума: Российский Путь к Военному Искусственному Интеллекту (The weapon of reason: the Russian path to military artificial intelligence)." Izvestia. https://iz.ru/815370/angelina-galanina-dmitrii-liudmirskii-roman-kretcul/oruzhie-razuma-rossiiskii-put-k-voennomu-iskusstvennomu-intellektu.

Елистратов, В.В. (Elistratov, V. V.). 2020. "ГУНИД МО РФ. Взаимодействие Предприятий ОПК и Заказчика (GUNID of the Ministry of Defence of the Russian Federation. Interaction between defence industry enterprises and the customer)." New Defence Order Strategy. https://dfnc.ru/arhiv-zhurnalov/2020-3-62/gunid-mo-rf-vzaimodejstvie-predpriyatij-opk-i-zakazchika/.

Заквасин, Алексей (Zakvasin, Alexey), and Елизавета, Комаров (Elizaveta, Komarova). 2020. "«Сети с Глубинным Обучением»: Какое Значение Для Российской Армии Имеют Программно-Аппаратные Комплексы ("Networks with deep learning": what is the significance of software and hardware complexes for the Russian army)." Russia Today. https://russian.rt.com/russia/article/791747-programmno-apparatnyi-kompleks-armiya-era.

Кашемиров, Максим (Kashemirov, Maxim). 2020. "На форуме «Армия» обсудили будущее искусственного интеллекта (The future of artificial intelligence was discussed at the army forum)." TVZvezda.ru. https://tvzvezda.ru/news/2020829848-yAWFx.html.

Корнев, Тимофей (Kornev, Timofey), and Галимова, Наталья (Galimova, Natalia). 2021. "«Единая Россия» Увидела Риски в Развитии Искусственного Интеллекта (United Russia saw risks in the development of artificial intelligence)." РБК. https://www.rbc.ru/technology_and_media/17/08/2021/611b6d7e9a79471ebe4288ec.

Комаров, Антон (Komarov, Anton). 2018. "Искусственный Интеллект Стал Оружием Современной Холодной Войны (Artificial intelligence has become a weapon of the modern cold war)." GearMix.Ru. http://gearmix.ru/archives/40224.

Круглов, Александр (Kruglov, Alexander), Алексей Рамм (Alexey Ramm), and Евгений Дмитриев (Evgeny Dmitriev). 2018. "Средства ПВО Объединят Искусственным Интеллектом (Air defence systems will be combined by artificial intelligence)." Izvestia. https://iz.ru/733333/aleksandr-kruglov-aleksei-ramm-evgenii-dmitriev/sredstva-pvo-obediniat-iskusstvennym-intellektom.

Курильченко, Алексей (Kurilchenko, Alexey). 2019. "«Стрелец» - Не Имеющий Аналогов Комплекс Разведки. И Не Только Разведки ("Strelets" is an unparalleled intelligence complex. And not only intelligence)." Zvezda Weekly. https://zvezdaweekly.ru/news/t/2019111182-OaG3w.html.

Морозова, Василиса (Morozova, Vasilisa). 2018. "Минобороны РФ Рассмотрит Стандарты Для Искусственного Интеллекта (The Ministry of Defence of the Russian Federation will consider standards for artificial intelligence)." TVZvezda.Ru. https://tvzvezda.ru/news/201803200846-bppv.htm.

Петров, Иван (Petrov, Ivan). 2020. "Впервые Вуз Минобороны Начнет Готовить Специалистов По Робототехнике (For the first time the University of the Ministry of Defence will begin to train specialists in robotics)." Rossiyskaya Gazeta. https://rg.ru/2020/10/23/vpervye-vuz-minoborony-nachnet-gotovit-specialistov-po-robototehnike.html.

Радыгин, Иннокентий (Radygin, Innokenty). 2020. "Нейросеть Для Управления Боевыми Роботами Представил «Ростех» (Rostec presented neural network for controlling combat robots)." Potokmedia.Ru. https://potokmedia.ru/russia_world/216863/rosteh-pokazal-miru-nejroset-upravljajushhuju-gruppami-boevyh-robotov/.

Телеканал Санкт-Петербург. 2018. "Фонд перспективных исследований предложил ввести стандарты для искусственного интеллекта (The Foundation for Advanced

Research proposed to introduce standards for artificial intelligence).” https://topspb.tv/news/2018/03/20/fond-perspektivnyh-issledovanij-predlozhil-vvesti-standarty-dlya-iskusstvennogo-intellekta/.

Тигров, Константин (Tigov, Konstantin). 2018. “В Минобороны Рассказали о Применении Искусственного Интеллекта в ВС РФ (The MoD speaks about the AI use in the Russian Armed Forces).” TVZvezda.Ru. https://tvzvezda-ru.turbopages.org/tvzvezda.ru/s/news/forces/content/201803151914-bcyl.htm.

Хроленко, Александр (Khrolenko, Alexander). 2017. “‘Периметр’: Как Устроена Российская Система Ответного Ядерного Удара (“Perimeter”: how the Russian System of Retaliatory Nuclear Strike works).” RIA-Novosti. https://ria.ru/20170821/1500527559.html.

ЯRobot. 2020a. “Круглый стол «Технологии искусственного интеллекта в интересах обороны и безопасности государства» (Round table “artificial intelligence technologies for the defence and security of the state).” https://ya-r.ru/2020/08/30/kruglyj-stol-tehnologii-iskusstvennogo-intellekta-v-interesah-oborony-i-bezopasnosti-gosudarstva/.

———. 2020b. “Виталий Давыдов, ФПИ: мы никуда не денемся от использования боевых роботов (Vitaly Davydov, ARF: we will not get away from the use of combat robots).” https://ya-r.ru/2020/04/22/vitalij-davydov-fpi-my-nikuda-ne-denemsya-ot-ispolzovaniya-boevyh-robotov/.

Ястребова, Светлана (Yastrebova, Svetlana). 2019. “Чем займется российский альянс по развитию искусственного интеллекта (What will the AI Alliance Russia do).” Vedomosti. https://www.vedomosti.ru/technology/articles/2019/11/09/815838-alyans.

8

MILITARY AI DEVELOPMENTS IN RUSSIA

Samuel Bendett

Over the past decade, artificial intelligence moved front and centre in the Russian military's thinking about new concepts and technologies for future wars. Public discourse has grown and accelerated following the adoption of the national AI strategy in 2019, a guiding document for the government, the industry, private sector and academia for the institution of federal projects aimed at accelerating the application of artificial intelligence across the country. Domestic state programmes and funding, ongoing academic research, growing private-sector development, and efforts across state-supported and state-funded corporations and enterprises all pointed to the Russian government's commitment to stick to its claims of soon becoming one of the leading AI powers (CNA Corporation 2021b). Concurrently, the Russian military's thinking about artificial intelligence has become a public conversation among the country's practitioners, developers and users.

This chapter will analyse how the Russian defence and security establishment thinks about AI and what role artificial intelligence plays in the nation's defence and security planning. The content will draw upon open-source materials such as Russian-language magazines, journals and periodicals. It worth noting that the bulk of the text was compiled prior to the Russian invasion of Ukraine in February 2022, and this chapter should serve as a reference of the Russian military's thinking about AI in general, and in some applications in particular. Following the Ukraine war, and the swift imposition of IT and high-tech sanctions on the Russian Federation as a result, many efforts described here may be paused, put on hold, revised or reworked altogether, as the Russian government and the Russian Ministry of Defence (MOD) are seeking ways to adapt to the resulting environment. Precisely settling on where AI fits with the MOD plans can be a moving target, given the growing slate of public opinions and analyses on the use of AI in the Russian armed forces and the fast-pacing changes in the technology

DOI: 10.4324/9781003218326-9

itself. At the same time, the Ukraine war will serve as a significant origin of new lessons and tactics learned and adopted, which should drive the Russian military debate and adaptation. It is likely that additional MOD sentiment and discussions in the coming months will become available by the time this book is printed, either supporting or overriding some of the arguments made in this chapter. Therefore, this chapter should be treated as part of the evolving and ongoing debate on military-use artificial intelligence in Russia to augment the growing work on this topic.

Defining the Importance of AI – Russian Government's Sentiment

Statements made by the Russian President Vladimir Putin and his government between 2017 and 2022 to communicate the importance of AI have reflected the national aim to become an AI RDTE&F (research, development, testing, evaluation and fielding) leader – an ambition that can certainly be thwarted going forward via Western global sanctions that have hammered Russian IT and high-tech industry during the Ukraine war (Funakoshi et al., 2022). In his speeches, the Russian head of state noted that AI is essential and pivotal to Russia's future, necessitating extensive domestic research and development effort. At the same time, appeals for some form of international governance with Russia's participation are at least part of the Russian government's strategy. In September 2020, while addressing the United Nations, Putin stated that digital technologies tend to spread uncontrollably and, like conventional weapons, can fall into the hands of radicals and extremists, giving rise to huge risks (Vladimir Putin, as cited in D-Russia.ru 2020). He called on the international community to use new technologies for the benefit of humanity – to find the right balance between incentives for the development of artificial intelligence and justified restrictive measures (Vladimir Putin, as cited in D-Russia.ru 2020). Putin's address implied, that the international community should come to an agreement on AI regulation to manage potential threats from the point of view of military and technological security and traditions, law and morality (Vladimir Putin, as cited in D-Russia.ru 2020).

Putin is not the only high-level Russian official to appeal for some form of international AI control and oversight. In April 2019, Russian Security Council Secretary Nikolai Patrushev called on the international community to develop a comprehensive regulatory framework that would prevent the use of technologies such as AI from undermining national and international security (Russian News Agency 2019). At the same time, such public appeals contrast with Putin defining artificial intelligence as a crucial element for safeguarding Russia's own place in the world – notably, equating the development and use of AI with protecting Russia's "unique civilisation" (Putin, as cited in Tass.ru 2020b). Despite appealing to the international community to develop rules and red lines for AI use, the very same technology also appears to be exempt for the Russian leadership when put in the context of "Russia-ness" and the country's uniqueness. By noting that

Russia is a separate civilisation, the Russian head of state drew a line between appeals to find common ground on AI and safeguarding Russia's exclusive place in the world with the help of specific technological developments (Putin, as cited in Tass.ru 2020b). In 2022, speaking at the AI Journey annual conference, Putin noted that the artificial intelligence competition among states is fierce, and Russia's place in the world, along with the nation's sovereignty and security depends on AI research and development results. (Putin, as cited in Tass.com 2022b) In the wake of its invasion of Ukraine, defining national uniqueness has evolved into arguing for Russia's "technological sovereignty", a concept best described as diminished dependence on imported Western technology and growing reliance on the domestic ability to produce key high-tech systems of importance to strategic industries, such as AI (Wilde and Sherman, 2022).

Arguing for AI as a key national asset is also reflected in earlier public statements. In a September 2019 speech, the Russian president stressed that new technologies are changing the world, with artificial intelligence and unmanned (uncrewed) vehicles forming the basis for Russia's future development and growth (Putin, as cited in Tass.ru 2020b). Also, in 2019, Putin noted that the country's future was impossible without the development of AI (IZ.ru 2020). By 2021, the Russian president made additional statements highlighting the importance of AI for the nation's military and national security as a whole (CNA Corporation 2021a).

These statements are indicative of the Russian leadership's recognition that it is engaged in a technological competition with the other leading powers (i.e., the United States) for its very survival, with artificial intelligence playing a key part as a pivotal defence and enforcement mechanism. This sentiment is part of the official MOD and government discourse. Speaking at the Army-2021 military-technical forum, Oleg Khramov, Deputy Secretary of the Russian Security Council, noted that global digitalisation trends indicate that artificial intelligence technologies were becoming instruments of geopolitical influence, provoking military-political confrontation (Mitrohina 2021). High-tech-enabled nations like the United States are actively promoting global approaches that are beneficial to themselves to form the foundations for creating AI systems and regulating their use, thus creating threats to Russia's national security.

Echoing these sentiments are Russian military experts and academics, such as Dr Aleksandr Bartosh, a corresponding member of the Russian Academy of Military Sciences, who noted that the explosive growth of new technologies and innovations forms the foundations of the next "technological order" that will require changes in global governance (Bartosh 2021). In this environment, a state that will be able to formulate a development model that best meets future challenges will be able to adapt its military and government structures to the challenges of modern conflicts (Bartosh 2021). In this competition, the leading place in military-scientific research and armed forces development should belong to artificial intelligence, and safeguarding the Russian state from future threats must include understanding what AI technologies mean for the military (Bartosh

2021). Likewise, Ruslan Tsalikov, First Deputy Minister of Defence, noted that artificial intelligence was viewed by all leading countries, particularly the United States, as a means of achieving global domination (Bratsky 2021) – therefore, Russia should take a leading position in artificial intelligence development to ensure national security (Bratsky 2021).

Drawing a line around Russia's special geopolitical position reinforced by AI could, according to the government's reasoning, allow the country to maintain its power, sovereignty and independence. How such ambitions will survive the ongoing adaptation to the IT and high-tech sanctions is an open question. At this point, the MOD is trying to lead the way by reinforcing existing and creating new partnerships in the nation's AI research and development ecosystem, parallel to the civilian efforts to establish "technical sovereignty mentioned earlier (Tass.ru 2022). Almost a year into its invasion of Ukraine, any potential international cooperation on AI between the Russian Federation and other states is at once pivotal to the survival of the Russian AI industry, and limited given that the bulk of high-tech nations are observing sanctions against the country. Earlier, Moscow was participating in international discussions and forums like the United Nations, where many AI standards and applications were discussed – going forward, such participation may be revised or put on hold indefinitely as the global community pushes back against Russian actions in Ukraine. If such isolation may be long-term, it may reinforce MOD's position that it is in fact stacking up its capabilities against unfriendly nations seeking to undermine Russian Federation's ability to defend and secure itself.

Russian Military Establishment on the AI Use and Implementation

Artificial intelligence is an integral part of the MOD discourse on the future of war (CNA Corporation 2021b). The Russian military establishment envisions that humans will be in the loop and will remain the decision-makers for such systems and processes (Malov 2018). For example, in August 2020, Ruslan Tsalikov confirmed that the introduction of AI technologies in military systems would not lead to replacing humans, but will expand their opportunities in obtaining information, get faster and more accurate data processing and transmission, as well as increase the speed of decision-making and improve control systems operations (YaRobot.ru 2020). This sentiment was confirmed a year later by Deputy Defence Minister Yunus-Bek Yevkurov, who noted in August 2021 that no matter the quality of artificial intelligence, the decision is always up to the human commander (Arkadiev 2021).

Within the MOD, using AI in autonomous and robotic systems is one of the most visible aspects of the country's high-tech RDTE&F. This technology is viewed as a critical mission multiplier that should ultimately replace human fighters in dangerous assignments and situations. For example, as far back as 2013, the Chief of the General Staff General Valery Gerasimov envisioned that fully robotic formations should be capable of conducting independent combat operations (Maslennikov et al. 2020). In an often-quoted 2020 statement, Vitaly Davydov, Deputy Director of the Advanced Research Foundation (ARF, Russia's DARPA-like organisation), remarked that human fighters will eventually be supplanted by military robots that can act faster, more accurately and more selectively than people (Vitaly Davydov, as cited in Ria.ru 2020b).

Broadly speaking, Russian military thinkers admit that AI technologies have already found applications in today's military roles, such as decision support systems, natural language processing, data mining and pattern recognition tools and algorithms (Burenok et al. 2018). In 2018, the ARF proposed developing AI for image recognition, speech recognition, control of autonomous military systems and support for weapons life-cycle technologies for the nation's military (Top-SPB.tv 2018; Ria.ru 2019). Today, MOD's AI RDTE&F follows these patterns when it comes to systems and weapons developments (CNA Corporation 2021a), such as technology for creating "intelligent" robotics, and for the creation and use of multi-agent systems such as drone swarms (Burenok et al. 2018). At the same time, the Russian military has not openly demonstrated this technology in actual combat, especially against the backdrop of the Ukrainian defence ministry starting to use Western facial recognition technology to identify Russian active and deceased soldiers fighting in the country (Dave and Dustin 2022). This may be partly due to the classified nature of some of the Russian AI research. Still, the public admission by Ukraine of its artificial intelligence use in this war is a stark juxtaposition with relative Russian silence on its own active combat AI use at this point in the war.

Public statements on artificial intelligence technologies in the Russian military systems and processes emphasise AI as a decision-making tool that collects and analyses vast quantities of data for the final human input. In a 2021 public report on the development of artificial intelligence and autonomy in Russia published by the CNA Corporation, key "digitisation" to "intellectualisation" processes described the evolution of Russian military artificial intelligence technology and concepts (CNA Corporation 2021a; Maslennikov et al. 2020, 67–77). Russian military thought points to the further development of digital processes in today's military that should naturally progress to the widespread adoption and use of AI systems that can perform creative functions traditionally considered the human prerogative (Burenok et al. 2018). This eventual "intellectualisation" of weapons systems, military tactics and procedures could result in the evolution of the human role towards primarily monitoring the combat environment, conducting a comprehensive analysis of decisions made by robotic systems, as well as monitoring the issuance of attack commands (CNA Corporation 2021a; Maslennikov et al. 2020, 67–77). This Russian military discourse is also similar to the Chinese MOD's strategic thought on AI implementation (Pollpeter and Kerrigan 2021).

These "human-in-the-loop" (Common definition) scenarios are grounded in today's technological reality. However, it may be challenging to foresee how the ever-increasing speed of decision-making in the coming multi-domain wars may affect a human operator's ability to make the correct final decision (McDermott 2019). Some Russian experts think that their military intends to fully evolve from human to machine decision-making, by noting that the decision-making in combat operations would eventually be carried out by robotic systems (Maslennikov et al. 2020, 67–77). Such sentiments about future Russian AI-enabled combat remain aspirational, as the current technology does not allow for this level of independence (Malov 2018). Russia's current war in Ukraine likewise adds to the growing gap between the theoretical and practical applications of technology in combat, potentially casting doubt on the implementation of MOD's future AI and robotics plans as articulated earlier (The Economist 2022).

At this point, the MOD claims to adopt existing AI technology as an evolving tool that retains a central human role. A key example often cited in the Russian media is the country's National Defence Coordination Centre (NDCC), tasked with daily, round-the-clock oversight of military and defence activity (Rogoway 2015). According to open-source data, the MOD will utilise AI at the NDCC to assist in decision-making by collecting and submitting the necessary information for the human operators to understand the status of Russian forces in the country and around the world (Regnum.ru 2020). The NDCC specifically noted that it would not outsource actual decision-making to AI (Regnum.ru 2020). At the same time, no timeline was given for such AI application, indicating a more conceptual approach rather than near-term artificial intelligence use. According to open sources, multiple AI projects for decision-making in air-, land- and sea-based platforms are in the works across the MOD, with the defence industry promising to field such capabilities in the coming years (CNA Corporation 2021a).

Numerous Russian MOD RDTE&F institutions and enterprises conceptualise AI in autonomous operations. An often-cited public example is the ARF's Marker unmanned ground vehicle concept, a testbed for coordinated autonomous action in an uncertain environment (Martyanov, as cited in Tass.ru 2020a). For that, ARF is testing deep neural networks to assist in vehicles' decision-making – to teach the machine to perform tasks independently at a great distance from the operator (Martyanov, as cited in Tass.ru 2020a). Other military AI developments are influenced by Russia's involvement in current and recent conflicts that use human-operated technology. For example, the MOD apparently deliberated how AI should eventually direct swarms of air-, land- and sea-based autonomous systems based on its Syrian combat experience (Milenin and Sinnikov 2019, 50–57). The ongoing testing and evaluation of Uran-9 uncrewed combat ground vehicle is part of this post-Syria evaluation, and the MOD wants to determine the best way to use this new technology in future conflicts (Tass.ru 2021e). These deliberations and tests, however, did not result in the Russian military fielding autonomous weapons in Ukraine. Instead, the Russian forces are using mostly remote-controlled uncrewed aerial and ground vehicles (UAVs) to gather intelligence, conduct surveillance and demining operations, with a growing loitering drone application that may have onboard AI for target designation and recognition, a subject open to intense international debate due to lack of physical evidence (Knight 2022; Zhang, 2022).

The MOD organisations and institutions working on the military AI development include the afore-mentioned Advanced Research Foundation (Tass.ru 2018); the ERA technopolis, the MOD-administered research city tasked with AI and breakthrough technology development (Bendett 2018); Rostec, Russia's largest defence-industrial conglomerate with numerous subsidiaries working on AI RDTE&F; and the MOD's own R&D centres, such as the 46th Central-Science Research Institute (TsNII) and the Main Directorate of Scientific Research and Technological Support of Advanced Technologies (GUNID), that are working on high-tech systems, robotics, autonomy, and AI problem sets. In the words of ERA Deputy Director Andrei Morozov, AI technologies are a "cross-cutting" topic in almost all the technopolis research (Zakvasin 2019). To that end, ERA opened an artificial intelligence laboratory in September 2020 (Zakvasin 2019). This new centre will work on developing, training and testing neural networks on military equipment's virtual counterparts or physical mock-ups (Zakvasin 2019). Today, ERA is one of the focal points for Russian military AI development under sanctions, within a growing military ecosystem involving multiple institutions and enterprises that aim to continue research and development on behalf of the country's armed forces (Tass.ru 2022).

Of special interest for the MOD is the development of UAVs, with artificial intelligence as their key C4ISR mechanism. Speaking at the ARMY-2021 military-technical forum, Nikolay Dolzhenkov, General Designer of Kronshtadt JSC (the maker of Orion and other long-range military UAVs), noted that achieving advantages in the development of artificial intelligence systems will define success in the development of unmanned systems in general (Tass.ru 2021a). His sentiment that the robotisation of weapons of war has become a major global trend is echoed across the MOD and the Russian government (CNA Corporation 2021a). Going forward, the MOD priorities for military UAV development include introducing AI elements into the drone control systems, swarm development and man-unmanned teaming, and integrating these systems in the common operating environment with manned aircraft (Biryulin 2020; Russian News Agency 2021b). AI tests to enable multiple ground and maritime robotic systems are also supposedly taking place across the Russian military industry and services (Ria.ru 2019 2020a, 2020c).

There is ongoing MOD AI RDTE&F in ISR, command and control, and high-precision weapons development as well (CNA Corporation 2021a). As the Russian military is seeking to gain an advantage over perceived NATO and US strengths like precision-guided weapons in multi-domain operations (Khramchikhin 2018), the need for Moscow to formulate and then incorporate some form of AI into military systems will grow – as a mission multiplier and a key defence mechanism. There may be an additional and very realistic impetus to this development going forward, given the Russian military's bungled advance into Ukraine and a high casualty rate among its forces, juxtaposed against Ukraine's more nimble approach to defence and the readiness to use commercial AI against the invading force. The MOD is also conceptualising the development and use of AI in infrastructure, logistics, early warning, electronic warfare (EW) and other uses across the military services and branches (CNA Corporation 2021a). Just as important is MOD's work to foresee the consequences of using AI in combat, to clearly predict the problems expected in future conflicts and to promote damage minimisation and risk management systems across autonomous and manned platforms (Ilnitsky and Losev 2019).

A complementary problem set to the above-mentioned developments is Russia's use of AI in the broadly defined information and cyber operations space. One of the public clues to Russia's willingness to develop AI for such capability comes from an earlier speech by the MOD Deputy Minister Yuri Borisov. In 2018, he noted that artificial intelligence technologies will help Russia to effectively counter in the information space and win cyber wars. He noted that cyberwar has already become a reality and that today's battles first play out in the information space, with victory depending on the party most capable of controlling and organising it (Russian Ministry of Defence 2018).

Russian society's perceived vulnerability to Western influence, an often-cited reason for developing technologies to protect Russia's unique geopolitical civilizational role, serves as an amplifier for efforts to build out capabilities in the information environment and cyberspace. As a nation that considers itself on the defensive against consistent Western efforts to "hack" their way into key domestic military, socio-cultural and civilian targets (Russian News Agency 2021a), using advanced technologies like AI for monitoring, evaluation and interdiction becomes a key Russian mechanism to safeguard the country and retain the position of relative safety from such perceived encroachment (Perla 2021). Russian MOD officials also recognise that AI as a powerful information tool could target societies and political establishments by impacting the content, speed and volume of data and information delivery and perception (Ilnitsky and Losev 2019). Andrei Ilnitsky, advisor to the Minister of Defence, noted that artificial intelligence is already capable of creating fake news, shaping artificial reality online, hacking social media accounts and distributing special information there to influence the consciousness of citizens and to force politicians to make certain decisions. For Ilnitsky, these processes could produce risks of real conflicts between countries (The Ministry of Defence 2021).

Concurrently, AI could become a significant mission multiplier for Russia's own information and cyber operations worldwide, either government-sanctioned or done by independent groups (Clayton 2021; Stubbs 2021). Even as the MOD is not openly discussing the details of using AI for cyber operations, the country's civilian discourse on this topic sheds light on how such efforts take place. The open-source discussion points to AI as a tool that could potentially automate hacking and cyberattacks, bringing their complexity to an unprecedented level that is difficult to counter, thus dramatically increasing the chances of success (Medvedovsky 2017). In this context, it is possible to endlessly automate and increase the efficiency of such AI-enabled scenarios. A military that can master such concepts can impact how societies think and respond to key developments like international crises, potentially raising the stakes MOD experts like Ilnitsky and others.

Russian AI Debate: Ethics, Human-in-the-Loop and Independent Action

Multiple MOD academic institutions are involved in the research and analysis of the role of AI in current and future warfare. Their public deliberations offer a glimpse of priorities in military AI development, and present an overview of current and future advantages and concerns about this technology. According to a key analysis by the MOD's Academy of Rocket and Artillery Sciences (the Rocket Academy), the most achievable Russian interim AI results are "intelligent" technologies for situational control of military robotics and uncrewed aerial vehicles, along with the development of decision-making methods in a real-time complex dynamic environment (Burenok et al. 2018). The Marker UGV tests mentioned earlier are conducted along these research and development priorities.

The Rocket Academy offers some of the most detailed public discourse on the uncertainty of the human-in-the-loop approach to the military environment articulated earlier, given the exponential growth of information today, along with rising data uncertainty and its poor structure. Considering the psychological, mental and other limitations of human decision-maker's abilities, as well as the currently modest role of automation in decision-making, there is a growing need to use "intelligent" systems for planning and managing daily and combat activities to transform unstructured data into knowledge ready for immediate use (Burenok et al. 2018). In this envisioned environment, multiple uncrewed and robotic systems may be utilising "intelligent" decision-making systems, echoing earlier ARF statements on this matter (Burenok et al. 2018).

This Rocket Academy analysis envisions artificial intelligence disseminated throughout the military force structure, with each soldier equipped with an "intelligent" information service to provide intelligence, assess the data, and plan and control combat operations (Burenok et al. 2018). This data is envisioned as part of the initial stage of information wars, collecting and analysing intelligence information, fake news, press releases and cyber-attacks (Burenok et al. 2018). Today, such tactical collection and analysis are evident in the "Strelets" personal command, control, communications and reconnaissance system apparently issued to Russian soldiers, with the goal of connecting air- and land-based assets for precision strikes (Russian Aviation 2021). Despite the system's high-profile use in Syria, the Russian media was mute on its potential application in the ongoing Ukraine war.

Notable AI usage risks include disadvantages and limitations with incomplete consideration of ethical standards; insufficient cognitive systems development, leading to inadequate communication between humans and machines; unrepresentative training samples and incorrect initial data for self-learning of artificial intelligence; and widespread illegal use of AI methods to manipulate data. Additional identified risks include the accidental and deliberate impact of enemy efforts on AI-enabled armaments and military equipment (Burenok et al. 2018). Such risks and their consequences could be catastrophic in the case of an "independent goal-setting" by the military artificial intelligence system. Today, this goal setting is a purely human prerogative, but since AI systems could be more and more scalable, the volume of "human" functions transferred to them would also increase (Burenok et al. 2018).

The ethical dilemma on the current and future use of military artificial intelligence is AI simulating human commanders' decision-making in combat. The Rocket Academy analysis notes that since today's neural networks training is carried out on a sample limited by the knowledge of experts, as well as by the amount of information in official documents and manuals, AI would not be able to copy actual human thinking (Burenok et al. 2018). This current level of training will lead to the adoption by the artificial intelligence of solutions that do not go beyond the boundaries of the training sample itself. At the same time, the ingenious, resourceful, creative and, as a rule, high-risk solutions usually associated with human thinking in critical and stressful situations would be ignored (Burenok et al. 2018). This means that there could be situations on the battlefield in which the AI, unlike the human commander, would not be able to make an actual "intelligent" decision (Burenok et al. 2018). The human, as a "biological prototype" of an artificial neural network, arrives at this knowledge throughout his or her life under the continuous influence of external and internal conditions and factors (Burenok et al. 2018). It is this large volume of the specified conditions and actions – that is, the entire lifetime experience – that "does not fit into any computer program in principle" (Burenok et al. 2018).

Therefore, if the human experience is a factor that any advanced intellectual system could not replicate, then AI would ultimately remain limited in its capability, even if it could offer quick and precise – but limited – calculations and conclusions. It is interesting to note that a similar debate is taking place in the Russian civilian AI research, development and implementation space, with private sector companies debating whether a neural network can replace a human worker. In such debates, the current general sentiment includes AI gradually replacing simple and routine tasks, while truly creative tasks influenced by the ongoing daily uncertainty remain the human prerogative (Bunina 2022). The sentiments expressed above also do not differ too much form the US thinking on the emerging role of AI in military and intelligence analysis applications. The US Intelligence Advanced Research Projects Activity (IARPA) recently indicated plans to develop AI tools to help its analysts write better quality reports. IARPA hinted that such tools will assist but not replace analysts, since no AI program, no matter how sophisticated, can equal the combined expertise of humans who have built lengthy experience on their intelligence topics (Vincent 2023). While these deliberations indicate a potential point in time when such technology is possible, today's military combat still relies heavily on human-centred decisions and actions, with soldiers operating largely legacy systems designed decades ago. Russia's current military performance in Ukraine is part of this trend, with military and commercial technology use impacting the decisions made at the tactical and operational levels. (The Economist 2022).

In a June 2020 analysis, several authors writing for the MOD's *Voyennaya Mysl* (VM) magazine discussed the Russian military's growing "digitisation" and its impact on the future of the Russian forces. They also noted that this "digitisation" leads over time to the impending lessening of human role. As the technology matures, the human role will primarily consist of monitoring the combat environment and issuing commands to attack (Maslennikov et al. 2020, 67–77). The authors noted that the formation and adoption of decisions is eventually given to artificial intelligence systems, with a human role included only in exceptional critical cases and would consist mostly of supervision and control (Maslennikov et al. 2020, 67–77).

VM's main arguments do not deviate much from the accepted thinking on the impending military automation and the role of AI found in Western, American and other sources (Rempfer 2020). The Russian experts argue that there is complete certainty for the Russian armed forces in the "intellectualisation" processes – using AI to increase Russian defence capability (Maslennikov et al. 2020, 67–77). They refer to a quote from President Putin's 2019 speech that "AI should be used in military affairs, but not to the extent that it replaces a person everywhere" (Maslennikov et al. 2020, 67–77). They conclude that "man plus the machine" is a preferable scenario, in a nod to the American thinking on this topic (Maslennikov et al. 2020, 67–77).

One of the most-cited Russian MOD officials on military AI and robotics is General Vladimir Zarudnitsky, chief of the Military Academy of the Russian Armed Forces General Staff. In August 2021, Gen Zarudnitsky noted that with the creation of hypersonic, robotic systems and weapons based on new physical principles, the development and implementation of artificial intelligence technologies play a key role (Zarudnitsky 2021, 34–47). Furthermore, military command and all forces must be prepared for the fact that the development of AI will "soon" lead to the massive use of aerial-, underwater-, surface- and space-based robotic systems that work in swarms, with the ability to independently achieve goals (Zarudnitsky 2021, 34–47). Such swarms would be capable of creating a direct threat to any adversary defensive systems. Likewise, Zarudnistky noted that getting the maximum effect during reconnaissance and strike missions can be achieved by synchronising fire, manoeuvring, and highly mobile forces and assets using robotic systems and artificial intelligence (Zarudnitsky 2021, 34–47). To Zarudnitsky, increasing Russian firepower means saturating battle formations with inexpensive robotic platforms and UAVs, with certain systems potentially operating independently with onboard AI technologies. This concept is far from reality today, even for the most advanced militaries like the United States. Neither Zarudnistky nor others can indicate when this technology's future will dawn on the Russian military. The ongoing IT and high-tech sanctions against Russia may impact how microelectronics and key software and hardware for such a future may be procured, developed and tested, potentially impacting the MOD timelines and moving implementation schedules "to the right" across the defense-industrial sector.(Bendett 2022).

When it comes to the AI in the MOD's R&D institutions, the discussion turns to specific developments aimed at a more effective combat scenario. In a 2021 interview with the Arsenal Otechestva military magazine, Major Andrey Koluzov, head of the ERA's AI testing laboratory, remarked that his institution's R&D only considers realistic technologies created today, or those that would be built relatively soon. When it comes to AI, this implies the so-called "weak" (or "narrow") specialised artificial intelligence built for specific tasks and missions (Murahovsky 2021).

Discussing the ethics of AI in combat, Koluzov explained that when comparing the results of specialised AI and trained military personnel, it becomes clear that the human specialist works better when solving tasks in close to ideal conditions. At the same time, the conditions for using AI in combat would most certainly be different: lack of time to make a proper decision, possibly poor settings for target recognition and identification, enemy countermeasures and the need to review large volumes of data (Murahovsky 2021). In such situations, specialised AI, such as a decision-making tool mentioned earlier, will be much more effective than a human. In what has become an emergent Russian stance on AI in combat, questions about the "human factor" and "inhumanity" of military AI are discussed not from the standpoint of philosophy, but from the perspective of specific tests and evaluation of weapons and military equipment developed today. Koluzov hints that once such tests are carried out, and their results are analysed, the Russian military establishment would then discuss whether to replace a person with an AI algorithm (Murahovsky 2021). To the point, in July 2022, the ERA hosted a discussion on robotics, concentrating on the technical vision, pattern recognition and use of AI for the weapons development. Specifically, the application of artificial intelligence in robotic complexes and information systems, improvement of information systems with the use of technologies for processing large data sets, as well as the formation of mechanisms for information and software research were high on the agenda, with main emphasis placed on the practical use and introduction of such technologies in the Armed Forces (Sosnitsky 2022).

Numerous Russian academics are also involved in the ongoing debate on the role of AI in combat. Dr Alexander Perendzhiev, Associate Professor at Plekhanov University, noted that artificial intelligence is not capable of performing creative functions that are inherent in humans that could be key to victory. AI is also not capable of purely human sentiment that often plays a role in combat, such as patriotism, comradeship and readiness to sacrifice oneself – therefore, artificial intelligence cannot be "humanised." (Almazov 2021). Today, narrow AI like the GPS works well under normal conditions, yet it cannot function in challenging and unpredictable situations. Therefore, a human cannot yet entirely rely on artificial intelligence in combat (Almazov 2021).

Even before the February 2022 invasion of Ukraine, Russian military leadership, its researchers and scientists were concerned with the state of current AI skills and knowledge base across the MOD, and in Russia as a whole. Defence Minister Shoigu discussed the MOD needing 300 new programmes to build new skills for developing and testing robotic and high-tech systems across the military, emphasising the emerging trends in digitisation and AI use in foreign armies (Shoigu, as cited in Tass.ru 2021d). While the MOD is publicly announcing that it is racing to address the dearth of specialists, other officials are less confident and openly note scientific and organisational problems that may prevent the country from achieving its desired goals.

Andrei Ilnitsky specifically addressed the shortage of such specialised skills in his public statements before the Ukraine invasion. He noted that projects involving the use of artificial intelligence technology require mandatory expertise of specialised government and MOD structures. Such an examination at the interdepartmental level should be entrusted to the competent personnel (Tass.ru 2021c). Insufficient technical and scientific competencies and the unpreparedness of key decision-makers to implement systems with AI elements are a serious management threat to the country today. Ilnitsky stressed that no matter how robust the AI is, the final decision must remain with the person (Tass.ru 2021c). In practice, however, there is a danger that, when making decisions, the recommendations of technical specialists responsible for the development and operation of AI in specific government departments and agencies will not be properly verified by such decision-makers, due to their lack of relevant knowledge, education and competencies (Tass.ru 2021c).

This situation may be significantly exacerbated in the near future by the sanctions' aftershocks, when tens of thousands of key IT workers and developers fled Russia after February 2022 (Ria.ru 2022). While the Russian government is pulling out all stops to keep its IT workforce in the country, its efforts may be impacted by the US administration's attempts to lure this workforce to the United States, especially those who work on artificial intelligence (Jacobs and Nardelli 2022). The fight for the IT workforce may impact Russia's domestic-industrial sector as well, and the government is seeking to ensure a pipeline of IT and high-tech university graduates to work at domestic enterprises. The uncertainty over the domestic IT market going forward may impact the development of the military-oriented workforce as well, even as the actual data on MOD's AI workforce is likely to remain classified for the near future.

Moreover, according to Dr Vasily Burenok, President of the Academy of Rocket and Artillery Sciences, Russia needs to form the regulatory legal framework for artificial intelligence development and use (Burenok 2021). There needs to be a determination and normative consolidation of priority tasks for the MOD in peacetime and wartime, where artificial intelligence systems (AIS) should be used (Burenok 2021). Currently lacking across the Russian military are correct mathematical descriptions for specific problems that need to be understood by AI's software developers. Further, Burenok noted that MOD needs to support the efforts to have more specialised AIS software developers and create a common AIS test system (Burenok 2021). Today, Russia's MOD research and development institutions also lack common R&D standards for AIS, and the Russian troops lack actual AIS specialists (Burenok 2021). It is unclear how such debate will be impacted by the sanctions and their after-effects, given current government priorities and actions (Ria.ru 2022).

Conclusion – The Evolving Debate on Military AI in Russia

The debate on the use of artificial intelligence in the Russian military is growing, drawing in military experts and officials, academics and key decision-makers. Not all the ideas and opinions expressed in this chapter line up neatly to portray an agreed-upon set of conclusions. Instead, there is much overlap in some aspects of where AI fits in the Russian military, while there is also plenty of room for a diverse set of principles and discussions. Today, major aspects of military AI involve decision-making capacity as a major element in the ongoing Russian RDTE&F. At the same time, there are some notable questions still unresolved, such as the extent of human control over the increasing sophistication of "intellectual" mechanisms and systems (Maslennikov et al. 2020, 67–77). The debate over human control over AI systems will probably dominate such discussions for years to come.

Speaking at the ARMY-2020 military expo, Deputy Prime Minister for Defence and Space Industry Yuriy Borisov stated that the role of the human factor will only continue to grow – no matter what new technologies could come to the aid of humans, including robotics and AI, since all these technologies are created and used by humans. Borisov – the same minister who spoke about AI's role in cyber and info operations – reiterated that these technologies simply do not work without humans (Vesti.ru 2020). Likewise, Ruslan Tsalikov also noted that artificial intelligence will not replace people but should become their assistant (TVZvezda.ru 2020).

Official Russian discourse does not explain the way out of the misbalance of current thinking that humans will be in the loop and the envisioned lessening of the human role as AI technology becomes more sophisticated.

In some ways, Russian developments will probably seek to mirror the image of its competitors like the United States. As the current leader in high-tech military-industrial developments, the United States often sets the stage for global technology by achieving fast implementation and incorporation of advanced tech into existing and prospective military platforms. Therefore, recent American efforts to utilise AI in air-, land- and sea-based autonomous platforms are probably very high on the Russian radar (Mayfield 2020). Likewise, the Russian MOD is establishing an Artificial Intelligence Department tasked with interdepartmental R&D and acquisition coordination, similar to the DoD's JAIC (Russian News Agency 2021c, Tass.com 2022). Its official role as the main AI node in the military's ecosystem points to the highest departmental authority on the nation's military AI use and implementation - managing technologies, efforts and lessons learned are part of its mission, which may include prioritizing the efforts that can be most useful in combat, including analysing data for better battlefield management.

At the same time, Russian military AI RDTE&F can be broadly divided into a pre- and post-February 2022 phases. The phase before the war in Ukraine is characterised by relatively steady growth in initiatives and diversity in debate and opinions on the role of military AI. The relatively opaque and classified nature of some of this work meant that public statements cited here drove the impression of the Russian military on the technological ascendancy, building on the military reforms launched in 2010–2011. The post-February 2022 phase is unfolding now, with the Russian high-tech sector battered by global sanctions and the government seeking ways to replace the physical, technical and intellectual assets lost since the Ukraine invasion. The Russian military also expressed interest in learning from the civilian AI developments, in order to avoid duplicating research and development efforts while benefiting from available solutions (Russian News Agency 2022). Given past public admissions that image recognition, speech recognition, data analysis and data management solutions have benefited the nation's financial, medical and retail sectors of the economy (CNA Corporation 2021a.), it's likely that these technical solutions may find application in the nation's military domain in the coming years. Russia's military performance in Ukraine may likewise inform the domestic debate on the use of AI in combat, given how Russian forces' conduct demonstrated the gap between the theoretical approaches described in this chapter, and the gruelling practicality of the war. With the Russian MOD on the record with the need to develop military AI that can serve as an advantage on the battlefield, and as more public research becomes available, more light can be shed in the coming years on how the nation's military intends to incorporate AI and prepare its force for broader combat quality improvement and sophistication of military elements and systems. For now, public data sampled in this chapter offers an overview of key aspects of Russian military thinking, a debate worth considering as the war in Ukraine continues...

References

Almazov, Kirill. 2021. "Rise of the machines: can artificial intelligence replace the living soldier (Восстание машин: сможет ли искусственный интеллект заменить живого солдата)". *Riafan.ru*. August 5, 2021. https://riafan.ru/1498688-vosstanie-mashin-smozhet-li-iskusstvennyi-intellekt-zamenit-zhivogo-soldata.

Arkadiev, Andrei. 2021. "Evkurov spoke about the role of the commander and the intelligent use of AI on the battlefield (Евкуров рассказал о роли командира и разумном использовании ИИ на поле боя)". *TvZvezda.ru*. August 23, 2021. https://tvzvezda.ru/news/20218231528-wfQJx.html.

Bartosh, A. 2021. "Who, with whom and with what will fight in the XXI century (Кто, с кем и чем будет воевать в XXI веке)". *NVO.ng.ru*. August 26, 2021. https://nvo.ng.ru/gpolit/2021-08-26/1_1155_prognosis.html.

Bendett, Samuel. 2018. "Russia wants to build a whole city for developing weapons". *WarisBoring.com*. March 29, 2018. https://warisboring.com/russia-wants-to-build-a-whole-city-for-developing-weapons/.

Bendett, Samuel. 2022. "Russia's artificial intelligence boom may not survive the war". *DefenseOne.com*. April 15, 2022. https://www.defenseone.com/ideas/2022/04/russias-artificial-intelligence-boom-may-not-survive-war/365743/.

Biryulin, Roman. 2020. "Interview with Alexey Krivoruchko, Deputy Minister of Defence of the Russian Federation (Интервью заместителя Министра обороны Российской Федерации Алексея Криворучко)". *Redstar.ru*. December 30, 2020. http://redstar.ru/oruzhie-rossii-operezhaet-vremya/.

Bratsky, Yan. 2021. "Tsalikov said that Russia can become one of the leaders in artificial intelligence (Цаликов заявил, что Россия может стать одним из лидеров в сфере искусственного интеллекта)". *TVZvezda.ru*. August 26, 2021. https://tvzvezda.ru/news/20218231628-4bOIi.html.

Bunina, Valeria. 2022. "No more need for 'juniors.' They will be replaced by a neural net. («Джуны» больше не нужны. Их заменит нейросеть)". *Gazeta.ru*. February 11, 2022. https://www.gazeta.ru/tech/2022/02/04_a_14498737.shtml?updated.

Burenok, V.M., Durnev, R.A., Krjukov, Y. K. 2018. "Intelligent armament: the future of artificial intelligence in military affairs (разумное вооружение: будущее искусственного интеллекта в военном деле)". *Vooruzhenia I Ekonomika*, 1(43), 2018. http://www.viek.ru/43/4-13.pdf.

Burenok, Vasily. 2021. "AI in military affairs". Arsenal Otechestva, Issue #3 2021.

Clayton, James. 2021. "Russia hacking claims pose challenge for Biden". *BBC*. July 7, 2021. https://www.bbc.com/news/technology-57745324.

CNA Corporation. 2021a. "Artificial intelligence and autonomy in Russia report". *CNA*. May 2021. https://www.cna.org/centers/cna/sppp/rsp/russia-ai.

CNA Corporation. 2021b. "Artificial intelligence in Russia biweekly newsletters by the CNA Corporation's Russia Studies Program". *CNA*. March 2020–March 2021. https://www.cna.org/centers/cna/sppp/rsp/.

Dave, Paresh, Dastin, Jeffrey. 2022. "Exclusive: Ukraine has started using Clearview AI's facial recognition during war". *Reuters.com*. March 14, 2022. https://www.reuters.com/technology/exclusive-ukraine-has-started-using-clearview-ais-facial-recognition-during-war-2022-03-13/.

D-Russia.ru. 2020. "Vladimir Putin at the UN urged to seek a balance in the regulation of AI - both in the military sphere and in terms of traditions, law, morality (Владимир Путин в ООН призвал искать баланс в регулировании ИИ - как в военной сфере, так и с точки зрения традиций, права, морали)". *D-Rusisa.ru*. September 23, 2020. https://d-russia.ru/vladimir-putin-v-oon-prizval-iskat-balans-v-regulirovanii-ii-kak-v-voennoj-sfere-tak-i-s-tochki-zrenija-tradicij-prava-morali.html.

Funakoshi, Minami, Lawson, Hue, Deka, Kannaki. 2022. "Tracking sanctions against Russia". *Reuters*. May 2, 2022. https://graphics.reuters.com/UKRAINE-CRISIS/SANCTIONS/byvrjenzmve/.

Ilnitsky, Andrei, Losev, Aleksandr. 2019. "Artificial intelligence is both risks and opportunities (Искусственный интеллект - это и риски, и возможности)". *RedStar.ru*. June 24, 2019. http://redstar.ru/iskusstvennyj-intellekt-eto-i-riski-i-vozmozhnosti/.

IZ.ru. 2020. "Putin demanded to provide a breakthrough in the field of artificial intelligence (Путин потребовал обеспечить прорыв в сфере искусственного интеллекта)". *Iz.ru*. January 15, 2020. https://iz.ru/964458/2020-01-15/putin-potreboval-obespechit-proryv-v-sfere-iskusstvennogo-intellekta.

Jacobs, Jennifer, Nardelli, Alberto. 2022. "Biden seeks to rob Putin of his top scientists with visa lure". *Bloomberg*. April 29, 2022. https://www.bloomberg.com/news/articles/2022-04-29/biden-seeks-to-rob-putin-of-his-top-scientists-with-visa-lure.

Khramchikhin, Aleksandr. 2018. "Rethinking the danger of escalation: the Russia-NATO military balance". *CarnegieEndowment*. January 25, 2018. https://carnegieendowment.org/2018/01/25/rethinking-danger-of-escalation-russia-nato-military-balance-pub-75346.

Knight, Will. 2022. "Russia's killer drone in Ukraine raises fears about AI in warfare". *Wired*. March 17, 2022. https://www.wired.com/story/ai-drones-russia-ukraine/.

Malov, Andrei. 2018. "Advisor to the Russian Ministry of Foreign Affairs, on the reasons for Moscow's skeptical attitude towards the ban on "combat robots" (Советник ДНКВ МИД РФ Андрей Малов — о причинах скептического отношения Москвы к запрету «боевых роботов»". *Kommersant.ru*. August 16, 2018. https://www.kommersant.ru/doc/3714110?from=doc_vrez.

Maslennikov, O.V., Aliev, F.K., Vassenkov, A.V., Tlyashev, O.M. 2020. "Intellectualization is an important component of digitalization of the Armed Forces of the Russian Federation (Интеллектуализация — важная составляющая цифровизации Вооруженных Сил Российской Федерации)". *Voennaya Mysl magazine*, pp. 67–77. June 2020.

Mayfield, Mandy. 2020. "Services infusing AI into air, land, sea robots". *National Defense Magazine*. October 26, 2020. https://www.nationaldefensemagazine.org/articles/2020/10/26/services-infusing-ai-into-air-land-sea-robots.

McDermott, Roger. 2019. "Russia tests network-centric warfare in Tsentr 2019". *Jamestown*. September 25, 2019. https://jamestown.org/program/russia-tests-network-centric-warfare-in-tsentr-2019/.

Medvedovsky, Ilya. 2017. "Robot hacker. How to apply artificial intelligence to cybersecurity (Робот-хакер. Как применять искусственный интеллект в кибербезопасности)". *Forbes.ru*. December 21, 2017. https://www.forbes.ru/tehnologii/354793-robot-haker-kak-primenyat-iskusstvennyy-intellekt-v-kiberbezopasnosti.

Milenin, O.V., Sinnikov, A.A. 2019. "O roli aviatsii vozdushno-kosmicheskikh sil v sovremennoi voine. Bespilotnye 'letatel'nye apparaty kak tendentsiia razvitiia voennoi aviatsii". *Voennaia 'mysl'*, 11: 50–57. https://dlib.eastview.com/browse/doc/55953437.

Mitrohina, Ekaterina. 2021. "The Security Council declared the danger of AI as a tool of geopolitical influence (В Совбезе заявили об опасности ИИ как инструмента геополитического влияния)". *Gazeta.ru*. August 24, 2021. https://www.gazeta.ru/politics/news/2021/08/24/n_16424636.shtml?updated.

Murahovsky, Victor. 2021. "Artificial intelligence in military affairs (Искусственный интеллект в военном деле)". *Arsenal Otechestva*, #4(54). https://arsenal-otechestva.ru/article/1513-iskusstvennyj-intellekt-v-voennom-dele-2

Perla, Andrei. 2021. "No rise of the machines: artificial intelligence is a weapon in a mental war against Russia (Восстания машин не будет. Искусственный интеллект - это оружие в ментальной войне против Росси)". *Tsargrad.ru*. August 24, 2021. https://tsargrad.tv/articles/vosstanija-mashin-ne-budet-iskusstvennyj-intellekt-jeto-oruzhie-v-mentalnoj-vojne-protiv-rossii_403336.

Pollpeter, Kevin, Kerrigan, Amanda. 2021. "The PLA and intelligent warfare: a preliminary analysis". *CNA*. October 2021. https://www.cna.org/CNA_files/PDF/The-PLA-and-Intelligent-Warfare-A-Preliminary-Analysis.pdf.

Rempfer, Kyle. 2020. "Automation doesn't mean soldiers will be out of a job, chief says". *Army-Times*. January 14, 2020. https://www.armytimes.com/news/your-army/2020/01/14/automation-doesnt-mean-soldiers-will-be-out-of-a-job-chief-says/.

Ria.ru. 2019. "Advanced Research Foundation discussed artificial intelligence projects (В ФПИ рассказали о проектах в области искусственного интеллекта)". *Ria.ru*. February 20, 2019. https://ria.ru/20190220/1551137812.html.

Ria.ru. 2020a. "Armata tank will get AI (Танк "Армата" получит искусственный интеллект)". *Ria.ru*. August 27, 2020. https://ria.ru/20210827/armata-1747538483.html.

Ria.ru. 2020b. "Vitaly Davydov: terminators will replace human fighters (Виталий Давыдов: живых бойцов заменят терминаторы)". *Ria.ru*. April 21, 2020. https://ria.ru/20200421/1570298909.html.

Ria.ru. 2020c. ""Vityaz" became the first "robot" to reach the bottom of the Mariana Trench (Аппарат "Витязь" стал первым "роботом", достигшим дна Марианской впадины)". *Ria.ru*. May 9, 2020. https://ria.ru/20200509/1571206567.html?in=t.

Ria.ru. 2022. "Chernyshenko denied information about the massive outflow of scientific personnel from Russia (Чернышенко опроверг информацию о массовом оттоке научных кадров из России)". *Ria.ru*, April 8, 2022. https://ria.ru/20220408/nauka-1782583365.html.

Rogoway, Tyler. 2015. "Look inside Putin's massive new military command and control centre". *FoxtrotAlpha*. November 19, 2015. https://foxtrotalpha.jalopnik.com/look-inside-putins-massive-new-military-command-and-con-1743399678.

Russian Aviation. 2021. "Unique method of guiding attack drones tested in Syria". *Russian Aviation*. April 5, 2021. https://www.ruaviation.com/news/2021/4/5/16037/?h.

Russian Ministry of Defence. 2018. "The development of artificial intelligence is essential for the successful conduct of cyberwarfare (Развитие искусственного интеллекта необходимо для успешного ведения кибервойн)". *Russian MOD*. March 2018. https://function.mil.ru/news_page/person/more.htm?id=12166660@egNews.

Russian News Agency. 2019. "Russia's security chief calls for regulating use of new technologies in military sphere". *Russian News Agency*. April 24, 2019. https://tass.com/defense/1055346.

Russian News Agency. 2021a. "Cyber-attacks against Russia carried out from US, Germany, the Netherlands, expert says". *Russian News Agency*. July 7, 2021. https://tass.com/defense/1311463.

Russian News Agency. 2021b. "Long-range UAVs of enhanced endurance to be provided for Russian army by end of 2021". *Russian News Agency*. December 23, 2020. https://tass.com/defense/1241331.

Russian News Agency. 2021c. "Russia's top brass to set up Artificial Intelligence Department". *Russian News Agency*. May 31, 2021. https://tass.com/defense/1296019.

Russian News Agency. 2022. "The Ministry of Défense said that the register of AI technologies will accelerate the adoption of equipment into service" ("В Минобороны заявили, что реестр технологий ИИ ускорит принятие техники на вооружение"), *Russian News Agency*, December 22, 2022. https://tass.ru/armiya-i-opk/16658635

Sosnitsky, Vladmir. 2022. "Innovation is Evaluated by Practice: ERA has become an effective platform for constructive research dialogue "(ИННОВАЦИИ ОЦЕНИВАЕТ ПРАКТИКА Технополис ЭРА стал эффективной площадкой конструктивного исследовательского диалога) https://dlib.eastview.com/browse/doc/78978635 Krasnaya Zvezda (RedStar.ru), No. 80, July 25, 2022.

Stubbs, Jack. 2021. "SolarWinds hackers are tied to known Russian spying tools". *VentureBeat*. January 11, 2021. https://venturebeat.com/2021/01/11/solarwinds-hackers-are-tied-to-known-russian-spying-tools/.

Tass.com. 2022a. "Russian defence ministry introducing AI technologies in army," Tass.com, August 24, 2022. https://tass.com/defense/1497995

Tass.com 2022b, "Russia's future largely depends on success in AI sphere — Putin," Tass.com, November 24, 2022. https://tass.com/economy/1541465

Tass.ru. 2018. "Most MOD scientific schools work on artificial intelligence and robotics (Большинство научных школ Минобороны работает над искусственным интеллектом и роботами)". *Tass.ru*. March 15, 2018. http://tass.ru/armiya-i-opk/5034153.

Tass.ru. 2019. "Era will open a microelectronics development centre for artificial intelligence (В "Эре" откроют центр разработки микроэлектроники для искусственного интеллекта)". *Tass.ru*. July 26, 2019. https://nauka.tass.ru/nauka/6706420.

Tass.ru. 2020a. "Oleg Martyanov: in the future, there will be not an army of terminators, but an army of smart "Markers" (Олег Мартьянов: в будущем будет не армия терминаторов, а армия умных "Маркеров")". *Tass.ru*. June 29, 2020. https://tass.ru/interviews/8831445.

Tass.ru. 2020b. "Putin: the future of Russian civilization depends on the success in the development of high technologies (Путин: будущее российской цивилизации зависит от успеха в развитии высоких технологий)". *Tass.ru*. May 17, 2020. https://nauka.tass.ru/nauka/8493647.

Tass.ru. 2021a. "Expert believes that artificial intelligence is becoming the main task in the development of UAVs (Эксперт считает, что искусственный интеллект становится главной задачей в развитии БЛА)". *Tass.ru*. August 22, 2021. https://tass.ru/armiya-i-opk/12189355.

Tass.ru. 2021b. "Expert said that the robotization of war has become the main global trend (Эксперт заявил, что роботизация средств ведения войны стала основным мировым трендом)". *Tass.ru*. August 23, 2021. https://tass.ru/armiya-i-opk/12189407.

Tass.ru. 2021c. "The Ministry of Defence said that projects with artificial intelligence technologies require expertise (В МО заявили, что проекты с технологиями искусственного интеллекта требуют экспертизы)". *Tass.ru*. August 22, 2021. https://tass.ru/armiya-i-opk/12190099.

Tass.ru. 2021d. "Shoigu: UAVs have become a powerful weapon that requires new approaches in training specialists (Шойгу: БПЛА стали мощным оружием, требующим новых подходов при подготовке специалистов)". *Tass.ru*. August 6, 2021. https://tass.ru/armiya-i-opk/12073127.

Tass.ru. 2021e. "Uran-9 combat robots were used for the first time during a special training in the Volga region (На спецучениях в Поволжье впервые при ведении обороны применены боевые роботы "Уран-9")". *Tass.ru*. August 27, 2021. https://tass.ru/armiya-i-opk/12236651.

Tass.ru. 2022. "ERA Technopops will develop AI for the Russian Armed Forces (В технополисе "Эра" будут развивать технологии искусственного интеллекта в интересах ВС РФ)". *Tass.ru*. April 8, 2022. https://tass.ru/armiya-i-opk/14321799.

The Economist. 2022. "How rotten is Russia's army?". *The Economist.* April 30, 2022. https://www.economist.com/leaders/2022/04/30/how-rotten-is-russias-army.

Regnum.ru. 2020. "The Russian National Defence Control Centre uses artificial intelligence (Национальный центр управления обороной РФ применяет искусственный интеллект)". *Regnum.ru.* January 27, 2020. https://regnum.ru/news/polit/2836730.html.

TopSPB.tv. 2018. "Advanced Research Fund proposes to introduce standards for artificial intelligence (Фонд перспективных исследований предложил ввести стандарты для искусственного интеллекта)". *TopSPB.tv.* March 20, 2018. https://topspb.tv/news/2018/03/20/fond-perspektivnyh-issledovanij-predlozhil-vvesti-standarty-dlya-iskusstvennogo-intellekta/.

TVZvezda.ru. 2020. "The future of Artificial Intelligence was discussed at the Army Forum (На форуме «Армия» обсудили будущее искусственного интеллекта)". *TVZvezda.ru.* August 29, 2020. https://tvzvezda.ru/news/forces/content/2020829848-yAWFx.html?utm_source=tvzvezda&utm_medium=longpage&utm_campaign=longpage&utm_term=v1.

Vesti.ru. 2020. "Interview with Deputy Defence Minister Yuri Borisov". *Vesti.ru.* August 25, 2020. https://www.vesti.ru/article/2449057.

Vincent, Brandi. 2023. "IARPA to develop novel AI that automatically generates tips to improve intel reports." Fedscoop.com. January 6, 2023. https://www.fedscoop.com/iarpa-to-develop-novel-ai-that-automatically-generates-tips-to-improve-intel-reports/

Wilde, Gavin and Sherman, Justin. 2022. "Putin's internet plan: Dependency with a veneer of sovereignty". Brookings.edu. May 11, 2022. https://www.brookings.edu/techstream/putins-internet-plan-dependency-with-a-veneer-of-sovereignty/

YaRobot.ru. 2020. "Artificial intelligence technologies for the defence and security of the state roundtable (Круглый стол «Технологии искусственного интеллекта в интересах обороны и безопасности государства»)". *YaRobot.ru.* August 30, 2020. https://ya-r.ru/2020/08/30/kruglyj-stol-tehnologii-iskusstvennogo-intellekta-v-interesah-oborony-i-bezopasnosti-gosudarstva/.

Zakvasin, Aleksei. 2019. "Artificial intelligence is a means, not an end in itself: the Era technopolis discussed work of its unique centre («Искусственный интеллект — средство, а не самоцель»: в технополисе «Эра» рассказали о работе уникального кластера)". *Russian.rt.* November 24, 2019. https://russian.rt.com/russia/article/686954-tehnopolis-era-intervyu.

Zarudnitsky, V.B. 2021. "Victory factors in future military conflicts (Факторы достижения победы в военных конфликтах будущего)". *Voennaya Mysl*, 8: 34, 47.

Zhang, Michael. 2022. "Ukraine opens Russian drone, finds Canon DSLR inside". *PetaPixel.* April 11, 2022. https://petapixel.com/2022/04/11/ukraine-opens-russian-drone-finds-canon-dslr-inside/.

9

COMPARING MILITARY AI STRATEGIC PERSPECTIVES

Japan and South Korea

Ryo Hinata-Yamaguchi

Across the world, Artificial Intelligence (AI) is making its mark as one of the key technologies of the Fourth Industrial Revolution, enabling greater levels of autonomy and processing power that will transform many aspects of our society. Likewise, AI is also bringing evolutionary, or even revolutionary, changes to national security, with an increasing number of states pursuing the technology to enhance their defence readiness in areas including, but not limited to, command, control, communications, computers, intelligence, surveillance, target acquisition and reconnaissance (C4ISTAR), unmanned systems, missile defence, cybersecurity, administrative and logistical tasks, and many others. While still in the early stages compared to the United States (US), China, and Russia, both Japan and the Republic of Korea (ROK or South Korea) have taken some critical steps in adopting and operationalising AI for national defence. Their efforts have involved technological advances and significant policy reconfigurations. However, information on the developments in Japan and the ROK remains somewhat limited, not simply due to the level of secrecy but also due to the nascent nature of emerging technologies.

This chapter aims to comparatively assess the developments in Japan and the ROK, exploring the perceptions towards military AI and its governance in the national defence context. The chapter begins with an overview of the rationales and applications of AI for defence in Japan and the ROK, followed by discussions on AI governance and applications to the defence sector. It then looks at the ethical debates concerning AI-based systems and research and development (R&D). The chapter will also discuss the impact of the COVID-19 pandemic on Seoul and Tokyo's defence planning, its strategic implications, and the key questions going forward.

DOI: 10.4324/9781003218326-10

Rationales for the Pursuit of AI for National Defence

Several internal and external factors rationalise Japan and the ROK's pursuit of the development and application of AI for defence. The first rationale is threat-based defence planning, eyeing the developments in China, Russia, and North Korea. The advancements in China and Russia are particularly notable, with significant investments and use of state resources and close coordination between the military and civilian sectors to enhance their AI capacity and military applications. Pyongyang has taken strides in information communications technology (ICT) since the 1990s and is undertaking incremental but steady developments to adopt AI. The developments in China, Russia, and North Korea concern both Japan and the ROK – as existential and potential threats to security – as AI can be integrated into the various military capabilities that consequently change the character of warfare.

The second driver is based on the universal recognition of AI as a vital technology to enhance defence readiness and operations, ranging from C4ISTAR to logistical management. In the information age, the management of military capabilities and operations pivots on the effective and efficient processing and usage of data. Simply put, AI significantly enhances the ability for real-time data processing in ways beyond human capacity, making it an essential technology to enhance the military's operations. Over the past decade, both Japan and the ROK have significantly accelerated the modernisation of their armed forces with assets that require or can be further enhanced by AI systems for more effective and efficient operations.

Third, AI and robotics also have particular importance for Japan and the ROK in relation to their demographic challenges. While both Seoul and Tokyo have made efforts to attract foreign labour, they have simultaneously turned to AI and robotics as a solution to offset the personnel burdens and fill the gaps in human resources. The demographic issues affect not only the society and economy profoundly but also national defence. In Japan, where the Japan Self-Defence Force (JSDF) is an all-volunteer force, the number of available (and willing) applicants has diminished following demographic circumstances. Even though the recession of the 1990s–2000s caused an uptick in applicants, the economic recovery since the 2010s has led to a downturn in the number of those applying to serve the JSDF, forcing the Ministry of Defence (MOD) to raise its maximum age limit for enlistment. In the ROK, although the conscription system is still in place, the demographic challenge has nonetheless shrunk the pool of human resources that the armed forces can scoop up. For both countries, the alternatives to compensate for the personnel shortages in the defence forces are much more challenging than in the civilian sector, given the restrictions on recruitment and retirement age and also citizenship requirements. The struggles in adequately staffing the forces while also facing the urgent need to sustain and strengthen their defence readiness have led to the emphasis on automation through the utilisation of AI and robotics technologies.

Fourth, advances in the ICT sector have served as an enabler and a driver of their military application of AI. Both Japan and ROK have a high penetration of computer and internet usage, and have pursued automation and computerisation as the essential enablers of economic growth over the past several decades. The computing technologies in Japan and the ROK are worthy of note. Japan has made significant advances in supercomputing, with the K Computer setting the record as the world's fastest supercomputer in June 2011, which Fugaku later broke in June 2020. While the ROK has not ventured into supercomputing to the same extent as Japan, the country has demonstrated advanced levels of online infrastructures and strong adaptability to network-based operations and services. Thus, although both Japan and the ROK are still behind in the pursuit of AI for military purposes compared to the US, Russia, and China, both countries certainly have the potential to make significant advancements in the coming years.

Fifth, AI-equipped systems are essential for arms exports – which are vital to boost the trade profiles of both Japan and the ROK. South Korea has rapidly pursued the modernisation of its defence industry and equipment to bolster its trading power. In recent years, the ROK's proactive efforts in arms trade have been notable, particularly with sales to Asian, Oceanian, European, and Middle Eastern states. Even for defence companies, Hanwha Aerospace, Korea Aerospace Industries, and LIG Nex1 have been particularly successful. As for Japan, steps are being taken to sell domestically produced defence equipment, especially after the former Abe Shinzo administration revised the arms export ban. Progress has been mixed, with some agreements and successful sales, particularly in Southeast Asia, but also some unsuccessful attempts in securing contracts – most notably with Australia in the export of submarines. While both Japan and the ROK may lack the profile compared to the more experienced arms exporters, their strong potential in AI and robotics could significantly enable them to become more successful in arms sales, enhancing their trade performance and defence innovation.

Developments in Governance of Defence Acquisitions

Compared to the US, China, and Russia, the issuance of strategies and policies relating to AI in Japan and the ROK has been relatively recent. At the same time, notable developments are seen in governance with the successive administrations in both Japan and the ROK – regardless of political origins – pursuing new and emerging technologies for national defence. The accelerated pursuit of AI has coincided with reconfigurations in the governance of defence-related R&D and procurements. Given the two countries' strong industrial and technological capacity and potential, the recent efforts by the two governments have set the proper framework to facilitate the development, acquisition, and operationalisation of new and emerging technologies such as AI.

In Japan, the Artificial Intelligence Technology Strategy issued in 2017 by the government's Strategic Council for AI Technology discussed the importance of AI for society, but made no references to the utility for national defence.

Moreover, the document primarily focused on the political, bureaucratic, and organisational framework to enable the advancement of AI-related R&D. Specific references to the utilisation of AI for national defence are made (albeit briefly) in the National Defence Programme Guidelines and Mid-Term Defence Programme issued in December 2018, citing AI as one of the "game-changing" technologies for the management of operations but also to enhance automated capabilities such as unmanned systems (Japan Ministry of Defence 2018a, 18; Japan Ministry of Defence 2018b).

Clear developments are seen in Japan's governance of defence-related R&D and acquisitions, particularly with the establishment of the Acquisition, Technology & Logistics Agency (ATLA) in 2015 to replace the Technical Research and Development Institute. The purpose of the structural reform was to centralise and integrate the various departments related to R&D and acquisitions, as well as establish more robust networks to collaborate with academic institutions and related industries. In particular, the defence budgets since FY2020 have allocated approximately JPY 10.1 billion (US$95.8 million) to apply cutting-edge civilian technologies to the defence sector under the Innovative Science & Technology Initiative for Security Programme (Japan Ministry of Defence 2020b, 29).

As for the ROK, the National Strategy for Artificial Intelligence released in 2019 clearly states national defence as one of the key areas in applying AI. The utilisation of AI for national defence is also present in the ROK's Defence Reform 2.0, unveiled in July 2018 by the then Moon Jae-in administration, vowing to "use scientific and technological advancements of the Fourth Industrial Revolution to overcome resource shortage and adapt to future battlefields" (ROK Ministry of National Defence 2018, 50). Indeed, the notion of implementing and utilising new and emerging technologies has been stressed by previous and current administrations. Nonetheless, what differs under the current defence reform plan is the substantial nexus with the nation's comprehensive AI strategy and the significant increase in military expenditures to strengthen the ROK's independent defence readiness.

As for the defence industry in the ROK, major reforms have taken place over the past couple of decades. The Defence Acquisition Programme Administration (DAPA) of the Ministry of National Defence (MND) was formed in 2006 to centralise and integrate the acquisition organs that were scattered across the MND and the different service branches. Significant changes occurred in operations, particularly in dealing with corruption and other problematic practices that have long plagued the ROK's defence acquisitions and the reputation of the defence sector overall.

In both Japan and the ROK, the pursuit of developments in AI has also led to changes in the defence industrial network, going beyond the industrial heavyweights and other manufacturers that traditionally supplied technologies to the defence sector. Start-ups and small-medium enterprises with expertise in new and emerging technologies, such as AI and robotics, have gained greater attention, making it essential for the defence ministries to expand their outreach.

The developments in Japan are particularly notable, with the MOD establishing several collaborative initiatives with start-ups specialising in AI. In May 2018, FRONTEO started a programme to train the JMSDF in AI-based technologies (PR Times 2018). Then in September 2020, ACES inked an agreement to advise the Japan Ground Self-Defence Force (JGSDF) on the utility of AI (PR Times 2020). As for the ROK, the MND is still dependent on the *chaebol* conglomerates, such as Hanwha Systems, that have been key players in many of the ROK Armed Forces' ICT-related programmes. However, in recent years, the MND has also teamed up with academic institutions like the Korea Advanced Institute of Science and Technology (KAIST) and several smaller companies specialising in AI and automated systems.

Furthermore, both Tokyo and Seoul have also reconfigured their recruitment programmes to employ specialists and technicians in various areas, including ICT (ROK Ministry of National Defence 2018, 94–95; Japan Ministry of Defence 2020a, 407). While hired under different processes from the "career-track" and other general recruits, technicians with expertise in new and emerging technologies have allowed the defence sector to draw on expertise that is otherwise unattainable in the MOD and MND. By doing so, the R&D programmes and the implementation and operationalisation of new and emerging technologies, including AI, have been significantly enhanced.

The reconfigurations and reforms of defence industry complexes and networks in both countries are much about improving the bureaucratic systems and establishing better means of technological R&D and acquisitions across the board and thus are not specifically about AI. Hence, many gaps need to be filled. In particular, the military application of new and emerging technologies, such as AI, requires proper coordination between the military sector and related industries and these industries' maturity. AI experts in Japan and the ROK have made pleas for industrial developments. For instance, Nakajima Hideyuki explains Japan's lag in AI, noting the small volume of data caused by the lack of proper business models and data collection systems and the shortage of funding in AI development (Majima 2017). Even for Korea, Hwang Ji-hwan argues that the AI-related investment and R&D are still insufficient, and the nascent nature of big data has impeded the military application of AI (Hwang 2019, 29–30).

Applications of AI in Defence

Despite the common rationales for implementing and operating AI in defence, there are notable differences between Japan and the ROK. The differences are based not only on strategic, operational, and tactical priorities but also on political factors that affect their defence planning and operations. Japan is still in the early stages of applying AI to defence, with many of the projects in the experimental and design stages of development. One key area where AI will be applied is C4ISTAR. The FY2020 defence budget allocated JPY 800 million (US$7.7 million) to "experiment with the application of AI to the radar image target identification" to enhance the effectiveness of ISTAR (Japan Ministry of Defence 2020b, 46). There is a particular focus on enhancing maritime patrols, with reports that the ATLA is collaborating with Hitachi Global to develop an AI-equipped system to identify vessels (The Straits Times 2018; Miki 2019). Developments are apparent, with reported plans to equip the Japan Maritime Self-Defence Force (JMSDF) Kawasaki P-1 maritime patrol aircraft with AI systems (Takahashi 2019).

AI is also expected to be applied to unmanned systems, as stated in the current Defence Buildup Programme that has outlined plans for various air, surface, and underwater capabilities (Japan Ministry of Defence 2022a). Plans for unmanned systems in the air and naval domains are already underway from previous defence plans, with the RQ-4B Global Hawk acquisition and studies on Unmanned Underwater Vehicles (UUV) (Japan Ministry of Defence 2019, 9–12, 26). Moreover, Japan is also working on the informed, intelligent, and instantaneous fighter project (i3 Fighter) that networks manned and unmanned tactical aircraft (Japan Ministry of Defence 2010). The project is planned to take place in three stages, with the first starting with trials of remote-controlled operations, the second to test swarm operations controlled by manned aircraft, and then the third to test autonomous operations (Kobara 2021). The project is already moving ahead, aiming to test the initial prototypes by 2024 and then work on the final product by 2035. While there is much to see regarding the actual progress of the i3 Fighter concept and other AI-related developments, the systems would undoubtedly be one of the keys to the JSDF's readiness against future threats and uncertainties.

Japan also plans to utilise AI for cybersecurity. Robust developments in the JSDF's cybersecurity operations have evolved over time, starting with establishing the JGSDF Cyber Defence Group in 2014. The MOD's plans to utilise AI for cybersecurity are more recent, with the research on the applications of AI to cybersecurity in 2018 and the plans to establish the AI/Cyber Security Promotion Office. Later, the FY2020 budget set aside JPY 30 million (US$277,700) to design a system that detects malicious e-mails and then determines the threat they pose (Japan Ministry of Defence 2020b, 5). The use of AI for cybersecurity is part of the government's growing efforts to protect the MOD's and JSDF's computer networks and AI systems from existential cyber threats – particularly after the defence industrial sector suffered several large-scale cyber-attacks in recent years.

Although Japan's application of AI in defence is still in its initial stages, the pace of development is expected to accelerate in the coming years. The FY2021 Draft Defence Budget devoted JPY 1 billion (US$9.5 million) to accelerating the application of AI and other cutting-edge civilian technologies in the next three to five years to meet "operational needs" (Japan Ministry of Defence 2021, 29), and the FY 2023 Draft Defence Budget has pledged to spend roughly a total of JPY 6.6 billion (US$50 million) on AI-related programs (Japan Ministry of Defence 2022). In particular, the current Defence Buildup Plan is pushing to develop an AI-based analysis system to aid commanders in making operational and tactical decisions, with the FY2023 defense budget devoting JPY 4.3 billion (US$32.5 million) to conduct R&D of the technology (Japan Ministry of Defence 2022b, 28).

Given the steady R&D developments in machine learning and bolder efforts by the previous Suga Yoshihide administration to advance ICT, Japan's potential capacity for the defence application of AI is growing, as already seen by the efforts of the Kishida Fumio administration. In particular, as Japan pursues more high-end capabilities and commits to more complex operations for multi-domain operations in the ground, maritime, air, cyber, space, and electromagnetic spectrum domains, the need for advanced information-based systems such as AI and quantum computing will grow in congruence.

In contrast, the developments in the ROK have been faster and more comprehensive, including advancements in automated weapons systems. The most notable is the development of AI-equipped sentry guns that first began in the early 2000s with the Samsung Techwin SGR-A1 (Korea Defence Acquisition Programme Institute 2017). Then in December 2010, DoDAAM unveiled the Super aEgis II "remote-controlled weapon station" equipped with a 12.7-mm machine gun and an optional 40-mm automatic grenade launcher (DoDAAM Systems 2021). While both the SGR-A1 and Super aEgis II are set to fire only with input from human operators, they can function as lethal autonomous weapons systems (LAWS) to autonomously survey, detect, track, and track fire on targets (Kumagai 2007; Parkin 2015).

The ROK also unveiled plans for the development of lethal unmanned aerial systems. In October 2020, DAPA announced it would acquire a range of lightweight UAVs, including those equipped with guns and platforms capable of conducting suicide missions (Yonhap News 2020a). At the same time, it also plans to build autonomous platforms for the naval domain. In December 2020, DAPA signed a contract with LIG Nex1 to develop an autonomous underwater mine detection platform (Yonhap News 2020b). While the level of autonomy the system will have is unknown compared to the SGR-A1 and the Super aEgis II, these platforms will likely enhance the efficiency in the detection and neutralisation of sea mines and submarines that remains to be some of the critical threats posed by North Korea.

Key developments are also seen in command and control, with the Intelligent ICT Surveillance and Reconnaissance System that improves the handling of ISTAR-related data, as well as in the long term to create "AI-based intelligent command and control system" that "analyse[s] and share[s] battlefield situations in real time" (ROK Ministry of National Defence 2018, 147). The MND and Hanwha Systems are already working on an "AI staff officer" system planned to be operational by 2025. According to the South Korean media, the system purports to assist commanders in making operational and tactical decisions by calculating and presenting data concerning the capabilities, location, and expected movements of adversarial forces (Joo 2017). Although the system is not designed to make decisions and issue orders autonomously, it increases the effectiveness and efficiency of operations by expediting the real-time processing of data to assist commanders. AI is also reported to be systemised in human resource management to recruit junior and non-commissioned officers, using bots to test and screen applicants and analyse their responses. Although the system is still in the trial phase, it is expected to offset the bureaucratic burdens in human resource management.

The distinctive applications of AI by Japan and the ROK are explained by the strategic demands and focus of the two countries. For Japan, improving ISTAR in the air and maritime domains is a priority given the archipelagic nature of the nation with a vast maritime territory and exclusive economic zones. Yet despite the demands, the personnel shortages in the air and maritime branches have been dire, where out of approximately 247,150 in the JSDF, about 150,850 are in the JGSDF while the Japan Air Self-Defence Force (JASDF) and JMSDF only have about 46,950 and 45,350 respectively (International Institute for Strategic Studies 2020, 279). Combined, much is about fielding the necessary assets to deal with the challenging security environment – most notably against China which has attained a quantitative and, in some areas, even qualitative edge in the military balance. For Japan, matching the Chinese People's Liberation Army (PLA) counterparts on one-on-one terms is beyond the JSDF capacity, requiring smart technologies to sharpen its assets and capabilities.

As for the ROK, much of the focus is on the varying North Korean threats, particularly guarding the inter-Korean border and nearby areas, including the Seoul metropolitan area. Although the ROK Army and ROK Marine Corp have 493,000 active personnel combined, the demographic issues and the burden from constant patrols have pushed the rationale for sentry drones and surveillance systems to guard against the North (International Institute for Strategic Studies 2020, 287–288). Even for the air and maritime capabilities, the focus is on North Korea – particularly against its submarines and small surface vessels, as well as unmanned systems. Although discreet, there are also concerns in the ROK about China. The sharpening and strengthening of defence assets would enhance ROK's defences against any undesirable actions by China.

Along with the technological developments in Japan and the ROK, questions emerged over how the forces will adapt to AI and transition into forces capable of conducting AI-enabled warfare. First, much depends on how AI will be adopted by their armed forces, including their operational doctrines, to ensure that emerging technologies improve their military readiness. The ROK has already taken some steps in this regard, with the establishment of the Artificial Intelligence Research and Development Centre under the ROK Army Training and Doctrine Command in early 2019, focusing on the application of AI as well as operational and tactical concepts and doctrines. For Japan, specific organisations dedicated to AI have yet to be established. However, each service branch of the JSDF has a Command and Staff College and the Joint Staff College that focus on developing new concepts and doctrines.

The second question concerns the actual effectiveness of AI in enhancing military operations. Indeed, AI would allow the processing of data at much greater speeds and volumes, allowing operators greater effectiveness and efficiency in collecting and processing battlefield information and engaging targets. Such attributes are critical given the time-pressing threats, such as attacks by ballistic missiles and hypersonic weapons, and other fast-paced threats, including cyber and electronic attacks, but also situations that are not programmed in the machine-learning systems. Still, at this stage, the above-mentioned capabilities are more about accelerating and enhancing the processes for achieving existing missions instead of creating new types of missions. Moreover, many also overlook potential challenges. In particular, AI does not guarantee accuracy and veracity. Consequently, the conclusions reached by AI systems would still need to be checked and even appropriated by human commanders – a process that would consume time regardless of how fast AI calculations were processed. Indeed, none of the above questions should discourage the utilisation of AI, as the technology would undoubtedly enhance defence capabilities in various ways. Nevertheless, Japan and the ROK would need to work out the relevant doctrines and procedures to ensure that AI properly enhances the readiness of the defence forces to carry out the missions effectively.

One problem is that many become over-captivated by the "humans versus AI" contests, often noting trials like the US's AlphaDogfight trials of the Defence Advanced Research Projects Agency (DARPA) Air Combat Evolution programme and similar programmes in other states like China. While various tests have shown how AI-driven systems have defeated human pilots, the question should be how humans can work with AI-equipped systems, not simply fight against them. Hence for Japan and the ROK (like other states), the key agenda is how they can formulate a practical, mission-capable operational framework.

The third question, relating to the second, is the actual effectiveness against the threats posed by China, North Korea, and Russia. While AI allows enhancements in readiness against the "guns and bombs" of the adversaries and competitors, dependence on AI-equipped systems also ups the vulnerabilities against threats in the cyber and electromagnetic spectrums – both of which are areas that Beijing, Moscow, and Pyongyang have pursued to inflict disruptive effects against technologically advanced opponents. Furthermore, there are bound to be greater complexities given that China, North Korea, and Russia have all pursued their means of hybrid warfare, which include greater readiness for both armed operations and counterstability operations with a strong emphasis on asymmetric effects, and with AI systems playing an important role. The developments point to the risks for both Japan and the ROK, where the operations executed by the opponents could be beyond the AI systems, thereby blunting the sharpness of readiness against the threats.

The fourth question is how AI systems can be tailored according to specific protocols and procedural caveats. For Japan, its constitution provides constraints on how Tokyo can use force. Specifically, systems with the ability to autonomously engage targets may work beyond the strict protocols concerning rules of engagement. Unless there are major revisions to the policies concerning the rules of engagement, or the constitution itself, the AI systems will be programmed with specific protocols that could, in turn, be counterproductive to the effectiveness of autonomous systems.

For the ROK, although there are no constitutional or legal restrictions that parallel those of Japan, there are sensitivities – particularly with North Korea. While focused on the North Korean threat, Seoul has also restrained itself from militarily responding to attacks and provocations by the Northern brethren as means of escalation control. Against this backdrop, autonomous systems that detect and engage targets along the border serve as a double-edged sword, where on the one hand they are critical assets for defence and border security, while on the other hand they could spark armed conflicts.

The fifth and final question concerns the implementation and operationalisation of AI systems that pivot on cultivating an AI culture within the ranks of the Japanese and ROK forces. Even though the systems currently pursued are not fully autonomous, transitioning to new systems requires a significant amount of education and training. Furthermore, the transition is not as easy as many may assume. While there may be overall support for AI systems that enhance defence readiness, the benefits and utilisation of AI may mean different things to different departments and roles within the forces. For instance, Japan's i3 Fighter programme could significantly alter the role of human aviators, where they take on roles more as coordinators of systems on top of their traditional roles as aerial combatants.

Ethical Controversies

Around the world, there have been many ethical controversies and debates concerning the military application of AI-equipped systems. Warfare itself is already filled with ethical questions, and the emergence of AI-equipped systems has raised even more concerns, particularly regarding autonomous "killer robots" and the manipulation of AI-equipped platforms. It is important to note that ethical questions concerning the use of AI for defence are far from straightforward and therefore need to be contextualised. The ethical debates are relatively narrow when it comes to the AI systems' ability to collect and process information, as well as mobility. Such features are already present in various consumer robots like autonomous vacuum cleaners and many other commercial platforms. However, there are undoubtedly sensitive and critical ethical questions regarding AI autonomously making decisions and taking actions – especially those that inflict damage and harm.

Both Japan and the ROK have participated in every Convention on Certain Conventional Weapons meeting regarding LAWS since 2014. Still, both have focused more on legal regulations and norms rather than taking any proactive steps to ban the technology. While Japan has been proactive in discussions on LAWS and has clearly stated it has no plans to develop such systems, they have shied away from calling for an international ban. The ROK has also concurred with the concerns over LAWS and denied the R&D of such systems. However, it simultaneously argued that it is "premature" to negotiate a legally binding instrument on LAWS and requested more meetings "to enhance our common understanding…without prejudging specific policy outcomes" (Government of the ROK 2018). The ROK's position has raised concerns, particularly given the development of platforms such as the SGR-A1 and Super aEgis II that have the ability to autonomously execute lethal actions.

Domestically, the debates in both Japan and the ROK concerning the military application of AI have been relatively low-key. While the usual debates over AI ethics and its impact on society are regularly heard in both Japan and the ROK, there is also the general recognition of AI and robotics as the inevitable and plausible means for development and modernisation – particularly given the demographic crises. Likewise, the military applications of AI and robotics are generally viewed as realistic, effective, and efficient means of enhancing and sustaining the readiness of the defence forces against threats. Moreover, the mild domestic reactions towards the military applications of AI can be explained by the lower levels of enthusiasm towards enlistment. The developments are not seen as zero-sum, with the employment of AI as the means of strengthening defence without increasing the human resource demands on the society. Hence, as long as the technology proves to be effective and safe, the level of resistance to applying AI for defence will remain mild.

Of course, some civil organisations and study groups by lawmakers have raised questions concerning the military application of AI – particularly regarding LAWS. The restrictions on LAWS have gained greater support, particularly in Japan, where there is a general bipartisan agreement not to pursue the R&D of LAWS. Still, the legislative debates on LAWS have been negligible, and broader discussions on the application of AI for defence remain limited. Hence while there is general opposition to "killer robots", the ethical concerns over the assistive role of AI in other areas such as C4ISTAR, human resources, cybersecurity, and others have not been adequately conceptualised and nuanced in the public and political domains. To a great extent, one could argue that the ethical debates over the military applications of AI have been outweighed by the need for automation and computerisation to fill the gaps and mount the optimum levels of readiness against the threats faced. At the same time, the weaponisation of AI has not been implemented nor conceptualised enough for a detailed, contextualised debate on ethics.

Controversies are seen in the academia-defence collaboration programmes, with growing concerns raised by opponents over what they see as the increase in the level of intervention and meddling by the government and militarisation of the academia. The controversies are most potent in Japan. In particular, a research funding programme known as the National Security Technology Research Promotion, established under the ATLA, has become a topic of significant controversy and led to divisions within the academic community regarding collaboration with the defence sector. The main opposition force is the Science Council of Japan (SCJ), which has historically opposed military-related projects and has not been shy in criticising the ruling Liberal Democratic Party. Tensions renewed in 2020 when the then Suga administration rejected six of the 105 scholars recommended by the SCJ to join an independent policy advisory group supposedly on political grounds. While the controversies are not specially about AI per se, they reveal the schisms that undermine the transfer of science and technology from the research to the defence sector.

Issues concerning academic-defence collaboration are also seen in the ROK, albeit to a lesser extent than Japan. Despite occasional tensions, academia-government collaboration for defence is not uncommon in the ROK, and robust industrial involvement in the defence sector has been a norm. However, there were international controversies in February 2018 concerning the R&D of autonomous systems through academia-defence collaboration programmes when Hanwha Systems and the KAIST established the Research Centre for the Convergence of National Defence and Artificial Intelligence. Soon afterwards, a group of AI researchers led by Toby Walsh of the University of New South Wales declared the boycott of KAIST over concerns that the joint research centre would lead to the creation of LAWS (Shalal 2018). While KAIST responded by claiming that it will not conduct R&D of LAWS, the issue nonetheless highlighted questions concerning the contents and direction of some of the academia-defence collaboration R&D projects.

There are also concerns over technological transfers to state and non-state actors, particularly given that the R&D of AI takes place in both the academic and private sectors. The risks of knowledge transfers to foreign and undesirable actors are not limited to cyber espionage but also through information-sharing via collaborative programmes. In the case of cyber, China, North Korea, and Russia are notorious for their cyber operations, raising grave concerns over the security of sensitive information relating to AI and other technological systems. As for collaborative programmes, there have been concerns in Japan regarding some universities' joint research programmes with Chinese counterparts linked to the People's Liberation Army (Gao et al. 2020). The implications are clear, with the potential transfer of scientific and technological knowledge that benefits the opponent's R&D but also creates numerous security vulnerabilities and potentially undermines the effectiveness of AI-based systems for Japan and the ROK. While there has been some progress in developing AI governance in the civilian sector, the defence sector has lagged behind. Like many states, the reconfigurations would span across various areas, including codes, laws, protocols, and education and training. Naturally, there are challenges, including the content of the changes and how smoothly and timely these can be implemented.

Impact of COVID-19

AI has gained renewed attention in the push to implement and utilise the technology during the pandemic, from contact tracing to the increased automation of operations under COVID-19 norms. Both Japan and the ROK have used big data in dealing with public health and safety crises. For the ROK, its robust response to COVID-19 can be attributed to exploiting big data to detect and trace the spread of the virus. Japan's use of big data has been much more moderate, given the legal limits in accessing and utilising citizens' information. Nevertheless, big data has been promoted as a more effective means of studying and simulating the general movement of people to better prepare for disruptions in critical infrastructures and non-traditional security crises such as natural disasters. Hence, while the approaches are different, COVID-19 has renewed Japan and the ROK's interest in AI to deal with non-traditional security threats and manage society during times of crisis.

In defence planning, there were some questions over the impact of COVID-19 on Japan and the ROK's defence modernization plans, given the economic contractions combined with the prioritisation of COVID-19 and economic recovery. While the economic effects of COVID-19 are long-term, the disruptive impact of COVID-19 on Japan and the ROK's defence plans have been relatively limited at this stage, albeit some delays and disruptions in the R&D, construction, and delivery of new systems. Defence budgets of both Japan and the ROK are continuing to increase at a remarkable rate. In Japan, the defence budget has continued to increase, particularly in 2022 when it announced a budget of JPY 6.82 trillion (US$51.5 billion) for FY2023 which is a 26% increase from the previous year as well as vowing to spend 2% of the GDP on defence by 2027. As for the ROK, Seoul overall has maintained its steady pace of increases in defence spending albeit with some disruptions. The draft defence outlays approved by the National Assembly in December 2020 were set at KRW 52.8 trillion (US$48.6 billion), only slightly less than the KRW 52.9 trillion (US$48.7 billion) requested by MND (Choi 2020). However, the FY2020 defence budget was cut by KRW 1.77 trillion (US$1.63 billion) – approximately 3.6% of the original budget – to deal with COVID-19 (Oh 2020). Nevertheless, Seoul's defence budget has continued to increase, standing at KRW 57.1 trillion (US$ 45.5 billion) for FY2023.

Despite the effects of COVID-19, both Japan and the ROK view the developments and application of AI for defence purposes as a strategic priority. At the same time, the extraordinary COVID-19 situation could cause delays in the implementation and delivery of the systems that would otherwise benefit from AI. The risks are particularly acute given that both Japan and the ROK are pursuing a cohort of heavy-duty acquisitions such as next-generation aircraft, advanced surface combatants and submarines, aircraft carriers, missile defence systems, and standoff capabilities that are already causing defence planning dilemmas and straining the budget. While many of the defence planning problems predate

COVID-19, there are still concerns over how the economic and logistical effects of the pandemic could create further complexities.

Questions Going Forward

The developments of AI and its application to defence in Japan and the ROK can be viewed through several aspects. There have been significant developments, with both countries issuing and executing various initiatives to advance AI and apply the technology to defence. Given that there is much work in progress, it is challenging to precisely assess the level of effectiveness from the defence readiness viewpoint. However, both countries are well positioned to make significant technological advances in the coming years. Despite the advanced technological capacity and potential, there are several issues that the two countries face. In particular, the strong insistence on indigenous developments in AI raises questions over the actual technological advances to meet the pressing demands to tackle new and emerging challenges. The questions are not simply about technological capacity and resources but also whether the necessary systems can be implemented and operationalised in time to meet the urgent challenges. Moreover, questions concerning ethics would grow and become embodied as AI technologies advance and are applied in both the civilian and defence sectors.

There are also several questions about the overall security strategy in the regional context. In particular, the developments in China, Russia, and North Korea certainly signify concerns for both Japan and the ROK. Despite their efforts, the volume and pace of the developments in Japan and the ROK in the military applications of AI are still inferior to those of China and Russia. Moreover, one also needs to consider the threats posed by new and emerging technologies, including AI, quantum computing, robotics, and hypersonic and laser weapons. Thus, the problem is not simply about "keeping up with the Joneses" but simultaneously developing defence and deterrence systems against those capabilities. The concerns are arguably more significant for Japan, which must face the Chinese, North Korean, and Russian military advances across all warfare domains. Problems are compounded by the high potential for an "AI arms race" that would accelerate as the states in the region all pursue the military applications of AI, raising concerns over collateral arms build-ups and sabre-rattling, as well as risks from the probability of errors (Scharre 2019). Such problems would lead to security dilemmas and risks that are far different from the arms races and "grey zone" situations ever experienced in the Asia-Pacific, further upping the dilemmas for both Japan and the ROK.

Regarding cooperation, both Japan and the ROK would need to work closely with their strategic partner – the US. Significant developments are already seen between Japan and the US, including closer alliance strategies and operations and growing attention to collaboration on new and emerging technologies (Nurkin and Hinata-Yamaguchi 2020). As for the ROK and the US, the alliance remains strong despite some periods of uncertainty. The demands to strengthen the partnership have grown, given the continued concerns over North Korea. Cooperation with the US is not limited to the transfer of technologies for future high-end systems equipped with AI but also standardised protocols and enhanced interoperability, which are critical to the alliances' readiness against both existential and emerging threats. Moreover, Japan-US and ROK-US cooperation would also be vital to deal with the regional implications of the developments in AI and its military applications.

Both Japan and the ROK will also need to work with one another. The fact that both countries are allies of the US already provides opportunities and justification for closer Japan-ROK-US trilateral cooperation. In particular, cooperation between Japan and the ROK would be most pivotal in air and maritime security, as well as ballistic missile defence and cybersecurity – areas where AI is anticipated to play significant roles. Yet, despite the many reasons for Japan-ROK cooperation from the regional security standpoint, the state of bilateral ties and differing approaches to regional security issues have significantly undermined the developments in defence cooperation between the two (Hinata-Yamaguchi 2016). Even if the relations are not adversarial, Seoul's and Tokyo's lack of effort to build a partnership is concerning.

Given the centrality of data to AI and the significance of AI in C4ISTAR, there are critical questions concerning information security. Stronger laws and measures are required in both Japan and the ROK to enhance their own national security, the alliance with the US, and cooperation with like-minded states. Japan is seeking to join the "Five Eyes" intelligence pact consisting of Australia, Canada, New Zealand, the UK, and the US. However, many legal and technical vulnerabilities in Japan remain, which paved the way for a number of cyber espionage and cyber-attacks. Even for South Korea, while having strict laws on information security, there have been notable cyber breaches to government, commercial, and industrial infrastructures in recent years – most notably from North Korea. Although it is easy to point towards the problems that need to be addressed, there are challenges, given that stricter information security measures could be met with opposition on the grounds of individual rights and excessive power to governments.

Both Japan and the ROK should also continue to work with other states to address matters concerning the use of AI in defence operations. In September 2020, both Japan and the ROK took part in the inaugural "AI Partnership for Defence" meeting hosted by the US DoD Joint AI Centre along with Australia, Canada, Denmark, Estonia, Finland, France, Israel, Norway, Sweden, the UK, and the US. The meeting was not an alliance pact but rather to discuss and bridge concepts on the "responsible use of AI, advance shared interests and best practices on AI ethics implementation, establish frameworks to facilitate cooperation, and coordinate strategic messaging on AI policy" (AI Partnership for Defence 2020). While international dialogues and initiatives on AI in defence are still in their early stages, Japan and the ROK need to continue working with other states.

Conclusion

For both Japan and the ROK, AI is critical for national defence. The characteristics of the technology allow greater levels of automation and computerisation that may significantly enhance the effectiveness and efficiency of their operations. Moreover, AI is vital for both Japan and the ROK to fill the gaps in personnel shortages and narrow the disadvantages caused by the quantitative deficit against their adversaries and competitors. Still, as discussed throughout this chapter, the developments in Japan and the ROK are indeed still in their early stages, and both states have significant potential to make substantial strides in the future. The question, therefore, is the direction and extent of the implementation and operationalisation of AI in national defence in the coming years. While much remains uncertain, the answers would become clearer through future defence plans that are expected to introduce and operationalise new capabilities and systems including AI, as well as better governance of the technology.

References

AI Partnership for Defence. Joint Statement. *AI Partnership for Defence (AI PfD)*. 15–16 September 2020.

Choi, Soo-hyang. "S. Korea's Defence Budget Rises 5.4 Pct to 52.8 tln Won in 2021." *Yonhap News*. 2 December 2020. https://en.yna.co.kr/view/AEN20201202010800325.

DoDAAM Systems. Super aEgis II. 29 August 2021. http://www.dodaam.com/eng/sub2/menu2_1_4.php.

Gao, Feng, Gigi Lee, and (Translated by Luisetta Mudie). "Japanese Universities' Ties to China's Military-Linked Schools Sparks Concern." *Radio Free Asia*. 30 November 2020. https://www.rfa.org/english/news/china/japan-pla-research-11302020174438.html.

Government of the ROK. "Statement to the Convention on Conventional Weapons Group of Governmental Experts on Lethal Autonomous Weapons Systems." 13 April 2018. https://conf.unog.ch/digitalrecordings/index.html?guid=public/61.0500/9DE8541C-724E-4B12-A25D-8AC1CB10FF42_15h23&position=1466.

Hinata-Yamaguchi, Ryo. "Completing the US-Japan-Korea Alliance Triangle: Prospects and Issues in Japan-Korea Security Cooperation." *The Korean Journal of Defence Analysis* 28 (3). Fall 2016: 383–402.

Hwang, Ji-hwan. 2019. "Applications of Machine Learning in North Korea and South Korea." In *The Impact of Artificial Intelligence on Strategic Stability and Nuclear Risk*, edited by Lora Saalman. Stockholm: SIPRI: 29–32.

International Institute for Strategic Studies. 2020. *The Military Balance 2020*. London: International Institute for Strategic Studies.

Japan Ministry of Defence. Medium Term Defence Programme (FY2019–FY2023). 18 December 2018a.

———. National Defence Programme Guidelines for FY 2019 and Beyond. 18 December 2018b.

———. 2022a. Defence Buildup Programme (Japanese version). Tokyo, Japan.

———. 2019. Defence Programmes and Budget of Japan - Overview of FY2019 Budget. Tokyo, Japan.

———. 2020a. Defence of Japan 2020. Tokyo, Japan.

———. 2020b. Defence Programmes and Budget of Japan - Overview of FY2020 Budget. Tokyo, Japan.

———. 2021. Defence Programmes and Budget of Japan - Overview of FY2021 Budget (Japanese version). Tokyo, Japan.

———. 2022b. Defence Programmes and Budget of Japan - Overview of FY2023 Draft Budget (Japanese version). Tokyo, Japan.

———. *shouraino sentoukini kansuru kenkyuukaihatsu bijon [Research and Development Vision of Future Fighters]*. Tokyo, Japan: Ministry of Defence Japan. 25 August 2010.

Joo, Kyung-don. "S. Korea Plans to Use AI to Assist Military Commanders." *Yonhap News*. 9 October 2017. https://en.yna.co.kr/view/AEN20171009001600315.

Kobara, Junnosuke. "Japan Aims to Deploy Unmanned Fighter Jets in 2035." *Nikkei Asia*. 1 January 2021. https://asia.nikkei.com/Politics/Japan-aims-to-deploy-unmanned-fighter-jets-in-2035.

Korea Defence Acquisition Programme Institute. 2017. *gukbang muinrobot siheompyeongga jeokyong bangan [Plan to Apply the Test Evaluations of Unmanned Systems for National Defence]*. Seoul: Korea Defence Acquisition Programme Institute.

Kumagai, Jean. "A Robotic Sentry for Korea's Demilitarized Zone." *IEEE Spectrum*. 1 March 2007.

Majima, Kayo. "AIkoushinkoku' nihon, sonogeninha gyousei? kigyou? kokuminsei? [Japan, the 'Underdeveloped Country in AI' Is the Cause the Administration? Corporates? Or the National Character?]." *JDIR*. 9 November 2017.

Miki, Rieko. "Eye in the Sky: Japan Seeks AI-Guided Surveillance for Patrol Planes." *Nikkei Asia*. 9 November 2019. https://asia.nikkei.com/Business/Aerospace-Defense/Eye-in-the-sky-Japan-seeks-AI-guided-surveillance-for-patrol-planes.

Nurkin, Tate, and Ryo Hinata-Yamaguchi. *Emerging Defence Technologies in the Indo-Pacific and the Future of US-Japan Cooperation*. Washington, DC: Atlantic Council. April 2020.

Oh, Seok-min. "300 bln Won of Defence Budget to be Cut for Extra Spending over Coronavirus." *Yonhap News*. 3 June 2020. https://en.yna.co.kr/view/AEN20200602011100325.

Parkin, Simon. "Killer Robots: The Soldiers That Never Sleep." *BBC Future*. 17 July 2015.

PR Times. FRONTEO, "kaijoujieitaiheno jinkouchinou 'KIBIT'wo mochiita koudokaisekigijyutsuno kensyuuwo kaishi [FRONTEO Starts Training JMSDF on 'KIBIT' AI-based Advanced Analysis Technology]." *PR Times*. 25 May 2018. https://prtimes.jp/main/html/rd/p/000000208.000006776.html.

———. "ACESga rikujoujieitaini AIgijyutsukatsuyounituiteno jogenwo okonaukotode goui [ACES Signs Agreement with JGSDF on Providing Advise to the JGSDF on Utility of AI Technologies]." *PR Times*. 29 September 2020. https://prtimes.jp/main/html/rd/p/000000014.000044470.html.

ROK Ministry of National Defence. 2018. *Defence White Paper 2018*. Seoul: ROK Ministry of National Defence.

Scharre, Paul. May/June 2019. "Killer Apps: The Real Dangers of an AI Arms Race." *Foreign Affairs* 98 (3): 135–144.

Shalal, Andrea. "Researchers to Boycott South Korean University over AI Weapons Work." *Reuters*. 5 April 2018. https://jp.reuters.com/article/us-tech-korea-boycott/researchers-to-boycott-south-korean-university-over-ai-weapons-work-idUSKCN1HB392.

Takahashi, Kosuke. "Japan to Outfit Kawasaki P-1 MPA with Artificial Intelligence." *Jane's Defence Weekly*. 13 November 2019.

The Straits Times. "Japan Developing Artificial Intelligence System to Monitor Suspicious Activity at Sea." *The Straits Times*. 31 August 2018. https://www.straitstimes.com/asia/east-asia/japan-developing-artificial-intelligence-system-to-monitor-suspicious-activity-at-sea.

Yonhap News. "Underwater Robot for Mine Detection." *Yonhap News*. 9 December 2020a. https://en.yna.co.kr/view/PYH20201209013300325.

———. "S. Korea to Acquire Suicide UAVs, Advanced Attack Drones for Future Warfare." *Yonhap News*. 19 October 2020b. https://en.yna.co.kr/view/AEN20201019005600325.

10

AUSTRALIA'S APPROACH TO AI GOVERNANCE IN SECURITY AND DEFENCE

S. Kate Devitt and Damian Copeland[1]

On 27 February 2021, Australia's Loyal Wingman military aircraft hinted at the possibility of fully autonomous flight at Woomera Range Complex in South Australia (Insinna 2021; Royal Australian Air Force 2021). With no human on board, the plane used a pre-programmed route with remote supervision to undertake and complete its mission. The flight's success and the Royal Australian Air Force's announcement to order six aircraft signalled an intention to incorporate artificial intelligence (AI) to increase military autonomous capability and freedom of manoeuvre. Air Vice-Marshal (AVM) Cath Roberts (Head of Air Force Capability) said, "The Loyal Wingman project is a pathfinder for the integration of autonomous systems and artificial intelligence to create smart human-machine teams" (de Git 2021). AVM Roberts also confirmed that "[w]e need to ensure that ethical and legal issues are resolved at the same pace that the technology is developed" (Department of Defence 2021b).

Just over six months later, on 25 September, Australia[2] won the silver medal at the 2021 DARPA Subterranean Challenge, also known as the *robot Olympics*. In the event, Australia used multiple robotics platforms equipped with AI to autonomously explore, map and discover models representing lost or injured people and suspicious backpacks or phones, or navigate tough conditions such as gas pockets. The outstanding performance confirms Australia's international reputation at the forefront of robotics, autonomous systems and AI research and development (Persley 2021).

In parallel to technology development, Australia is navigating the challenge of developing and promoting AI governance structures inclusive of Australian

DOI: 10.4324/9781003218326-11

values, standards, and ethical and legal frameworks. National initiatives have been led by:

1 Australia's national research organisation, CSIRO Data61 (Hajkowicz et al. 2019);
2 Government (Department of Industry Innovation and Science 2019; Department of Industry Science Energy and Resources 2020a, 2020b, 2021) in the civilian domain;
3 Defence Science and Technology Group, Royal Australian Air Force and Trusted Autonomous Systems in Defence (Devitt et al. 2021; Department of Defence 2021b).

Two large surveys of Australian attitudes to AI were conducted in 2020. Selwyn and Gallo Cordoba (2021) found that, based on over 2,000 respondents, Australian public attitudes towards AI are informed by an educated awareness of the technologies affordances. Attitudes are generally positive, and respondents are proud of their scientific achievements. However, Australians are concerned about the government's trustworthiness in using automated decision-making algorithms due to incidents such as the Robodebt (Braithwaite 2020) and #CensusFail (Galloway 2017) scandals. A second study of over 2,500 respondents found that Australians have low trust in AI systems but they generally accept or tolerate AI (Lockey et al. 2020). They found that Australians trust research institutions and defence organisations the most to use AI, and they trusted commercial organisations the least. Australians expect AI to be regulated and carefully managed (Lockey et al. 2020).

This chapter will begin with Australia's strategic position, Australia's definition of AI and identifying the Australian Defence Organisation's (ADO) AI priorities. It will then move into AI governance initiatives and specific efforts to develop frameworks for ethical AI in both civilian and military contexts. The chapter will conclude with likely future directions for Australia in AI governance to reshape military affairs and Australia's role in international governance mechanisms and strategic partnerships.

Australia's Strategic Position

Australia's current strategic position has been shaped by two major developments: (1) the announcement of AUKUS on 15 September 2021 (Morrison, Johnson and Biden, as stated in The White House 2021a, c), and (2) public commitment to NATO and AUKUS allies through sanctions, supply of humanitarian support and lethal weapons to Ukraine to defend against the invasion of Russia (Prime Minister, and Minister of Defence 2022). AUKUS confirmed a shift in strategic interests for the United States to the Asia-Pacific and away from the Middle East with the withdrawal from Afghanistan.

> Recognizing our deep defense ties, built over decades, today we also embark on further trilateral collaboration under AUKUS to enhance our joint capabilities and interoperability. These initial efforts will focus on cyber capabilities, artificial intelligence, quantum technologies, and additional undersea capabilities.
>
> *(The White House 2021c)*

Commitment to defend Ukraine signals a strengthening global alliance among liberal democracies, of which Australia is a part. The Prime Minister calls the conflict "'a very big wake-up call' that reunites liberal democracies to meet a polarising and escalating threat" (Kelly 2022). The 2020 Strategic Update identified new objectives for ADO.

TEXT BOX 10.1 NEW OBJECTIVES FOR AUSTRALIAN DEFENCE 2020

1 to **shape** Australia's strategic environment;
2 to **deter** actions against Australia's interests;
3 to **respond** with credible military force, when required.

These new objectives will guide all aspects of ADO's planning, including force structure planning, force generation, international engagement and operations.
To implement these objectives, ADO will:

- Prioritise our immediate region (the north-eastern Indian Ocean, through maritime and mainland South East Asia to Papua New Guinea and the South-West Pacific) for the ADF's geographical focus;
- Grow the ADF's self-reliance for delivering deterrent effects; expand defence's capability to respond to grey-zone activities, working closely with other arms of government;
- Enhance the lethality of the ADF for the sorts of high-intensity operations that are the most likely and highest priority in relation to Australia's security; maintain the ADF's ability to deploy forces globally where the government chooses to do so, including in the context of US-led coalitions;
- Enhance ADO's capacity to support civil authorities in response to natural disasters and crises.

(Department of Defence 2020a, 24–25)
(Department of Defence 2020a, 2.12)

With these in mind, Australia's global position has been elevated with the announcement of a new Australia, United Kingdom and United States (AUKUS) science and technology, industry and defence partnership (Morrison, Johnson, and Biden, as stated in The White House 2021a, c). This partnership is likely to increase data, information and AI sharing and align AI governance structures and interoperability policies (Deloitte Center for Government Insights 2021) to manage joint and cooperative military action, deterrence, cyber-attacks, data theft, disinformation, foreign interference, economic coercion, attacks on critical infrastructure, supply chain disruption and so forth (Hanson and Cave 2021). In addition to the AUKUS, Australia has a number of strategic partnerships, including the global "five-eyes" network of the United Kingdom, United States, Australia, Canada and New Zealand (Office of the Director of National Intelligence, 2022); the Quad – India, Japan, Australia and the United States (Shih and Gearan 2021); and local partnerships, including the Association of Southeast Asian Nations (ASEAN) (Thi Ha 2021) and Pacific family (Blades 2021).

The strategic issues identified in both the *Defence White Paper* (Department of Defence 2016) and the *2020 Strategic Update* (Department of Defence 2020a) put AI among priority information and communications technology capabilities, e.g.

> Over the next five years, Defence will need to plan for developments including next-generation secure wireless networks, artificial intelligence, and augmented analytics.
>
> *(Department of Defence 2020a, 41)*

Australia's Definition of Artificial Intelligence

Australia (Department of Industry Science Energy and Resources 2021) defines AI as follows:

> AI is a collection of interrelated technologies that can be used to solve problems autonomously and perform tasks to achieve defined objectives. In some cases, it can do this without explicit guidance from a human being (Hajkowicz et al. 2019). AI is more than just the mathematical algorithms that enable a computer to learn from text, images or sounds. It is the ability for a computational system to sense its environment, learn, predict and take independent action to control virtual or physical infrastructure.

Australia defines AI by its functions (sensing, learning, predicting, independent action), focus and degree of independence in achieving defined objectives with or without explicit guidance from a human being. The Australian definition encompasses the role of AI in digital and physical environments without discussing any particular methodology or technology that might be used. In doing so, it aligns itself with the OECD's Council on Artificial Intelligence's definition of an AI system:

> An AI system is a machine-based system that can, for a given set of human-defined objectives, make predictions, recommendations, or decisions influencing real or virtual environments. AI systems are designed to operate with varying levels of autonomy.
>
> *(OECD Council on Artificial Intelligence 2019)*

Australian Defence AI Priorities

While the Australian Department of Defence has not formally adopted a Defence AI Roadmap or Strategy, Australia has prioritised developing sovereign AI capabilities, including robotics, autonomous systems, precision-guided munitions, hypersonic weapons, integrated air and missile defence systems, space technology, information warfare and cyber capabilities (Australian Government 2021). Australia notes that AI will play a vital role in ADO's future operating environment, delivering on strategic objectives of shape, deter and respond (Department of Defence 2021a). AI will contribute to Australia in maintaining a capable, agile and potent ADO.

TEXT BOX 10.2 AUSTRALIAN SOVEREIGN INDUSTRY CAPABILITY PRIORITY: ROBOTICS, ARTIFICIAL INTELLIGENCE AND AUTONOMOUS SYSTEMS

Robotics and autonomous systems are important elements of military capability. They act as a force multiplier and protect military personnel and assets.

The importance of these capabilities will continue to grow over time. Robotics and autonomous systems will become more prevalent commercially and in the battlespace.

Australian industry must have the ability to design and deliver robotic and autonomous systems. This will enhance the ADF's combat and training capability through:

- improving efficiency;
- reducing the physical and cognitive load to the operator;
- increasing mass;
- achieving decision-making superiority;
- decreasing risk to personnel.
- These systems will comprise of:
  advanced robots;
  sensing and artificial intelligence encompassing algorithms;
  machine learning and deep learning.

These systems will enhance bulk data analysis. This will facilitate decision-making processes and enable autonomous systems.

(Australian Government 2021)

Potential military AI applications have been taxonomised into *warfighting functions* – force application, force protection, force sustainment, situational understanding – *and enterprise functions* – personnel, enterprise logistics, and business process improvement (Devitt et al. 2021). Operational contexts help discern the range of purposes of AI within ADO as well as diverse legal, regulatory and ethical structures required in each domain to govern AI use. For example, the use of AI in ensuring abidance with workplace health and safety risk management (Australian Institute of Health and Safety 2021; Centre for Work Health and Safety 2021) is relevant to Defence People Group,[3] whereas the use of AI within new weapons systems and the Article 36 review process is within the portfolio for Defence Legal (Commonwealth of Australia 2018). AI will also be needed to manage Australia's grey zone threats (Townshend et al. 2021).

The ADO acknowledges that they need to effectively use their data holdings to harness the opportunities of AI technologies. The Defence Artificial Intelligence Centre (DAIC) has been established to accelerate Defence's AI capability (Department of Defence 2021a, 35; 2020b). The ADO has launched *The AI for Decision Making Initiative* (Defence Science Institute 2020a, 2021; Defence Science & Technology Group 2021a) and a Defence Artificial Intelligence Research Network (DAIRNET) to develop AI "to process noisy and dynamic data in order to produce outcomes to provide decision superiority" (Defence Science & Technology Group 2021b).

These efforts include human-centred projects such as *human factors for explainable AI* and studies on AI bias in facial recognition (Defence Science Institute 2020b). The Department of Defence has committed to developing guidelines on the ethical use of data (Department of Defence 2021a), and the Australian government has committed to governance and ethical frameworks for the use of artificial capabilities for intelligence purposes (Attorney-General's Department 2020, Recommendation 154). Ethics guidelines will help Australia respond to a public debate on the ethics of facial recognition for military purposes even if biases are reduced (van Noorden 2020).

AI Governance in Australia

AI governance includes social, legal, ethical and technical layers (algorithms and data) that require norms, regulation, legislation, criteria, principles, data governance, algorithm accountability and standards (Gasser and Almeida 2017). Australia's strategic, economic, cultural, diplomatic and military use of AI will be expected to be governed according to Australian attitudes and values and international frameworks.

TEXT BOX 10.3 AUSTRALIAN VALUES

- Respect for the freedom and dignity of the individual
- Freedom of religion (including the freedom not to follow a particular religion), freedom of speech and freedom of association
- Commitment to the rule of law, which means that all people are subject to the law and should obey it
- Parliamentary democracy whereby our laws are determined by parliaments elected by the people, those laws being paramount and overriding any other inconsistent religious or secular "laws"
- Equality of opportunity for all people, regardless of their gender, sexual orientation, age, disability, race or national or ethnic origin
- A "fair go" for all that embraces:
  - mutual respect;
  - tolerance;
  - compassion for those in need;
  - equality of opportunity for all
- The English language as the national language, and as an important unifying element of Australian society

(Department of Home Affairs 2020)

Australia is positioning itself to be consistent with emerging best practices internationally for ethical, trustworthy (Ministère des Armées 2019), responsible AI (Fisher 2020) and allied frameworks for ethical AI in Defence (Lopez 2020; Stanley-Lockman 2021). To this end, Australia is a founding member of the Global Partnership on AI (GPAI),[4] an international and multi-stakeholder initiative to undertake cutting-edge research and pilot projects on AI priorities to advance the responsible development and use of AI built around a shared commitment to the *OECD Recommendation on Artificial Intelligence*.[5] The OECD has demonstrated a considerable "ability to influence global AI governance through epistemic authority, convening power, and norm- and agenda-setting" (Schmitt 2021). Since 2018, Australia has used a consultative methodology and public communication of evidence-based ethics frameworks in civil and military domains. The civil domain work is driven by CSIRO's Data61 (Dawson et al. 2019), and the military work is driven by Defence Science and Technology Group (DSTG) (Devitt et al. 2021).

AI Ethics Principles

In 2019, the Australian government sought public submissions in response to a CSIRO Data61AI Ethics discussion paper (Dawson et al. 2019). A voluntary AI Ethics Framework emerged from the Department of Industry Innovation and Science (2019) (DISER) to guide businesses and governments in developing and implementing AI in Australia. The framework includes eight AI ethics principles (AU-EP) to help reduce the risk of adverse impacts from AI and ensure the use of AI is supported by good governance standards – see Text Box 10.4.

TEXT BOX 10.4 AUSTRALIA'S AI ETHICS PRINCIPLES (AU-EP)

1 **Human, societal and environmental well-being**: AI systems should benefit individuals, society and the environment.
2 **Human-centred values**: AI systems should respect human rights, diversity and the autonomy of individuals.
3 **Fairness**: AI systems should be inclusive and accessible and should not involve or result in unfair discrimination against individuals, communities or groups.
4 **Privacy protection and security**: AI systems should respect and uphold privacy rights and data protection and ensure the security of data.
5 **Reliability and safety**: AI systems should reliably operate in accordance with their intended purpose.
6 **Transparency and explainability**: There should be transparency and responsible disclosure so people can understand when they are being significantly impacted by AI and can find out when an AI system is engaging with them.
7 **Contestability**: When an AI system significantly impacts a person, community, group or environment, there should be a timely process to allow people to challenge the use or outcomes of the AI system.
8 **Accountability**: People responsible for the different phases of the AI system lifecycle should be identifiable and accountable for the outcomes of the AI systems, and human oversight of AI systems should be enabled.

(Department of Industry Innovation and Science 2019)

Case studies have been undertaken with the industry to evaluate the usefulness and effectiveness of the principles. Many of the findings and due diligence frameworks will be helpful in the dialogue between defence industries, the Australian Defence Force and the Department of Defence. Key findings from Industry (Department of Industry Science Energy and Resources 2020b) include the following:

- AU-EP are relevant to any organisation involved in AI (private, public, large or small).

- Organisations expect the Australian government to lead by example and implement AU-EP.
- Implementing AU-EP can ensure that businesses can exemplify best practices and be ready to meet community expectations or any changes in standards or laws.
- Ethical issues can be complex, and businesses may need more help from professional or industry bodies, academia or experts and the government.
- Businesses need training and education, certification, case study examples and cost-effective methods to help them implement and utilise AU-EP.

The case studies revealed that the responsibilities of AI purchasers and AI developers differ. Each group needed internal due diligence, communication and information from external stakeholders, including vendors or customers, to establish accountability and responsibility obligations. Businesses found some principles more challenging to implement practically. The advice given by the government is that businesses ought to document the process of managing ethical risks (despite ambiguity) and to refer serious issues to relevant leaders. To support ethical AI, businesses are advised by the DISER to:

- Set appropriate standards and expectations of responsible behaviour when staff deploy AI. For example, via a responsible AI policy and supporting guidance;
- Include AI applications in risk assessment processes and data governance arrangements;
- Ask AI vendors questions about the AI they have developed;
- Form multi-disciplinary teams to develop and deploy AI systems. They can consider and identify impacts from diverse perspectives;
- Establish processes to ensure clear human accountability for AI-enabled decisions and appropriate senior approvals to manage ethical risks. For example, a cross-functional body to approve an AI system's ethical robustness;
- Increase ethical AI awareness-raising activities and training for staff.

The Australian government commits to continuing to work with agencies to encourage greater uptake and consistency with AU-EP (Department of Industry Science Energy and Resources 2020b). In the *2021 AI Action Plan*, Australia hopes that widespread adoption of AU-EP among business, government and academia will build trust in AI systems (Department of Industry Science Energy and Resources 2021). AU-EP are included in the *Defence Method for Ethical AI in Defence* report (Devitt et al. 2021, 48–50). However, some have questioned the value of AU-EP without them being embedded in policy, practice and accountability mechanisms. Contentious uses of AI in government, such as facial recognition by police, have not gone through ethical review and do not have institutional ethical oversight (ASPI 2022). While federal frameworks may not have seen effective operationalisation, New South Wales (NSW) has published its own AI Assurance Framework that mandates AI projects undergo ethical risk assessment (NSW Government 2022).

Standards

The Future of Humanity Institute at the University of Oxford recommends developing international standards for ethical AI research and development (Dafoe 2018; Cihon 2019). This is consistent with Standards Australia's *Artificial Intelligence Standards Roadmap: Making Australia's Voice Heard* (2020). Standards Australia seeks to increase cooperation with the US National Institute for Standards & Technology (NIST) and other Standards Development Organisations (SDOs). Australia aims to participate in ISO/IEC/JTC 1/SC 42, and the National Mirror Committee (IT-043) regarding AI. Standards Australia notes the importance of improving AI data quality and ensuring Australia's adherence to both domestic and international best practices in privacy and security by design.

TEXT BOX 10.5 ARTIFICIAL INTELLIGENCE STANDARDS ROADMAP: MAKING AUSTRALIA'S VOICE HEARD

Recommendations:

1 Increase the membership of the Artificial Intelligence Standards Mirror Committee in Australia to include participation from more sectors of the economy and society.

2 Explore avenues for enhanced cooperation with the US National Institute for Standards & Technology (NIST) and other Standards Development Organisations (SDOs) with the aim of improving Australia's knowledge and influence in international AI Standards development.

3 The Australian government nominate government experts to participate in ISO/IEC/JTC 1/SC 42 and the National Mirror Committee (IT-043). The Australian government should also fund and support their participation, particularly at international decision-making meetings where key decisions are made, within existing budgetary means.

4 Australian businesses and government agencies develop a proposal for a direct text adoption of ISO/IEC 27701 (Privacy Information Management), with an annex mapped to local Australian privacy law requirements. This will provide Australian businesses and the community with improved privacy risk management frameworks that align with local requirements and potentially those of the General Data Protection Regulation (GDPR), Cross-Border Privacy Rules (CBPR) and other regional privacy frameworks.

5 Australian government stakeholders, with industry input, develop a proposal to improve data quality in government services in order to optimise decision-making, minimise bias and error, and improve citizen interactions.
6 Australian stakeholders channel their concerns about inclusion, through participating in the Standards Australia AI Committee (IT-043), to actively shape the development of an international management system standard for AI as a pathway to certification.
7 The Australian government consider supporting the development of a security-by-design initiative, which leverages existing standards used in the market, and which recognises and supports the work being carried out by Australia's safety-by-design initiative.
8 Develop a proposal for a Standards hub setup to improve collaboration between standards-setters, industry certification bodies and industry participants, to trial new more agile approaches to AI Standards for Australia.

(Standards Australia 2020)

Human Rights

A report by the Australian Human Rights Commissioner (AHRC) (Santow 2021) concerning human rights and AI in Australia makes a suite of recommendations, including the establishment of an AI Safety Commissioner (Sadler 2021). Of relevance to this chapter are the recommendations to:

- Require human rights impact assessments (HRIA) before any government department or agency uses an AI-informed decision-making system to make administrative decisions [Recommendation 2];
- The government needs to make AI decision-making transparent and explainable to affected individuals and give them recourse to challenge the decision [Recommendations 3, 5, 6, 8];
- AU-EP should be used to encourage corporations and other non-government bodies to undertake a human rights impact assessment before using an AI-informed decision-making system.

Human rights impact assessments of AI in Defence will vary depending on the context of deployment, e.g. whether the AI is deployed within the warfighting or rear echelon functions. Notably, Defence has established precedence working collaboratively with AHRC, e.g. on "Collaboration for Cultural Reform in Defence" examining human rights issues, including gender, race and diversity; sexual orientation and gender identity; and the impact of alcohol and social media on the cultural reform process (Jenkins 2014). Thus, it is possible that Australia could work again with the AHRC on AI decision-making in the Australian Defence Force. As algorithms could unfairly bias recommendations, honours and awards, promotion, duties or postings against particular groups, e.g. women or LGBTIQ+. While not documented in the military yet, tech giants, including Amazon, have withdrawn AI-powered recruitment when they found that it was biased against women (Parikh 2021). There are also new methods to debias the development, use and iteration of AI tools in human resources (Parikh 2021).

Australian AI Action Plan

In the *Australian AI Action Plan* (Department of Industry Science Energy and Resources 2021), the Australian government commits to:

- Developing and adopting AI to transform Australian businesses;
- Creating an environment to grow and attract the world's best AI talent;
- Using cutting-edge AI technologies to solve Australia's national challenges;
- Making Australia a global leader in responsible and inclusive AI.

To achieve the final point, Australia commits to the AI ethics principles (Department of Industry Innovation and Science 2019) and the OECD principles (2019) on AI to promote innovative, trustworthy AI that respects human rights and democratic values. The OECD AI principles (2019) are given as follows:

1 AI should benefit people and the planet by driving inclusive growth, sustainable development and well-being.
2 AI systems should be designed in a way that respects the rule of law, human rights, democratic values and diversity, and they should include appropriate safeguards – for example, enabling human intervention where necessary – to ensure a fair and just society.
3 There should be transparency and responsible disclosure around AI systems to ensure that people understand AI-based outcomes and can challenge them.
4 AI systems must function in a robust, secure and safe way throughout their life cycles, and potential risks should be continually assessed and managed.
5 Organisations and individuals developing, deploying or operating AI systems should be held accountable for their proper functioning in line with the above principles.

In 2021, the OECD released a report on how nations are responding to AI ethics principles. In the report, Australia is noted as:

- Deploying a myriad of policy initiatives, including establishing formal education programmes in STEM and AI-related fields to empower people with the skills for AI and prepare for a fair labour market transition;

- Offering fellowships, postgraduate loans and scholarships to increase domestic AI research capability and expertise and retain AI talent. Australia has dedicated AUD 1.4 million to AI and machine learning PhD scholarships;
- Australia and Singapore, building on their pre-existing trade agreement, also signed the Singapore-Australia Digital Economy Agreement (SADEA), where Parties agreed to advance their cooperation on AI.

Recently the United States and Europe confirmed their commitment to OECD principles in a joint statement that:

> The United States and European Union will develop and implement AI systems that are innovative and trustworthy and that respect universal human rights and shared democratic values, explore cooperation on AI technologies designed to enhance privacy protections, and undertake an economic study examining the impact of AI on the future of our workforces.
>
> *(The White House 2021b)*

Australia will likely remain aligned with the AI frameworks of allies, particularly the United Kingdom (AI Council 2021) and the United States (National Security Commission on Artificial Intelligence 2021).

AI Governance in Defence

While Australia has not released an overarching AI governance framework for Defence, this chapter outlines an argument for such a framework that draws from publicly released concepts, strategy, doctrine, guidelines, papers, reports and methods relating to human, AI and data governance relevant to Defence and Australia's strategic position. Australia is a founding partner in the US's AI Partnership for Defense (PfD) that includes Canada, Denmark, Estonia, France, Finland, Germany, Israel, Japan, the Republic of Korea, Norway, the Netherlands, Singapore, Sweden, the United Kingdom and the United States (JAIC Public Affairs 2020, 2021). In doing so, Australia has aligned its AI partnerships with AUKUS, five eyes (minus New Zealand), the Quad (minus India) and ASEAN via Singapore.[6] In particular, Australia is seeking to increase AI collaboration with the United States and United Kingdom through AUKUS (Nicholson 2021).

AI in Weapons Systems

Computer software designed to perform computational or control functions has been used in weapons systems for over 40 years (Department of Defense 1978). Such weapons require thorough tests and evaluation to identify and mitigate risks of computer malfunction. This resulted in a recent drive for digital engineering (88th Air Base Wing Public Affairs 2019; National Security Commission on Artificial Intelligence 2021). AI and autonomous weapons systems

(AWS) do not necessarily coincide, but the application of Australia's international and domestic legal obligations to AI weapons systems will almost certainly affect Australia's ability to develop, acquire and operate autonomous military systems. Australia has stated that it considers a sweeping prohibition of AWS to be premature (Australian Permanent Mission and Consulate-General Geneva 2017; Commonwealth of Australia 2018; Senate Foreign Affairs Defence and Trade Legislation Committee 2019, 65) and emphasises the importance in compliance with the legal obligation to undertake Article 36 reviews to manage the legal risks associated with these systems (see International Committee of the Red Cross, 2006).

Article 36 of the Protocol Additional to the Geneva Conventions of 12 August 1949, and relating to the Protection of Victims of International Armed Conflicts, 8 June 1977 (Additional Protocol 1), provides:

> In the study, development, acquisition or adoption of a new weapon, means or method of warfare, a High Contracting Party is under an obligation to determine whether its employment would, in some or all circumstances, be prohibited by this Protocol or by any other rule of international law applicable to the High Contracting Party.

The Article 36 process requires Australia to determine whether it can meet its international legal obligations in operating AWS. Performing a thorough Article 36 review requires consideration of International Humanitarian Law (IHL) prohibitions and restrictions on weapons, including Customary International Law, and an analysis of the normal or expected use of the AWS against the IHL rules governing the lawful use of weapons (i.e. distinction, proportionality and precautions in attack). This includes ensuring weapon operators understand their functions and limitations as well as the likely consequences of their use. Thus, users of AWS are legally required to be reasonably confident about how they will operate before deploying them (Liivoja et al. 2020). The ADF Concept for future robotics and autonomous systems (Vine 2020) states:

> 3.10 Existing international law covers the development, acquisition and deployment of any new and emerging capability, including future autonomous weapons systems.
>
> 3.44 Australia has submitted two working papers to the LAWS GGE in an attempt to demonstrate how existing international humanitarian law is sufficient to regulate current and envisaged weapon systems; the first (Commonwealth of Australia 2018) explained the article 36 weapon review process and the second (Australian Government 2019) outlined the 'System of Control' which regulates the use of force by the ADF. Within the domestic legal system, the RAS (particularly drones) is being considered in the development and review of legislation on privacy, intelligence services and community safety.

Australia argues that "if states uphold existing international law obligations… there is no need to implement a specific ban on AWS, at this time" (Commonwealth of Australia 2019). However, the 2015 Senate Committee Report on unmanned platforms said,

> the committee is not convinced that the use of AWS should be solely governed by the law of armed conflict, international humanitarian law and existing arms control agreements. A distinct arms control regime for AWS may be required in the future.
>
> *(see para 8.30)*

The report recommended that:

> …the Australian Government support international efforts to establish a regulatory regime for autonomous weapons systems, including those associated with unmanned platforms.

Australia welcomes discussion (e.g. McFarland 2020, 2021) around international legal frameworks on autonomous weapons and how technological advances in weapons systems can comply with international humanitarian law (Senate Foreign Affairs Defence and Trade Legislation Committee 2019).

Ethical AI Statements across the Services

Different defence institutions in Australia have addressed the importance of ethical and legal aspects of AI in their operations. The Royal Australian Navy (2020) stated that the "development of trusted autonomous systems is expected to increase accuracy, maintain compliance with Navy's legal and policy obligations as well as regulatory standards, and if utilised during armed conflict, minimise incidental harm to civilians". The Army (2018) said it would "remain cognisant of the ethical, moral and legal issues around the use of RAS technologies as this strategy evolves and is implemented". Finally, the Royal Australian Air Force (RAAF) (2019, 10–11) mentioned that it would explore ways to ensure ethical and moral values and legal accountabilities remain central, including continuously evaluating which decisions can be made by machines and which must be made by humans. The exploration and pursuit of augmented intelligence must be transparent and accountable to the RAAF's legal, ethical and moral values and obligations. Greater engagement with risk and opportunity must be matched by accountability and transparency.

It is assumed that the governance of AI will dovetail with aspects of human governance, particularly where AI augments or replaces human decision-makers, and, in some parts, similarly to technology governance and following best practices in data governance. Australian Defence has confirmed commitments to non-AI governance of humans and technology, as detailed in the section below.

Human Governance in Defence

Expectations of human decision-makers are likely to be applied if not extended whenever AI influences or replaces human decision-making, including moral and legal responsibilities. The Australian definition of Command ADDP 00.1 Command and Control AL1 (Department of Defence 2019, 1-1):

Command: The authority which a commander in the military Service lawfully exercises over subordinates by virtue of rank or assignment.

1 Command includes the authority and responsibility for effectively using available resources and for planning the employment of organising, directing, coordinating and controlling military forces for the accomplishment of assigned missions.
2 It also includes responsibility for health, welfare, morale and discipline of assigned personnel.

Within the Definition of Command is authority and responsibility for military decision-making, including using physical or digital resources such as how and when AI is deployed. When making decisions, the Australian Defence Force Leadership Doctrine (ADF-P-0, Ed. 3) (2021a) states, "Ethical leadership is the single most important factor in ensuring the legitimacy of our operations and the support of the Australian people". Suggesting that Command is expected to

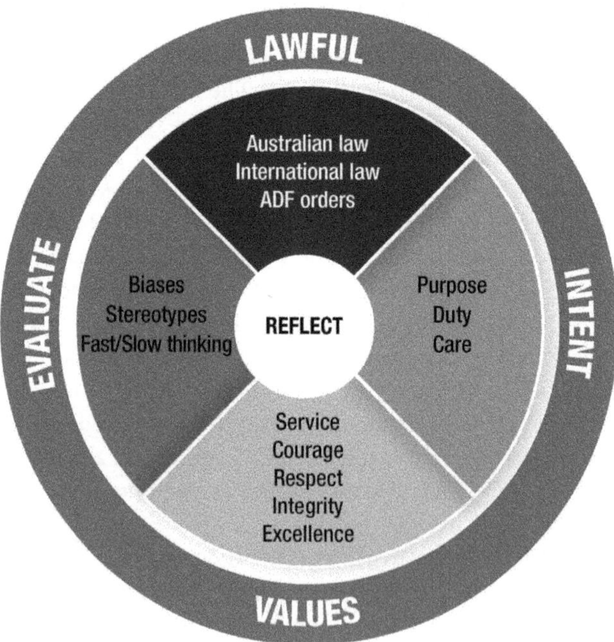

FIGURE 10.1 Australian Defence Force ethical decision-making framework.

deploy digital assets ethically, the Leadership Doctrine argues in no uncertain terms that "your responsibility as a leader is to ensure the pursuit of your goals is ethical and lawful. There are no exceptions" (Australian Defence Force 2021a, 7). The Australian Defence Force – Philosophical – 0 Military Ethics Doctrine (Australian Defence Force 2021b) breaks down ethical leadership into a framework, including intent, values, evaluate, lawful, and reflect (see Figure 10.1).

The *Lead the Way: Defence Transformation Strategy* articulates that Defence wants human decision-makers to be agile, adaptive and ethical with a continuous improvement culture "embedding strong Defence values and behaviours, clear accountabilities and informed and evidence-based decision-making" (Department of Defence 2020c, 21). ADF-P-7 "The Education Doctrine" (Australian Defence Doctrine Publication 2021) emphasises the importance of "Innovative and inquiring minds" that are "better equipped to adapt to fast-changing technological, tactical and strategic environments". Abilities sought include:

- Objectively seek and identify credible information;
- Accurately recognise cues and relationships;
- Quickly make sense of information and respond appropriately.

Ethical AI could contribute to and augment human capabilities for a faster and more agile force. Australian Defence personnel using AI to augment decision-making will be expected to use it ethically and lawfully, to increase the informativeness and evidence base for decisions, and for decision-makers to be agile and accountable both with and without AI.

Ethics in Australian Cybersecurity and Intelligence

Key strategic threats for Australia are cybercrime, ransomware and information warfare. Cyber security incidents are increasing in frequency, scale and sophistication, threatening Australia's economic prosperity and national interests (White 2021). AI is likely to play a role in decision-making support and autonomous defence and offensive campaigns to thwart those who seek to undermine Australia's interests. Australia has not published ethics of AI policy for cybersecurity or intelligence. However, ethical behaviours are highlighted in publicly available value statements, such as "we always act legally and ethically" (Australian Signals Directorate 2019a, 2019b), and communications suggest that Australia would expect strong governance of AI systems used in these operations, including abidance with domestic and international law and the values of government organisations. For example, speaking to the Lowy Institute Director-General of Australian Signals Directorate (ASD), Mike Burgess (2019) highlighted that "rules guide us when people are watching; values guide us when they're not" (Lowy Institute 2019, 51:46) and that ASD is "an organisation that is actually incredibly focused on doing the right thing by the public and being lawful that's an excellent part of our culture born out of our values we put a lot of effort focusing on that" (Lowy Institute 2019, 52:27).

A comprehensive review of the legal framework of the national intelligence community highlights the importance of accountability, transparency and oversight of how the Australian government collects and uses data (Richardson 2020). The government response to the Richardson report (Attorney-General's Department 2020, 40–41) agrees that governance and ethical frameworks should be developed for the use of artificial capabilities for intelligence purposes (recommendation 154), citing values including control, oversight, transparency and accountability (recommendations 155–156). The Australian government noted the importance of human-in-the-loop decision-making where a person's rights or interests may be affected or an agency makes an adverse decision concerning a person (recommendation 155). The Australian government is also committed to working with businesses on potential legislative changes, including the role of privacy, consumer and data protection laws (Cyber Digital and Technology Policy Division 2020).

Defence Data Strategy

In 2021, Defence released a *Defence Data Strategy*. The strategy promises a Data Security Policy to ensure the adoption of a risk-based approach to data security that allows Defence more latitude to respond to the increase in grey-zone activities, including cyber-attacks and foreign interference, and a renewed focus on data security and storage processes. Defence identified ethical considerations as a critical component of their data strategy. While they commit to being informed by *The Australian Code for the Responsible Conduct of Research and the National Statement on Ethical Conduct in Research* (Australian Research Council 2020), neither of these codes provides any guidance on the development of AI for Defence or security purposes. Nevertheless, Defence is committed to producing training so that personnel are "equipped to treat data securely and ethically" by 2023 (Department of Defence 2021a, 13).

TEXT BOX 10.6 ETHICAL DATA, DEFENCE DATA STRATEGY 2021–2023

Guidelines around the ethical use of data will be developed to ensure we have a shared understanding of our legislative and ethical responsibilities

...

The Australian Code for the Responsible Conduct of Research and the National Statement on Ethical Conduct in Research will inform these guidelines. The ethical use of data guidelines will form part of the Defence Human and Animal Research Manual and policies.

(Department of Defence 2021a, 42)

Framework for Ethical AI in Defence

Australia has not adopted an ethics framework specifically for AI use in Defence. However, a Defence Science and Technology technical report based on outcomes from an evidence-based workshop[7] has recommended a method for ethical AI in Defence (MEAID) (Department of Defence 2021b; Devitt et al. 2021) and an Australia-specific framework to guide ethical risk mitigation. MEAID draws from the workshop for further consideration and does not represent the views of the Australian government. Rather than stipulating principles, MEAID identifies five facets of ethical AI and corresponding questions to support science and technical considerations for the potential development of Defence policy, doctrine, research and project management:

- **Responsibility** – who is responsible for AI?
- **Governance** – how is AI controlled?
- **Trust** – how can AI be trusted?
- **Law** – how can AI be used lawfully?
- **Traceability** – how are the actions of AI recorded?

MEAID notes that facets of ethical AI for Defence and the associated questions align with the unique concerns and regulatory regimes to which Defence is subject. For example, in times of conflict, Defence is required to comply with international humanitarian law (IHL, *lex specialis*) and international human rights law (*lex generalis*) in armed conflict (*jus in bello*[8]). Defence is also required to comply with international legal norms concerning using force when not engaged in armed conflict (*jus ad bellum*) when applying military force. Australia's inclusion of "Law" as an ethical facet highlights the values Australia promotes through abidance with international humanitarian law, particularly the concepts of proportionality, distinction and military necessity which have no direct non-military equivalent and as such require consideration of a specific set of requirements and responsibilities.

Responsibility: Who Is Responsible for AI?

MEAID notes two critical challenges of understanding and responsibility that must be addressed when operating with AI systems. First, to effectively and ethically employ a given system (AI or not), the framework argues that a commander must sufficiently understand its behaviour and the potential consequences of its operation (Devitt et al. 2021, 11). Second, there can be difficulty in identifying any specific individual responsible for a given decision or action.

Responsibility for critical decisions is spread across multiple decision-makers, offering opportunities to exercise authority and make mistakes. The allocation of ethical and legal responsibility could be distributed across the nodes/agents in the human-AI network causally relevant for a decision (Floridi 2016). However, legal responsibility ultimately lies with humans. Additionally, AI could help reduce mistakes and augment human makers who bear responsibility (Ekelhof 2018). Decisions made with the assistance of or by AI are captured by accountability frameworks, including domestic and international law.[9]

The Department of Defence can examine legal cases of responsibility in the civilian domain to guide some aspects of the relevant frameworks, e.g. the apportioning of responsibility for the test driver in an Uber automated vehicle accident (Ormsby 2019). Defence could also consider arguments that humans within complex systems without proactive frameworks risk being caught in *moral crumple zones* (Elish 2019), where the locus of responsibility falls on human operators rather than the broader system of control within which they operate. Defence must keep front of mind that humans, not AI, have legal responsibilities and that individuals – not only states – can bear criminal responsibility directly under international law (Cryer et al. 2019).

Governance – How Is AI Controlled?

MEAID suggests that AI creators must consider the context in which AI is to be used and how AI will be controlled. The point of interface through which control is achieved will vary, depending on the nature of the system and the operational environment. There must be work conducted to understand how humans can operate ethically within machine-based systems of control in accordance with Australia's commitment to the Article 36 reviews of all new means and methods of warfare (Commonwealth of Australia 2018).[10] With regard to the control of lethal autonomous weapons, Australia notes the legal, policy, technical and professional forms of controls imposed systematically throughout the "life" cycle of weapons over nine stages:

System of Control of Weapons (Commonwealth of Australia 2019):

Stage One: Legal and Policy Framework
Stage Two: Design and Development
Stage Three: Testing, Evaluation and Review
Stage Four: Acceptance, Training and Certification
Stage Five: Pre-deployment Selection
Stage Six: Weapon Use Parameters
Stage Seven: Pre-deployment Certification and Training
Stage Eight: Strategic and Military Controls for the Use of Force
Stage Nine: After-Action Evaluation

MEAID supports the governance framework of IEEE's Ethically Aligned Design by the IEEE Global Initiative on Ethics of Autonomous and Intelligent Systems (2019). Human-machine collaboration should be optimised to safeguard against poor decision-making, including automation bias and/or mistrust of the system (Hoffman et al. 2018; Alexander 2019). AI should provide confidence and uncertainty in an AI's information or choices (McLellan 2016; Christensen and Lyons 2017).

Trust – How Can AI Be Trusted?

Human-AI systems in Defence need to be trusted by users and operators, commanders and support staff, and the military, government and civilian population of a nation. MEAID points out that the *High-Level Expert Group on Artificial Intelligence of the European Union* "believe it is essential that trust remains the bedrock of societies, communities, economies and sustainable development" (High-Level Expert Group on Artificial Intelligence 2019). They argue that trustworthy AI must be lawful, ethical and robust.

MEAID suggests that trust is a relation between human-human, human-machine and machine-machine, consisting of two components: competency and integrity. Competence comprises skills, reliability and experience; integrity comprises motives, honesty and character (Devitt 2018). This framework is consistent with the emphasis on character and professional competence in ADF-P-0 ADF Leadership Doctrine (Australian Defence Force 2021a, 4). It is noted that the third value of ADF leadership is *understanding*, which falls within the responsibility facet discussed above.

Operators will hold multiple levels of trust in the systems they use depending on what aspect of trust is under scrutiny. In some cases, users may develop a reliance on low integrity technology that they can predict easily, such as using the known flight path of an adversary's drone to develop countermeasures. Users may also depend on technologies because of convenience rather than trust. Finally, individual differences exist in the propensity to trust, highlighting that trust is a relational rather than an objective property. To be trusted, AI systems need to be safe and secure within the Nation's sovereign supply chain. Throughout their lifecycle, AI systems should reliably operate in accordance with their intended purpose (Department of Industry Innovation and Science 2019).

Law: How Can AI Be Used Lawfully?

AI developers should be cognizant of the legal obligations within their anticipated use of the technology. Law within a Defence context has specific ethical considerations that must be understood. International humanitarian law (IHL) (*lex specialis*) and international human rights law (*lex generalis*) were forged from ethical theories in just war theory: *jus ad bellum* governing the resort to force, *jus in bello* regulating the conduct of parties engaged in lawful combat (Coates 2016) and *jus post bellum* regarding obligations after combat. The legal frameworks that accompany Defence activities are human-centred, which should mean that AI compliance with them will produce more ethical outcomes (Liivoja and McCormack 2016). Using AI to support human decision-making could lead to better humanitarian outcomes. There are many policies and directives that may apply, some of which have the force of law. In a military context, there will also typically be an extant set of rules called the *rules of engagement*, which specify the conditions that must be met to fire upon a target.

Legal compliance may be able to be "built into" AI algorithms, but this relies on legal rules being sufficiently unambiguous and well specified that they can be encoded as rules that a computer can interpret and that meet stakeholder expectations. In practice, laws are not always that clear, even to humans. Laws can intentionally be created with ambiguity to provide flexibility. In addition, they can have many complicated conditions and have many interconnections to other laws. Further work is needed to clarify how AI can best enable abidance with applicable laws.

Traceability: How Are the Actions of AI Recorded?

MEAID notes that there are legislative requirements for Defence to record its decision-making. However, the increasing use of AI within human-AI systems means the manner of records must be considered. Records can represent the systems, the causal chain of events, and the humans and AIs engaged in decisions. MEAID suggests that information needs to be accessible and explanatory; the training and expertise of humans must be open to scrutiny; and the background theories and assumptions, training, test and evaluation process of AIs must be retained. Information on AI systems should be available and understandable by auditors. Just as some aspects of human decision-making can be inscrutable, some aspects of the decisions of AIs may remain opaque. Emerging transparency standards may guide best practice for Defence (Winfield et al. 2021).

When decisions lead to expected outcomes or positive outcomes, the factors that lead to those decisions may not come under scrutiny. However, when low likelihood and/or negative outcomes occur, organisations should be able to "rewind" the decision process to understand what occurred and what lessons might be learned. Noting that decisions made under uncertainty will always have a chance of producing adverse outcomes, even if the decision-making process is defensible and operators are acting appropriately. No matter how an AI is deployed in Defence, data, training, theoretical underpinning, decision-making models and actions should be recorded and auditable by the appropriate levels of government and, where appropriate, made available to the public.

Method for Ethical AI in Defence

MEAID recommends assessing ethical compliance from design to deployment, requiring repeated testing, prototyping and reviewing for technological and ethical limitations. Developers already must produce risk documentation for technical issues. Similar documentation for ethical risks ensures developers identify, acknowledge and attempt to mitigate ethical risks early in the design process and throughout test and evaluation (Devitt et al. 2021). MEAID closely with the IEEE Standard Model Process for Addressing Ethical Concerns during System Design (IEEE 2021) – see Text Box 10.7.

TEXT BOX 10.7 IEEE 7000-2021 STANDARD

IEEE 7000-2021 standard provides:

- A system engineering standard approach integrating human and social values into traditional systems engineering and design;
- Processes for engineers to translate stakeholder values and ethical considerations into system requirements and design practices;
- A systematic, transparent and traceable approach to address ethically oriented regulatory obligations in the design of autonomous intelligent systems.

Australia has developed a practical methodology (Devitt et al. 2021) that can support AI project managers and teams in managing ethical risks in military AI projects, including three tools:

1 An AI Checklist for the development of ethical AI systems;
2 An Ethical AI Risk Matrix to describe identified risks and proposed treatment;
3 For larger programs, a data item descriptor (DID) for contractors to develop a formal Legal, Ethical and Assurance Program Plan (LEAPP) to be included in project documentation for AI programs where an ethical risk assessment is above a certain threshold.

AI Checklist

The main components of the checklist are:
A To describe the military context in which the AI will be employed;
B To explain the types of decisions supported by the AI;
C To explain how the AI integrates with human operators to ensure effectiveness and ethical decision-making in the anticipated context of use and countermeasures to protect against potential misuse;
D To explain framework/s to be used;
E To employ subject matter experts to guide AI development;
F To employ appropriate verification and validation techniques to reduce risk.

Ethical AI Risk Matrix

An Ethical AI Risk Matrix will:

- Define the activity being undertaken;
- Indicate the ethical facet and topic the activity is intended to address;
- Estimate the risk to the project objectives if issue is not addressed;

- Define specific actions you will undertake to support the activity;
- Provide a timeline for the activity;
- Define action and activity outcomes;
- Identify the responsible party(ies);
- Provide the status of the activity.

Analysis

MEAID offers practical advice and tools for defence industries and Defence to communicate, document and iterate design specifications for emerging technologies and identify operational contexts of use considering ethical and legal considerations and obligations. MEAID also offers entry points to explain system function, capability and limits to both expert and non-expert stakeholders on military technologies. MEAID aims to practically ensure accountability for: (a) considering ethical risks, (b) assigning person(s) to each risk and (c) making humans accountable for decisions on how ethics are de-risked. It has been mentioned on the International Committee of the Red Cross blog (Copeland and Sanders 2021) as establishing an iterative process to engage industry during the design and acquisition phase of new technologies to increase IHL abidance and reduce civilian harms.

Developed by Defence Science and Technology Group, Plan Jericho Air Force (Department of Defence 2020b) and Trusted Autonomous Systems,[11] the MEAID framework has been adopted by industry[12] and is the ethics framework used in a case study of Allied Impact (Gaetjens et al. 2021) and being trialled by Australia in the TTCP AI Strategic Challenge (Stanley-Lockman 2021, 43–44). A side-by-side comparison between AU-EP, MEAID and OECD shows significant overlap in responsibility and trust but also gaps where military uses of AI encounter ethical considerations not applicable to the civilian realm, such as the application of just war principles of distinction and proportionality (Law) and military control of weapons systems (Governance). The AU-EP share many similarities with the OECD. For example, contestability is equivalent to the OECD requirement that humans can understand and intervene in AI-based outcomes as well as challenge them.

While not a formally adopted view of the Australian government, MEIAD establishes tools to assess ethical compliance that "[e]ven as an opinion, the Method is the clearest articulation of ethical AI for defence among the Indo-Pacific allies" (Stanley-Lockman 2021, 21). As Stanley-Lockman (2021) states:

> The [MEAID] tools offer a process to validate that contractors have indeed taken the ethical risks they identified into account in their design and testing prior to later acquisition phases....The incorporation of ethics in design through the acquisition lifecycle also intends to build trust in the process and, by extension, the systems by the time they go into service.

Like many countries, ADO undertakes a formal capability acquisition process to assist the government in identifying and meeting its military capability needs. This process, known as the Product Life Cycle, consists of four phases (strategy and concepts, risk mitigation and requirement setting, acquisition, and in-service and disposal) separated by government decision gates (Commonwealth of Australia 2020). This process ensures that government's strategic objectives (see Text Box 10.1) drive Defence's acquisition priorities.

Australia's Sovereign Industry Capability Priorities reflect the government's realisation that future Defence AI capabilities will increasingly rely on research and development in the civil sector. This necessitates closer collaboration between Defence and defence industry to ensure the timely delivery of cutting-edge technology that reflects Australia's values and ethical AI principles and ensures legal and ethical risks associated with military AI technology are identified and mitigated in the earliest stages of development.

Australia's Department of Defence may inform the defence industry of its legal and ethical requirements to enable AI developers to introduce design measures to mitigate or remove the risks before entering the Defence procurement process, rather than attempting to address legal and ethical risks during the acquisition process. This provides efficacies for both Defence and industry by allowing the industry to better focus their development priorities and assisting Defence in streamlining its AI capability acquisition process. MEAID provides Defence with a practical approach that can readily integrate into the existing Product Life Cycle process to inform and enable the transfer of legal and ethical AI technology from the defence industry into Defence. MEAID tools such as the LEAPP provide Defence with visibility of a contractor's plan to mitigate legal and ethical risk and, together with the facets of ethical AI and the Article 36 weapon review process, can inform government decisions to acquire military AI technology that is both legal and aligns with Australia's ethical principles.

Australia can play a leadership role by integrating legal and ethical considerations into its Defence AI capability acquisition process. This requires a policy framework that defines its legal and ethical requirements, is informed by defence industry stakeholders and provides a practical methodology to integrate legal and ethical risk mitigation strategies into the acquisition process.

Conclusion

This chapter explored Australia's public positioning on AI and AI governance 2018–2021 through published strategies, frameworks, action plans and government reports. While these provide a top-down view, high-level national AI strategies may align with the lived experience of public servants and personnel encountering AI in Defence or Australian Defence Force commanders and operators using AI systems (Kuziemski and Misuraca 2020). Australia is a leading AI nation with strong allies and partnerships. It has prioritised the development of robotics, AI and autonomous systems to develop a sovereign capability for the military. Australia commits to Article 36 reviews of all new means and methods of warfare to ensure weapons and weapons systems are operated within acceptable systems of control.

Additionally, the country has undergone significant reviews of the risks of AI to human rights and within intelligence organisations and has committed to producing ethics guidelines and frameworks in security and defence (Department of Defence 2021a; Attorney-General's Department 2020). Australia is committed to OECD's values-based principles for the responsible stewardship of trustworthy AI and adopting a set of national AI ethics principles. While Australia has not adopted an AI governance framework specifically for Defence, *A Method for Ethical AI in Defence* (MEAID) published by Defence Science includes a framework and pragmatic tools for managing ethical and legal risks for military applications of AI.

The chapter's key findings are that Australia has formed strong international AI governance partnerships likely to reinforce and strengthen strategic partnerships and power relations. Like many nations, Australia's commitment to civilian AI ethics principles does not provide military guidance or governance. The ADO has the opportunity to adopt a robust AI ethical policy for security and defence that emphasises commitment to existing international legal frameworks and can be applied to AI-driven weapons. A risk-based ethical AI framework suited for military purposes and aligned with best practices, standards and frameworks internationally can ensure that defence industries consider ethics-by-design and law-by-design ahead of the acquisitions process. Australia should continue to invest, research and develop AI governance frameworks to meet the technical potential and strategic requirements of military uses of AI.

Notes

1 Acknowledgements: Tim McFarland, Eve Massingham, Rachel Horne and Tara Roberson.
2 The team included Commonwealth Scientific and Industrial Research Organisation (CSIRO) Data61 and Emesent, with international partner the Georgia Institute of Technology.
3 See https://www1.defence.gov.au/about/people-group.
4 Other GPAI countries include Canada, France, Germany, India, Italy, Japan, Mexico, New Zealand, Korea, Singapore, Slovenia, the United Kingdom, the United States and the European Union. In December 2020, Brazil, the Netherlands, Poland and Spain joined GPAI (Department of Industry Science Energy and Resources 2020a; Gobal Partnership on AI 2021).
5 GPAI working groups are focused on four key themes: responsible AI, data governance, the future of work, and innovation and commercialisation.
6 Note there is little representation from remaining ASEAN nations Brunei, Cambodia, Indonesia, Laos, Malaysia, Myanmar, the Philippines, Thailand and Vietnam or Pacific Nation[s]
7 Workshop held in Canberra from 30 July to 1 August 2019 with 104 people from 45 organisations, including representatives from Defence, other Australian government agencies, the Trusted Autonomous Systems Defence Cooperative Research Centre (TASDCRC), civil society, universities and Defence industry.

8 'jus in bello' usually refers specifically to IHL even though human rights law still operates in conflict.
9 There is sometimes considerable uncertainty about exactly how to apply legal frameworks to decisions made with significant AI involvement.
10 The Protocol Additional to the Geneva Conventions of 12 August 1949, and relating to the Protection of Victims of International Armed Conflicts, 8 June 1977 (Protocol I), refers alternately to "methods or means of warfare" (Art. 35(1) and (3), Art. 51(5)(a), Art. 55(1), "methods and means of warfare" (titles of Part III and of Section I of Part III), "means and methods of attack" (Art. 57(2)(a)(ii)) and "weapon, means or method of warfare" (Art. 36) (International Committee of the Red Cross 2006).
11 See https://tasdcrc.com.au/.
12 See Athena AI at https://athenadefence.ai/software.

References

88th Air Base Wing Public Affairs. 23 December, 2019. "Digital engineering transformation coming to Air Force weapons enterprise." https://www.af.mil/News/Article-Display/Article/2046599/digital-engineering-transformation-coming-to-air-force-weapons-enterprise/.

AI Council. 2021. "AI roadmap." United Kingdom. https://www.gov.uk/government/publications/ai-roadmap.

Alexander, Donovan. 2019. "Is our reliance on technology creating a new dark age?" *Interesting Engineering*, 10 May, 2019. https://interestingengineering.com/is-our-reliance-on-technology-creating-a-new-dark-age.

Army. 2018. "Robotic and autonomous systems strategy." https://researchcentre.army.gov.au/library/other/robotic-autonomous-systems-strategy.

ASPI. 2022. "Russia-Ukraine war, policing and AI, and an Australian DARPA." 4 March, 2022, in *Policy, Guns and Money*. https://www.aspistrategist.org.au/policy-guns-and-money-russia-ukraine-war-policing-and-ai-and-an-australian-darpa/.

Attorney-General's Department. 2020. "Government response to the comprehensive review of the legal framework of the National Intelligence Community." https://www.ag.gov.au/national-security/publications/government-response-comprehensive-review-legal-framework-national-intelligence-community.

Australian Defence Doctrine Publication. 2021. "ADF-P-7 learning."

Australian Defence Force. 2021a. "ADF-P-0 ADF leadership, edition 3." *The Forge*. https://theforge.defence.gov.au/adf-philosophical-doctrine-adf-leadership.

———. 2021b. "ADF-P-0 military ethics, edition 1, 2021." https://theforge.defence.gov.au/ethics.

Australian Government. 2019. "Australia's system of control and applications for autonomous weapon systems." Group of governmental experts on emerging technologies in the area of Lethal Autonomous Weapons Systems, Geneva, 25–29 March, 2019 and 20–21 August, 2019. https://docs-library.unoda.org/Convention_on_Certain_Conventional_Weapons_-_Group_of_Governmental_Experts_(2019)/CCWGGE.12019WP.2Rev.1.pdf.

———. 2021. "Four new Sovereign Industrial Capability Priorities announced." 7 September, 2021. https://business.gov.au/cdic/news-for-defence-industry/four-new-sovereign-industrial-capability-priorities-announced.

Australian Institute of Health and Safety. 2021. "How will artificial intelligence and machine learning impact OHS?" Australian Institute for Health and Safety. Last Modified 21 June. https://www.aihs.org.au/news-and-publications/news/how-will-artificial-intelligence-and-machine-learning-impact-ohs.

Australian Permanent Mission and Consulate-General Geneva. 2017. "Australian statement - General exchange of views, LAWS GGE 13–17 November 2017." https://geneva.mission.gov.au/gene/Statement783.html.

Australian Research Council. 2020. "Codes and guidelines." https://www.arc.gov.au/policies-strategies/policy/codes-and-guidelines.

Australian Signals Directorate. 2019a. "ASD corporate plan 2019–2020." https://www.asd.gov.au/sites/default/files/2019-08/ASD_Corporate_Plan_final_12.pdf.

———. 2019b. "Values." Accessed 25 September. https://www.asd.gov.au/about/values.

Blades, Johnny. 2021. "Aukus pact strikes at heart of Pacific regionalism." *Radio New Zealand Pacific*. https://www.rnz.co.nz/international/pacific-news/451715/aukus-pact-strikes-at-heart-of-pacific-regionalism.

Braithwaite, Valerie. 2020. "Beyond the bubble that is Robodebt: How governments that lose integrity threaten democracy." *Australian Journal of Social Issues* 55 (3): 242–259.

Burgess, M. 2019. "What ASD cyber operatives really do to protect Australian interests." 28 March, 2019. https://www.themandarin.com.au/106332-mike-burgess-director-general-asd-speech-to-the-lowy-institute/.

Centre for Work Health and Safety. 2021. "Ethical use of artificial intelligence in the workplace - AI WHS scorecard." NSW Government. https://www.centreforwhs.nsw.gov.au/knowledge-hub/ethical-use-of-artificial-intelligence-in-the-workplace-final-report.

Christensen, James C., and Joseph B. Lyons. 2017. "Trust between humans and learning machines: Developing the gray box." *Mechanical Engineering* 139 (06): S9–S13. https://doi.org/10.1115/1.2017-Jun-5. https://doi.org/10.1115/1.2017-Jun-5.

Cihon, Peter. 2019. "Standards for AI governance: International standards to enable global coordination in AI research & development." *Future of Humanity Institute. University of Oxford*. https://www.fhi.ox.ac.uk/wp-content/uploads/Standards_-FHI-Technical-Report.pdf.

Coates, A. J. (2016). *The ethics of war* (2nd ed.). Manchester University Press.

Commonwealth of Australia. 2018. "The Australian Article 36 review process." United Nations group of governmental experts of the high contracting parties to the convention on prohibitions or restrictions on the use of certain conventional weapons which may be deemed to be excessively injurious or to have indiscriminate effects, 30 August, 2018. https://docs-library.unoda.org/Convention_on_Certain_Conventional_Weapons_-_Group_of_Governmental_Experts_(2018)/2018_GGE%2BLAWS_August_Working%2Bpaper_Australia.pdf.

———. 2019. "Australia's system of control and applications for autonomous weapon systems." Group of governmental experts on emerging technologies in the area of lethal autonomous weapons systems, 25–29 March, 2019 and 20–21 August, 2019, Geneva, 26 March, 2019. https://www.unog.ch/80256EDD006B8954/(httpAssets)/16C9F75124654510C12583C9003A4EBF/$file/CCWGGE.12019WP.2Rev.1.pdf.

———. 2020. Capability Life Cycle Manual (V.2.1). Edited by Investment Portfolio Management Branch.

Copeland, D., and L. Sanders. 2021. "Engaging with the industry: Integrating IHL into new technologies in urban warfare." *Humanitarian Law and Policy* (blog), *ICRC*, 8 October. https://blogs.icrc.org/law-and-policy/2021/10/07/industry-ihl-new-technologies/.

Cryer, Robert, Darryl Robinson, and Sergey Vasiliev. 2019. *An introduction to international criminal law and procedure*. Cambridge: Cambridge University Press.

Cyber Digital and Technology Policy Division. 2020. "2020 cyber security strategy." Department of Home Affairs. https://www.homeaffairs.gov.au/about-us/our-portfolios/cyber-security/strategy.

Dafoe, Allan. 2018. "AI governance: A research agenda." *Governance of AI Program, Future of Humanity Institute, University of Oxford: Oxford, UK* 1442:1443.

Dawson, D., E. Schleiger, J. Horton, J. McLaughlin, C. Robinson, G. Quezada, J. Scowcroft, and S. Hajkowicz. 2019. *Artificial intelligence: Australia's ethics framework: A discussion paper.* Data61 CSIRO, Australia (Data61 CSIRO, Australia: Australia Data61 CSIRO). https://consult.industry.gov.au/strategic-policy/artificial-intelligence-ethics-framework/.

de Git, Melanie. 2021. "Loyal Wingman uncrewed aircraft completes first flight." *Innovation Quarterly, Boeing*, 12 April, 2021. https://www.boeing.com/features/innovation-quarterly/2021/04/loyal-wingman.page.

Defence Science & Technology Group. 18 November, 2021a. "AI to enable military commanders to make better decisions." https://www.dst.defence.gov.au/news/2021/11/18/ai-enable-military-commanders-make-better-decisions-faster.

———. 2021b. "Defence Artificial Intelligence Research Network (DAIRNET) research call." Accessed 1 November. https://www.dst.defence.gov.au/partner-with-us/opportunities/defence-artificial-intelligence-research-network-dairnet-research-call.

Defence Science Institute. 19 May, 2020a. "The artificial intelligence for decision making initiative." https://www.defencescienceinstitute.com/news/the-artificial-intelligence-for-decision-making-initiative.

———. 2020b. "'Artificial intelligence for decision making' initiative." https://www.defencescienceinstitute.com/component/sppagebuilder/?view=page&id=29&highlight=WyJhcnRpZmljaWFsIiwiJ2FydGlmaWNpYWwiLCJpbnRlbGxpZ2VuY2UiLCJhcnRpZmljaWFsIGludGVsbGlnZW5jZSJd.

———. 10 May, 2021. "Applications open for the artificial intelligence for decision making initiative round 2." https://www.defencescienceinstitute.com/news/initiatives/applications-open-for-the-artificial-intelligence-for-decision-making-initiative-round-2.

Deloitte Center for Government Insights. 2021. "The future of warfighting." Deloitte. https://www2.deloitte.com/global/en/pages/public-sector/articles/future-of-warfighting.html.

Department of Defence. 2016. "Defence white paper." https://www1.defence.gov.au/about/publications/2016-defence-white-paper.

———. 2019. ADDP 00.1 Command and Control AL1. Edited by Department of Defence.

———. 2020a. "2020 defence strategic update." https://www1.defence.gov.au/about/publications/2020-defence-strategic-update.

———. 2020b. "Artificial intelligence enhances the impact of air and space power for the Joint Force." Department of Defence annual report 2019–2020. https://www.transparency.gov.au/annual-reports/department-defence/reporting-year/2019-20-31.

———. 2020c. "Lead the way: Defence transformation strategy." https://www1.defence.gov.au/about/publications/lead-way-defence-transformation-strategy.

———. 2021a. "Defence data strategy 2021–2023." https://www1.defence.gov.au/about/publications/defence-data-strategy-2021–2023.

———. 16 February, 2021b, "Defence releases report on ethical use of AI." https://news.defence.gov.au/media/media-releases/defence-releases-report-ethical-use-ai.

Department of Defense. 1978. Managing weapon system software: Progress and problems (unclassified digest of a classified report).

Department of Home Affairs. 2020. "Australian values." https://www.homeaffairs.gov.au/about-us/our-portfolios/social-cohesion/australian-values.

Department of Industry Innovation and Science. 2019. "Australia's artificial intelligence ethics framework." Accessed 25 September. https://www.industry.gov.

au/data-and-publications/australias-artificial-intelligence-ethics-framework/australias-ai-ethics-principles.

Department of Industry Science Energy and Resources. 16 June, 2020. 2020a. "The global partnership on artificial intelligence launches." https://www.industry.gov.au/news/the-global-partnership-on-artificial-intelligence-launches.

———. 2020b. "Testing the AI ethics principles." https://www.industry.gov.au/data-and-publications/australias-artificial-intelligence-ethics-framework/testing-the-ai-ethics-principles.

———. 2021. "Australia's artificial intelligence action plan." https://www.industry.gov.au/data-and-publications/australias-artificial-intelligence-action-plan.

Devitt, S. K. 2018. "Trustworthiness of autonomous systems." In *Foundations of trusted autonomy*, edited by Hussein A. Abbass, Jason Scholz and Darryn J. Reid, 161–184. Cham: Springer International Publishing.

Devitt, S. K., M. Gan, J. Scholz, and R. S. Bolia. 2021. *A method for ethical AI in defence*. Defence Science and Technology Group (Defence Science and Technology). https://www.dst.defence.gov.au/publication/ethical-ai.

Ekelhof, M. A. (2018). "Lifting the fog of targeting." *Naval War College Review* 71 (3): 61–95.

Elish, M. C. (2019). "Moral crumple zones: Cautionary tales in human-robot interaction." *Engaging Science, Technology, and Society* 5: 40–60.

Fisher, Erik. 2020. "Necessary conditions for responsible innovation." *Journal of Responsible Innovation* 7 (2): 145–148. https://doi.org/10.1080/23299460.2020.1774105. https://doi.org/10.1080/23299460.2020.1774105.

Floridi, L. (2016). "Faultless responsibility: On the nature and allocation of moral responsibility for distributed moral actions." *Philosophical Transactions of the Royal Society A: Mathematical, Physical and Engineering Sciences, 374*(2083), 20160112.

Gaetjens, D., S. K. Devitt, and C. Shanahan. 2021. Case Study: A Method for Ethical AI in Defence Applied to an Envisioned Tactical Command and Control System (DSTG-TR-3847). Canberra: Defence Science & Technology Group. https://www.dst.defence.gov.au/publication/case-study-method-ethical-ai-defence-applied-envisioned-tactical-command-and-control

Galloway, Kate. 2017. "Big data: A case study of disruption and government power." *Alternative Law Journal* 42 (2): 89–95.

Gasser, Urs, and Virgilio A. F. Almeida. 2017. "A layered model for AI governance." *IEEE Internet Computing* 21 (6): 58–62.

Gobal Partnership on AI. 2021. "The global partnership on AI." Accessed 25 September https://gpai.ai/.

Hajkowicz, S. A., S. Karimi, T. Wark, C. Chen, M. Evans, N. Rens, D. Dawson, A. Charlton, T. Brennan, C. Moffatt, S. Srikumar, and K. J. Tong. 2019. *Artificial intelligence: Solving problems, growing the economy and improving our quality of life*. CSIRO Data61 and the Department of Industry, Innovation and Science, Australian Government. https://data61.csiro.au/en/Our-Research/Our-Work/AI-Roadmap.

Hanson, Fergus, and Danielle Cave. 2021. "Australia well placed to turbocharge its strategic tech capability." Australian Strategic Policy Institute. https://www.aspi.org.au/opinion/australia-well-placed-turbocharge-its-strategic-tech-capability.

High-Level Expert Group on Artificial Intelligence. 2019. *Ethics guidelines for trustworthy AI*. European Commission. https://ec.europa.eu/digital-single-market/en/news/ethics-guidelines-trustworthy-ai.

Hoffman, Robert R., Nadine Sarter, Matthew Johnson, and John K. Hawley. 2018. "Myths of automation and their implications for military procurement."

Bulletin of the Atomic Scientists 74 (4): 255–261. https://doi.org/10.1080/00963402.2018.1486615.

IEEE. 2021. "IEEE 7000™-2021-IEEE standard model process for addressing ethical concerns during system design." https://engagestandards.ieee.org/ieee-7000-2021-for-systems-design-ethical-concerns.html.

IEEE Global Initiative on Ethics of Autonomous and Intelligent Systems. 2019. *Ethically aligned design: A vision for prioritizing human well-being with autonomous and intelligent systems (EADe1).* IEEE. https://standards.ieee.org/content/ieee-standards/en/industry-connections/ec/autonomous-systems.html.

Insinna, Valerie. 2021. "Australia makes another order for Boeing's Loyal Wingman drones after a successful first flight." *DefenceNews*, 3 March, 2021. https://www.defensenews.com/air/2021/03/02/australia-makes-another-order-for-boeing-made-loyal-wingman-drones-after-a-successful-first-flight/.

International Committee of the Red Cross. 2006. "A guide to the legal review of new weapons, means and methods of warfare: Measures to implement Article 36 of Additional Protocol I of 1977." *International Review of the Red Cross* 88 (864). https://www.icrc.org/eng/assets/files/other/irrc_864_icrc_geneva.pdf.

JAIC Public Affairs. 16 September, 2020. 2020. "JAIC facilitates first-ever international AI dialogue for defense." https://www.ai.mil/news_09_16_20-jaic_facilitates_first-ever_international_ai_dialogue_for_defense_.html.

———. 28 May, 2021, "DoD Joint AI Center facilitates third international AI dialogue for defense." https://www.ai.mil/news_05_28_21-jaic_facilitates_third_international_ai_dialogue_for_defense.html.

Jenkins, K. 2014. "Collaboration for cultural reform in Defence." https://defence.humanrights.gov.au/.

Kelly, Paul. 2022. "New world disorder: Ukraine redefines global landscape." 4 March, 2022. https://www.theaustralian.com.au/inquirer/a-new-world-disorder-morrison-calls-on-the-west-to-unite-against-russia-and-china/news-story/433b6ff74637c45454393030f827f1e7.

Kuziemski, Maciej, and Gianluca Misuraca. 2020. "AI governance in the public sector: Three tales from the frontiers of automated decision-making in democratic settings." *Telecommunications policy* 44 (6): 101976.

Liivoja, Rain, Eve Massingham, Tim McFarland, and Simon McKenzie. 2020. "Are autonomous weapons systems prohibited?" Game Changer. Trusted Autonomous Systems. https://tasdcrc.com.au/are-autonomous-weapons-systems-prohibited/.

Liivoja, R., & McCormack, T. (Eds.). (2016). *Routledge Handbook of the Law of Armed Conflict*. Routledge.

Lockey, S., N. Gillespie, and C. Curtis. 2020. *Trust in artificial intelligence: Australian insights 2020.* The University of Queensland and KPMG Australia. https://assets.kpmg/content/dam/kpmg/au/pdf/2020/public-trust-in-ai.pdf.

Lopez, C. T. 2020. "DOD adopts 5 principles of artificial intelligence ethics." *DOD News.* https://www.defense.gov/Explore/News/Article/Article/2094085/dod-adopts-5-principles-of-artificial-intelligence-ethics/.

Lowy Institute. 2019. "Mike Burgess, Director-General on the Australian Signals Directorate (ASD) - Offensive cyber." YouTube. https://youtu.be/Th6EKCwhGrs.

McFarland, Tim. 2020. *Autonomous weapon systems and the law of armed conflict: Compatibility with international humanitarian law.* Cambridge: Cambridge Core.

———. 2021. "Autonomous weapons and the Jus Ad Bellum." *Law School Policy Review.* https://lawschoolpolicyreview.com/2021/03/20/autonomous-weapons-and-the-jus-ad-bellum-an-overview/.

McLellan, Charles. 2016. "Inside the black box: Understanding AI decision-making." *ZDNet*, 1 December, 2016. https://www.zdnet.com/article/inside-the-black-box-understanding-ai-decision-making/.

Ministère des Armées. 2019. *Artificial intelligence in support of defence: Report of the AI task force.* https://www.defense.gouv.fr/sites/default/files/aid/Report%20of%20the%20AI%20Task%20Force%20September%202019.pdf

National Security Commission on Artificial Intelligence. 2021. "Final report." United States of America. https://www.nscai.gov/wp-content/uploads/2021/03/Full-Report-Digital-1.pdf.

Nicholson, B. 2021. "Morrison says AUKUS will strengthen cooperation on critical technologies." *The Strategist, Australian Strategic Policy Institute*, 17 November, 2021. https://www.aspistrategist.org.au/morrison-says-aukus-will-strengthen-cooperation-on-critical-technologies/.

NSW Government. 2022. "NSW AI assurance framework." NSW Government. Accessed 5 March. https://www.digital.nsw.gov.au/policy/artificial-intelligence/nsw-ai-assurance-framework.

OECD. 2019. "The OECD AI principles." https://www.oecd.org/going-digital/ai/principles/.

OECD Council on Artificial Intelligence. 2019. *Recommendation of the Council on Artificial Intelligence.* https://legalinstruments.oecd.org/en/instruments/OECD-LEGAL-0449

Office of the Director of National Intelligence. 2022. "Five Eyes Intelligence Oversight and Review Council (FIORC)." https://www.dni.gov/index.php/ncsc-how-we-work/217-about/organization/icig-pages/2660-icig-fiorc.

Ormsby, G. (2019, 11 March). "Uber fatality unveils AI accountability issues." *Lawyers Weekly.* https://www.lawyersweekly.com.au/biglaw/25213-uber-fatality-unveils-ai-accountability-issues

Parikh, Nish. 2021. "Understanding bias in AI-enabled hiring." *Forbes Magazine*, 2021. https://www.forbes.com/sites/forbeshumanresourcescouncil/2021/10/14/understanding-bias-in-ai-enabled-hiring/?sh=33f2d7997b96.

Persley, Alexandra. 2021. "Australia claims historic top two spot in the 'Robot Olympics'." https://www.csiro.au/en/news/News-releases/2021/Australia-claims-historic-top-two-spot-in-the-Robot-Olympics.

Prime Minister, and Minister of Defence. 1 March, 2022. 2022. "Australian support to the Ukraine." Prime Minister of Australia. https://www.pm.gov.au/media/australian-support-ukraine.

Richardson, D. 2020. "Report of the comprehensive review of the legal framework of the national intelligence community." Attorney-General's Department. https://www.ag.gov.au/national-security/consultations/comprehensive-review-legal-framework-governing-national-intelligence-community.

Royal Australian Air Force. 2019. "At the edge: Exploring and exploiting our fifth-generation edges." https://www.airforce.gov.au/our-mission/plan-jericho.

———. 2021. "Loyal Wingman first flight." *YouTube*, 2 March, 2021. https://youtu.be/BiSHVl7UMRk.

Royal Australian Navy. 2020. "RAS-AI strategy 2040: Warfare innovation navy." https://www.navy.gov.au/media-room/publications/ras-ai-strategy-2040.

Sadler, Denham. 2021. "HRC calls for an AI Safety Commissioner." *InnovationAus*, 27 May, 2021. https://www.innovationaus.com/hrc-calls-for-an-ai-safety-commissioner/.

Santow, E. 2021. "Human rights and technology final report." Australian Human Rights Commission. https://tech.humanrights.gov.au/downloads.

Schmitt, Lewin. 2021. "Mapping global AI governance: A nascent regime in a fragmented landscape." *AI and Ethics*. https://doi.org/10.1007/s43681-021-00083-y. https://doi.org/10.1007/s43681-021-00083-y.

Selwyn, Neil, and Beatriz Gallo Cordoba. 2021. "Australian public understandings of artificial intelligence." *AI & Society*: 1–18. https://link.springer.com/article/10.1007/s00146-021-01268-z.

Senate Foreign Affairs Defence and Trade Legislation Committee. 2019. "Official Committee Hansard Senate Foreign Affairs, Defence and Trade Legislation Committee Estimates Wednesday, 23 October 2019." https://parlinfo.aph.gov.au/parlInfo/search/display/display.w3p;query=Id%3A%22committees%2Festimate%2F53068544-efe7-4494-a0f2-2dbca4d2607b%2F0000%22.

Shih, Gerry, and Anne Gearan. 2021. "As Biden hosts first Quad summit at the White House, China is the background music." *The Washington Post*, 24 September, 2021. https://www.washingtonpost.com/world/2021/09/24/quad-us-india-australia-japan-china/.

Standards Australia. 2020. *Artificial intelligence standards roadmap: Making Australia's voice heard*. https://www.standards.org.au/news/standards-australia-sets-priorities-for-artificial-intelligence.

Stanley-Lockman, Z. 2021. "Responsible and ethical military AI allies and allied perspectives: CSET issue brief." Centre for Security and Emerging Technology, Georgetown University's Walsh School of Foreign Service. https://cset.georgetown.edu/wp-content/uploads/CSET-Responsible-and-Ethical-Military-AI.pdf.

The White House. 2021a. "Remarks by President Biden, Prime Minister Morrison of Australia, and Prime Minister Johnson of the United Kingdom announcing the creation of AUKUS." The White House. https://www.whitehouse.gov/briefing-room/speeches-remarks/2021/09/15/remarks-by-president-biden-prime-minister-morrison-of-australia-and-prime-minister-johnson-of-the-united-kingdom-announcing-the-creation-of-aukus/.

———. 2021b. "FACT SHEET: U.S.-EU establish common principles to update the rules for the 21st century economy at Inaugural Trade and Technology Council meeting." https://www.whitehouse.gov/briefing-room/statements-releases/2021/09/29/fact-sheet-u-s-eu-establish-common-principles-to-update-the-rules-for-the-21st-century-economy-at-inaugural-trade-and-technology-council-meeting/.

———. 2021c. "Joint leaders statement on AUKUS." https://www.whitehouse.gov/briefing-room/statements-releases/2021/09/15/joint-leaders-statement-on-aukus/.

Thi Ha, Hoang 2021. "The Aukus challenge to Asean." *The Straits Times*, 2021. https://www.straitstimes.com/opinion/the-aukus-challenge-to-asean.

Townshend, Ashley, Thomas Lonergan, and Toby Warden. 2021. "The U.S.-Australian alliance needs a strategy to deter China's gray-zone coercion." *War on the Rocks*, 2021. https://warontherocks.com/2021/09/the-u-s-australian-alliance-needs-a-strategy-to-deter-chinas-gray-zone-coercion/.

van Noorden, Richard. 2020. "The ethical questions that haunt facial-recognition research." *Nature*, 18 November, 2020. https://www.nature.com/articles/d41586-020-03187-3.

Vine, R. 2020. *Concept for robotics and autonomous systems.* Australian Defence Force. https://www.defence.gov.au/vcdf/forceexploration/adf-concept-future-robotics-autonomous-systems.asp.

White, L. 2021. "Tackling the growing threats to Australia's cyber security." *2021 Mandarin defence special report.* https://www.themandarin.com.au/169281-tackling-the-growing-threats-to-australias-cyber-security/.

Winfield, Alan F. T., Serena Booth, Louise A. Dennis, Takashi Egawa, Helen Hastie, Naomi Jacobs, Roderick I. Muttram, Joanna I. Olszewska, Fahimeh Rajabiyazdi, Andreas Theodorou, Mark A. Underwood, Robert H. Wortham, and Eleanor Watson. 2021. "IEEE P7001: A proposed standard on transparency." *Frontiers in Robotics and AI* 8 (225). https://doi.org/10.3389/frobt.2021.665729. https://www.frontiersin.org/article/10.3389/frobt.2021.665729.

ABOUT THE CONTRIBUTORS

Samuel Bendett is an Analyst at the Center for Naval Analyses' Russia Studies Program. His work involves analysis of Russian defence and security technology, as well as Russian unmanned systems, robotics, and AI development and application. He is also an Adjunct Senior Fellow at the Center for a New American Security (CNAS). He is a Member of CNA's Center for Autonomy and Artificial Intelligence, and an honorary "Mad Scientist" with the US ARMY TRADOC's Mad Scientist Initiative. He is also a Russian military autonomy and AI SME for the DOD's Defense Systems Information Analysis Center. Prior to joining CNA, Mr Bendett worked at the National Defense University on emerging and disruptive technologies for the Department of Defense response in domestic and international crisis situations. His previous experience includes working for the US Congress, the private sector, and non-profit organisations on foreign policy, international conflict resolution, defence, and security issues. Samuel Bendett received his MA in Law and Diplomacy from the Fletcher School, Tufts University and BA in Politics and English from Brandeis University.

Cansu Canca is a philosopher and the Founder+Director of AI Ethics Lab, where she leads teams of computer scientists, philosophers, and legal scholars to provide ethics analysis and guidance to researchers and practitioners. She is also the Ethics Lead and Research Associate Professor at the Institute for Experiential AI at Northeastern University, co-leading their Responsible AI practice. Cansu serves as an AI Ethics and Governance Expert consultant to the United Nations, working with UNICRI Centre for AI & Robotics and the Interpol in building a "Toolkit for Responsible AI Innovation in Law Enforcement". Cansu has a PhD in philosophy, specialising in applied ethics. She primarily works on ethics of technology, having previously worked on ethics and health. She serves as an ethics expert in various ethics, advisory, and editorial boards.

Prior to AI Ethics Lab, she was on the full-time faculty at the University of Hong Kong, and an ethics researcher at the Harvard Law School, Harvard School of Public Health, Harvard Medical School, National University of Singapore, Osaka University, and the World Health Organization. She was listed among the "30 Influential Women Advancing AI in Boston" and the "100 Brilliant Women in AI Ethics".

Damian Copeland is a Senior Research Fellow with the TC Beirne School of Law, The University of Queensland in the Law and Future of War project. Damian's research focuses on the application of export control, arms trade, and sanctions regimes relevant to the export and brokering of trusted autonomous military systems and associated technology. His broader research and teaching interests include international humanitarian law and domestic counter-terrorism law. Damian completed his Bachelor of Law (Hons) at the Queensland University of Technology and Masters in Law (Merit) at the Australian National University. He is completing a PhD at the Australian National University on the Article 36 weapon review of autonomous weapon systems. Damian is serving member of the Australian Defence Force (Army Legal Corps) and has served in Iraq, Afghanistan, East Timor, Cambodia, and Somalia.

S. Kate Devitt is the Chief Scientist of Trusted Autonomous Systems Defence CRC, Brisbane Australia; adjunct Associate Professor at Human-Computer Interaction, ITEE, University of Queensland, Australia; and CEO of BetterBeliefs, an evidence-based social platform. She worked as a social and ethical robotics researcher for Defence Science & Technology Group during 2018–2021 and was on the ADF COVID-19 task force 2020, providing specialised advice regarding social and ethical aspects of data, technology, and AI systems that may be considered, developed, and employed as part of the Operation. Kate is the lead author of the "Trust and Safety" chapter for Australia's Robotics Roadmap (V.2). She is a co-editor of the book *Good Data* (Institute of Network Cultures, The Netherlands, 2019) with realistic methods on how data can be used to progress a fair and just digital economy and society. With a diverse background in the history and philosophy of science, epistemology, cognitive science ethics, science communication, decision support, and human factors, Dr Devitt helps build technologies that enable the development of autonomous systems for Defence that incorporate ethical, legal, and regulatory structures to achieve social licence to operate and trusted adoption.

Qi Haotian is an Assistant Professor at the School of International Studies of Peking University, and Secretary General of the Institute for Global Cooperation and Understanding (iGCU) of Peking University. His research interests centre around and cut across three areas: technological transitions and world politics, international security and conflict management, methodology and philosophy of social science. At Peking University, he teaches courses in international security, international public policy, and game theory.

Ryo Hinata-Yamaguchi is a Project Assistant Professor at the Research Center for Advanced Science and Technology in the University of Tokyo and Executive Director at ROLES, and is also an Adjunct Fellow at the Pacific Forum. Ryo has presented, published, and consulted on a variety of topics relating to defence and security, and transport governance in the Indo-Pacific. Ryo previously served as a Non-Commissioned Officer in the Japan Ground Self-Defence Force (reserve) and also held positions at the Pusan National University, Universitas Muhammadiyah Malang, FM Bird Entertainment Agency, International Crisis Group Seoul Office, Sasakawa Peace Foundation, Embassy of Japan in Australia, and the Japan Foundation Sydney Language Centre. Ryo received his PhD from the University of New South Wales, MA in Strategic and Defence Studies and BA in Security Analysis from the Australian National University and was also a Korea Foundation Language Training Fellow.

Vadim B. Kozyulin is the Director of the Centre for Global Studies & International Relations at the Institute of Contemporary International Studies of the Diplomatic Academy of the Russian Ministry of Foreign Affairs. His research interests focus on military artificial intelligence, new weapons systems, arms control, Russia's military-technical cooperation with foreign states, strategic stability, Russia-US and Russia-NATO relations, Central Asia and Afghanistan, and illicit arms trade. He is a member of the Expert Council on the International Humanitarian Law of the State Duma of the Russian Federation, a participant in the International Panel on the Regulation of Autonomous Weapons Systems (IP-RAW), and a participant in the Russian-American Dartmouth dialogue. Since 1994 he has been a Research Fellow at the PIR Center, a Moscow-based think tank. He graduated from the MGIMO University.

Federico Mantellassi is a Research and Project Officer at the Geneva Centre for Security Policy (GCSP), where he has worked since 2018. Federico conducts research on the security, societal, and ethical impacts of emerging technologies such as artificial intelligence, synthetic biology, and neurotechnology. He also coordinates the GCSP's Polymath Initiative. Previously, he assisted in the organisation of executive education activities and was the project coordinator of the annual Geneva Cyber 9/12 Strategy Challenge. He holds a Master's degree in Intelligence and International Security from King's College London, and a Bachelor's degree in International Studies from the University of Leiden. Federico speaks Italian, French, and English.

Tate Nurkin is a Non-Resident Senior Fellow with the Center for Strategic and Budgetary Assessments and the founder of OTH Intelligence Group LLC, a defence consulting and research firm. He is also a Non-Resident Senior Fellow at the Atlantic Council. He is a frequent author and speaker on defence technology and the future of military capabilities, Indo-Pacific defence, security, and geopolitical issues, and the global defence industry and markets. Prior to establishing the OTH Intelligence Group in March 2018, Tate spent 12 years at Janes, where he served in a variety of roles, including from 2013 as the Executive Director of Strategic Assessments and Futures Studies. He holds a Master of Science degree in International Affairs from the Sam Nunn School of International Affairs at Georgia Tech and a Bachelor of Arts degree in history and political science from Duke University.

Jean-Marc Rickli is the Head of Global and Emerging Risks at the Geneva Centre for Security Policy (GCSP) in Geneva, Switzerland. He is also the co-chair of the NATO Partnership for Peace Consortium (PfPC) on Emerging Security Challenges Working Group and a senior advisor for the Artificial Intelligence Initiative at the Future Society. He represents the GCSP in the United Nations in the framework of the Governmental Group of Experts on Lethal Autonomous Weapons Systems (LAWS). He is a member of the Geneva University Committee for Ethical Research and of the advisory board of Tech4Trust, the first Swiss startup acceleration programme in the field of digital trust and cybersecurity. Prior to these appointments, Dr Rickli was an assistant professor at the Department of Defence Studies of King's College London and at the Institute for International and Civil Security at Khalifa University in Abu Dhabi. In 2020, he was nominated as one of the 100 most influential French-speaking Swiss by the Swiss newspaper Le Temps. Dr Rickli received his PhD in International Relations from Oxford University.

Simona R. Soare is a Research Fellow for Defence and Military Analysis at the International Institute for Strategic Studies. Simona analyses trends in emerging and disruptive technologies and their impact on transatlantic and European security and defence. Before joining the IISS, Simona was a Senior Associate Analyst for transatlantic defence and EU-NATO cooperation with the European Union Institute for Security Studies (EUISS) in Paris. She previously served as security and defence adviser to the vice president of the European Parliament and as a defence analyst with the Romanian Ministry of Defence. Simona is the author and editor of numerous books, articles, and chapters on transatlantic and European security, defence innovation, and technology transfers. She holds a PhD in Political Science/International Security from the National School of Political Studies and Public Administration and is a US Department of State fellow and a James S. Denton fellow. Simona lectures in international security, NATO, and EU defence.

Zoe Stanley-Lockman fulfilled the chapter in her capacity as an Associate Research Fellow in the Military Transformations Programme at the Institute of

Defence and Strategic Studies at the S. Rajaratnam School of International Studies in Singapore. Her research interests are in the areas of military innovation, responsible military AI, emerging and disruptive technologies, defence innovation ecosystems, and military capability development. Previously, she was a defence analyst at the European Union Institute for Security Studies in Paris and Brussels. She holds a Master's degree in International Security with a focus on Defence Economics from Sciences Po Paris, and a Bachelor's degree from Johns Hopkins University. Throughout her studies, her practical experience included working on dual-use export controls with the US government and consulting for US government systems integrators. In addition to completing studies commissioned by government stakeholders, her work has been published by the *Journal of Strategic Studies*, Oxford University Press, Center for Security and Emerging Technology, the Bulletin of the Atomic Scientists, and think tanks in Europe and Asia.

The Editors

Richard A. Bitzinger is an Independent International Security Analyst. He was previously a senior fellow with the Military Transformations Programme at the S. Rajaratnam School of International Studies (RSIS), Nanyang Technological University. His work focuses on security and defence issues relating to military modernisation and force transformation, defence industries, and armaments production. He previously served as the Coordinator of the Military Transformations Programme. Formerly with the RAND Corp. and the Defence Budget Project, he has been writing on Asian aerospace and defence issues for more than 20 years.

Michael Raska is an Assistant Professor and Coordinator of the Military Transformations Programme at the S. Rajaratnam School of International Studies, Nanyang Technological University in Singapore. His research interests and teaching focus on emerging technologies, strategic competition, and future warfare in the Indo-Pacific; theories and strategies relating to defence and military innovation; and plotting cyber conflicts and information warfare. He is the author of *Military Innovation and Small States: Creating Reverse Asymmetry* (Routledge, 2016), and a co-editor of two volumes: *Defence Innovation and the 4th Industrial Revolution: Security Challenges, Emerging Technologies, and Military Implications* (Routledge, 2022), and *Security, Strategy and Military Change in the 21st Century Cross-Regional Perspectives* (Routledge, 2015). He has published in journals such as the *Journal of Strategic Studies*, *Strategic Studies Quarterly*, *Journal of Complex Operations*, *Air Force Journal of Indo-Pacific Affairs*, *Korea Journal of Defence Analysis*, and also in *Sirius – Zeitschrift für strategische Analysen* (in German). His academic contributions also include chapters and policy reports in cooperation with the International Institute for Strategic Studies (IISS); the Center for New American Security (CNAS); the Norwegian Institute of Defence Studies (IFS); the Strategic Studies Institute (SSI) at the US Army War College; the European Union Institute for Security

Studies (EUISS); the Swedish Defence University (FHS); and in Germany, the Institut für Sicherheitspolitik an der Universität Kiel (ISPK). In Singapore, he has lectured at the Goh Keng Swee Command and Staff College of the Singapore Armed Forces. Dr Raska attained his PhD from the National University of Singapore, where he was a recipient of the President's Graduate Fellowship.

INDEX

Note: **Bold** page numbers refer to tables; *italic* page numbers refer to figures and page numbers followed by "n" denote endnotes.

For Product Safety Concerns and Information please contact our EU representative GPSR@taylorandfrancis.com
Taylor & Francis Verlag GmbH, Kaufingerstraße 24, 80331 München, Germany

www.ingramcontent.com/pod-product-compliance
Ingram Content Group UK Ltd.
Pitfield, Milton Keynes, MK11 3LW, UK
UKHW021451080625
459435UK00012B/456

* 9 7 8 1 0 3 2 1 1 0 7 5 2 *